UNDERSTANDING

Dying, Death, and Bereavement

———

UNDERSTANDING

Dying, Death, and Bereavement

SECOND EDITION

MICHAEL R. LEMING
St. Olaf College, Northfield, Minnesota

GEORGE E. DICKINSON
College of Charleston, Charleston, South Carolina

HOLT, RINEHART AND WINSTON, INC.
Fort Worth   Chicago   San Francisco   Philadelphia
Montreal   Toronto   London   Sydney   Tokyo

Publisher   Ted Buchholz
Aquisitions Editor   Christopher P. Klein
Project Editors   Christine Caperton, Mary K. Bridges
Production Manager   Tad Gaither
Art & Design Supervisor   John Ritland
Text Designer   Janet Bollow
Cover Illustration   Paul Micich

Address for editorial correspondence: Holt, Rinehart and Winston, Inc., 301 Commerce Street, Suite 3700, Fort Worth, TX 76102

Address for orders: Holt, Rinehart and Winston, Inc., 6277 Sea Harbor Drive, Orlando, Florida 32887. 1-800-782-4479, or 1-800-433-0001 (in Florida)

Library of Congress Cataloging-in-Publication Data

Leming, Michael R.
   Understanding dying, death, and bereavement / Michael R. Leming,
   George E. Dickinson. — 2nd ed.
   Includes bibliographical references.
   ISBN 0-03-028377-9
   1. Death—Social aspects—United States.   2. Death—Psychological
aspects.   3. Bereavement—Social aspects—United States.
4. Bereavement—Psychological aspects.   5. Funeral rites and
ceremonies—United States.   I. Dickinson, George E.   II. Title.
HQ1073.5.U6L45   1990
306.9—dc20   89-29924

PRINTED IN THE UNITED STATES OF AMERICA

0 1 2 3   118   9 8 7 6 5 4 3 2 1

Holt, Rinehart and Winston, Inc.
The Dryden Press
Saunders College Publishing

Photo Credits
p. 12 Robert Harbison; **p. 20** Jeffrey J. Foxx; **p. 28** © Joel Gordon 1984; **p. 36** © Joel Gordon 1983; **p. 66** © Joel Gordon 1978; **p. 85** © Spencer Grant; **p. 96** © Ed Lettau; **p. 108** UPI/

continues on page 462

MICHAEL R. LEMING

Michael R. Leming is Professor and Chair of the Department of Sociology at St. Olaf College in Northfield, Minnesota. He holds degrees from Westmont College (B.A.), Marquette University (M.A.), and the University of Utah (Ph.D.), and has done additional graduate study at the University of California in Santa Barbara. He is the co-author with George E. Dickinson of *Understanding Families: Diversity, Continuity, and Change* (Allyn and Bacon, 1990), and is co-editor with Raymond DeVries and Brendan Furnish of *The Sociological Perspective: A Value-Committed Introduction* (Zondervan, 1989).

Leming is the founder and director of the St. Olaf College Social Research Center, member of the board of directors of the Minnesota Coalition on Terminal Care, and steering committee member of the Northfield AIDS Response. He also serves as a hospice educator, volunteer, and grief counselor.

GEORGE E. DICKINSON

George E. Dickinson is Professor and Chair of the Department of Sociology and Anthropology at the College of Charleston in Charleston, South Carolina. He holds degrees from Baylor University (B.A. and M.A.) and Louisiana State University (Ph.D.). He has also done postdoctoral work in gerontology at Pennsylvania State University. Dickinson is the co-author with Michael R. Leming of *Understanding Families: Diversity, Continuity, and Change* (Allyn and Bacon, 1990), and has published more than thirty articles in journals such as *Death Studies, Omega, Journal of Medical Education, Journal for the Scientific Study of Religion, Medical Care, Family Practice Research, Journal of Family Issues,* and *Journal of Marriage and the Family.*

Dickinson has been teaching courses in death and dying for more than fifteen years and conducting research on physicians' and other medical personnel's attitudes toward terminally ill patients. He is also actively involved with hospice.

Preface

───

Since the publication of the first edition of *Understanding Dying, Death, and Bereavement* we have received many comments from students, faculty, and clinical practitioners with suggestions for improvements and additions to be incorporated into the second edition. These suggestions proved to be a tremendous resource for us in our task of producing the "new and improved" version of our textbook. We want all of you to know that your input is both encouraging and very valuable to us.

This second edition includes more than cosmetic changes. At least 80 percent of the manuscript has been rewritten or is entirely new. This new edition also includes four additional chapters: Understanding the Social Meanings of Dying and Death (Chapter 2); Euthanasia and Biomedical Issues (Chapter 7); Suicide (Chapter 8); and the Bereavement Process (Chapter 13).

Our goal has been to produce a book that is informative, practical, multidisciplinary in orientation, inclusive of the major foci of the interdisciplinary subject of social thanatology, and yet humanistic. We have tried to equip the reader with the necessary information to both *understand* and *cope* with the social processes of dying, death, and bereavement. Because both of us have taught courses on this subject for fifteen years, we realize that *every* student comes with both academic and personal agendas when approaching this subject.

In our first edition we brought together nine national authorities who had extensive academic experience and personal involvement in the topical areas on which they wrote. However, we discovered that differences in writing styles and levels of treatment created some problems for our readers. Therefore, with the exceptions of Chapter 11 and parts of Chapters 8 and 12, we have rewritten every chapter which was previously contributed by our professional colleagues (see Acknowledgments).

Though we collaborated throughout the twenty-four months of revising this book, a division of labor was established from the outset. Chapters 2, 4, 6, 7, 12, and 13 were primarily the responsibility of Michael Leming. George Dickinson was responsible for writing Chapters 1, 3, 5, 8, 9, 10, and 14. Thus, if you occasionally encounter a reference to "I" in a chapter, the first person singular refers to the primary author of that particular chapter. It is our hope that these personal accounts throughout the text will give a more personal touch to the chapters and make the reading seem less "textbookish."

We believe that *Understanding Dying, Death, and Bereavement*, Second Edition, will make a significant contribution to your class because it is comprehensive, dealing with the full range of topics in social thanatology; scholarly and academically sound; represents a unified effort informed by 30 years of experience; and, finally, practical to the student, being concerned with personal issues relating to an individual's ability to cope with the social and psychological processes of dying, death, and bereavement.

This book is intended for undergraduate and graduate university students, although it also would be appropriate for use in professional courses in medicine, nursing, mortuary science, social work, and pastoral counseling. The book could be used in sociology, psychology, nursing, social work, physical education, religion, health science, and education courses. It could also be used as a primary or a supplementary text in courses on gerontology, health, human development, counseling, and medical sociology. We believe that this edition will appeal to a vast audience, not only because of its wide adoptability on college and university campuses, but also because of its practical implications for all persons who must cope with dying, death, and bereavement.

The following features have been included in this edition to make it interesting and personally relevant to the student: (1) Boxed inserts present timely readings and articles that illustrate issues covered in the text; (2) Chapter Summaries serve as study aids to outline the important points of each chapter; (3) Discussion Questions highlight important issues in the chapters; (4) Annotated bibliographies provide information on suggested readings to students who wish to do further research; and (5) Glossaries of unfamiliar terms are contained within each chapter. There is also an Instructor's Manual with Test Bank available from Holt, Rinehart and Winston that includes suggestions for teaching activities and student projects; recommends audiovisual materials; and provides a test bank of more than 700 true–false, multiple-choice, and essay questions.

We would welcome suggestions and feedback from readers which might improve future editions of this book. We would also appreciate correspondence from instructors concerning pedagogy related to the teaching of this subject.

ACKNOWLEDGMENTS

Looking back over the past ten years, we are struck by the degree to which this book is the result of a very large team effort. We are indebted to the work of the contributing authors for the first edition. We continue to be grateful for the original contributions of Professors Robert Bendiksen, Nils C. Friberg, and Ann L. Overbeck even though their chapters have been rewritten. Chapter 11, on the history of American bereavement, is entirely the work of Professor James J. Farrell (Department of History, St. Olaf College). Portions of chapters dealing with the social meanings of dying and death (Chapter 2), hospice (Chapter 6) and the funeral (Chapter 12) contain sections of the earlier chapters written, respectively, by Glenn M. Vernon (Professor of Sociology, University of Utah [deceased]), John W. Abbott (Director of Educational Services and Public Information, Connecticut Hospice), and Robert C. Slater (Professor Emeritus of Mortuary Science, University of Minnesota). We could not have produced a book of this quality without their earlier contributions.

We are also indebted to Judy Langemo and Lisa Schmidt for their secretarial assistance and to Kristen Olson, Chris Klein, Stacy Emerick, Christine Caperton, John Ritland, Mary K. Bridges, and Karee Galloway at Holt, Rinehart and Winston, and copyeditor Kathy Nevils Bunnell for their work in producing this manuscript and for the confidence and encouragement they invested in this project.

Our appreciation is also extended to the psychologists, sociologists, gerontologists, and social thanatologists who reviewed the manuscript in its several drafts and who contributed to its improvement, coherence, and overall refinement. They are: Dale Lund, University of Utah; Tillman Rodabough, Baylor University; Gerry R. Cox, Fort Hays State University; and John R. Earle, Wake Forest University.

Finally, we acknowledge the support of our families during the past three years. Many times this required them to share in our struggle as we "walked in the valley of the shadow of death" and as we encountered what seemed to be insurmountable obstacles. They know how much strength we have gained from reflecting upon our death-related experiences. They have also been able to observe "our mourning changed into dancing." We hope that our readers will also experience a renewed appreciation for life as they begin to understand, intellectually and emotionally, more fully the social-psychological processes of dying, death, and bereavement.

Michael Leming

George Dickinson

Contents

—

4   Religion and Death Attitudes   93

11 The History of Bereavement and Burial Practices in American Culture 325

12 The Funeral: Expression of Contemporary American Bereavement 369

ONE

Understanding Dying and Death

CHAPTER 1

The American Way of Dying

—

I mourn not those who lose their vital breath
But those who, living, live in fear of death.

THE ANCIENT GREEK ANTHOLOGY

1 People who relate to any aspect of dying and death are thought by many to be weird and "out of it." Just note the reactions of others when you tell them you are taking a course on death and dying. The startled reactions of others when told that I teach a course on death and dying are interesting, to say the least. One woman, when informed that I offer a course on death and dying, reacted by asking, "How could you do such a thing?"

Imagine the responses to people who are funeral directors or who work in a nursing home or on a cancer ward of a hospital. From the reactions that most people have to these death-related issues, it appears that death discussions are considered in bad taste and something to be avoided.

Dying in the United States today occurs offstage, away from the arena of familiar surroundings of kin and friends. Seventy percent of current deaths in the United States occur in institutional settings—hospitals and nursing homes. Grandfather dies not at home today, where he has spent most of his life, but in an impersonal institutional setting. Such removal of death from the usual setting prompted Richard Dumont and Dennis Foss (1972:2) to raise the question, "How is the modern American able to cope with his own death when the deaths he experiences are infrequent, highly impersonal, and viewed as virtually abnormal?"

CURRENT INTEREST IN THANATOLOGY

The realization of the question posed by Dumont and Foss in the early 1970s brought about a concerted effort to talk about and study dying and death. Certainly death, like sex, was not a new event, but both had been rarely discussed openly. In fact, sex, as a subject of discussion, came out of the closet sooner in the 1960s, followed by death in the 1970s.

Why the Increased Interest?

This increased interest in **thanatology** (the study of dying, death, and bereavement) was due to several reasons. First, with the majority of Americans dying in hospitals and nursing homes—not the case at the turn of the century—an aura of mystery developed. One is taken to the hospital or nursing home and is brought back dead. As one little boy said, "I don't want to go to the hospital because that's where you go to die." He had seen Grandfather "taken away" to a hospital alive; and the next time he saw him, Grandfather was dead. Often small children are not allowed to go into certain parts of a hospital; thus the taboo nature of a hospital setting makes one wonder what is going on in there. A desire to examine this mysterious thing called death has contributed to a growing interest in thanatology.

Second, with individuals living longer today because of life-support equipment, organ transplants, penicillin, and other antibiotics, an interest has developed in the topic of dying and death. Such prolongation of life has raised ethical issues (e.g., Karen Ann Quinlan and Baby Jane Doe) involving the right to die, causing a furor in philosophy, law, and medicine. With the media highly publicizing these cases, the public was alerted to moral and legal questions about death not previously posed. Whether or not to disconnect life-supporting equipment presented questions for which ready answers were not found.

The whole issue of when death occurs evolves from these medical and ethical developments. The question of who determines when one is alive or dead has been addressed by physicians, lawyers, philosophers, and theologians. These questions, along with the controversy over abortion rights, were a few of the significant ethical issues of the 1970s that helped to open the forum for discussion and debate concerning the topic of dying and death.

Third, fewer individuals are raised on farms today than at the turn of the century. Being brought up in a rural environment gave one direct exposure to birth and death as an everyday event. Children were surrounded by the alpha and omega of the life cycle. Kittens, puppies, piglets, calves, chicks, and colts were born—and also died. Thus, it was commonplace to see death and to deal with these situations accordingly. With less than 10 percent of the United States population living on farms today, these birth and death scenes have largely been removed from the experience of most individuals.

Fourth, the Space Shuttle disaster in 1986 brought death to the attention of millions of school children around the country. In so doing, the catastrophe forced adults to deal with the issue. While the astronauts and the teacher were not visible to television viewers, their space ship was shown. The live television coverage brought sudden death into the living room. The media continued the coverage for weeks following this event. Television had previously brought death into the home during the Vietnam conflict in the 1960s and 1970s.

While dying and death have now become issues of intellectual concern, our society has done little formal **socialization** of its members to deal with death on the personal and emotional levels. Hospitals have traditionally excluded visitors under the age of fourteen. Parents have often tried to shield "innocent" children from death scenes. Medical and theology schools, which train people who will work with the dying, have not had significant curricular offerings to prepare their students for this death-related work. Overall, our socialization to dying and death situations has been unsystematic and ineffective.

The Media and Death

As a child growing up in Texas, I have fond memories of spending the night with my grandparents on Fridays and going to the movies with my grandfather. The movie was always a western with basically the same theme—the "good guys" were cowboys who wore white hats, and the "bad guys" were the Indians. Just as it appeared that the good guys were going to be wiped out, military reinforcements would *always* come to the rescue at the last minute! The guys in the white hats would be rescued, and the bad guys would receive their just reward—death.

In the early 1970s, however, Hollywood began to produce films revolving around the theme of death in which the good guy died. For example, in *Love Story* one of the two main characters is dying throughout much of the film, and does, in fact, die during the film. Since that time numerous films have been produced with death as a principal theme. Certainly, Woody Allen films are filled with references to death.

Many situational comedies on prime-time television in the 1970s and 1980s also addressed the topic of death. While many viewed death in a serious vein, others took a humorous approach. After all, both death and sex are topics of jokes. They are uneasy topics, so laughter is a way of coping.

Numerous television specials in the early 1970s addressed dying and death in one- and two-hour programs viewed at prime times. "Living with Death" presented various death-related situations observed through the eyes of a CBS reporter. ABC's "Right to Die" addressed moral questions concerning mercy killing and suicide.

The National Endowment for the Humanities sponsored a program entitled "Dying" in the mid-1970s. For two hours this program sensitively portrayed four cancer patients, ranging in age from the late twenties to the early seventies, interacting with others. Each died during the course of the filming. A PBS documentary in 1979 showed the last three years of Joan Robinson's life. This three-hour film revealed the experience of a woman and her husband as they tried to live with her cancer of the breast and uterus.

Death appears to be more abstract for those growing up today than for previous generations. By the age of 15, some media experts say, the average American has seen 13,000 murders on television and has been exposed to an endless stream of war, famine, and holocaust in the daily news (Bordewich, 1988:34). Because we are unlikely to know the deceased people, however, the effect of this death news upon us is minimal. Robert Kavanaugh (1972:13) makes the following observation that demonstrates this problem:

> Over a two-week period of nighttime [television] viewing, I counted an average of 34 deaths at close range, countless more at a distance. Not one death raised as much as a slight tremor in me. Television feeds our fantasy of forever being a spectator. Even a bloody nose or a fainting spell by a fellow viewer would have aroused more emotion in me than a hundred deaths on the tube.

The AIDS epidemic, frequently reported by the media, will likely force more and more schools and colleges to acknowledge the problems of death. By the age of 18, one in 20 students has had to cope with the death of a parent, and nearly half with the loss of a parent through divorce or separation (Bordewich, 1988:34). Thus, a need for thanatology seems apparent in today's society.

The Discipline of Thanatology

The interdisciplinary study of dying, death, and bereavement called *thanatology* flourished in the academic world in the 1970s and 1980s. Literally hundreds of courses on dying and death were offered in high schools and colleges. According to Dan Leviton (1977), the number of death-education college courses increased from 20 in 1970 to 1,100 in 1974.

One of the early thanatology texts, published in 1959, was an anthology by psychologist Herman Feifel entitled *The Meaning of Death*. In 1963 Jessica Mitford's *American Way of Death* was very critical of the funeral industry. Elisabeth Kübler-Ross's *On Death and Dying*, published in 1969, and Ernest Becker's *Denial of Death*, published in 1973, both became bestsellers. It was Elisabeth Kübler-Ross, a physician, who was a catalyst in making the medical profession realize that the terminally ill patient is more than the cancer patient in Room 713, but a warm, living human being with personal needs. Both these books alerted the public to the issue of dying in America.

While three professional journals in thanatology emerged in the 1970s, only two survived into the 1980s: *Death Studies* (formerly *Death Education*) and *Omega: The Journal of Death and Dying*. The number of articles on death also expanded considerably in education, medicine, health, nursing, psychology, social work, and sociology journals.

Fergus Bordewich (1988) observes that a generation ago death was a subject less likely than sex to be found in the curricula of American public schools. If death was acknowledged at all, it was usually discussed within the context of literary classics. In the past decade courses treating dying and death far more explicitly have appeared in schools across the country. Though the actual number is unknown, thousands of schools are involved, according to groups that either oppose or support death education. Many schools have blended some of the philosophies and techniques of death education into health, social studies, gerontology, literature, and home economics courses. Others have introduced suicide-prevention programs.

An argument for death education noted by Bordewich (1988:31) from *The School Counselor* in 1977 said:

> An underlying, but seldom spoken, assumption of much of the death-education movement is that Americans handle death and dying poorly and that we ought to be doing better at it. As in the case of many other problems, many Americans believe that education can initiate change. Change is evident, and death education will play as important a part in changing attitudes toward death as sex education played in changing attitudes toward sex information and wider acceptance of various sexual practices.

What effects do courses on dying and death have on students? As noted in pre- and post-tests of the attitudes of 184 students enrolled in a college course on dying and death (Dickinson, 1986), the majority of responses revealed less fear of death and death-related events at the end of the course.

While these students had higher death anxieties on entering the course than did four similar studies of other populations, including one of coal miners just prior to entering the mines (Dickinson, 1986), they had changed by the end of the course: these students revealed death anxieties much lower than the other four populations. Perhaps students coming into an elective course in thanatology have a high fear of the topic anyway, and enter the course to alleviate it. Nonetheless, this study did reveal less anxiety in the students of dying and death after discussing, reading, seeing films, visiting a funeral home, and going to a cemetery. Exposure seemed to make them less anxious about death-related matters.

DEFINING DEATH

On page 10, the "Wizard of Id" defines death as a once in a lifetime experience." While one cannot refute the Wizard's answer, such a response would not suffice in the medical or legal professions.

A recent headline in a newspaper (*News and Courier*, September 22, 1988, Charleston, SC) read "Doctors 'Kill' Patient to Save Her Life." The article went on to say that surgeons had put the patient in a coma, stopped her heart, chilled her by 40 degrees, and drained her body of blood for forty minutes to save her from the aneurysm pressing on her brain. She was placed in a sort of suspended animation that allowed surgeons to repair a hard-to-reach, high-risk aneurysm once considered inoperable. As one surgeon noted, "It may be the surgery of the future in cases where bleeding poses the greatest risk to the operation." Thus, the headline said the physicians "killed" in order to "*save* the patient." Defining death is indeed a confusing issue.

International Definitions of Death

Defining death is a difficult assignment. In the 1950s the United Nations and the World Health Organization proposed the following definition: "Death is the permanent disappearance of all evidence of life at any time after birth has taken place" (United Nations, 1953). Thus, as death can take place only after a birth has occurred, any deaths prior to a (live) birth cannot be included in this definition. The latter is called a *fetal death* and is defined (Stockwell, 1976) as:

> Death (disappearance of life) prior to the complete expulsion or extraction from its mother or a product of conception irrespective of the duration of pregnancy; the death is indicated by the fact that after such separation the fetus does not breathe or show any other evidence of life, such as beating of the heart, pulsating of the umbilical cord, or definite movement of voluntary muscles.

Not all countries follow the definition of death recommended by the United Nations. In some countries, infants dying within twenty-four hours after birth are classified as stillbirths rather than deaths, or are disregarded altogether. In some other countries infants born alive, who die before the end of the registration period (which may last several months), are considered stillbirths or are excluded from all tabulations. Thus, one is not "alive" until officially registered, and one cannot be legally "dead" if never alive. The whole question of life and death is more complicated than might initially appear on the surface.

BOX 1.1   **"DEAD" CANCER PATIENT**
AWAKENS IN MORTUARY

HARARE, ZIMBABWE   After being pronounced dead in the hospital, a cancer patient later awoke in a mortuary. She said her superstitious relatives were afraid to visit her.

The family of Beauty Shitto had made funeral arrangements to bury her, after doctors at the hospital in Gweru had declared her dead and sent her body to the mortuary.

Adapted from the *News and Courier*, Charleston, SC, June 22, 1988, p. 9A. Copyright Associated Press, used by permission.

American Definitions of Death

Leon Kass (1971:699) simply defines death as "the transition from the state of being alive to the state of being dead." Simple enough, yet the issue is clouded by many factors.

By traditional definitions, death occurs when heartbeat and breathing stop, "the irreparable cessation of spontaneous cardiac activity and spontaneous respiratory activity" (Ramsey, 1970:59). Medical advances, however, have made this heartbeat definition of death obsolete. Under this definition many people living today would have once died since their hearts stopped beating and breathing stopped as a result of heart attacks. With respirators to artificially breathe for a patient, along with other life-support equipment, many lives are saved. A diagnosis of brain death allows respirators to be turned off when the brain is "totally and irreversibly" dead (Cope, 1978).

In 1968, a committee of the Harvard Medical School (Beecher, 1968) claimed that the ultimate criterion for death should be brain activity rather than the functioning of heart and lungs. The Harvard Report notes that death should be understood in terms of "a permanently nonfunctioning brain," for which there are many tests. With brain death the body would not be able to

Reprinted by permission of Johnny Hart and NAS, Inc.

breathe on its own because breathing is controlled in the brain. If the brain is dead, any artificially induced heartbeat is merely pumping blood through a dead body.

Various tests can be given to detect any signs of brain activity (Cope, 1978). Physicians search for any hint of normal brain-controlled reflexes. They turn the head, and even put cold water in the ear, to look for any sign of movement. They search for any sign of the eye pupils responding to light. One test is to touch the cornea of the eye and see whether this triggers a blink. The respirator is also stopped briefly to look for any sign of spontaneous breathing. Absence of brain activity, as signified by a flat electroencephalogram (EEG), is another criterion for brain death. The tests can be repeated 24 hours later to make certain that the absence of these life signs is not temporary.

According to one neurologist (Cope, 1978), when death occurs on the basis of cessation of breathing and heartbeat, the brain is deprived of blood supply and dies within a matter of minutes. Death of the brain is what is final and absolute. On the other hand, while one may lose all brain function, the loss may not be irreversible. For example, a person having taken an overdose of barbiturates may have a temporary absence of any signs of brain activity, but this is not brain death because it is reversible.

With a lack of consensus regarding the definition of death, determining death continues to be controversial. Kansas was the first state to legislate a definition of death in 1970. Since then a number of other states have adopted similar statutes.

BOX 1.2 **MAN REVIVED AFTER OBITUARY PUBLISHED**

CINCINNATI A man whose obituary was published after doctors declared him "brain dead" revived and was returned to intensive care in critical condition. Physicians at the University of Cincinnati Hospital

(continued on next page)

declared John Birckhead, 41, of Cincinnati brain dead Wednesday morning.

Funeral arrangements had been made by that evening, and a death notice was purchased for Birckhead, who had been hospitalized in a coma after being found hanging by his T-shirt at a jail. Meanwhile, breathing was detected during a final medical evaluation and Birckhead was returned to intensive care at the hospital.

A misunderstanding between hospital officials and members of Birckhead's family resulted in the publication of John Birckhead's obituary Thursday morning in the *Cincinnati Enquirer*. The family was told that before a legal declaration of death, a second medical evaluation had to be performed.

DENYING DEATH

Though some evidence exists to suggest that Americans accept death (the majority have life insurance policies and many have wills), it has been suggested that we are a death-denying society (Dumont and Foss, 1972). Such evidence of death-denying in the United States includes the following six examples.

First, we tend to use euphemisms for death, rather than using the words *death* and *dead* and *dying*. Examples of such euphemisms are: succumbed, passed away, was taken, went to heaven, departed this life, bit the dust, kicked the bucket, croaked, passed on, was laid to rest, cashed in, expired, ended his/her days, is no more, checked out, signed off, breathed his/her last breath, returned to dust, went out like a light, ran out of time, brought down the curtain, went on to glory, is pushing up daisies, was taken by the Grim Reaper, heard the trumpet call, and is six feet under. It is less painful to use euphemisms as buffers, rather than use the stark words *death, dead, and dying*.

Second, we have a taboo on death conversation. A friend recently wrote a two-page letter describing her summer activities. She noted that she and her husband had been on vacation, and he became ill. He was taken to the hospital for surgery. She said, "He had the best of care. I lov*ed* him so." She never said that her husband had died, but it was obvious. It is difficult to say those words—dead, dying, and death.

Third, **cryonics** (body freezing) suggests a denial of death. The person's body is frozen in dry ice and liquid nitrogen. Being a very expensive process

The creation of the Vietnam Memorial in Washington, D.C., was the result of a popular movement whose goal was to recognize the many men and women who lost their lives in a very unpopular war. This social movement ran contrary to the death denial sentiment typically found in American society.

initially, with additional high annual costs, cryonics has not caught on. It is based on the idea that someday a cure will be found for the illness of the "deceased," and that he or she can then be treated with the "cure" and thawed out. Thus, one does not die, but is put in the cooler and brought back at a later date.

As many as 40 people have had their bodies frozen after death in hopes that new technology would someday be able to restore them to health (Adams, 1988:332). The first was James Bedford, a 73-year-old psychologist from Glendale, California, who was frozen in 1967. Many of the 40 were thawed after their estates ran out of money, and allegedly only 11 are still in cryonic suspension.

BOX 1.3 **CHILLING ANSWER TO LIFE AFTER DEATH**

BY KATHERINE BISHOP

SAN FRANCISCO   Everyone knows that you can't take it with you. But if members of the American Cryonics Society Inc. have their way, they are going to come back and get it.

Last week the organization, which is dedicated to the proposition that death is an imposition on life and ought to be eliminated, celebrated its 20th anniversary here with a $100-a-plate dinner attended by 65 people. The Speaker of the State Assembly, Willie Brown, showed up at the Fairmont Hotel to cut the cake, and Angela Alioto, a newly elected member of the San Francisco Board of Supervisors, made an appearance, testifying to the fact that no group is too eccentric to be ignored here.

Since the term was coined in 1965, cryonics has taken some small steps from the realm of science fiction and has even come up with its own independent religion known as Venturism. Cryonics (derived from the Greek word for cold) refers to the practice of freezing the body of a person after death to preserve it for possible revival in some distant future after a cure has been found for whatever killed the poor soul. Adherents make arrangements to have their bodies placed in cryonic suspension, meaning preservation at extremely low temperatures using liquid nitrogen in stainless steel capsules.

As it turns out, members are planning to come back to a body vastly better than the one they left in. "Usually the body is shot and they don't want to come back in that kind of shape," said H. Jackson Zinn, a San Francisco lawyer who is the organization's president.

Many members believe science will be able to restore their body and build a better one as long as the basic "information" of the person remains properly stored. Thus one popular choice is the "neuro only" option, in which only the head is preserved.

Such practices are not without problems. Last year, six people from Alcor Life Extension Foundation in Riverside, a nonprofit cryonics storage center independent of the Cryonics Society, were handcuffed and taken away for questioning on suspicion of homicide after they removed and froze the head of one client after her heart stopped beat-

(continued on next page)

ing but without having a doctor present at Alcor to pronounce her legally dead.

While criminal charges have not been filed, a grand jury investigation is continuing and Alcor has sued the State Department of Health Services, which believes that cryonics does not qualify as a "scientific" use of human remains and refuses to issue required forms. The lawsuit's outcome will affect the work of all existing storage centers, said Alcor's Manager, Michael Federowicz, who goes by the name Mike Darwin.

Should cryonics prove to work, it might lead to a host of social issues, including what is to be done about overpopulation if people continue to be born while others refuse to stay dead. The organization believes that space will be colonized, opening up vast new adventures in living for millions of humans, new or reconstituted.

"To think that we must be confined to this planet is, come on, too parochial," said Jerry White, a founder of the Cryonics Society.

Another problem is where to store all the stainless steel capsules holding the "suspension members," as the frozen bodies are called. Thus far, there are fewer than a half dozen storage centers in the country, with two of them in this state.

Mr. White suggested that there are a number of existing structures that could be adapted for such use, including an abandoned Titan missile site the group has toured in Northern California.

"I was envisioning these big silos just full of liquid nitrogen, the liquid nitrogen generators busy 24 hours a day just spewing stuff in there," he said. "And you could see thousands of patients in there, see them bobbing around."

Cryonics also involves a host of moral and philosophical problems that have not been addressed by society. The most immediate one might be faced by the survivors of the suspended, who might not agree with their loved ones' choice of body preservation and might bring legal challenges to them.

"If I'm frozen, will my wife say, 'Gee, I should have gotten that insurance money,'" mused Irving Rand, a New York City insurance salesman. Mr. Rand is president of Cryonics Coordinators of America, which helps people obtain insurance to cover the cost of freezing and storage.

A more weighty issue to ponder grows out of the fact that if future technology makes it possible to duplicate a person from those parts that have been frozen, it follows that a frozen person could not only be restored, but could also have complete copies made of himself as a sort of human floppy disk.

(continued on next page)

As Mr. Darwin states the issue, "If you duplicate and store yourself as a backup copy, is that copy you?"

And there is also the question of what the state of the world will have become over time. As Mr. Rand said, "Who knows what the world is going to be like 100 years from now, if it's even worth coming back."

But Mr. Zinn is more upbeat about the prospects. "One hundred years from now, anything that's fun, I don't want to miss it."

Fourth, we do not die in America, we simply take a long nap. Caskets have built-in mattresses, some strawlike and others innerspring. The room in the funeral home where the body is laid out is referred to by some as the slumber room. Certainly, no one ever heard of having pets *killed* by veterinarians; we have them put to sleep. Dying does not occur in America, one just goes to sleep.

Fifth, unlike nonliterate societies, we call in a professional when someone dies. The funeral director takes the body away, and we do not see it again until it is ready for viewing. When we see the body again, the cosmetic job is such that the person looks as alive as possible under the circumstances. When viewing a body at a funeral home, I have heard people make the comment that the person "looks better than I have seen him/her look for years." This is the dying of death that is discussed in Chapter 11.

Sixth, in many places in the United States, the casket is not lowered into the ground until after the family and friends have left the cemetery. It is not easy to watch a casket lowered into the ground because this reminds the viewers of the finality of death. There are several bad moments when a significant other dies—initially being told of the death, seeing the body for the first time, seeing the casket closed for the last time, and seeing the casket lowered into the ground. One can avoid the last moment by leaving the cemetery.

Thus, examples of denial of death can be found in the United States. We are not suggesting that this is all bad. It is simply a way of coping and simply seems to be evident in the American way of dying.

MORTALITY STATISTICS

Ask an individual how he or she wishes to die. With the exception of the comical reply, "When I'm 92 and at the hands of a jealous lover," most people will respond, "When I'm very old, at home, unexpectedly, in my own

bed, while sleeping—and with my full mental and physical capabilities."
Unfortunately for most of us, we will not die as we would like. For some,
this may be a source of apprehension and anxiety.

As noted earlier, most Americans die in institutionalized settings, not at
home. According to Box 1.4 "Please Notify," we should be more considerate
about our dying, whether at home or away.

BOX 1.4   **PLEASE NOTIFY**

> A lecturer was about to address a business association in Los Angeles
> when the association director reminded its members: "Every week we
> pay return postage for mail that goes to our members and is not deliv-
> erable because you have moved, changed your post office box number,
> or died without letting us know."
>
> *Mountaineer*, Waynesville, NC, April 11, 1980.

Death Etiology and Life Expectancy

As noted in Table 1.1, most of us (69 percent) will die of one of two **chronic
illnesses**—heart disease and cancer. With these chronic diseases, deaths are
usually prolonged and are not sudden and unexpected, as most people
would desire.

Life expectancy has increased considerably in the past 50 years. Life
expectancy for males in the United States has increased from 54 years to
nearly 70 years over the past half century. Females' life expectancy during
this same period has increased from 55 to 77 years. Whites live nearly five
years longer than blacks in the United States. These differences in life expectancy are shown in Table 1.2.

THE WIZARD OF ID   by Brant parker and Johnny hart

Reprinted by permission of Johnny Hart and NAS, Inc.

TABLE 1.1

Ten Leading Causes of Death in the United States, 1900 and 1985
(in Death Rates per 100,000 Population)

CAUSES OF DEATH	DEATH RATES PER 100,000 POPULATION	PERCENT OF ALL DEATHS
	1900*	
1. Pneumonia	191.9	12.5
2. Consumption (tuberculosis)	190.5	12.5
3. Heart disease	134.0	8.3
4. Diarrheal diseases	85.1	5.6
5. Diseases of the kidneys	83.7	5.5
6. All accidents	72.3	4.7
7. Apoplexy (stroke)	66.6	4.3
8. Cancer	60.0	3.9
9. Old age	54.0	3.5
10. Bronchitis	48.3	3.2
All other causes		36.0
	1985	
1. Major cardiovascular diseases	409.6	46.9
2. Malignancies	193.3	22.1
3. Accidents	39.1	4.5
4. Pulmonary diseases	31.3	3.6
5. Pneumonia and influenza	28.3	3.2
6. Diabetes	15.5	1.8
7. Suicide	12.3	1.4
8. Chronic liver disease	11.2	1.3
9. Nephritis	8.9	1.0
10. Homicide	8.3	1.0
All other causes		13.2

*These data are limited to the registration area that included 10 registration states and all cities having at least 8000 inhabitants. In 1900 this represented 38 percent of the entire population of the continental United States. Since accidents were not reported in the 1900 census, this rate was taken from Lerner (1970).   Sources: *Abstract of the Twelfth Census of the United States, 1900,* Table 93. Washington, D.C.: U.S. Government Printing Office, 1902, and *Statistical Abstract of the United States, 1988,* 108th edition, Table 117. Washington, D.C.: U.S. Government Printing Office, 1988.

Monroe Lerner. 1970. "When, Why and Where People Die." In O. G. Brim, H. E. Freeman and N. A. Scotch, Eds. *The Dying Patient.* New York: Russel Sage Foundation, p. 14.

Gender Differences in Mortality Rates

Why females outlive males is a long-debated topic. This pattern tends to exist in most parts of the world except for a few nonliterate societies where a high maternal mortality rate exists. The suggestions that females traditionally have both engaged in less strenuous work and have not been allowed to work in occupations with high accident rates, such as coal mining and steel manu-

TABLE 1.2
Expectation of Life by Race, Age, and Sex, 1985

| | | EXPECTATION OF LIFE IN YEARS | | | |
| | | White | | Black and Other | |
AGE (IN YEARS)	Total	Male	Female	Male	Female
At birth	74.7	71.9	78.7	65.3	73.5
1	74.5	71.6	78.4	65.7	73.8
2	73.6	70.7	77.4	64.7	72.8
3	72.6	69.7	76.5	63.8	71.9
4	71.7	68.7	75.5	62.9	70.9
5	70.7	67.8	74.5	61.9	70.0
6	69.7	66.8	73.5	60.9	69.0
7	68.7	65.8	72.5	59.9	68.0
8	67.7	64.8	71.5	59.0	67.1
9	66.8	63.8	70.6	58.0	66.1
10	65.8	62.9	69.6	57.0	65.1
11	64.8	61.9	68.6	56.0	64.1
12	63.8	60.9	67.6	55.0	63.1
13	62.8	59.9	66.6	54.1	62.1
14	61.8	58.9	65.6	53.1	61.1
15	60.9	58.0	64.6	52.1	60.2
16	59.9	57.0	63.7	51.2	59.2
17	58.9	56.1	62.7	50.2	58.2
18	58.0	55.1	61.7	49.3	57.2
19	57.0	54.2	60.7	48.4	56.3
20	56.1	53.3	59.8	47.4	55.3
21	55.1	52.3	58.8	46.5	54.3
22	54.2	51.4	57.8	45.6	53.4
23	53.3	50.5	56.9	44.7	52.4
24	52.3	49.6	55.9	43.8	51.4
25	51.4	48.7	54.9	42.9	50.5
26	50.4	47.7	53.9	42.1	49.5
27	49.5	46.8	53.0	41.2	48.6
28	48.5	45.9	52.0	40.3	47.6
29	47.6	44.9	51.0	39.4	46.7
30	46.7	44.0	50.1	38.5	45.8
31	45.7	43.1	49.1	37.7	44.8
32	44.8	42.2	48.1	36.8	43.9
33	43.8	41.2	47.1	36.0	43.0
34	42.9	40.3	46.2	35.1	42.0
35	42.0	39.4	45.2	34.3	41.1
36	41.0	38.4	44.3	33.5	40.2
37	40.1	37.5	43.3	32.6	39.3
38	39.2	36.6	42.3	31.8	38.4
39	38.2	35.7	41.4	31.0	37.5

Expectation of Life by Race, Age, and Sex, 1985

		EXPECTATION OF LIFE IN YEARS			
		White		Black and Other	
AGE (IN YEARS)	*Total*	*Male*	*Female*	*Male*	*Female*
40	37.3	34.7	40.4	30.2	36.6
41	36.4	33.8	39.5	29.4	35.7
42	35.5	32.9	38.5	28.6	34.8
43	34.5	32.0	37.6	27.8	33.9
44	33.6	31.1	36.6	27.0	33.0
45	32.7	30.2	35.7	26.3	32.1
46	31.8	29.3	34.8	25.5	31.3
47	31.0	28.4	33.9	24.7	30.4
48	30.1	27.6	32.9	24.0	29.6
49	29.2	26.7	32.0	23.3	28.8
50	28.3	25.8	31.1	22.5	27.9
51	27.5	25.0	30.2	21.8	27.1
52	26.6	24.2	29.4	21.1	26.3
53	25.8	23.3	28.5	20.5	25.5
54	25.0	22.5	27.6	19.8	24.7
55	24.2	21.7	26.7	19.1	24.0
56	23.4	21.0	25.9	18.5	23.2
57	22.6	20.2	25.0	17.8	22.5
58	21.8	19.5	24.2	17.2	21.7
59	21.1	18.7	23.4	16.6	21.0
60	20.3	18.0	22.6	16.0	20.3
61	19.6	17.3	21.8	15.4	19.6
62	18.8	16.6	21.0	14.9	19.0
63	18.1	15.9	20.2	14.4	18.3
64	17.4	15.3	19.4	13.8	17.6
65	16.7	14.6	18.7	13.3	17.0
70	13.5	11.6	15.0	10.8	13.8
75	10.6	9.0	11.7	8.7	11.1
80	8.1	6.8	8.7	6.8	8.6
85 and over	6.0	5.1	6.4	5.7	6.9

Source: *Statistical Abstract of the United States, 1988,* 108th edition, Table 109. Washington, D.C.: U.S. Government Printing Office, 1988.

facturing, actually do not explain this greater longevity of females. Traditional housework involves the lifting of many pounds of laundry, daily picking up and keeping up with small children, the handling of foodstuffs, and walking several miles within the house performing daily chores. No, housework is not a plush job.

Differences in life expectancies for males and females create a situation where there are twice as many females as males at age 80. Is America ready for polygyny as a reward (or punishment) for octogenarians?

Perhaps it would be more correct to suggest that females historically have watched their diet more carefully than males due to their knowledge about food and the special cultural emphasis on weight maintenance. With more current emphasis on diet and exercise for both genders, however, this argument may no longer be completely accurate.

Anthropologist Ashley Montagu (1968) suggests that women use their emotions in a more positive way because they are more likely to cry than men. Since it is not "macho" to cry, men generally refrain from such behavior, resulting in more psychosomatic disorders such as peptic ulcers. Montagu asks, "Is this a superior use of emotions?" Perhaps being freer to express themselves through the release of emotional feelings contributes to a decrease of stress for women.

Males have traditionally been involved in more risk-taking activities through masculine behaviors like smoking (the rugged Marlboro man, for example) and drinking. Males have also historically been more inclined to drive fast cars and live the James Dean happy-go-lucky life.

On the biological side of the argument, the conception ratio (projected to be higher than 120 males per 100 females) favors males, as does the **sex ratio** at birth (105 males per 100 females). In the early teens the sex ratio levels off, and after age 80, the ratio is less than 50 males per 100 females.

Perhaps females simply have better-built bodies. Their bodies must be capable of carrying and supporting new life. Thus, it appears they are the "Porsche" model, whereas males are the more "thrown-together" model.

The debate goes on. Whether females outlive males in the United States because of biological or cultural reasons, we will not settle here. The fact is, females outlive males. As gender roles continue to change and females are found in greater numbers and in a greater variety of nontraditional occupations; as males share more in domestic tasks; and as the sexes come together in more unisex behaviors (smoking, drinking, the "fast" life), stresses and strains of life should be more equally distributed between the genders. The argument of biology versus culture as influencing life expectancy can then be better addressed.

BOX 1.5 **PUTTING A PRICE ON HUMAN LIFE**

Putting a price tag on human life is a common activity among life insurance companies, airlines, courts, industries, and agencies. Being required by law (Executive Order 12291 issued by President Ronald Reagan in February of 1981), the federal government routinely calculates the value of a life. Ordinary citizens make much the same determination when they choose small cars over larger, take jobs hundreds of feet below the ground for higher pay, or buy inexpensive houses in a flood plain instead of more expensive ones in safer areas.

People have been calculating the worth of their lives and the lives of others for as long as archaeologists, anthropologists, and historians can document human existence. The Aztecs in the 15th century and the Code of Hammurabi of ancient Babylonia created elaborate systems of compensation for injuries and deaths. In both ancient and medieval law a sum of money was paid by a guilty party to satisfy the family of the person injured or killed.

A fundamental difference exists, however, between calculating the value of a life to compensate for its loss, a common practice throughout the centuries, and determining whether it is worth saving, a practice growing more common today. Some philosophers argue that the value of human life is infinite or incalculable. However, insurance agents, economists, legal experts, scientists, and agency administrators are assigning life values ranging from a few dollars to many millions of dollars, depending on the formulas used.

(continued on next page)

One way of figuring value is to break down the body into chemical elements—5 pounds calcium, 1½ pounds phosphorus, 9 ounces potassium, 6 ounces sulfur, 6 ounces sodium, a little more than 1 ounce magnesium, and less than an ounce each of iron, copper, and iodine. On that basis a human life today is worth $8.37, up $1.09 in six years because of inflation.

Another approach is to look at the going price of contract murder. Andreas Santiago Hernandez, 22, recently told the Los Angeles Police Department that he was paid $5,000 to kill Lorraine Keifer, the 67-year-old widow of a San Fernando Valley executive. Lt. Fahey says that in New York City a murder contract can cost nothing, if it is "for practice," or $10,000 and up.

The life insurance industry determines what people would have earned had they lived. It is their earning power over the course of their working life.

Adapted from William R. Greer, "Putting a Price on Human Life Is Being Questioned." *The Courier-Journal,* Louisville, KY, June 30, 1985, p. 1D.

COPING WITH THE AMERICAN WAY OF DYING

Human beings do not respond to all deaths in the same manner. As noted in Chapter 2, humans ascribe meanings to death and then respond to these meanings. The American way of dying places higher values on some causes of deaths and ascribes less status to other causes. Likewise, coping with the death of a significant other will be influenced by the cause of the death.

There are special problems associated with deaths caused by a chronic disease such as heart disease or cancer. These include the increasing dependence of the patient and the physical and psychological fatigue of the caregiver, who must observe the patient's deterioration. There are some real advantages, however. The following is a partial list of the opportunities provided by a slow death caused by a chronic disease:

1. The dying person is given an opportunity to attend to unfinished business—make out a will, complete incomplete projects.

2. The dying person and his or her family can attempt to heal broken family relationships, can say their final farewells, and can all participate in constructing a meaningful and dignified death.

3. Funerals and other arrangements can be made with the consent and participation of the dying person.

4. Anticipatory grief on the part of the survivors and dying patient can take place.

Deaths due to **acute illnesses** (e.g., pneumonia), accidents, and heart attacks also provide special problems and advantages to survivors. For all quick deaths there is the problem of being unprepared for the death. Some of the grieving that has preceded the death due to a chronic disease cannot be expressed in deaths of this type. Consequently, grief is usually more intense when the dying takes place in a short period of time. Survivors may also experience more intense guilt—"If only I had done something, she wouldn't have died." Suicide creates special problems for survivors because they can become stigmatized by having a relative commit suicide—"They drove him to it." Finally, when people die without warning, survivors often are troubled because they did not have a chance to mend a broken relationship or say good-bye.

On the other hand, survivors of deaths due to acute diseases and accidents are less likely to experience the following problems associated with chronic diseases:

1. Dying persons may not be willing to accept death, and when learning of their fates, may act in unacceptable ways.

2. Families may be unwilling to accept the death.

3. The dying process may be a long and painful process, not only for the dying patient, but for the family as well.

4. The cost of dying from a chronic disease can be, and usually is, very expensive. The entire assets of a family can be wiped out by the medical bills of a chronically ill patient.

Thus, there seem to be advantages and disadvantages of dying a sudden death and of dying a lingering death. Since we have limited choices in the matter (unless one intervenes), we will simply have to be prepared to cope with the varied possibilities. Who knows? Perhaps death will come "while sleeping in one's own bed at home at night in old age and with full mental and physical capabilities."

CONCLUSION

While the American way of dying is being discussed and researched more today than in previous decades, discussion often poses as many questions as answers. The following questions do not have simple and straightforward answers: When does death take place? Who should determine the timing of a particular death? Who in society should be responsible for defining the meaning of life and death? When is a death an accident and when is it a suicide?

Americans have developed a paradoxical relationship with death—we know more about the causes and conditions surrounding death, but we have not equipped ourselves emotionally to cope with dying and death. The American way of dying is such that avoiding direct confrontation with dying and death is a real possibility for many persons. What we need is the ability to both understand and cope with these processes. The purpose of this book is to provide an understanding of dying, death, and bereavement that will assist individuals to better cope with and understand their own deaths and the deaths of others.

SUMMARY

1. The American way of dying is typically confined to institutional settings and removed from usual patterns of social interaction.

2. American society has done little to formally socialize its members to deal with dying and death on the personal and emotional levels.

3. The "thanatology movement" was a concerted effort in the 1970s to bring about an open discussion and awareness of behaviors and emotions related to dying, death, and bereavement.

4. An increased emphasis on dying and death is reflected in today's media.

5. The issue of when death occurs is a difficult one to resolve because consensus does not exist in America regarding the definition of life and death.

6. The American way of dying has changed considerably since 1900. Relative to earlier times, Americans are less likely to die of acute diseases. Currently more than 75 percent of the deaths taking place in the United States can be attributed to chronic diseases.

7. In the past 50 years, life expectancy has increased 20 years. Serious consequences have followed affecting Americans' understanding and ability to cope with dying and death.

8. The manner in which an individual dies will influence the way in which his or her survivors cope with the death. Chronic and acute diseases have advantages and disadvantages for the coping abilities of dying patients and their families.

9. The United States is basically a death-denying society.

10. The "value" of human life can be "calculated" in various ways.

DISCUSSION QUESTIONS

1. Why did death "come out of the closet" in the 1970s? What events related to the thanatology movement helped change the American awareness of dying and death?

2. What factors have contributed to the American avoidance of death and dying?

3. Discuss whether you think the United States is basically a death-denying or a death-accepting society.

4. How has the definition of death changed over the years? What complications has this created for the American way of dying?

5. Compare and contrast the relative advantages and disadvantages of dying from acute and chronic diseases. What effects do each of these causes have on the abilities of families to cope with the death of a family member?

6. Discuss why women outlive men in the United States and most countries of the world.

GLOSSARY

Acute illness   A communicable disease caused by a number of microorganisms including viruses, fungi, and bacteria. Acute illnesses last for a relatively short period of time and either result in a cure or death. Examples of acute illnesses include smallpox, malaria, cholera, influenza, and pneumonia.

Chronic illness   A noncommunicable, self-limiting disease from which the individual rarely recovers, even though the symptoms of the disease can often be alleviated. Chronic illnesses usually result in deterioration of organs and tissues, making the individual vulnerable to other diseases, often leading to serious impairment and even death. Examples of chronic illnesses include cancer, heart disease, arthritis, emphysema, and asthma.

Cryonics   A method of subjecting a corpse to extremely low temperatures through the use of dry ice and liquid nitrogen.

Death etiology   The cause of death.

Sex ratio   The number of males per 100 females.

Socialization   The social process by which individuals are integrated into a social group by learning its values, goals, norms, and roles. This is a life-long process that is never completed.

Thanatology   The interdisciplinary study of death-related behavior, including actions and emotions concerned with dying, death, and bereavement.

REFERENCES

Adams, Cecil. 1988. *More of the Straight Dope*. New York: Ballantine Books.

Beecher, Henry K. 1968. "A Definition of Irreversible Coma." *Journal of the American Medical Association*, 205 (August 5):85–88.

Bordewich, Fergus M. 1988. "Mortal Fears: Courses in 'Death Education' Get Mixed Reviews." *Atlantic Monthly*. February, 261:30–34.

Cope, Lewis. 1978. "Is Death, like Pregnancy, an All-or-Nothing Thing?" *Minneapolis Tribune*, June 22, pp. 1 and 6A.

Dickinson, George E. 1986. "Effects of Death Education on College Students' Death Anxiety." Unpublished paper presented at the Forum for Death Education and Counseling, Atlanta, GA, April 18–20.

Dumont, Richard G. and Dennis C. Foss. 1972. *The American View of Death: Acceptance or Denial?* Cambridge, MA: Schenkman.

Kass, Leon R. 1971. "Death as an Event: A Commentary on Robert Morison." *Science*. 173:698–702.

Kavanaugh, Robert E. 1972. *Facing Death*. Baltimore: Penguin Books.

Leviton, Dan. 1977. "The Scope of Death Education." *Death Education*, 1:41–56.

Montagu, Ashley. 1968. *The Natural Superiority of Women*, Rev. Ed. New York: Collier Books.

News and Courier. 1988. "Doctors 'Kill' Patient to Save Her Life." Charleston, SC, September 22, p. 1A.

Ramsey, Paul. 1970. *The Patient As Person: Explorations in Medical Ethics*. New Haven: Yale University Press.

Stockwell, Edward G. 1976. *The Methods and Materials of Demography*, Condensed Edition. New York: Academic Press.

United Nations. 1953. *Principles for a Vital Statistics System*, Statistical Papers, Series M, No. 19 (August):6.

SUGGESTED READINGS

Dumont, Richard G. and Dennis C. Foss. 1972. *The American View of Death: Acceptance or Denial?* Cambridge, MA: Schenkman.

Presents American attitudes and experience related to the fear of death. Suggests that Americans both accept and deny death simultaneously.

Farrell, James J. 1980. *Inventing the American Way of Death, 1830–1920.* Philadelphia: Temple University Press.

An historical account of death in America.

Rosenberg, Jay F. 1983. *Thinking Clearly about Death.* Englewood Cliffs, NJ: Prentice-Hall.

A philosophical treatise of death and dying.

Wolinsky, Fredric D. 1988. *The Sociology of Health: Principles, Practitioners, and Issues,* 2nd edition. Belmont, CA: Wadsworth.

Presents the sociology of health and the health care delivery system.

CHAPTER 2

Understanding the Social Meaning of Dying and Death

—

The symbols of death say what life is and those of life define what death must be. The meanings of our fate are forever what we make them.

W. LLOYD WARNER, *THE LIVING AND THE DEAD*

2 This chapter focuses on one of the basic themes of this book—the social meaning of dying, death, and bereavement. Social meaning is the most important component of every aspect of dying and death considered in this text. If dying is perceived to be primarily a biological process, then defining dying and death simply as a biological or physical process would seem to be appropriate. Most people would likely agree with the "biology-is-primary, social meaning-is-secondary" interpretation. *We do not.*

Dying, in fact, is much more than a biological process. It is truly one of the most individual things that can happen to the body, and what happens takes place exclusively within the skin of the one person. However, with reference to the *meaning of dying,* the dying process is one of the most social experiences one can have—no human body exists in a vacuum or outside a social context. When a person dies, many things other than internal biological changes take place. For nearly all human beings, every act of dying influences others. Consequently, the act of dying is a social or shared event.

The sociological perspective emphasizes the social-symbolic nature of human interaction. The key factor that unites biological entities into a social group or multiperson entity is shared meaning: many of the goals one person wants to achieve, and many of the experiences a person wants to have, require shared and coordinated meanings and situations. Symbols are the means by which socially created meaning is shared in the process of human interaction. Symbols are words or gestures that stand for something else by reason of association.

A specific death has distinct meanings wherever the deceased had meaningful relationships, and the death of one person has extensive social consequences. With a death in a husband–wife **dyad,** half of that entity dies. If the couple has two children, one fourth of the family dies. One 30,000th of the community dies, and one two hundred fifty-millionth of a nation dies.

BOX 2.1   **THE FREE FALL**

> When I die, my husband loses his wife, his lover, his confidante. My children lose their mother. Each friend loses me as a friend. But I lose all human relationships. That's the meaning of the free fall. That's the meaning of being alone.
>
> JoAnn Kelley Smith (a dying person), *Free Fall* (Valley Forge, PA.: Judson Press, 1975), p. 36.

If a person is identified with many social roles or positions, and that death creates a situation where many roles or positions are vacated, then many persons or role occupants die in a single death. Furthermore, we may agree that while one biological body dies, ownership of that body is difficult to determine. "Who owns my body?" is a question often posed by people who are dying. Related to the basic ownership question are "Who is qualified to make decisions about *my* body?" and "If I am the one who is dying, what right do any others have to tell me what to do with my body?" Because humans are social animals, ownership is a creation of symbol-using people. Joint ownership patterns are created and exist for most people. Therefore, body ownership might be considered shared and the decisions related to it would be joint decisions.

The elimination or departure of a person from the ranks of "the living" leaves a hole in the midst of the living. Certain meaning is lost, while new meaning is added—behavior that previously involved the dead is literally no longer possible for it also has ceased to exist. Established interaction or behavior patterns are disrupted, an event that demands attention. The **funeralization** process involves activities, rites, and rituals associated with the final disposition of the dead. This process usually reduces the social disruption caused by death insofar as the rituals are acceptable to those involved and are performed according to societal norms.

The living are not only concerned with the death of a person, but also with what happens to the living as a result of that death. While the biological person may be gone, the meaning remains just so long as the living grant the "symboled immortality" or "meaning immortality" to the deceased (Lifton and Olson, 1974).

The granting or creating of such immortality is one of the things symbol-using beings can do. In fact, a given person may even take on more significance after dying than before. For the bereaved, changing the meaning of lost relationships is essential and may be done with varying degrees of ease, depending upon the nature of the relationship (see Chapter 4 for further treatment of this subject).

This book will try to counter the widespread tendency to interpret dying as primarily a biological process—something the body does to the person. We are concerned, rather, with what people *do* about these processes. For example, biologists and medical personnel (or anyone else, including social scientists) respond to the meaning of the biology rather than to the biology *per se*. The physician's decisions are made on the basis of what the biological condition means to that physician. Making a medical diagnosis is the process by which the physician decides the meaning of the biological factors. This diagnosis, then, represents the process of transposing biological factors into meaning factors.

Death-related meaning has extensively changed since the early 1970s. With reference to past knowledge about death, much of what was known was either untrue or incompatible with contemporary knowledge. While ignorance may cause problems, greater harm stems from people's convictions. The sociological statement made popular by W. I. Thomas illustrates this principle—whatever is *defined* as being real to the physician will *become* real in its consequences for diagnoses. Thus, the "biology-is-primary" perspective on dying and death creates a **self-fulfilling prophecy.**

A recurring dramatic illustration of the fact that the behavior of the physician and others stems from the meaning rather than from the biology *per se* can be seen each time the news media reports that a corpse in the morgue has come back to life after wrongly being pronounced dead by the experts. The physician's belief that a body is dead does not guarantee that it is. Behavior follows from the meaning, not from the biological factors *per se*—a *living* body was sent to the morgue.

Finally, the dying process almost always occurs in a social situation to which meanings are ascribed. Physically, everyone dies in some place, and that place is given symbolic meanings by those involved. Therefore, in this book we will focus on the fact that dying is more than a biological or physical event because it is shared, symboled, and situated.

The Social Nature of Meaning

To understand the role of meaning in death-related behavior, it is necessary to understand the influence of meaning in all human behavior. We use words to tell ourselves and each other what something means. This book consists of words about dying and death. Words consist of configurations of symbols. The words or symbols are not inherently embedded in the things named—we do not somehow extract words or meaning from the things we see as meaningful. Rather, we create symbols or words to represent the things named. In fact, the symbols re-present (present in a different way) the phenomena of concern. For example, the symbol C-A-S-K-E-T represents the container into which a dead body is deposited before burial.

The fact that all symbols are **empirical** means that they can potentially be shared or understood by more than one person. The meaning of a CASKET can be shared by many—the CASKET *per se* cannot. Meaning is created from symbols that are socially constructed, transmitted, and used.

Some symbols have empirical referents. These are the symbols—especially names or labels—that people use to identify, talk, or think about the aspects of the empirical world. Some symbols, however, do not refer to anything empirical. These types of symbols would include beauty, humor, indignity, and evil. Such nonempirically referented words have an exceptionally meaningful impact upon behavior because they are involved in the human process of making choices. To engage in social behavior, we employ both types of symbols or meanings.

Thus, we have attempted to recognize distinct differences between the empirical world and the meaning world. We have attempted to emancipate the words (symbols or meaning) from the world. Most people do just the reverse: They enslave the words by joining, locking, or laminating them to the empirical world so strongly that their separate identity is lost or hardly recognized.

Most discussions of words (symbols or meaning) involve people who think primarily in terms of the world. They have an empirical-world bias, even though they are talking to each other about things that are not physically present and that have no empirical existence. They effectively execute a symbol by-pass.

Creating and Changing Meaning

Biological bodies are *created, live,* and *die.* Bodies of meaning are also *created, live,* and *die.* Biological continuity occurs through a process of biological transmission or transference. Meaning (culture) continuity occurs through a process of social-symboled transmission. The socialization process occurs as biological bodies are transformed into social beings and as we teach our children how to behave in what our society considers to be a human way.

Creation of new meaning is always possible. Death-related meaning is no different from any other type of meaning. It is important to remember that this meaning is also created by humans, and is not discovered in the world. All meanings, including death-related meanings, are subject to change. However, well-established meaning is difficult to change. Meaning, for example, is frequently defined as sacred and, therefore, more likely to be protected and perpetuated than changed. Crises or traumatic conditions may be necessary for the acceptance of change in death-related meaning.

As noted in Chapter 11, many of the contemporary death-related meanings, including the rituals involved in adjustment, were created by ancestors who experienced dying in quite different social circumstances than those found in contemporary society. Furthermore, considering the dramatic changes in health, longevity, and health care, our ancestors experienced death in somewhat different biological bodies. Therefore, it is not surprising that discontinuities have developed in American death-related meanings and experiences.

Any aspect of death-related behavior can be changed if there is enough societal (or subsocietal) support. One person can change death-related meaning for him- or herself, but it is difficult to maintain and sustain the new vision if significant others do not support, legitimate, or validate this meaning system.

As in the ripples caused by dropping a stone into the lake, changes in death-related meaning will inevitably have consequences that move into and penetrate other areas of living. Change in the sacred components of dying and death may come in through the back door, so to speak. Cremation may gain increased acceptance, not as a direct result of changes in religion, but as a result of the unavailability of space for earth burials. Likewise, changes in life-prolonging, or dying-prolonging, procedures may result more from availability of technological devices than from changes in religion or **mores.**

A SOCIAL SCIENCE UNDERSTANDING OF DYING AND DEATH

In this book we will present many research findings produced in the social sciences to help provide an understanding for death-related experiences. We will also provide sociological, psychological, religious, historical, and cross-cultural perspectives for interpreting contemporary American customs dealing with dying, death, and bereavement. Finally, in providing an awareness of the many ways in which humans deal with death-related phenomena, we hope to give the perspective that different does not necessarily mean bad or good but simply different, and that death-related behavior can only be evaluated in reference to its social context.

It is our goal to provide multidisciplinary perspectives on dying, death, and bereavement from the bodies of knowledge developed in the social sciences. Chapters 3 and 9 will emphasize a psychological viewpoint to understanding death awareness and meanings; Chapters 4 and 10 utilize an anthropological or comparative approach in providing a cross-cultural perspective on death rituals; Chapters 11 and 12 review the history of American bereavement and funeralization; and Chapter 14 discusses some of the practical or economic aspects of dying, death, and bereavement issues. In the remainder of this chapter we will focus upon the sociological approach in providing a conceptual understanding of dying and death.

The Sociological Approach to Understanding Dying and Death

Sociology has been defined in many ways. We define sociology as *the scientific study of human interaction.* There are two parts of this definition that we will explore—sociology as (1) a scientific endeavor, with (2) human interaction as the subject of investigation.

George C. Homans (1967:7) in *The Nature of Social Science* claims that any science has two basic jobs to do: *discovery* and *explanation.* By the first we judge whether it is a science, and by the second, how successful a science it is. The first job is to state and test more or less general relationships between empirical events of nature. The second task is to explain these relationships within a theoretical context. A scientific explanation will tell us why, under a given set of conditions, a particular phenomenon will occur (Homans, 1967:22). In the process of discovery, the scientist is attempting to formulate general statements concerning empirical variables that can be verified by systematic observation.

Even though the claim has often been made that sociology and the other social sciences differ from the natural sciences because they use a radically different technique for doing research, Richard Rudner (1966:5) contends that the differences between the natural and social sciences are much less fundamental than a difference in methodology. Both the natural and social sciences use the same empirical methodology. This empirical methodology is based on observation and reasoning, not on supernatural revelation, intuition, appeals to authority, or personal speculation.

Sociology, as a science, aims at both discovering empirical regularities and explaining these regularities by referring to an interrelated set of empirical **propositions.** The goal of sociology is to produce a body of knowledge that will not only provide an understanding of the causal processes influencing human interaction, but will enable the sociologist to predict future social behaviors.

This is the basis for George C. Homans' (1967:4) contention that sociology is scientific.

> What makes a science are its aims, not its results. If it aims at establishing more or less general relationships between properties of nature, when the test of the truth of a relationship lies finally in the data themselves, and the data are not wholly manufactured—when nature, however stretched out on the rack, still has a chance to say "No!"—then the subject is a science. By these standards all the social sciences qualify.

Sociology shares with the other social sciences the scientific epistemology (study of knowledge) and a concern for understanding human interaction. The success of sociology, like any other science, is judged by the explanatory power and predictive ability of the body of knowledge produced by the research efforts within the discipline.

A body of scientific knowledge is a collection of those statements of relationship (or propositions) for which there is empirical evidence. It is organized in two ways. The first is the unsystematic collection of all research studies dealing with a particular content area published in research periodicals. For example, one might expect to find all social science research investigations concerned with death-related behavior to be published in a broad range of sociological and psychological journals. However, one would be more likely to find them in one of the following periodicals: *Omega: The Journal of Death and Dying, Death Studies, The Gerontologist, The American Sociological Review, The American Psychological Review, Human Organization, The Journal of Social Psychology,* and *The Journal of Abnormal and Social Psychology.* Knowledge of this type is there for all who will make use of it, and the only organization of these findings would be found in the theoretical frameworks of other research investigations and textbooks citing these studies.

The second method by which a body of knowledge is organized is through a theoretical **paradigm.** Research studies sharing general commitments to methodological techniques, research assumptions, and levels of analysis are brought together to form theoretical paradigms. According to George Ritzer (1975:7):

> A paradigm is a fundamental image of the subject matter within a science. It serves to define what should be studied, what questions should be asked, how they should be asked, and what rules should be followed in interpreting the answers obtained. The paradigm is the broadest unit of consensus within a science and serves to differentiate one scientific community (or sub-community) from another. It subsumes, defines, and interrelates the examples, theories, methods, and instruments that exist within it.

Sociology, like most other scientific disciplines, is a multiparadigm science. There is much debate over the number of paradigms existing within the field of sociology, yet sociologists would agree that no single paradigm is dominant within the discipline. Paradigms are further divided into subparadigms or theoretical orientations. Examples of these theoretical traditions (discussed later in this chapter) would include structural–functional theory, conflict theory, social exchange theory, and symbolic interaction theory.

George Ritzer (1975) divides sociological knowledge into three basic paradigms—social factist, social definitionist, and social behavioralist. The social

This picture is much more than a hole in the ground. Consider the emotional reaction you have to this photograph: your society has helped produce this response.

behavioralist paradigm is more concerned with psychological issues, influenced by the work of B. F. Skinner, and will not be discussed here. The social factist and definitionist approaches are the two central paradigms within the discipline of sociology and serve to organize contemporary sociological knowledge related to death and dying issues. The first paradigm is generally concerned with group actions and societal structures, and the second focuses on analysis of the behavior, attitudes, meanings, and values of individuals. For the purpose of simplicity, we will discuss these two general paradigms and the following four subparadigms: structural–functional theory, conflict theory, social exchange theory, and symbolic interaction theory.

The Social Factist Paradigm

Emile Durkheim's work served as the primary foundation for the social factist paradigm. In attempting to differentiate sociology from social philosophy, Durkheim defined the discipline as the study of social facts. For Durkheim (1964) social facts are "any way of doing things (fixed or not) which are capable of exercising restraint upon the individual." He advocated that sociologists should study social facts *as if* they were things. To accomplish this end, Durkheim (1964) formulated the following four guidelines in his *Rules of the Sociological Method* (originally published in 1895):

1. All preconceptions must be eradicated.

2. The subject matter for sociological research must be social facts directly observed.

3. Social facts must be viewed as a product of group experiences and not individual actions.

4. The cause of any given social fact must be sought in its preceding social facts.

The social factist paradigm is primarily concerned with group actions and societal structures. This point is exemplified in Emile Durkheim's (1964) claim that "society is a social system which is composed of parts which, without losing their identity and individuality, constitute a whole which transcends its parts." From the social factist point of view, a particular nuclear family cannot be reduced to merely a collection of individuals—social phenomena have a reality of their own.

Therefore, sociological research from this perspective will study group-related phenomena (e.g., death rituals, structures that provide care for dying patients, and professional groups of funeral functionaries) rather than behaviors of particular individuals.

Durkheim advocated the use of historical and comparative methods in sociological research. An example of this type of death-related research

DEELISH, MY LITTLE KUMQUAT

"I get uncomfortable watching dead people endorse things on TV."

might be comparison of the size, structure, and function of colonial funerals in Concord, Massachusetts, with a similar contemporary analysis of funerals in the same city.

Unlike Durkheim, however, many contemporary social factists employ the survey research design. The use of the latter technique creates a problem for some; as George Ritzer (1975:27) says, "How can one study social facts (cultural patterns) by asking individuals questions?" This issue might be more clearly understood by considering the analogy of the relationship between forests and trees. One can study forests in the United States and describe their sizes and distribution, their rates of reproduction, morbidity, and mortality, and the impact of acid rain upon them. However, to adequately understand a forest one must look at a few trees. The same may be true of cultural and social patterns and the behaviors of individuals.

Subsumed under the social factist paradigm are the subparadigms of structural–functional theory and conflict theory. The former is concerned with explaining the persistence of social facts, social institutions and structures, and the stability of society. Conflict theory focuses upon the competition between the various parts, institutions, and/or structures within a given society and the coercive forces which allow societies to perpetuate themselves at times and change at others.

STRUCTURAL–FUNCTIONALIST THEORY

Structural–functionalists view society as a social system of interacting parts in which death-related behavior is analyzed from two perspectives:

1. How do death-related meaning systems and death institutions contribute to the maintenance of the larger social system?

2. In what ways are death-related meaning systems and death institutions affected by their relationships to the larger social system?

Functionalists are interested in positive (eufunctional) and negative (dysfunctional) results of social interaction as well as the intended (manifest) and unintended (latent) consequences of death-related behavior. When family members commit themselves to care for a dying family member, it is eufunctional for emotional ties within the family; however, this behavior (especially if family members must interrupt their employment) may be dysfunctional for the security of family financial resources. A manifest function of attending a funeral is to support the bereaved as they attempt to adapt to the loss of a loved one, but a latent function is to strengthen the relationships that exist within social groups.

If structural–functionalist theorists were interested in the funeral rites and rituals, they might investigate one or more of the following research questions:

1. How do funerals help to celebrate and maintain society's most salient social values?

2. How do funerals help to promote relationships within kinship groups (grandparents, parents, aunts and uncles, cousins, brothers, sisters, etc.)?

3. How do funerals contribute to and/or affect the relationships between bereaved families and the larger society?

4. How do funerals facilitate the grieving process as one mourns the death of a loved one?

5. How do death-related rituals help return bereaved persons to their normal social responsibilities?

6. How are funeral rituals employed to socially differentiate families regarding social status?

Box 2.2's research example, written by Kathy Charmaz (1980:183–187), describes the strategies employed by coroners' deputies in maintaining the routine character of their work as they attempt to get surviving family members to take over the responsibility for the care of the dead body and the financial obligations related to final disposition. In this description we can observe that if each party performs his or her socially prescribed role, the social system runs efficiently and social equilibrium is maintained.

BOX 2.2 **THE ANNOUNCEMENT OF DEATH BY THE CORONER'S DEPUTY**

In these coroners' departments, the ways in which deaths are announced to heretofore unsuspecting relatives are strategically constructed with an eye toward accomplishing the objectives of getting the relatives to quietly accept both the burial costs and the death without the deputy's personal involvement. Burial costs are likely to be the "real" issue in countries without access to inexpensive burials. Then, the deputies feel constrained to handle the notification of death strategically in order for the family to readily assume the costs of disposal of the body.

Consequently, the strategies employed in announcing the death to relatives differ according to the necessity of getting them to pay for burial costs. When this is necessary, and therefore an important part of the deputy's work, special techniques are likely to be employed. Notable, strategic control of the encounter is enhanced by making the announcement in person. The deputies then lay the grounds for ensuring that an uneventful and speedy disposition of the body is made at the expense of the family.

The other objective, to induce the relative to accept the death as real, coincides with the deputy's interest in making the announcement of death efficiently without eliciting a subsequent fuss from the bereaved or becoming involved themselves. Part of doing that means constructing situations in which the deputy's sense of self is protected, in addition to his or her control over the encounter in which he or she is engaged. Self-protection strategies are employed to maintain the routine character of the work and to keep the deputies from feeling personally involved in the ongoing scene. Part of the self-protection strategy consists of the effort to remain the polite, sincere, authoritative, but basically disinterested, official.

The strategies for making the announcement help the deputies remain in control of the situation and handle the special problems that

(continued on next page)

emerge in the course of interaction. Not the least of these problems is the necessity of deputies to construct the contextual properties of the announcing scene, besides constructing the announcement itself. In other words, they must create the kind of ambience and interactional circumstances wherein the announcement logically fits so that it is effective and believable; they have no ready-made scene to serve as an official backdrop for their proclamation.

Compared to physicians who announce "bad news" to the relative, deputies have a weighty problem. Besides their much lesser amount of authority and prestige, deputies lack the advantages typically possessed by physicians of a prior relationship with the relative, a fitting organizational setting for giving the news, and a series of prior interactional cues that serve to prepare the relative.

Since deputies have neither the structural supports provided by the hospital situation nor the physician's status, they must devise tactics to get their work done without incident. Typically, their objectives are to announce quickly, to turn the responsibility of the body and its subsequent burial expense over to the family, and to determine that the person who received the news is holding up well or is with someone. But all these tasks may be embellishments to their main task of the disposition of the body and getting the family to assume the expenses, when this is their real objective.

Deputies try to create an authoritative context by rapidly supplying one meaningful cue after another that brings the relatives into interaction as they prepare to move into the announcement. Compared to the medical scene, the cues come much more rapidly and sharply. Thus, the cues cannot be easily dismissed, although the survivor has little time to think about them.

Skillful deputies can be expected to handle the situation in such a way that cues will neither be missed or misinterpreted. The relatives are not permitted enough time to disattend to them and, should they attempt to, the deputies will alter their presentation accordingly. For example, a deputy stated, "Sometimes I'm stern, sometimes I'm sympathetic, sometimes I even shout a little bit louder than they can."

The deputies who telephone find they get a better response when they successively lead the relative into questioning them. By doing so, the officials set the conditions wherein they can impart progressively unpromising news. For example:

> I tell them that he collapsed today while at work. They asked if he is all right now. I say slowly, "Well, no, but they took him to the hospital." [. . .] They

(continued on next page)

ask if he is there now. I say, "They did all they could do—the doctors tried very hard." They say, "He is dead at the hospital?" Then I tell them he's at the coroner's office.

Most deputies expressly avoid the word "dead" when first imparting the news, since they feel it is too harsh. Substitutes are used, such as "fatally injured" and "passed away," if they must refer directly to it at all. A preferred technique is to control the interaction so that the relative refers to the person as "dead." Those making telephone announcements attempt to manipulate the conversation so that the relative says the word "dead." Several deputies remarked that having the survivors themselves say it made the announcement more meaningful to them and the death more "real." Describing a close family member as "dead" becomes symbolic and sets the stage for treating the deceased as such. The deputies then reaffirm the survivor's statements and elaborate on them. Consequently, when the deputies' strategies work, the transition from perceiving one's relative from alive to dead can be made rapidly. The symbolic shift is likely to occur so quickly during the encounter that the relative may remain unaware of how the interaction was managed. Indeed, in an encounter deputies deem successful, the relative is likely to express appreciation for their "sensitivity."

Deputies state that the relatives always ask about the circumstances of dying. The coroners give them what information they have and can release, then turn the situation around by asking about funeral and burial arrangements. To illustrate: "They always ask what happened. Then we reverse it and ask what type of arrangements they are going to make."

Or in the case of the telephone notification, the relative typically inquires, "What can I do [to help]?" The deputies simply state, "All you need to do now is call your family funeral director, and he'll direct you." In both situations, this approach gets the relatives down to business and usually results in their agreement to "help" while in the midst of the initial encounter with the deputies. Likely, the relatives have unwittingly volunteered to underwrite the expenditures before they have any conception of the implications or expense. Simultaneously, the deputies have played the role of officials who cut through the survivor's grief and shock by pointing to the work that has to be done. Moreover, the deputies have strategically managed the situation in ways that foster the relatives' acceptance of their directives.

CONFLICT THEORY

While structural–functional theory focuses upon the issue of societal maintenance and social equilibrium, conflict theory is primarily concerned with issues related to social change and disequilibrium. Conflict theorists focus upon competition, conflict, and dissension resulting from individuals and groups competing over limited societal resources.

In emphasizing social competition over limited scarce resources, conflict theorists interested in death-related behavior would point out the inequality in the availability and quality of medical care and the differential death rates. For example, the poor are deprived of optimal care, in general, and of life-saving procedures, in particular (Charmaz, 1980:37).

This same theoretical perspective (Charmaz, 1980:39) goes on to suggest that American society, which has an individualistic perspective on death (as it does on most other social issues), abdicates most of its social responsibilities to the dying and their family members. In the following quotation, Kathy Charmaz (1980:39) claims we are assured of an inequitable distribution of health care and a lack of social concern for the dying precisely because Americans value individualism and privacy.

> Beliefs in individualism, self-reliance, privatism, and stoicism are ideological and justify the ways in which dying is handled. The ideological view of dying as a private affair, something that *should* be the responsibility of the family, relieves other social institutions, notably health and welfare organizations, from the necessity of providing comprehensive services. Such beliefs are justified by ideological views that human beings deserve privacy in their problems, and in order to maintain self-respect, they wish to rely on themselves to handle them whenever possible. When it is not possible, failure may be conferred upon those unable to handle their situations.

If conflict theorists were interested in funeral rites and rituals, they might investigate one or more of the following research questions:

1. What are the dysfunctional consequences of attending funerals?

2. What role conflicts and family disputes arise as a result of planning a funeral for family members?

3. How does not attending a funeral create conflicts between adults in neighborhood, friendship, and occupational groups?

4. What are the problems created by the presence of children at funerals?

5. How do particular family relationships contribute to increased competition for status among family members as they participate in the funeral of a family member?

6. How do methods of planning a funeral and the related expenditures contribute to increased family conflict and competition for scarce financial resources within the family?

7. How does the death of a parent create sibling rivalry among the children, and how does the death of a child create marital problems for the parents?

Box 2.3's reading is an example of conflict theory's approach applied to family behavior related to the division of family property and the reading of the will.

BOX 2.3　**WHAT'S FAIR IS FAIR**

Even where a will or the law of intestacy calls for equal division of a bequest among a group of beneficiaries and the beneficiaries accept the principle of equal division, conflict may occur. Some possessions are indivisible but desirable to more than one person, such as a prized antique clock. Problems may arise in the attempt to divide valuables equally. Under what circumstances can a treasured rocking chair and a family Bible be divided equally between two or more family members?

If all beneficiaries want fair treatment and a will attempts fair treatment, conflict may occur because beneficiaries have different perceptions of what is fair. Fairness can mean that something is divided equally, but fairness also takes into account various principles of deservingness or right; a division of an estate can be fair without being equal. Because fairness can be determined on many different bases, there may be many competing interpretations on what is fair. The following list, derived from the work of Marvin Sussman et al. (1970) and from interviews carried out during our research, indicates some of the competing principles for determining if the outcome in inheritance is fair.

1. Long residence in a house confers some right to it.

2. Last name identity with the deceased confers some rights to the property of the deceased.

3. Blood relationship confers some rights.

4. High frequency of contact with the deceased confers some rights.

5. Material support of the deceased confers some rights.

6. Coresidence with the deceased confers some rights.

7. Having given the deceased a thing confers rights to its return.

(continued on next page)

---

8. Need arising from relative poverty, handicap, minorhood, orphan status, or infirmity confers rights.

9. Contribution in building the deceased's estate increases rights.

10. Kinship closeness confers rights.

11. Previous perceived underinheritance increases rights.

12. Overinheritance reduces rights.

13. Hostile relationship with the deceased reduces rights.

14. Congenial relationship increases rights.

In addition to people having discrepant interpretations of what is equal or what is fair, there will be instances where equality and fairness may be competing principles. Some individuals will believe that the estate should be divided equally, while other individuals will believe that it should be divided on the basis of what is fair, though fairness may be perceived differently by different persons.

Because there are so many possible interpretations of what is fair or what is equal and because people often seek fairness or equality, a dispute may not be resolved easily. Disputes over inheritance may be one of the major reasons for adult siblings to break off relationships with each other. In some cases the inheritance dispute may be the final battle between competitive siblings, and in that sense it resembles the "last straw" reported in breakups in other close relationships (Hill, Rubin, and Peplau, 1976; Nevaldine, 1978).

Sandra L. Titus, Paul C. Rosenblatt, and Roxanne M. Anderson, "Family Conflict over Inheritance of Property," *The Family Coordinator,* July 1979, pp. 337–338. Copyrighted 1979 by the National Council on Family Relations, 3989 Central Ave. N. E., Suite #550, Minneapolis, MN 55421. Reprinted by permission.

The Social Definitionist Paradigm

The social definitionist paradigm differs from the social factist paradigm at two crucial points: The first is that the definitionist would contend that the essential feature of society is its subjective character. Social facts do not have any inherent meaning other than that which humans attribute to them. W. I. Thomas argues that if people define situations as real, they will be real in their consequences. This argument is a basic premise of the social definitionist paradigm. The social definitionist would contend that all social facts are either intrasubjective or intersubjective.

BOX 2.4 **WORDS AND MEANINGS**

Blood,
and Pus . . .
Entrails,
Vomit,
Dung, Spit and Afterbirth.
Disgusting words.

Love,
And Soft.
Mother.
Kiss, Mood, and Friendship.
Tender words.

Spring,
And Smile.
Dance,
Play,
Fun, Sing, and Beachball.
Happy Words.

Death,
And Fire.
Pain,
War,
Divorce, Poverty, Hospital.
Sad Words.

No. That's not right at all. You cannot
String words together
And say They're bad
Or good.

Where are the verbs?
Who are we talking about?
What are the circumstances?

Vomit is beautiful to a mother whose child
Had just swallowed a pin.
Love is pain if you are a third party,
Outside, looking in.

Death is very nice for someone very old,
Very ill, and ready.

And surely you've danced with a clod.
Or had a sad spring.

(continued on next page)

The second distinguishing feature of the social definitionist paradigm is the methodological unit of analysis—the individual. The social definitionist will emphasize individual behavior over group actions and societal structures.

George Ritzer (1975:85–86) rightly credits the writings of Max Weber as the exemplar of the social definitionist paradigm. The essence of Weber's analysis of social action was the *meaningful action of individuals.* Weber (1966:88) defines social action as human behavior to which the acting individual attaches subjective meaning and which takes into account the behaviors of others.

Weber advocated *"interpretative understanding" (Verstehen)* as the research methodology for investigating social action. The interpretative understanding approach requires the researcher to develop an empathy for the subjects he or she studies. At times this will require the investigator to enter the subjective world of the subject by participating in this person's life experience. A Native American proverb encourages us not to judge the behavior of others until we have walked a mile in their moccasins. In this context, interpretative understanding attempts to describe and explain social behavior from the perspective of the subjective meanings of the actors' intentions for their behavior. Today, contemporary sociologists utilize the *Verstehen* approach as they employ participant observation research techniques.

Reprinted by permission of Johnny Hart and NAS, Inc.

We will now consider social exchange theory and symbolic interaction theory as two theoretical traditions that might be implied by the social definitionist paradigm.

SOCIAL EXCHANGE THEORY

There are two traditions followed by social exchange theorists. The first is consistent with principles of behavioral psychology and stresses psychological reductionism and behavioral reinforcement techniques. The second type of social exchange theory has been influenced by the work of Peter Blau (1964) and is committed to many of the assumptions held by symbolic interactionists and the social definitionist paradigm. Social exchange theories of this type would contend that human behavior involves a subjective and interpretative interaction with others that attempts to exchange symbolic and nonsymbolic rewards. It is important that such social exchange involve reciprocity so that each interacting individual receives something *perceived* as equivalent to what is given.

From this perspective, individuals will continue to participate in social situations so long as they perceive that they derive equal benefits from their participation. For example, the social exchange theorist would contend that individuals will attend funerals (even though they tend to feel uncomfortable in such situations and find body viewing distasteful and anxiety-producing) because they perceive social benefit in being supportive of bereaved friends.

Box 2.5, a research summary of George C. Homans' work, provides an analysis of human behavior that draws on both types of social exchange's theoretical traditions.

BOX 2.5   **RELIGIOUS RITUAL OBSERVANCE AND ANXIETY**

George C. Homans (1965:87–88) concludes his synthesis of the theories of Malinowski and Radcliffe-Brown by citing seven elements related to the study of religious ritual and anxiety. The seven are the following:

1. Primary anxiety. Whenever individuals desire the accomplishment of certain results and do not possess the techniques which will make for success, they feel sentiments which we call anxiety.

2. Primary ritual. Under these circumstances, they tend to perform actions which have no practical result and which we call ritual. But these persons are not simply individuals—they are members of a

(continued on next page)

society with definite traditions. Among other things society determines the form of rituals and expects individuals to perform the rituals on appropriate occasions.

3. Secondary anxiety. When these people follow the technical procedures and perform the traditional rituals, their primary anxiety remains latent. We say that the rites give them confidence. Under these circumstances, they will feel anxiety only when the rites themselves are not properly performed. In fact, this attitude becomes generalized, and anxiety is felt whenever any of the traditions of society are not observed. This anxiety may be called secondary or displaced anxiety.

4. Secondary ritual. This is the ritual of the purification and expiation which has the function of dispelling secondary anxiety. Its form and performance, like those of primary ritual, may or may not be socially determined.

5. Rationalization. This element includes a system of beliefs which are associated with the rituals. They may be very simple: such statements as that the performance of a certain magic does ensure the catching of fish, or that if an Andaman mother and father do not observe the food taboos they will be sick. The statements may be very elaborate. Such are the statements which accompany the fundamental rituals of any society: the equivalents of the Mass of the Catholic Church.

6. Symbolization. Since the form of the ritual is not determined by the nature of a practical result to be accomplished, it can be determined by other factors. We say that it is symbolic, and each society has its own vocabulary of symbols. Some of the symbolism is relatively simple; for example, the symbolism of sympathies and antipathies. Some are complicated. In particular, certain of the rituals of a society, and those the most important, make symbolic reference to the fundamental myths of that society just as surely as the Mass makes reference to Christ's sacrifice on Calvary.

7. Function. Ritual actions do not produce a practical result on the external world—that is one reason why we call them ritual. But to make this statement is not to say that ritual has no function. Its function is not related to the world external to the society but to the inter-

(continued on next page)

nal constitution of the society. It gives the members of the society confidence; it dispels their anxieties; it disciplines the social organization.

In this seven-step conclusion, we can see that Homans has carefully brought together the major points of both Malinowski and Radcliffe-Brown. His basic contention is that when individuals experience anxiety in life crisis events, such as death, ritual will be instrumental in making sentiment latent. However, the fear of violating ritual obligations will again make anxiety manifest. This new anxiety will call for institutionalized ritual. Once individuals have fulfilled these religious magical ceremonies required by society, they will experience a reduction of anxiety.

Having discussed Homans' explicit theory of anxiety and ritual, we shall now turn to his implicit theory of these phenomena. In elaborating upon an implicit theory we must extrapolate Homans' position from his earlier theoretical treatises found in *The Human Group* (1950) and *Social Behavior: Its Elementary Forms* (1961). While any exegesis adds to the substantive writings of the author, it is believed that our elaboration will not distort Homans' exchange theory (in the tradition of psychological behaviorism) which is predicated upon belief in utilitarian self-interest. Abstracting Skinnerian behaviorism, the basic principle of Homans' theory is that if the individuals have needs they will manifest behaviors which have in the past satisfied these needs. To this basic theorem Homans (cited by Turner, 1974:233) adds the following corollaries:

1. individuals will avoid unpleasant experiences, but will endure limited amounts of them as the cost of emitting these behaviors satisfies overriding needs;

2. individuals will continue to perform activities as long as they continue to produce desired and expected effects;

3. as needs are satisfied by particular behaviors, individuals are less likely to emit these behaviors until the needs are again present.

Applying this theorem and its corollaries and Homans' explicit theory to the study of religion and anxiety, we have the following analysis. If individuals encounter an anxiety-producing situation, such as a death of a significant other, and they have utilized religious symbolizing in

(continued on next page)

the past to define death and dispel anxiety, they will engage in religious activity to meet their psychological needs in the present situation. Assuming that their sentiment of anxiety was latent before this present encounter with death, they may have been inactive in religious ritual behavior. The return to religious experience may cause anxiety due to the non-observance of religious obligations. While anxiety may be increased at this time (as Radcliffe-Brown would suggest) individuals will continue to perform religious rituals as long as they perceive them as having a potential for anxiety reduction. When the requirements for proper religious observance have been met (as determined by the group), death anxiety will again become latent.

In conclusion, Homans' social exchange theory states that religion functions to relieve anxiety associated with life-crisis situations. Death anxiety calls forth religious activity which serves to make anxiety latent. However, in order to maintain the external system of religious activity (which eventually becomes institutionalized), the group must continually reaffirm the potential threat of anxiety to unite individuals through a "common concern." This secondary anxiety may be effectively relieved through the group rituals of purification and expiation. However, primary reduction of anxiety is operative within the internal system of individual religion.

Michael R. Leming. 1977. "Social Exchange: Providing an Understanding of Religion and its Function." In Glenn Vernon (Ed.), *A Time to Die.* Washington, D.C.: University Press of America.

If exchange theorists were interested in funeral rites and rituals, they might investigate one or more of the following research questions:

1. Why do individuals attend funerals?

2. Why do some individuals not attend funerals?

3. What social and personal benefits do families derive from wakes, funerals, and other death-related rites of passage?

4. What are the social and personal costs for families when they provide wakes, funerals, and other death-related rites of passage?

5. What are the social and personal costs for families when they do not provide wakes, funerals, and other death-related rites of passage?

6. Why would the average American family spend approximately $4000 in burying their dead, when they could accomplish the same purpose at a fraction of the cost?

The foundation of symbolic interaction theory is that symbols (meaning) are a basic component of human behavior. People interact with each other based on their understanding of the meanings of social situations and their perceptions of what others expect of them within these situations. Stressing the symbolic nature of social interaction, Jonathan Turner (1985:32) says: "Symbols are the medium of our adjustment to the environment, of our interaction with others, of our interpretation of experiences, and of our organizing ourselves into groups."

From the symbolic interactionist perspective, human beings are autonomous agents whose actions are based upon their subjective understanding of society as socially constructed reality. Randall Collins (1985:200) makes this point in the following statements:

> Each individual projects himself or herself into various future possibilities; each one takes the role of the other in order to see what kind of reaction there will be to this action; as a result each aligns his or her own action in terms of the consequences he or she foresees in the other person's reactions. Society is not a structure, but a process. Definitions of situations emerge from this continuous negotiation of perspectives. Reality is socially constructed. If it takes on the same form over and over again, it is only because the parties to the negotiation have worked out the same resolution and because there is no guarantee that they cannot do it differently next time.

The symbolic interactionist perspective can be summarized in what some have called the **ISAS** paradigm statement—*Individual*-level behavior is in response to *Symbols*, relative to the *Audience*, and relative to the *Situation*. "ISAS" stands for the four basic components (see Vernon & Cardwell, 1981). Death-related behavior of the one dying, and of those who care about that person, is in response to meaning, relative to the audience and to the situation. Death-related behavior is shared, symboled (given meaning), and situated. It is socially created and not biologically predetermined.

Symbols Interaction is a dynamic, flexible, and socially created phenomenon. Meaning is socially created and socially perpetuated; it is preserved in symbols or words. However, preserved words have to be rediscovered and reinterpreted if they are to be continually used in human interaction. Generation after generation repeats the process with a somewhat different content—no book means the same to every reader. Similarly death-related behavior and meanings are dynamic phenomena.

BOX 2.6 **CONFLICTING DEATH-RELATED MEANINGS**

BY GLENN VERNON

Some Believe:

They are dying when they are not.
They are not dying when they are.

They should refuse to let some people die who want to die.
They, or maybe the state, should kill some people who want to live.

It would be good for a specific person to die.
It would be wrong for that specific person to die.

Dying is caused by the moral condition of the person dying.
Dying has nothing to do with the moral condition of a person.

God causes particular deaths.
God created universal death (thus everyone dies at some time) but does not
    influence particular deaths.

Wishing another person to die caused that death.
Wishing it were so cannot make it so.

Death is terminal—there is nothing beyond death.
Death is transition—it involves movement to another type of existence.

There is nothing for the person beyond death.
Death is transition—it involves movement to another type of existence.

An individual's dying time is predestined—a person dies when his or her
    time is up.
An individual's dying time is emergent—a person's time is up when death
    occurs.

Every person should fight to stay alive.
You should not fight that which is inevitable.

Dying is the worst thing that can happen to a person.
Certain types of living, such as living in an incapacitated and dependent
    state are worse than dying.

Keeping the biological body alive is the greatest value.
Humans in fact have a God-given instinct for such preservation. The well-
    being of the person is of greater value than just keeping the body alive.

Quantity of biological life is an overriding value.
Quality of life is an overriding value.

Nothing is of greater value than preserving one's life.
All have something for which they would give their life.

(continued on next page)

They can help the dying most by telling them the "real" meaning of death—"Let me tell you what dying should mean to you."
They can help the dying most by helping them decide what dying means to them—"Let me help you live fully while you are dying."

Dying is inherently fearful.
Dying can be welcomed and may be beautiful.

If death could be eliminated from our society, it would be wonderful—a step toward the creation of heaven on earth.
If death could be (and were) eliminated from our society it would be awful—a step toward the creation of a hell on earth.

A genuine concern with the dying person qualifies one as an effective care-giver.
Good intentions alone do not automatically qualify one as an effective care-giver.

Death would be welcomed—they want to die.
Death would be undesirable—they do not want to die.

Audience-Related Behavior   We constantly relate to each other; talking is the most common form of interaction. Even if we do not convey meaning to others with words, other people understand our meanings with their own words.

In making decisions about the meaning of death, one can, in effect, consult established words, other people, the self, or situational conditions. If one is dying, one can make decisions about dying behavior by observing the treatment by others. The audience involved may be family, physicians, clergy, nurses, peers, or even strangers walking down the hall of the hospital. How the patient is treated by these people reveals something about the patient. This treatment includes, but is not limited to, the following:

1. What people are willing to talk about with me—and what they avoid.

2. Whether they are willing to touch me, and how they touch me when they do.

3. Where I am, or maybe where others have located me—hospital, nursing home, intensive care unit, isolation unit, my room at home.

4. Tangible and verbal gifts others give me.

5. What people will let me do, or expect me to do, or will not let me do.

6. The tone of voice people use when they talk to me.

7. Frequency and length of visits from others.

8. Excuses these people make for not visiting.

9. The reactions of others to my prognosis.

Dying with dignity or self-respect does not always happen. Self-meaning can be created and sustained with the help of others. Dying as an unloved person, however, makes the dying an extremely difficult experience.

How you treat another also influences how that person will treat you. If another thinks you are leveling with him or her, he or she will treat you one way. If one thinks you want to engage in a game of let's pretend, one may be willing to play, as a favor to you. In death-related behavior, as in all behavior, one watches others for cues in deciding how to act.

BOX 2.7   **WHAT CAREGIVERS SHOULD NOT ASSUME ABOUT THE DYING**

BY GLENN M. VERNON

For the terminally ill person, the significant meaning that is taken into account in decision-making concerning self and others is the meaning she or he realizes. It is suggested that priority attention be given to meaning in any confrontation with death. Likewise the caregiver's behavior is influenced by the meaning the caregiver realizes. The same is also true of all people who are in social situations where dying and death occur.

Working from this perspective, it may be helpful to identify some frequently accepted assumptions that need to be questioned. It is

(continued on next page)

Box 2.7, continued

accordingly suggested that those working with the dying and the bereaved **SHOULD *NOT* ASSUME THAT:**

1. Those with whom you work necessarily share your meaning of death.

2. Meanings that were helpful to earlier generations are equally functional today.

3. Meaning remains constant and does not change.

4. Dying biologically is all that is happening.

5. Knowing about the biological aspects of dying will in and of itself provide knowledge about how humans expect to behave in death-related situations.

6. Pretension or deception, which you believe will help you cope with those who are dying, will help those with whom you are working.

7. The terminal patient is the only person who has death adjustment problems.

8. Persons facing bereavement have to wait until the death actually occurs before they can start working on their bereavement—meaning adjustment.

9. The person who is dying has somehow stopped meaningful living during the terminal period.

10. A death that is defined as meaningless, from the perspective of the person dying, cannot be given meaning in the last stages.

11. The terminal period without an extended future is necessarily one of no hope.

12. Talking is the only way for the caregiver to communicate "I care."

The audience to which the dying person relates may also be supernatural. Symbol users are not restricted to the natural–empirical world. Neither are they restricted to the world of the living. If believers realize that those who have died have an existence in another realm, or that there is a life after death, this belief is real to them and has consequences for their behavior.

People who are approaching death may involve themselves in a gradual replacement of a living audience with a supernatural, or other-world audience. As we have demonstrated, the dying relate to many audiences.

The Situation Where a person dies is also given meaning. As patients come to grips with the terminal condition, the manner in which they define the situation (and respond to it) will have a tremendous impact upon their dying. Dying in a nursing home or hospital is different from dying in the home, in bed, surrounded by a loving family and feelings of belonging. If patients view the institutional death setting as a supportive environment, their coping behavior may be helped. On the other hand, if they feel all alone, and if they have defined the place of dying as a foreign environment, adjustment will not be facilitated (Leming et al., 1977).

Like other meanings, the definition of the situation is an attempt by the individual to bring meaning to the world. Since the situational definition always involves selective perception, the terminal patient will assign meaning to the environment and will respond to this symbolic reality. The thing to which the patient responds does not have existence independent of his or her definition. Therefore, each terminal patient will interpret the dying environment differently. This accounts for the different experiences of dying patients (Leming et al., 1977). This point will be elaborated upon further in Chapter 5.

If symbolic interactionists were interested in funeral rites and rituals, they might investigate one or more of the following research questions:

1. What are the social meanings that give rise to the attendance of funerals?

2. How are death-related behaviors influenced by the social audiences of the American funeral?

3. In what ways do families utilize the funeral service to project an image of family value commitments and group cohesiveness?

4. How do families use the funeral in order to demonstrate status differentiation?

5. What is the influence of location of the funeral upon the meaning of the funeralization process?

6. How does the size of the funeral audience convey meaning to the bereaved and attribute social importance to the life of the deceased?

CONCLUSION

Why study death from a sociological perspective? The answers are many. While the primary goal of your course is *not* to prepare you for your own death or the deaths of loved ones, you may still learn many things that will be personally beneficial. Given the fact that you will have death-related experiences, it will be important for you to use a sociological perspective to acquire valuable insights into your own life and the lives of people about whom you care.

Secondly, as you read about the history of death-related customs in the United States and elsewhere, and comprehend social class and ethnic variations in bereavement customs, the sociological perspective may provide you with a new appreciation for your own life experiences and family traditions as they relate to issues of dying, death, and bereavement.

Thirdly, as you consider the ways the family socializes its members to develop death conceptualizations, attitudes, and feelings, the sociological perspective may help you to understand more fully how your own abilities to cope are a function of your upbringing. Furthermore, as you study the material in this book, you may attain a more objective perspective on some of the decisions that may confront you and your family as, one day, you attempt to deal with death-related situations. The sociological perspective, then, can make you more aware of the many options available to you regarding death-related decisions.

Finally, the study of dying, death, and bereavement is an important and interesting area of study to which social and behavioral scientists have much to contribute. A good reason to study death and dying from a sociological perspective is to learn more about the discipline of sociology. Social thanatology provides the student with an opportunity to investigate the meaning and application of many concepts developed in sociology and the other behavioral sciences.

SUMMARY

1. The goal of this chapter is to emphasize the extensive involvement of meaning in what many consider to be primarily a biological process—that is, dying.

2. Meaning consists of symbols that are socially created and socially used. Some symbols refer to something else or have an empirical referent. Some do not. The major function of both types of symbols is to permit humans to relate to each other and thus create shared behavior and meaning.

3. Death-related meaning permits sharing death-related behavior. The death-related behavior of the dying individual and those who are significant to that person is in response to meaning, relative to the audience and to the situation. It is a phenomenon that is socially created, not biologically predetermined.

4. Since most people participate in various social groups, they are involved in many different interaction patterns. Consequently, even though it is

but one biological body that dies, many "role holes" or vacancies are left with the death of a single individual. Bodies die—so do social relationships and social networks.

5. Death meaning includes evaluations of whatever those involved decide to evaluate. Evaluators may include values believed to be absolute, abstract, and situational. Defining values such as "living is always preferable to dying" as abstract rather than absolute helps explain the relativity of situational values and is likely to lead to fewer adjustment problems when confronting dying.

6. Dying is a social process. The person who is dying is living and is involved in living experiences with others.

7. Evolving death meanings are part of the general cultural changes taking place in contemporary society. Much of this change is centered around a discounting of biological influences upon social behavior.

8. Research studies that share general commitments to methodological techniques, research assumptions, and levels of analysis are brought together to form theoretical paradigms.

9. Sociology, like most other scientific disciplines, is a multiparadigm science.

10. The social factist paradigm is primarily concerned with group actions and societal structures. From the social factist point of view, society cannot be reduced to a collection of individuals—social phenomena have a reality of their own. Sociological research from this perspective will study group-related phenomena (social institutions and structures) rather than behaviors of particular individuals.

11. Structural–functionalists view society as a social system of interacting parts. Structural-functional theory focuses upon the issue of societal maintenance and social equilibrium.

12. Conflict theory is primarily concerned with issues related to social change and disequilibrium. Conflict theorists focus upon competition, conflict, and dissension resulting from individuals and groups competing over limited societal resources.

13. The social definitionist paradigm would contend that the essential feature of society is its subjective character. The social definitionist will emphasize individual behavior over group actions and societal structures.

14. Social exchange theory contends that human behavior involves a subjective and interpretative interaction with others that attempts to exchange symbolic and nonsymbolic rewards. Social exchange will

always involve reciprocity so that each individual involved in the interaction receives something perceived as equivalent to what is given.

15. From the symbolic interactionist perspective, human beings are autonomous agents whose actions are based on their subjective understanding of society as socially constructed reality.

DISCUSSION QUESTIONS

1. Discuss the differences between biological and symbolic death.

2. What arguments are offered in the rejection of the premise: In death, biology is primary, meaning is peripheral? Evaluate and discuss.

3. Each act of dying has three interconnected characteristics: shared, symboled, and situated. How does this relate to the statement that more dies than a biological body?

4. Answer the question "Who or what dies?"

5. Discuss the implications of the following quote: "Even though it is but one biological body that dies, many 'role holes' or vacancies are left with the death of that one person."

6. In making decisions about the death meaning, how does the treatment of the dying patient affect that patient's understanding of death and his or her role in the dying process?

7. As one faces imminent death, one becomes increasingly aware of the social nature of life. This change in awareness can lead to a life review where the individual realizes how extensively he or she lives with, through, and for others. Speculate as to why this change in perspective takes place.

8. Discuss the implications of the following quote: "I die for whatever it was for which I lived."

9. What are some of the meanings of "not dying"?

10. What are paradigms, and what are their functions for social science research?

11. Compare and contrast the social factist and social definitionist paradigms within the field of sociology.

12. Compare and contrast the structural–functional and conflict orientations in death-related research.

13. Compare and contrast the symbolic interactionist and exchange orientations in death-related research.

GLOSSARY

Dyad   Two units regarded as a pair (e.g., a husband and wife).

Empirical   Based on experience, sensory observation, or experimentation.

Funeralization   A process involving activities, rites, and rituals associated with the final disposition of the deceased's body.

ISAS   A shorthand presentation of the symbolic interactionist's paradigm statement: Behavior of the Individual is in response to Symbols, relative to the Audience, and relative to the Situation.

Mores   Ways of society felt to be for the good of society. "Must" behaviors that have stronger sanctions than a folkway (e.g., eating three meals per day) but not as severe as a law.

Paradigm   A set of shared general commitments to methodological techniques, research assumptions, and levels of analysis that unify bodies of knowledge produced by empirical research.

Proposition   A statement of relationship between two or more empirical variables.

Self-fulfilling prophecy   When a situation is defined as real, it becomes real in its consequences when individuals act to make it so.

Significant other   A person to whom special significance is given in the process of reaching decisions.

Symbol   Anything to which socially created meaning is given.

REFERENCES

Armbruster, W. A. 1972. *Bag of Noodles.* St. Louis: Concordia.

Blau, Peter M. 1964. *Exchange and Power in Social Life.* New York: Wiley.

Charmaz, Kathy. 1980. *The Social Reality of Death.* Reading, MA: Addison-Wesley.

Collins, Randall. 1985. *Three Sociological Traditions.* New York: Oxford University Press.

Durkheim, Emile. 1964. *The Rules of the Sociological Method.* New York: The Free Press.

Hill, C. T., Z. Rubin, and L. A. Peplau. 1976. "Breakups Before Marriage: The End of 103 Affairs." *Journal of Social Issues,* Vol. 32: 147–168.

Homans, George C. 1950. *The Human Group.* New York: Harcourt Brace Jovanovich.

Homans, George C. 1961. *Social Behavior: Its Elementary Forms.* New York: Harcourt Brace Jovanovich.

Homans, George C. 1965. "Anxiety and Ritual: The Theories of Malinowski and Radcliffe-Brown." In William A. Lessa and Evon Z. Vogt (Eds.), *Reader in Comparative Religion: An Anthropological Approach.* New York: Harper & Row. 83–88.

Homans, George C. 1967. *The Nature of Social Science.* New York: Harcourt Brace and World.

Leming, Michael R. 1977. "Social Exchange: Providing an Understanding of Religion and its Function." In Glenn Vernon (Ed.) *A Time to Die.* Washington, D.C.: University Press of America.

Leming, Michael R., Glenn M. Vernon, and Robert M. Gray. 1977. "The Dying Patient: A Symbolic Analysis." *International Journal of Symbology,* Vol. 8 (July): 77–86.

Lifton, Robert J. and E. Olson. 1974. *Living and Dying.* New York: Praeger.

Nevaldine, A. 1978. *Divorce: The Leaver and the Left.* Unpublished doctoral dissertation, University of Minnesota.

Ritzer, George. 1975. *Sociology: A Multiple Paradigm Science.* Boston: Allyn and Bacon.

Rudner, Richard S. 1966. *Philosophy of Social Science.* Englewood Cliffs, New Jersey: Prentice-Hall.

Sussman, M. B., J. N. Cates, and D. T. Smith. 1970. *The Family and Inheritance.* New York: Sage.

Titus, Sandra L., Paul C. Rosenblatt, and Roxanne M. Anderson. "Family Conflict over Inheritance of Property," *The Family Coordinator,* July 1979, 337–338.

Turner, Jonathan H. 1974. *The Structure of Sociological Theory.* Homewood, IL: Dorsey.

Turner, Jonathan H. 1985. *Sociology: A Student Handbook.* New York: Random House.

Vernon, Glenn M. and Jerry D. Cardwell. 1981. *Social Psychology: Shared, Symboled, and Situated Behavior.* Washington, D.C.: University Press of America.

Weber, Max. 1966. *The Theory of Social and Economic Organization.* New York: The Free Press.

SUGGESTED READINGS

Charmaz, Kathy. 1980. *The Social Reality of Death.* Reading, MA: Addison-Wesley.

An important book that provides phenomenological, interactionist, and Marxist interpretations of death-related behavior.

Collins, Randall. 1985. *Three Sociological Traditions.* New York: Oxford University Press.

Ritzer, George. 1975. *Sociology: A Multiple Paradigm Science.* Boston: Allyn and Bacon.

Two books on sociological theories that will provide more information and analysis on the four theoretical perspectives discussed in this chapter.

Feifel, Herman, Ed. 1977. *New Meanings of Death.* New York: McGraw-Hill.

Eighteen articles emphasizing the meaning of a wide variety of various aspects of death-related behavior.

Frankl, Viktor. 1959. *Man's Search for Meaning*. Boston: Beacon Press.

An outstanding book that examines the human desire to find meaning in both life and death.

Vernon, Glenn M. and Jerry D. Cardwell. 1981. *Social Psychology: Shared, Symboled, and Situated Behavior*. Washington, D.C.: University Press of America.

A book that explores the symbolic nature of social life and provides a detailed analysis of the symbolic interactionist perspective.

TWO

Understanding
Death Attitudes

—

CHAPTER 3

Developmental Perspective on Dying and Death

Adolescence through Older Adulthood

——

I, too, am trying to find some answers.
I, too, am troubled and sad. Did you know that?
Are you surprised that I don't know all the answers
      about death?
Don't be.

Even though no one really understands it,
      death is something we must accept.
We can talk about it.
You can learn something from me.
I can learn something from you.
We can help each other.

EARL A. GROLLMAN, *TALKING ABOUT DEATH*

3

In the verse above, Rabbi Grollman suggests that, even though no one really understands death, it is something we must accept. We can talk about death, can learn from each other, and can help each other. In this chapter we will talk about death with the hope that we can help each other better understand death conceptualizations at different stages of the life cycle. Since death conceptualizations of children are discussed specifically in Chapter 9, this chapter will be limited to adolescence through old age.

Sigmund Freud traced our conceptions of death to our earliest feelings concerning sexuality and fears of being punished for them. Alfred Adler had several brushes with death himself, and suffered seriously from a debilitating disease as a child. When Adler formulated his theories concerning the human psyche and its development, he attributed our need to strive and overcome to our early sensitivity to weakness and death.

The **ego psychologists** later departed somewhat from Freud and credited the individual with greater ability to manage the stresses and problems of life. Yet, they recognized that humans raise a whole set of defenses against the idea of death. Both children and adults, for example, have the power to distort their perceptions according to their needs: they have ways of denying harsh or painful thoughts. For example, people often believe and see what they want to believe and see, thus transforming images of their imaginations into reality.

In his Pulitzer Prize–winning book entitled *The Denial of Death,* Ernest Becker (1973) argued that fear and denial of death are basic dynamics for everyone. He asserted that we struggle to find meaning in life through heroic efforts. If we discover that heroic efforts are not possible, however, the dilemma can be avoided by building elaborate systems to explain the problem away. Some even flee into neurosis or a psychotic break. Becker felt that the fear of death was a basic problem of meaning with which we all struggle.

Though the subject of death was not a major concern in his writings, Swiss developmental psychologist Jean Piaget was probably instrumental in nudging psychologists to employ better methods of research in the developmental approach to understanding concepts of death (see Ginsburg & Opper, 1979). Through keen observations of his children and others, Piaget postulated that it is not until the early teen years that one is capable of genuinely abstract thought processes.

Since the publishing of Herman Feifel's *The Meaning of Death* in 1959, interest in and research on the conceptualization of death have grown. Representing **psychoanalytic, behavioristic,** humanistic, and other points of view, much has now been written on a developmental approach to death attitudes and awareness.

It is not the intent of this chapter to suggest that age should be seen as the sole determinant of one's death concept. Many other factors influence cognitive development, such as level of intelligence, physical and mental well-being, previous emotional reactions to various life experiences, religious background, other social and cultural forces, personal identity and self-worth appraisals, and exposure to or threats of death. Though an age-based approach is followed in this chapter, other important factors should not be ignored.

ADOLESCENCE

Adolescence is the "training period" between childhood and adulthood in the life experience of humans. It is often a time fraught with anxiety, rebellion, and indecision. Adolescence, from age 12 to 19, is composed of two significant periods (Gordon, 1986:17–18). The first period, from 12 to 15 (with 11 as the threshold), encompasses the acquiring of formal logical thought, the onset of biological sexuality, the growth of the physical structure, and the accomplishment of a myriad of psychosocial tasks. The second period, from 16 to 19, with transition around 15, is characterized by the completion of physical maturation, increasing intimacy with the opposite sex, continued acquisition of adult social skills, clarification of ethics and values, and the ability to make long-term commitments to persons and goals.

For adolescents, death is an unlikely event. Consequently, when a young person is dying it is disturbing for all those concerned. Death becomes real and must be taken into account.

Adolescents generally do not think in terms of their distant future in relation to their own lives. Their struggle with present life experiences, especially their own identity and anxiety about successes during the immediate future, virtually precludes thinking about what life will be like at age 45 or 70.

According to Jean Piaget (1958) and his followers, at about 11 or 12 years of age, young people are able to move from the use of language that is concretely oriented to an abstract level of thought. The adolescent can now use conditional statements like "if–then." Ideas can be taken apart and put back together again in new ways.

BOX 3.1   **BLACK ADOLESCENTS AND DEATH**

The black community generally keeps its dying family members at home far more frequently than does the white community, perhaps a reflection of socio-economic variables as well as a strong tradition of family and religious networking. Thus, black adolescents are typically more socialized at an earlier age to the rituals surrounding death and dying than are most white adolescents. Young black children are routinely taken to funerals and encouraged to interact with family members who are dying in the home. Also, the strong religious background of most black families helps to develop a belief about survival after death that makes death less threatening than it is for the more secularized white middle class.

This is not to suggest that the black culture does not have its fears and superstitions about death. On the whole, however, dying and death are not taboo subjects among black adolescents.

Adapted from Audrey K. Gordon, "The Tattered Cloak of Immortality," in *Adolescence and Death,* ed. by Charles A. Corr and Joan N. McNeil. New York: Springer, 1986, p. 28. Copyright © Springer Publishing Company, Inc., New York 10012. Used by permission.

An Identity Crisis

Being gripped by questions such as "Who am I?" and "How do I fit into the scheme of things?", the adolescent struggles with good and evil, love and hate, belonging and loneliness, and thoughts of life and death. These can be disturbing issues to the adolescent, who is not sure if he or she is a child or an adult, since conflicting identity signals are coming from all directions, further adding to the confused self-concept.

The adolescent has a vivid awareness of the dialectic between being and not being, according to psychologist Robert Kastenbaum (1986:11). Daily experience provides occasions for assertions of a new self, of "dyings" of the old self, and apparent abortions of the new self, notes Kastenbaum. Thus, it is precisely when the adolescent is most endangered by the polarities of being and not being that the concept of self emerges with singular force. The perception of a self under construction and then reconstruction occurs most notably as one experiences the possibility of failure, loss, catastrophe, and death.

One research study (Koocher, O'Malley, Foster, and Gogan, 1976) demonstrated that high school students experience much more anxiety, depression, and death fear than either junior high students or adults. They propose that it is the "identity crisis" of the adolescent years that could be largely responsible for this. Psychiatrist Robert Lifton (1976) also notes that adolescence is the time when a sense of great potential for disintegration, separation, and instability occupies the mind and brings about greater death anxiety.

Socialization to Death Fears

Like masturbation, adolescent death fears are universally experienced and discussed with equally uninformed peers, notes Audrey Gordon (1986:20–21). One of the tasks of adolescence is to begin to grapple with the meaning of life and death and to emerge with a philosophical stance that promotes optimism for the future. This is not an easy assignment, especially since one's attitude toward the future may involve pessimism more than optimism.

Our society's discomfort with the process of aging, illness, and death does not contribute positively toward the adolescent's image of a future (Gordon, 1986:22). Because youth is envied and aging is feared in America, Robert Browning's "grow old along with me" may *not* entail "the best yet to be" in the minds of adolescents. Consequently, a callousness toward physical deterioration and death often develops at this time. When the death of a significant other occurs, previous experience has probably not prepared the adolescent for the feelings of rage, loneliness, guilt, and disbelief that accompany a personal loss. If peers have not experienced a similar loss, they may have difficulty being supportive.

Adolescents often see death and dying depicted in the media as excessively "violent, macabre, distant, or unnaturally beautiful" (Gordon, 1986:22). Brutal death results from chain saws (*The Texas Chain Saw Massacre*, 1974), power tools (*The Toolbox Murders*, 1978), and even blenders and microwave ovens (*Gremlins*, 1984). *The Big Chill* (1983) opens with the dressing of a body for a funeral as the titles flash past. *Rambo* movies of the 1980s are filled with rapid-fire violence and death. *The Faces of Death* movies (I, II, and III), allegedly depicting actual human decapitation, autopsies, and executions by injection and electrocution, were overflowing with bizarre death scenes.

This picture, drawn by an adolescent, depicts death as a violent act committed by a deranged person in a bathroom.

In short, there seems to be a fascination with death. One perhaps builds up a sense of invulnerability by seeing other people dead or dying, notes psychologist Fred Hinker (*El Dorado Times,* 1985). Hinker says that watching these movies is like teenagers riding motorcycles at extremely high speeds. They are saying, "It can't happen to me. I'm proving it by flirting with death."

"What prepares the adolescent for an embalmed, cosmeticized body, and how does the teenager learn what to do at the time he or she is gripped by powerful emotions that threaten self-control?" asks Audrey Gordon (1986:24). How embarrassing it is to lose emotional control and perceive yourself as a child again, rather than a maturing young adult.

How do people in society, let alone the young, deal with such fears? Society is created and held together by rituals—for morning wake-up, going to school/work, eating, religion, politics, and so on (Gordon, 1986:23). Ritualization provides sanctioned boundaries within which the self can be safely expressed. Dying, death, and grief are all ritualized by society as a way to contain and give meaning to feelings of loss. The granting of adult responsibility and privilege to adolescents varies from culture to culture and group to group. Certainly in the United States, elders all too often do not teach children the adult rituals for handling dying, death, and grief. It, therefore, becomes one of the personal tasks of adolescence to acquire this knowledge.

BOX 3.2

DEATH THEMES IN ADOLESCENT MUSIC

THOMAS ATTIG

One key to understanding adolescents is cultivating an understanding of the music that occupies a central place in their lives. Music provides adolescents with mirrors of who they and society are and intimations of what they and society might become.

The stark aversion to old age in some of the music is startling. The lead singer of The Who in "My Generation" (1970) repeatedly asserts a wish to die before becoming old seemingly in part because of a repugnance that is attached to old age itself. Some songs, by contrast, express wonder about what it is like to be old and to see life from its end. The Beatles, for example, in "When I'm Sixty-Four" (1967) wonder about connections with others in old age when they ask whether they will still be needed and cared for as elderly people. Paul Simon in "Old Friends" (1968) sketches a lonely scene of two old friends sitting on a park bench, "winter companions . . . waiting for the sunset."

A theme with the need for continuity is found in Paul Simon's "Flowers Never Bend with the Rainfall" (1966). He offers a song that gives testimony to the extreme difficulty of thinking of oneself as anything but immortal. In "Eleanor Rigby" (1966) the Beatles paint a stark portrait of alienation and meaningless life. The concept of survival after death is treated in Joan Baez' 1969 rendition of the folk hymn "Will the Circle Be Unbroken?" The singer anticipates being reunited with her dead mother in a life to come.

Though a desire for symbolic immortality is noted in Neil Diamond's "Morningside" (1972), apparently the wish was not fulfilled by the survivors. After an account of how an old man spent his last days lovingly making a table so his children would remember him, the song reports that when he did die, no one wept and no one claimed the legacy that he had left behind.

The theme of loss and grief is prominent in adolescent music. Songs of tribute are among the best known: countless songs about Elvis Presley have been written and Dion's "Abraham, Martin, and John" (1975) refers to Abraham Lincoln, Martin Luther King, Jr., and John F. Kennedy. Also noteworthy is Don McLean's "American Pie" (1972) which views the death of Buddy Holly and other early rockers as a turning point in rock's loss of innocence.

Many songs express alarm over the potentially, sometimes all too real, lethal results of drug use. Lynyrd Skynyrd's "The Smell" (1977)

(continued on next page)

describes the smell of death in the air in the aftermath of the deaths from drug overdoses of many prominent performers including Janis Joplin, Jimi Hendrix, and Jim Morrison. Paul Simon's "Save the Life of My Child" (1968) depicts a scene in which a crowd is gathered beneath a young man perched on a ledge and under the influence of drugs.

Pornographic rock, where fantasy has taken over and death is dehumanized and distorted, is equivalent to the "slasher" movies. Warren Zevon's "Excitable Boy" (1968) describes the rape and killing of "Susie" after a junior prom date and cynically explains that the boy was just "excitable." The Rolling Stones' "The Midnight Rambler" (1969) salutes the Boston Strangler, and Thin Lizzy pays tribute to Jack the Ripper with "Killer on the Loose" (1980).

Death themes in adolescent music afford an opportunity for identification with cultural heroes, values and ideals, hopes and aspirations. It provides communication currency and social connection with peers and provides an alternative frame of reference within which their concerns can be and are addressed.

Adapted from "Death Themes in Adolescent Music: The Classic Years," in *Adolescence and Death,* ed. by Charles A. Corr and Joan N. McNeil. New York: Springer, 1986, pp. 32, 34–35, 37–39, 48, 51. Copyright © Springer Publishing Company, Inc., New York 10012. Used by permission.

Helping Adolescents Cope with Death

Whenever an individual is going through an unstable or trying period—especially when the stress involves basic feelings about self-worth, identity, and capability—the thought of death is particularly difficult to manage. Crucial to positive outcomes is the manner in which parents, friends, peers, teachers, and others enable the adolescent to process positively the ideas of the overwhelming threats of death to self and significant others.

Audrey Gordon (1986:23) notes that adolescents need not stumble around in a darkness that adults have helped to create. With proper preparation and support, young adolescents can be helped quite effectively by adults to become aware of death. Similarly, adults can help to impart to older adolescents a meaning to death and life that transcends everyday events and infuses the future with hope.

Below are some suggestions from Joan McNeil (1986:197–198) about improving family communication about death:

1. Adults must usually take the lead, at least in heightened awareness of the teenager's concerns about death and in openness to discussion of anything the adolescent feels like exploring.

2. Listen actively and perceptively, keeping your attention on the other person and the apparent feelings underlying his or her words.

3. Accept the other's feelings as real, important, and "normal."

4. Use supportive responses that reflect your acceptance and understanding of what the teenager is trying to say.

5. Project a belief in the other person's worth by indicating that you are not attempting to solve his or her problems, but are instead trying to help the adolescent find his or her own solutions.

6. Be willing to take time to enjoy each other's company and to provide frequent opportunities for talking together.

INTRODUCTION TO ADULTHOOD

We have already observed that one of the main problems with following a developmental scheme in the explanation of how people think, feel, and integrate life's experiences is that there are so many possible combinations of factors in any given life. The longer one lives, the more complex the picture becomes as the probability of additional factors influencing a particular person increases.

In addition to this limitation, caution is needed when attempting to generalize about what is true concerning any stage of life, and especially when looking at people beyond the adolescent stage of life. The premise behind this warning is that research findings describing a particular population, age group, or cross-section of people are just this—they should *not* be seen as more than a description of that particular sample of people. Research findings are influenced by the theoretical approach of the researcher and limitations of present knowledge, methodologies, and conclusions.

Another implication of this cautionary attitude toward understanding adulthood is that accurate conclusions could be drawn concerning any one person at any stage of life if more attention were paid to the many forces at work in, and features of, that particular person's life history. Another limitation to studying adults' concepts of death is the lack of a satisfactory definition of "maturity" in relation to the concepts of death—there is no way to know when one has arrived at a "mature" view of death.

Developmental psychologists are also limited in that they have not researched enough in the area of adulthood to draw firm conclusions about the changes in death conceptualization that might develop within an age category. For example, Freud concentrated on infancy and childhood. Erik Erikson, however, was able to move far beyond Freud to describe theoretically how the person develops over the entire lifespan. Some longitudinal studies of men have been published, but few of women. The relationship between these studies and ways of conceiving death is seldom discussed, except in research on aging. It seems to be assumed, for example, that we only need to pay attention to the death concepts of children and the elderly. Death research, therefore, is not taking place in as proportionately great a scale concerning the period of young adult to later middle age as the periods of childhood and old age. The major exceptions to this rule are found in studies of mentally and terminally ill populations.

Finally, a limitation is faced in determining what *adult* actually means. Biologically, though we may stop growing any taller at a certain age, great changes continue in the human body. Psychologically, it is even more difficult to arrive at any definition of adulthood that will be generalizable to a significant percentage of the population. One must conclude that the word *developmental* takes on a more individualistic character. Thus, one should expect that age will be less influential in explaining death conceptualizations for adult populations than other age groups.

BOX 3.3   **ECCLESIASTES 3:1–8**

For everything there is a season,
and a time for every matter under heaven:

a time to be born, and a time to die;
a time to plant, and a time to pluck up what is planted;
a time to kill, and a time to heal;
a time to break down, and a time to build up;
a time to weep, and a time to laugh;

a time to mourn, and a time to dance;
a time to cast away stones, and a time to gather stones together;
a time to embrace, and a time to refrain from embracing;
a time to seek, and a time to lose;
a time to keep, and a time to cast away;
a time to rend, and a time to sew;
a time to keep silence, and a time to speak;
a time to love, and a time to hate;
a time for war, and a time for peace.

The Holy Bible. Revised Standard Version. New York: Oxford University Press, 1962.

YOUNG ADULTHOOD

From the discussion of the development of the adolescent's intellectual understanding of death, one could expect the young adult (someone in the 20s or 30s) to have a good grasp of the universality, inevitability, and finality of death. The young adult should know, at least intellectually, that death is an entirely possible event for anyone at any moment. Unless forced to do so, however, one should not expect that every adult person would normally think of death constantly nor take it into consideration with each decision of importance.

Remember Death

In his book entitled *Man's Concern with Death*, historian Arnold Toynbee (1968) wrote:

> From the moment of birth there is the constant possibility that a human being may die at any moment, and inevitably this possibility is going to become an accomplished fact sooner or later. Ideally, every human being ought to live each passing moment of his life as if the next moment were going to be his last. He ought to be able to live in the constant expectation of immediate death and to live like this, not morbidly, but serenely. Perhaps this may be too much to ask of any being.

There have existed certain monastic Christian orders that practiced greeting each other daily with the words, "Remember death!" The fact that one tends to recoil from such a practice, however, is evidence that one would rather not take this advice.

The young adult would appear to especially reject the admonition to remember death. At this stage of life, one is just entering the arena of a somewhat independent life where capabilities and skills can be tested and pride can be taken in positive results. Hopes, aspirations, challenges, and preparation for success in life are the focus at this age. This means that dealing with dying or death would mean to face rage, disappointment, frustration, and despair (Pattison, 1977).

Young adults struck with serious disability or life-threatening disease have demonstrated that an almost universal sense of injustice and resultant anger exists when the young person is forced to "remember death." Along with all the international political issues involved, the protests against the Vietnam conflict in the 60s and 70s probably contained a good deal of repugnance to the idea of risking one's personal future at this stage of life. A walk through the wards of any major veterans' hospital or pediatric cancer unit would soon convince the most stubborn observer that significant physical and mental losses, and death itself, seem most abhorrent when suffered by the young adult.

The Novice Phase

Daniel Levinson (1978) labeled the young adult stage "the novice phase" since there is a strong sense of the need to learn, practice, and train oneself in the art of reaching one's fullest potential as a person and contributor to self-fulfillment, family, and society. Achieving something worthwhile would be devastatingly contradicted by any thought of serious limitation, sickness, or death.

Marjorie Lowenthal and her colleagues (Lowenthal, Thurnher, & Chiriboga, 1975) evaluated 216 people grouped in four stages of the life cycle: high school seniors, young newlyweds, middle-aged parents, and an older group about ready to retire. Each person was asked specific questions concerning concepts and thoughts about death. Older people thought of death mainly in connection with specific and personal circumstances such as the death of a friend, while younger people were likely to have death thoughts in response to general events such as accidents, earthquakes, or war.

Again, it is evident that though age may have some influence over the way one thinks, individual circumstances and external forces have a more powerful effect upon an individual's thoughts about death. The older one grows, the more apparent it becomes that one needs to reflect on life as much as one needs to engage in it. Such a practice can provide the individual with greater life satisfaction. As one moves into middle adulthood, however, it can have both positive and negative results.

MIDDLE-AGED ADULTHOOD

While there appears to be no agreement among social scientists as to the exact beginning of middle age, most seem to suggest that this period of life starts between ages 40 and 45. The U.S. Census Bureau defines middle age as being ages 45 to 64, while Vera in the Broadway play "Mame" describes middle age as being "somewhere between 40 and death."

For the person who has lived 40 or 50 years, life brings with it the advantages of experience. Promotion to supervisor, foreman, or analogous status rankings in work or social milieu demonstrates the greater political and social power achievable during middle age. Everyone is not promoted, however, and even those who are, as well as their less fortunate colleagues, become gradually aware that physical vitality has now begun to wane.

The Panic Begins

The "panic" begins once one realizes that the idealized self with dreams of accomplishment or fulfillment for so many years may not actually come to pass. Those whose job or self-concept depends upon youthful physical vigor especially suffer from this recognition. No amount of jogging reverses the effects of time. No patent medicine can undo the damage from wear and tear. The only hope is to make the best of what energies and experience remain and to focus on what one does best.

Those whose strengths lie in intellectual and social skills will be less threatened, since there is a cultural–social time clock that one is able to impose over the biological time clock (Neugarten, 1968). This seems to make more actual difference in the way one lives and how much satisfaction one is able to derive from life. Jack Riley (1968) found a stronger correlation between education and more positive views concerning death than between age and positive death views. Stated negatively, people with less education appear more often to have more negative views concerning death. One must remember, however, that a correlation does not prove a *causal* connection.

According to developmental theorists, death is a salient issue for midlife adults. Failing health, deaths of parents, loss of close friends, and changes in physical appearance contribute to a heightened awareness of death. As long as one's parents are living, there is a buffer between the person and death— one's parents are "supposed" to die first. When one's parents die, however, this buffer is gone and one's own generation becomes the genealogical line of descent to die.

In analyzing the relationships between death anxiety, age, developmental concerns, and socioeconomic status in a sample of 74 middle-aged women, Richardson and Sands (1987:327, 338) found that developmental factors were the salient issues with death concern, death as interpersonal loss, and death as a dimension of time. Age was the sole predicator of death anticipation, and death denial and income were significant with the physical aspects of death. For example, low-income respondents, more concerned about economic and physical matters, considered the material aspects of death more than the high-income group. No variable predicted death as depressing. These results revealed the multidimensionality of death attitudes and the significance of considering both developmental and socioeconomic influences in predicting death attitudes.

A More Philosophical Outlook Develops

Elliott Jacques (1965) observed that awareness of death changes people's lives in middle age, causing them to become more philosophical about their lives and to reevaluate values and priorities. In the process of confronting their own mortality, people deepen their capacities for love and enjoyment, and ultimately acquire more meaning in their lives. Carl Jung (1933) also believed that adults become more introspective and concerned with meaning during midlife and concluded that they experience an inner transformation after recognizing previously suppressed aspects of their personality. He maintained that those who successfully resolve these conflicts become more androgenous and more individuated.

Age differences in types of death concerns were observed by Stricherz and Cunnington (1982). The middle-aged emphasize the pain of dying and dying before being ready. The young adults focused on losing persons they cared for, and the elderly worried about being helpless, taking a long time to die, and having to depend on others. This study found that all age groups consider death, but they do so in different ways and contexts.

Middle-aged adults are aware of getting closer to the "day of reckoning" and will need to evaluate values, meanings, and sense of self-worth in the face of finitude. The individual becomes increasingly conscious of thoughts of painful death, the dying process, and of ceasing to be as a person. An awareness of the meaning of absence to significant others—spouse, children, and others—develops.

Thus, death at this point in life often carries with it some of the same sense of injustice and anger that the younger adult experiences with thoughts of death. Now, however, these thoughts are tempered with the recognition that many more forces exist that could bring death "home" to the individual.

Personal Growth Continues

While the mature adult needs to give up fantasies of immortality, omnipotence, and grandiosity, there still needs to be a sense of accomplishment—a fulfilling of oneself and one's plans for family and personal enterprises. Consciousness of time and death, therefore, makes little difference for the middle-aged adult. One strives to put all one's skills and experiences to the best possible use.

Once into the decade of the fifties, however, a turning point is reached in which one's finitude becomes even more evident. The individual becomes more conscious that time is no longer measured from birth so much as until death or until the end of one's most productive years. Focusing upon what one wants most to do before retirement or death causes one to avoid those things considered extraneous and/or uninteresting. All of this is not to say that increase in age means cessation of personal growth. To the contrary, as long as there is life, growth can occur for the individual who has the will to live and the will to give of self to others.

All is not lost in middle age, however. Bernice Neugarten (1968) points to evidence that people in their forties see the world in a more positive way than those in their sixties. Possibilities for the 60-year-old are more likely to be faced in passive modes of coping than in active modes. She suggests that women tend to cope increasingly in affective and expressive terms, while men at this stage will increasingly employ abstract and cognitive modes of coping.

OLDER ADULTHOOD

While some have observed that "growing old is hell," others look forward to the autumn of their lives. As Goethe stated, "To grow old is in itself to enter upon a new venture." An aging professional athlete noted that growing old is really mind over matter—as long as you do not mind, it does not matter.

Another division regarding old age has appeared in recent years—a division between the young-old and the old-old (Neugarten, 1974). The young-old come from the age group composed of those between 55 and 75; the old-old are 75 and over. Neugarten pictures the young-old as possessing relatively good health, education, purchasing power, free time, and being politically involved.

The young-old are distinguished from the middle-aged primarily by the fact of retirement. While 65 has been the marker of old-old since the beginning of the Social Security system, age 55 is becoming a meaningful lower age limit for the young-old because of the lowering age of retirement. Obviously, employment and health status have a tremendous effect upon placement in either older category.

Life can be compared to a train traveling through a tunnel. There is a point at which the train is leaving the tunnel rather than entering it. As our older relatives and friends die, we cannot help but become aware that we are not immune from death. As noted earlier, when no older generation exists, and the members of our own generation die with increasing frequency, the awareness of the scarcity of time becomes a reality. Therefore, for the person over the age of 60, the end of the tunnel is in sight.

Box 3.4 shows a letter sent to the author and his wife by Lucie Reid, who suggests that the "end of the tunnel is in sight" for her. She seems accepting of the fact and ready to die.

BOX 3.4

My Dear Children,

This seems a strange *gift* for this time of the year. This lovely ball was given me by the friend who made it, and I want it to hang for many years on your happy tree. If I live until another Christmas, I would be 97 which is too long to stay in this devastated world which my generation has made. I am ready to depart any time. God has been wonderfully good to me. I have had all any one could ask for—love and care and now every comfort in this shadowing time. I say with Cardinal Newman, "So long thy hand hath led me, sure it will lead me on."

I know that you are leading lives full of meaning, and my blessings go with this bright ball. I believe a circle has no beginning and no end.

Sincerely your friend,
Lucie Reid

(continued on next page)

Having lived next door to Lucie Reid for two years in western Pennsylvania, we moved. For several years after that, my wife and I received a beautiful hand-decorated Christmas ball from her. The ball usually arrived in mid-December. One year, however, the ball arrived in mid-July. The above note was enclosed in the package.

Lucie Reid died before "another Christmas."

Erikson's Final Stage of Life

Erik Erikson's theory of human development (1959) divides the life cycle into eight stages from infancy to old age. Each stage of development presents a crisis in understanding of oneself, of one's purposes, and of relationships with others. The developmental task at each stage is to resolve the crisis successfully; then the person can progress to the next stage of maturity. The eight stages are infancy, early childhood, play age, school age, adolescence, young adulthood, adulthood, and senescence. Erickson argues that a person must have been successful to some degree in solving the seven crises that come before in order to resolve the eighth stage of **senescence.** The task of the final stage of life is to achieve integrity—a conviction that one's life has meaning and purpose and that having lived has made a difference.

Hannelore Wass (1979:186) observed that the **life review,** a concept advanced by Robert Butler, is in close harmony with Erikson's eighth stage of the life cycle. The life review is triggered by the realization that one has reached the end of life and that death is near. The life review serves to prepare a person for dying—preparation that may decrease the fear of death.

Death Taboo and the Elderly

The death taboo is still in practice with respect to the elderly in the United States (Wass, 1979:190). There seems to be much reluctance to talk about death with the elderly. Since the elderly are nearing the end of their life cycle and dying is in the near future, one might assume that older adults would not want to talk about death. I can remember an undergraduate student of mine in the early 1970s wanting to do a research project and to interview the elderly on their attitudes toward dying. I even thought at the time that the elderly might not wish to talk about death. Was I ever wrong! She had a 100 percent response from those she contacted.

Even the experts on aging largely avoid the subject of death. Wass and Scott (1977) found in a survey that 90 percent of the scholarly and textual books examined on aging devote less than 5 percent of their space to a discussion of death. About 65 percent of the books give less than 1 percent, and nearly 20 percent of the books with a total of 3476 pages (average of 386 pages per book) make no mention of death whatsoever.

Wass (1979:190) speculates as to why death discussions are avoided with the elderly. Some believe that younger adults avoid the topic because it reminds them too chillingly of their own eventual demise. Others believe the topic is avoided so as not to upset an older person unduly. Others think that death is not brought up with the elderly because of some kind of embarrassment, particularly when an inheritance is involved.

To show how the topic of death is still taboo to many, several years ago, I was invited to serve as keynote speaker on death and dying at the annual spring banquet of the local American Association of Retired Persons. As we were sitting at the head table overlooking the 150 members of the local chapter of AARP, the moderator for the banquet turned to me just moments before he was to introduce me and said, "I told them you were going to speak on the aging process. Would you mind introducing your topic of death and dying to them?" Apparently, the person in charge, who had invited me to speak on death and dying, could not bring himself to disclose the topic beforehand. He, therefore, had previously announced the topic to be the aging process.

Death Fears

Like their younger contemporaries, older adults will have some anxieties and concerns as they approach death. There is empirical evidence that suggests older persons think of death more often than younger adults, but the elderly appear to have less actual **death fear** and **anxiety** (see Kalish, 1976; Kalish & Reynolds, 1976; Kastenbaum, 1969; Leming, 1980; Lund & Leming, 1975). While the elderly tend to have less fear of death than younger groups, they are more often aware of dying and death on a daily basis because of the high rate of death of friends and associates.

According to Richard Kalish (1976), several factors account for the lower death anxiety levels found in older adults: (1) Older adults see their lives as having fewer prospects for the future and less value; (2) older adults who live longer than they expected have a sense of living on "borrowed time"; and (3) dealing with the deaths of friends can help socialize older adults toward acceptance of their own death.

Richard Dumont and Dennis Foss (1972) suggest that, since older people are more likely to have fulfilled their goals in life, they are less fearful of death—for others, the possibility of death might threaten personal achievement, since many of their goals are yet to be realized. For those elderly who have not attained their goals, they are more likely to have either made their goals more modest or somehow rationalized their lack of achievement. It is also possible that older people come from an age cohort that was better socialized as children to deal with death. They are more likely to come from rural backgrounds and to have had earlier encounters with deaths of siblings, family members, and friends.

BOX 3.5   **SOCRATES ON THE FEAR OF DEATH**

> To fear death is nothing other than to think oneself wise when one is not; for it is to think one knows what one does not know. No man knows whether death may not even turn out to be the greatest of blessings for a human being; and yet people fear it as if they knew for certain that it is the greatest of evil.
>
> *Great Dialogues of Plato.* Trans. by W.H.D. Rouse. "The Apology (The Defense of Socrates)." Bergenfield, NJ: Mentor Books, 1971, p. 435.

Wass (1979:193) reports that few studies have examined gender differences in the fear of death among the elderly. The available studies show no such differences in noninstitutionalized, in institutionalized, and in acute geriatric patients. A study by Wass and Sisler (1978) of noninstitutionalized older persons, however, showed significant gender differences: Women have more fear of death than males. When only institutionalized versus noninstitutionalized elderly have been studied to determine if death fears vary with these two populations, Wass (1979:193) cites studies which show that the institutionalized elderly in nursing homes tend to be more fearful than those living out in the community in an apartment or house.

In a study of terminal cancer patients, Lund and Leming (1975) found that older patients had less anxiety concerning their diseases and terminal conditions than did younger persons. Older patients tended to experience greater depression, however.

Wass (1979:193–194) further reports that some evidence exists to suggest that the widowed tend to be more fearful of death than are the elderly married or remarried. Persons living alone have greater fear of death than those living with a family. The elderly with a grade school education have a greater fear of death than those elderly who are college graduates. The elderly with low incomes (less than $5000 annually) exhibit a greater fear of death than those with higher incomes (above $15,000 annually). High levels of death anxiety for the elderly seem to be associated with poor physical and mental health.

There is evidence (see Kalish 1976; Leming, 1980; McKenzie, 1980; Norman & Scaramelli, 1980) that differences in death anxiety and fear appear to

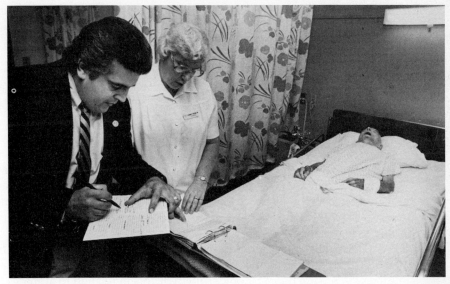

A coroner's office investigator gathers routine information following a nursing home death. Approximately 70 percent of all deaths take place in institutional settings.

be more a function of religiosity than age. Since older persons are more likely to be religious, a sense of comfort should be provided as they approach death. The older person is more likely to believe in an afterlife and rely on a faith in God as a coping strategy in dealing with death.

The Place of Death

Death for the older person becomes a normal and expectable event. The crisis for the elderly is not so much death, but how and where the death will take place. The prospect of dying in a foreign place in a dependent and undignified state is a very distressing thought for the older adult. They do not wish to be a financial or physical burden on anyone, yet the options of care may be limited.

While most elderly individuals would prefer to die in their homes in familiar surroundings, the majority continue to die in hospitals and nursing homes (Kalish, 1965). These institutionalized settings are better equipped to handle dying individuals, and the family is removed from the considerable strain of caring for a dying family member in the home. Thus, while the elderly might prefer to die at home, they are not likely to be allowed to do so.

The elderly are more likely to be separated from family and friends as they die. For them, the dying process may involve a fear of isolation and loneliness. Younger, terminally ill patients are usually more concerned about the pain, indignity, and dependency of the dying process, leaving loved ones and not accomplishing their goals (Leming, 1980).

CONCLUSION

Psychosocial studies of developmental concepts of death are themselves in a stage of infancy. Significant progress is being made, however, in an understanding of how children and adolescents experience loss at various stages of their development. Adolescence is a particularly vulnerable period with regard to facing death. A strong sense of injustice is not uncommon when one dies who has not seemed to reach fullest potential or even the opportunity to experience life.

Thinking about death is powerfully influenced by experience with death or threats of death. Mental health, ability to manage anxiety, and meaningfulness in life are the most powerful predictors in relation to attitudes toward death. Broad cultural–religious influences also enter significantly into each of these features.

People can and do manage much of what happens within their minds. One gathers information and insights, learns to better cope, and gives aid to others in need. At whatever stage of the life cycle, one can be helped to face both life and death more positively.

More research is needed to explore the relationships between death conceptualizations, gender differentiation, and position within the adult life cycle. Some stereotypes are beginning to fade concerning older men and women, but our conclusions are tentative, and more empirical research is needed.

Growing older pushes one to depend more upon educational, intellectual, and social skills than upon physical prowess. Feeling that one is useful and is contributing to the well-being of others, as well as having a healthy understanding of death, all contribute significantly to meaningful living and dying. As Robert Kavanaugh (1972:226) says, "I am ashamed how little I know about death and dying, but never have I enjoyed life more, dreamed more beautiful dreams each night, than when I began having courage to begin facing death."

Some pessimism can be found in older people, for willing disengagement from life is not necessarily a universal trait. While the fear of death lessens with age, the thought of death increases. The way time is used changes, as does the meaning one finds in life's experiences. Yet, living a happy and meaningful life is one of the ways to develop a positive and healthy view of death. Perhaps Alex Keaton of the television show "Family Ties" best sums up the developmental approach to death when he said,

"Children die with opportunities and dreams; old people die with achievements and memories."

SUMMARY

1. An overall psychosocial theory of death acceptable to a majority of researchers is still lacking.

2. The older the person, the more complex is the task of understanding what causes one to think about death in a particular way.

3. During adolescence the sense of personal identity is most vulnerable, and concepts and feelings of death are powerfully influenced by that vulnerability.

4. The young adult stage has been labeled "the novice phase" since a strong sense of need to train oneself in the art of reaching one's fullest potential is contradicted by any thought of death.

5. "The panic phase" begins during the middle years when one realizes that the idealized self one longs to develop may not actually happen.

6. Research concerning the conceptualization of death in middle adulthood is difficult to find.

7. Most people are capable of thinking of death more often and more profoundly than they do, but psychological defenses sometimes prevent this from happening.

8. According to Erik Erikson, the task of the final stage of life, senescence, is to achieve integrity.

9. In the United States a taboo exists with respect to discussing death-related topics with the elderly.

10. The crisis of the elderly is not so much death, but how and where the death will take place.

DISCUSSION QUESTIONS

1. What are some of the factors, other than age, that influence death conceptualizations? Why are these factors important in understanding the ways people conceptualize death?

2. Why do high school- and college-aged students have a higher level of death anxiety than junior high school students?

3. Both death and sex education are viewed by many as problems. Cite any current trends that may suggest that death and sex education are more in vogue in institutional settings today.

4. In your opinion, have death conceptualizations changed much in the past few decades? Do you see death conceptualizations changing much in the next few decades?

5. What are some of the limitations of the developmental approach to the understanding of death conceptualizations?

6. What are some death themes in contemporary adolescent music? How do you explain death themes in music?

7. How do you explain the popularity of some of the movies depicting brutal death scenes?

8. Why would young adults appear to reject the admonition to remember death?

9. Why would education tend to reduce one's anxiety about death?

10. Why does the death taboo exist with respect to the elderly in the United States?

GLOSSARY

Behaviorists   A school of psychology that focuses chiefly on overt behavior rather than upon inner psychological dynamics which cannot be clearly identified or measured.

Death anxiety/Death fear   A learned emotional response to death-related phenomena that is characterized by extreme apprehension.

Ego psychologists   A school of theorists and therapists who moved away from Freud in the direction of making more emphasis fall in therapy upon the coping strategies and strengths of the person rather than upon the more elusive dynamics of the libido and the unconscious.

Life review   Robert Butler's term that suggests a reverence for what one was and a time for judgment. The process involves looking back over one's life and perhaps tracing back one's steps in earlier years. Other meanings are a review of one's life, done as death draws near; and a therapeutic technique in helping the elderly.

Psychoanalysis   A school of theory and therapy that concentrates upon the unconscious forces behind overt behavior, dealing principally with instinctual drives and their dynamics in the individual's inner psyche; uses interplay of transference and resistance between psychoanalyst and client as principal foci.

Senescence   Erik Erikson's last stage of the life cycle; the task is to acheive integrity, a conviction that one's life has meaning and purpose and that having lived has made a difference.

REFERENCES

Becker, Ernest. 1973. *The Denial of Death.* New York: The Free Press.

Dumont, Richard G., & Dennis C. Foss. 1972. *The American View of Death: Acceptance or Denial?* Cambridge, MA: Schenkman.

El Dorado Times. 1985. "Death Films Popular, Store Manager Says." December 13, p. 16.

Erikson, Erik. 1959. "Identity and the Life Cycle: Selected Papers." *Psychological Issues, 1*:1–171.

Feifel, Herman. 1959. *The Meaning of Death.* New York: McGraw-Hill.

Ginsburg, Herbert, & Sylvia Opper. 1979. *Piaget's Theory of Intellectual Development,* Second Ed. Englewood Cliffs, NJ: Prentice-Hall.

Gordon, Audrey. 1986. "The Tattered Cloak of Immortality." In Charles A. Corr & Joan N. McNeil (Eds.), *Adolescence and Death.* New York: Springer, pp. 16–29.

Grollman, Earl A. 1970. *Talking About Death: A Dialogue between Parent and Child.* Boston: Beacon Press.

Jacques, Elliott. 1965. "Death and the Mid-Life Crisis." *International Journal of Psychoanalysis, 46*:502–514.

Jung, Carl. 1933. *Modern Man in Search of a Soul.* New York: Harcourt and Brace.

Kalish, Richard A. 1965. "The Aged and the Dying Process: The Inevitable Decisions." *Journal of Social Issues, 21*:87–96.

Kalish, Richard A. 1976. "Death and Dying in a Social Context." In Robert Binstock & Ethel Shanas (Eds.), *Handbook of Aging and Social Sciences.* New York: Van Nostrand-Reinhold.

Kalish, Richard A., & D. K. Reynolds. 1976. *Death and Ethnicity: A Psycho-cultural Investigation.* Los Angeles: University of Southern California Press.

Kastenbaum, Robert. 1969. "Death and Bereavement in Later Life." In Austin H. Kutscher (Ed.), *Death and Bereavement.* Springfield, IL: Thomas.

Kastenbaum, Robert. 1986. "Death in the World of Adolescence." In Charles A. Corr & Joan N. McNeil, (Eds.), *Adolescence and Death.* New York: Springer, pp. 4–15.

Kavanaugh, Robert E. 1972. *Facing Death.* Baltimore: Penguin.

Koocher, Gerald P., John E. O'Malley, Diane Foster, & Janis L. Gogan. 1976. "Death Anxiety in Normal Children and Adolescents." *Psychiatric Clinics, 9*:220–229.

Leming, Michael R. 1980. "Religion and Death: A Test of Homans' Thesis." *Omega, 10*:347–364.

Levinson, Daniel J. 1978. *The Seasons of a Man's Life.* New York: Knopf.

Lifton, Robert J. 1976. "The Sense of Immortality: On Death and the Continuity of Life." In Robert Fulton & Robert Bendiksen, (Eds.), *Death and Identity,* Rev. Ed. Bowie, MD: Charles Press.

Lowenthal, Marjorie F., Majda Thurnher, & David Chiriboga. 1975. *Four Stages of Life.* San Francisco: Jossey-Bass.

Lund, Dale A., & Michael R. Leming. 1975. "Relationship Between Age and Fear of Death: A Study of Cancer Patients." Paper presented at the Annual Scientific Meeting of the Gerontological Society," Louisville, KY (October).

McKenzie, Sheila C. 1980. *Aging and Old Age.* Glenview, IL: Scott, Foresman.

McNeil, Joan N. 1986. "Talking about Death: Adolescents, Parents, and Peers." *Adolescence and Death.* Charles A. Corr & Joan N. McNeil (Eds.). New York: Springer, pp. 185–199.

Neugarten, Bernice L. 1968. *Middle Age and Aging: A Reader in Social Psychology.* Chicago: The University of Chicago Press.

Neugarten, Bernice L. 1974. "Age Groups in American Society and the Rise of the Young-Old." *Annals of the American Academy of Political and Social Science,* 415:187–198.

Norman, William H., & Thomas J. Scaramelli. 1980. *Mid-Life: Developmental and Clinical Issues.* New York: Brunner/Mazel.

Pattison, E. Marshall. 1977. *The Experience of Dying.* Englewood Cliffs, NJ: Prentice-Hall.

Piaget, Jean. 1958. *The Growth of Logical Thinking from Childhood to Adolescence.* New York: Basic Books.

Richardson, Virginia, & Roberta Sands. 1987. "Death Attitudes among Mid-Life Women." *Omega,* 17:327–341.

Riley, Jack W. 1968. "Attitudes toward Aging." In M. W. Riley, et al. (Eds.), *Aging and Society: An Inventory of Research Findings.* New York: Russell Sage Foundation.

Stricherz, M., & L. Cunnington. 1982. "Death Concerns of Students, Employed Persons, and Retired Persons." *Omega,* 12:373–379.

Toynbee, Arnold. 1968. *Man's Concern with Death.* London: Hodder and Stoughton.

Wass, Hannelore. 1979. "Death and the Elderly." In Hannelore Wass (Ed.), *Dying: Facing the Facts.* Washington, DC: Hemisphere.

Wass, Hannelore, & M. Scott. 1977. "Aging without Death." *The Gerontologist* (August) 17:377–390.

Wass, Hannelore, & H. Sisler. 1978. "Death Concern and Views on Various Aspects of Dying among Elderly Persons." Paper presented at the International Symposium on the Dying Human, Tel Aviv, Israel (January).

SUGGESTED READINGS

Charles A. Corr & Joan N. McNeil. 1986. *Adolescence and Death.* New York: Springer. An excellent anthology composed of 17 chapters including contemporary interactions of adolescents and death; coping with dying, grief, and bereavement; suicide and adolescents; prevention, intervention, and post-intervention; and annotated resources.

Robert Kastenbaum & Ruth Aisenberg. 1976. *The Psychology of Death.* New York: Springer. Though somewhat technical in scope, this book discusses developmental concepts of death.

Edna LeShan. 1978. *Learning to Say Good-by: When a Parent Dies*. New York: Macmillan.

Aimed at a teen audience, yet helpful for young adults and parents as a model for explaining death to teenagers.

Dale A. Lund. 1989. *Older Bereaved Spouses: Research with Practical Applications*. New York: Hemisphere.

Summarizes and integrates the findings from the most recent studies in the United States on how older adults cope with the death of a spouse.

CHAPTER 4

Religion and Death Attitudes

Religion provided me with answers to problems I didn't even know I had.

ANONYMOUS ST. OLAF COLLEGE STUDENT, CIRCA 1977

Death radically challenges all *socially objectivated definitions of reality—of the world, of others, and of self. . . . Death radically puts in question the taken-for-granted, "business-as-usual" attitude in which one exists in everyday life. . . . Religion maintains the socially defined reality by legitimating marginal situations in terms of an all-encompassing sacred reality.*

PETER BERGER, *Sacred Canopy*

4   When one thinks of **religion** as a cultural system of meaning, an important question becomes relevant: Why did religion come into existence? Since this question attempts to discover the **etiology** of religious behavior and since we have no scientific record of the first religious activity, any answers must be speculative in nature. They are based on an *ex post facto* analysis of universal human needs that find fulfillment in a transcendent frame of reference. Such answers are also predicated on the assumption that humans have a need for religious expression. Saint Augustine has said, "Thou hast made us for thyself, O God, and our hearts are restless until they find their rest in thee." This idea is also reflected in the following statement by Pascal, the 17th-century French mathematician–philosopher: "There is a God-shaped vacuum in the heart of each man, which cannot be satisfied by any created thing but only by God, the creator, made known through Jesus Christ." Such answers, however, raise another, more fundamental question of why humans have this need.

DEATH AND THE ORIGIN OF RELIGION

From a symbolic interactionist perspective (Chapter 2), meanings are created and reproduced by humans. These meanings supply a base for activities and actions (behavior is in response to meanings) and provide order for the people who share a given culture. Peter Berger (1969) suggests that the human world has no order other than that created by humans. To live in a world without the order contributed by one's culture would force one to experience a meaningless existence. Sociologists refer to this condition as **anomie**—a term that literally means "without order."

There are many situations in life that challenge the order on which social life is based. Most of these situations are related to what Thomas O'Dea (1966) refers to as the three fundamental characteristics of human existence—uncertainty, powerlessness, and scarcity.

Uncertainty refers to the fact that human activity does not always lead to predictable outcomes. Even after careful planning, most people recognize that they will not be able to achieve all of their goals. Less optimistically, the 20th century's Murphy's Law states "Anything that can go wrong, will go wrong." The human condition is also characterized by *powerlessness*. We recognize that there are many situations in life, and events in the universe, over which humans have no control—among them are death, suffering, coercion, and natural disasters. Finally, in *scarcity,* humans experience inequality with regard to the distribution of wealth, power, prestige, and other things that make a satisfying life. This inequality is the basis for the human experience of relative deprivation and frustration.

The three experiences of uncertainty, powerlessness, and scarcity are situations that challenge the order of everyday life, and are, therefore, marginal to ordinary experiences. According to O'Dea (1966:5), such experiences "raise questions which can find an answer only in some kind of 'beyond' itself." Therefore, **marginal situations,** which are characteristic of the human condition, force individuals to the realm of the transcendent in their search for meaningful answers.

Peter Berger (1969:23, 43–44) claims that death is the marginal situation *par excellence.*

> Witnessing the death of others and anticipating his own death, the individual is strongly propelled to question the *ad hoc* cognitive and normative operating procedures of "normal" life in society. Death presents society with a formidable problem not only because of its obvious threat to the continuity of human relationships, but because it threatens the basic assumptions of order on which society rests. Death radically puts in question the taken-for-granted, "business-as-usual" attitude in which one exists in everyday life. . . . Insofar as knowledge of death cannot be avoided in any society, legitimations of the reality of the social world *in the face of death* are decisive requirements in any society. The importance of religion in such legitimations is obvious.

It is religion, or a transcendent reference, that helps individuals remain reality-oriented when the order of everyday life is challenged. Contemplating death, we are faced with the fact that we will not be able to accomplish all our goals in life. We also realize that we are unable to extend the length of our lives and/or control the circumstances surrounding the experience and cause for our deaths. We are troubled by the fact that some must endure painful, degrading, and meaningless deaths, while others find *more* meaning and purpose in the last days of their lives than they experienced in the years preceding "the terminal period." Finally, the relative deprivation created by differential life spans raises questions that are unanswerable from a "this world" perspective.

Religious-meaning systems provide answers to these problems of uncertainty, powerlessness, and scarcity created by death. O'Dea (1966:6–7) illustrates this function of religion:

> Religion, by its reference to a beyond and its beliefs concerning man's relationship to that beyond, provides a supraempirical view of a larger total reality. In the context of this reality, the disappointments and frustrations inflicted on mankind by uncertainty and impossibility, and by the institutionalized order of human society, may be seen as meaningful in some ultimate sense, and this makes acceptance of and adjustment to them possible. Moreover, by showing the norms and rules of society to be part of a larger supraempirical ethical order, ordained and sanctified by religious belief and practice, religion contributes to their enforcement when adherence to them contradicts the wishes or interests of those affected. Religion answers the problem of meaning. It sanctifies the norms

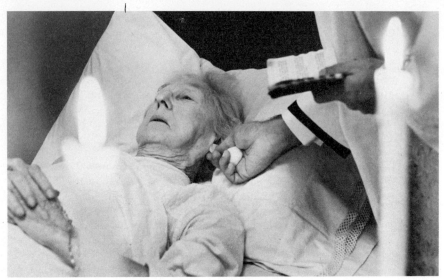

Religious-meaning systems help provide individuals with a transcendent point of reference whereby the loss created by death is compensated by a system of other-worldly gains.

of the established social order at what we have called the "breaking points," by providing a grounding for the beliefs and orientations of men in a view of reality that transcends the empirical here-and-now of daily experience. Thus not only is cognitive frustration overcome, which is involved in the problem of meaning, but the emotional adjustments to frustrations and deprivations inherent in human life and human society are facilitated.

RELIGION AS A MEANS OF PROVIDING UNDERSTANDING OF DEATH

Fifteen years ago, while on a class field trip to a funeral home, I complimented the funeral director on the beautiful pastoral scene hanging on a wall there. He said it was a very unusual wall hanging and took it down to show me the framed, velvet, reverse side that could also be displayed. He then took out a box containing a cross, a crucifix, and a Star of David that could be hung on the velvet backing. The funeral director told the class that he changed the hanging as the religious affiliation of the deceased varied.

Since the time of that field trip, I have become very conscious of the way funeral homes extensively employ religious symbols in attempting to create a religious ambiance. Consider the following:

1. Within the funeral home, "chapel" is the name given to the room where the funeral is held.

2. Most memorial cards have the 23rd Psalm on them.

3. The music one hears on the sound systems within most funeral homes is religious in nature.

4. Wall hangings found in most funeral homes usually have religious content.

5. Funeral homes often provide Christmas calendars, complete with Bible verses and religious scenes, for religious groups and other interested members of the community.

As discussed in the last section of this chapter, religious systems provide a means to re-establish the social order challenged by death. Our society has institutionalized the continued importance of religion by creating funeral **rituals** that have a religious quality about them.

There have been many attempts to explain the methods by which religion influences death meanings. Most discussion in this area has been strongly influenced by the theoretical writings of Malinowski, Radcliffe-Brown, and Homans.

Stated briefly, anthropologist Bronislaw Malinowski held that religion functioned to relieve the anxiety caused by the crisis experiences that people encounter in their lifetimes. Religion has its origin in the crisis experience in death because it provides individuals with a means of dealing with extraordinary phenomena. Religion functions to bring about a restoration of normalcy for the individual.

Malinowski (1965:70) says:

> Every important crisis of human life implies a strong emotional upheaval, mental conflict and possible disintegration. Religion in its ethics sanctifies human life and conduct and becomes perhaps the most powerful force of social control. In its dogmatics it supplies man with strong cohesive forces.

In elaborating on his theory that religion is the "great anxiety reliever," Malinowski (1965:71) claims that "death, which of all human events is the most upsetting and disorganizing to man's calculations, is perhaps the main source of religious belief." From Malinowski's perspective, death is not only the greatest source of anxiety, it is also the primary crisis event that calls forth religious behavior. Such theorizing leads us to ask the empirical question, Does religion provide humans with a solace in their attempts to cope with death? From the pragmatic perspective of the funeral industry, the question becomes, Are attempts on the part of the funeral home to merge religious and death meanings necessary and effective in assisting the bereaved?

Anthropologist A. R. Radcliffe-Brown (1965) disagrees with Malinowski's contention that religion functions primarily as an anxiety reliever, and claims, rather, that religion gives people fears and anxieties from which they would otherwise be free—the fear of spirits, God's judgment, the devil, hell.

From Radcliffe-Brown's perspective, we would be led to expect that the non-religious individual would have relatively less **death anxiety** and would cope better with his or her death and the deaths of others. We might also be led to the conclusion that from the point of reference of personal death anxiety, religious beliefs have **dysfunctional** consequences.

George Homans (1965) has attempted to resolve this problem by declaring that both Malinowski and Radcliffe-Brown are correct in their theorizing about the role of religion in death anxiety. Rather than pitting Radcliffe-Brown against Malinowski, he argues that Radcliffe-Brown's hypothesis is a supplement to Malinowski's theory. According to Homans (1965), Malinowski is looking at the individual, Radcliffe-Brown at the community. While Malinowski says that the individual tends to feel anxiety on certain occasions, Radcliffe-Brown says that society *expects* the individual to feel anxiety on certain occasions.

If we start with a psychological frame of reference (as does Malinowski), we focus our attention on the function of religion for the individual. From this perspective, patterns of social integration are contingent upon psychological processes—what works for the individual is functional for society. Therefore, since religious actions and rituals may help some individuals find meaning for death, and consequently dispel anomie in death-related situations, the social function of religion must be anxiety reduction. This point of view is illustrated in the following statement by Malinowski (1965:72):

> Religion in its ethics sanctifies human life and conduct and becomes perhaps the most powerful force of social control. In its dogmatics it supplies man with strong cohesive forces. It grows out of every culture, because life-long bonds of cooperation and mutual interest create sentiments, and sentiments rebel against death and dissolution. The cultural call for religion is highly derived and indirect but is finally rooted in the way in which the primary needs of man are satisfied in culture.

Turning to the perspective of Radcliffe-Brown, we find the following statement, which poses an alternative to Malinowski's reasoning (Radcliffe-Brown, 1965:81):

> I think that for certain rites it would be easy to maintain with equal plausibility an exactly contrary theory, namely, that if it were not for the existence of the rite and the beliefs associated with it the individual would feel no anxiety, and that the psychological effect of the rite is to create in the individual a sense of insecurity and danger.

In this quotation, Radcliffe-Brown argues that religion might serve to increase anxiety for the individual rather than reduce it as Malinowski would contend. Radcliffe-Brown (1965:81) begins with a societal perspective and declares that the function of religion is to create a sense of anxiety that will maintain the social structure of the society:

> Actually in our fears or anxieties, as well as in our hopes, we are conditioned by the community in which we live. And it is largely by the sharing of hopes and fears, by what I have called *common concern* in events or eventualities, that human beings are linked together in temporary or permanent associations.

George Homans' (1965) thesis is that when individuals encounter death, the anxiety they experience is basically socially ascribed, or learned. Death fears can be likened to the fears of other things—snakes, electricity, communism, or whatever. If we believe we are in a dangerous setting, we react accordingly. Religion, with its emphasis on immortality of the soul and its belief in a coming judgment, increases the level of death anxiety for individuals who follow the teachings of the religion. However, once individuals have fulfilled the requisite religious or magical ceremonies, they experience only a moderate amount of anxiety.

Homans (1965) brings both the perspectives of Malinowski and Radcliffe-Brown together by making four conclusions:

1. Religion functions to relieve anxiety associated with death-related situations.

2. Death anxiety calls forth religious activities and rituals.

3. In order to stabilize the group of individuals who perform these rituals, group activities and beliefs provide a potential threat of anxiety in order to unite group members through a "common concern."

4. This secondary anxiety may be effectively removed through the group rituals of purification and expiation.

Summarizing the relationship between **religiosity** and death anxiety, we can arrive at the following theoretical assumptions:

1. The meanings of death are socially ascribed—death *per se* is neither fearful nor nonfearful.

2. The meanings that are ascribed to death in a given culture are transmitted to individuals in the society through the socialization process.

3. Anxiety reduction may be accomplished through social cooperation and institutional participation.

4. Institutional cohesiveness in religious institutions is fostered by giving participants a sense of anxiety concerning death and uniting them through a common concern.

5. If the religious institutions are to remain viable, they must also provide a means for anxiety reduction.

6. Through its promise of a reward in the afterlife, and its redefinition of the negative effects of death upon the **temporal** life of the individual, religion diminishes the fear that it has ascribed to death and reduces anxieties ascribed to death by secular society.

In order to test the empirical validity of these assumptions, Michael Leming (1979–1980) surveyed 372 randomly selected residents in Northfield, Minnesota, concerning death anxiety and religious activities, beliefs, and experiences. Subjects were divided into four groups based on a religious commitment scale developed by Charles Glock and Rodney Stark (1966) and Joseph Faulkner and Gordon DeJong (1966). Approximately 25 percent of the respondents were placed in each category—the first group consisted of those persons who were the least religious and the fourth group contained the people who were the most religious.

Figure 4.1 gives the mean fear of death scores for each of the levels of religious commitment. The relationship between the variables of religiosity and death anxiety is **curvilinear**—persons with a moderate commitment to religion have added to the general anxiety that has been socially ascribed to

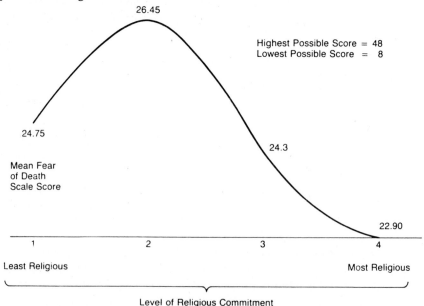

FIGURE 4.1 **Mean Fear of Death Scale Scores by Level of Religious Commitment**

death from secular sources. The person with a moderate commitment receives only the negative consequences of religion—what Radcliffe-Brown calls a "common concern." These persons acquire only the anxiety, which religion is capable of producing, and none of the consolation. On the other hand, the highly committed individual has the least anxiety concerning death. Religion, as Malinowski predicts, provides individuals with a solace when they attempt to cope with death attitudes.

In conclusion, religiosity seems to serve the dual function of "afflicting the comforted" and "comforting the afflicted." We have discovered that religion, when accompanied with a high degree of commitment, not only relieves the dread it engendered, but dispels much of the anxiety caused by the social effects of death.

RELIGIOUS INTERPRETATIONS OF DEATH

Until this point, we have provided a functional perspective on religion—we have defined religion in terms of what religion does *for* the individual and society. This approach focuses on the *consequences* of religion rather than on the *content* of religious belief and practice. In this section we will attempt to provide substantive perspectives on religion and death.

The substantive approach to religion attempts to establish what religion *is.* Substantive definitions of religion endeavor to distinguish religious activities from nonreligious behaviors by providing necessary criteria for inclusion as religious phenomena. The substantive definition of religion that has been used most frequently by sociologists is the one formulated by Emile Durkheim in his *Elementary Forms of Religious Life,* first published in 1915.

> A religion is a unified system of beliefs and practices relative to sacred things, that is to say, things set apart and forbidden—beliefs and practices which unite into one single moral community called a Church, all those who adhere to them.

In this definition, Durkheim designates four essential ingredients of religion—a system of beliefs, a set of religious practices or rituals, the sacred or supernatural as the object of worship, and a community or social base. Most substantive definitions of religion employed by contemporary sociologists will incorporate these four key elements. However, some sociologists have argued that in order to be inclusive of phenomena that most people consider religious, it might be proper to exclude the necessity of having a sacred point of reference. Buddhism, for example, does not have a supernatural being to which beliefs and rituals are oriented.

We will now consider five religious traditions and explain how each tradition attempts to interpret the meaning of death-related experiences and provides funeral rites and rituals for the bereaved. The five religious traditions considered are Judaism, Christianity, Islam, Hinduism, and Buddhism.

Judaism

Death in the Jewish tradition came into being as a result of Adam and Eve's sin, which caused them to be expelled from the Garden of Eden. When Adam and Eve ate the fruit from the "Tree of Conscience," they received the curse of pain in childbirth, the burden of work, and the loss of physical immortality.

According to the Biblical account in Genesis (2:4–3:24), while death was a punishment, it also brought the ability to distinguish between good and evil as well as the power and responsibility to make decisions that have a future consequence. According to J. Carse (1981:221):

> Adam and Eve lost their immortality, but acquired consciousness instead. God drove them out of paradise into death, but also into history. God's design for the people of Israel is not to save them from death, but to save them from their enemies in order that their history might continue.

In this description we gain an understanding of the importance of God's covenant with Abraham—that Abraham would become the father of many nations, and God would have a special relationship with his descendants forever (Genesis 17). Consequently, immortality was to be found in one's identity with the group.

Among contemporary Jews, including those who consider themselves religious, opinion differs regarding personal immortality. Some contend that there is no after*life* only an after*death*—the dead go to *Sheol*, where nothing happens, and the soul eventually slides into oblivion. Other Jews believe in a resurrection of the soul, when individuals are brought to a final judgment (Carse, 1981:221). Still, for others there is a real ambivalence regarding the immortality of the soul. Carse (1981:221) cites the writings of Rabbi Leona Modena (1571–1648), who states:

> It is frightening that we fail to find in all the words of Moses a single indication pointing to man's spiritual immortality after his physical death. Nonetheless, reason compels us to believe that the soul continues.

Regardless of the content of Jewish beliefs regarding the immortality of the soul, Jewish funeral customs and rituals emphasize the point that "God does not save us, as individuals, from death, but saves Israel for history, regardless of death" (Carse 1981:221).

According to Knobel (1987:396), traditional Jewish burial customs require that the body be cleansed by members of the Jewish burial society (*hevra'qaddisha'*, "holy society") in a washing process called *tahorah*, or "purification." Custom forbids embalming, cremation, and autopsy unless local laws require these procedures. The body is then dressed in plain linen shrouds *(takhrikhim)*; men are usually buried with their prayer shawls *(tallit)*. The body is then placed in a plain wooden casket and buried before sunset on the day of death, if at all possible. Reform Judaism allows for cremation and entombment, but burial is the most frequent form of body disposition. Throughout this process, it is considered inappropriate to use the funeral as a means for displaying one's social position and wealth.

BOX 4.1   # JEWISH GROUP BURIES ITS OWN

When a Jewish congregation here first began the practice of offering simple, inexpensive burials for its dead, some members were upset. But they now increasingly condone it.

Back in 1977, some people had felt it was barbaric when the body of a devout member, Al Sudit, 75, was lowered into his grave in a plain wooden box, with mourners themselves shoveling on the dirt. But recently, when another respected member, Morris Weiner, 81, was given the same sort of elemental funeral, relatives say they neither sensed nor heard any criticism.

Rabbi Arnold M. Goodman, spiritual leader of Adath Jeshurun Congregation, says volunteers of its society to honor the dead—*Chevra Kevod Hamet*—now handle about half the funerals of members.

Goodman, recently elected president of the Rabbinical Assembly, representing the nation's 1,200 Conservative rabbis, regards his congregation as a pioneer in setting up a model for traditional, simplified funerals.

He says congregations in Highland Park, Illinois, Portland, Oregon, and Washington, D.C., have adapted the method for their own use. But some other rabbis remain dubious.

The Chevra was formed in 1976 after Goodman, in a sermon, dealt with the impact of American values upon the funeral practices of Jewry. He suggested a committee study the requirements of the *Halacha*, or Jewish law, for responding to death.

Months of study convinced committee members that a simple wood coffin should be used, the body should be washed in a ritual process called *tahara* and, because dust is to return to dust as quickly as possible, there should be no formaldehyde in the veins, no nails on the coffin.

(continued on next page)

Box 4.1, *continued*

The society decided to offer traditional funerals free to Adath Jeshu-run members. The congregation provided seed money. Memorial dona-tions and voluntary contributions from the bereaved are accepted.

Here's how the Chevra functions:

> A congregation member signs a revokable agreement, asking for the *Chevra's* service when needed. When death occurs, *chaverim* (friends) call on the fam-ily, aid in writing the obituary, explain death benefits, aid in other ways and remain available for help.

Chevra Kadisha (sacred society), people of the same sex as the deceased and usually five in number, wash the body at the mortuary while saying prayers. The body is dressed in a shroud sewn by Chevra members and placed in a wooden coffin.

Shomrin (guards) watch over the body, in blocks of two hours, until burial. The coffin with rope handles is light enough to be borne by pall-bearers, including women. Spurning mechanical contrivances, the pall-bearers lower the coffin into the grave. Chaverim, the rabbi and cantor shovel in dirt. Family members may participate.

Judaism historically insists that the greatest commandment is to take personal involvement in burying the dead, Goodman says, but afflu-ence enables people to pay surrogates to do it.

Goodman says a funeral costs the Chevra less than $500. A compa-rable no-frills funeral handled by professionals would cost about $1,500, says Elliot Pinck, a local funeral home director.

Associated Press story in the *Rocky Mountain News* (Denver, Colorado), June 25, 1982.

For the bereaved, the Jewish mourning ritual begins by the rending (tearing) of garments. For some, the ripping of a black ribbon, which is then attached to the clothing, has symbolically replaced the process of rending garments. From the death until burial, mourners are exempt from normal religious obligations (e.g., morning prayers) and must *not* engage in the fol-lowing activities: drinking wine, eating meat, attending parties, and engaging in sexual intercourse (Knobel, 1987:396).

The liturgy for the funeral will consist of the recitation of psalms, a eulogy, and the following *El Male' Rahamin* memorial prayer (Knobel, 1987:396):

> *O God full of compassion, You who dwell on high! Grant perfect rest beneath the sheltering wings of Your presence, among the holy and pure who shine as the*

brightness of the heavens, unto the soul of _____ [the deceased] who has entered eternity and in whose memory charity is offered. May his/her repose be in the Garden of Eden. May the Lord of Mercy bring him/her under the cover of His wings forever and may his/her soul be bound up in the bond of eternal life. May the Lord be his/her possession and may he/she rest in peace. Amen.

During the interment service the body is lowered into the grave and covered with earth. The interment service consists of an acclamation of God's justice, a memorial prayer, and the recitation of *Qaddish*—a doxology reaffirming the mourner's faith in God despite the fact of death. After the burial service, the people in attendance form two lines between which the primary mourners pass. Those present comfort the mourners as they pass saying, "May God comfort you among the rest of the mourners of Zion and Jerusalem" (Knobel, 1987:397).

The *shiv'ah* is a period of seven days following the death in which the mourners act as if they were themselves dead. During this period they are forbidden to engage in work, have sexual intercourse, read the Bible, bathe, shave, or have their hair cut. It is expected that during the *shiv'ah* expressions of emotion and grief are to be of lesser intensity than during the funeral and burial rituals.

After the *shiv'ah*, mourners continue to avoid social gatherings until 30 days after the death. When one is mourning the death of a parent, the restrictions are observed for one year. After one year, all ritual expressions of grief cease with the exception of the *Yahrzeit*—the yearly commemoration of the person's death. *Yahrzeit* is observed by lighting a memorial light, performing memorial acts of charity, and attending religious services to recite the *Qaddish* prayer (Carse, 1981:221; Knobel, 1987:397).

Christianity

While Christianity shares much of the historical and mythical foundations found in Judaism, there are many distinct differences in the Christian approach to death, afterlife, and funeral rituals. For the Christian, death is viewed as the entrance to eternal life and, therefore, preferable to physical life. There is a strong belief in the immortality of the soul, the resurrection of the body, and a divine judgment of one's earthly life after death resulting in the eternal rewards of heaven or the punishments of hell.

For the Roman Catholic there are four potential dispositions of the soul after death—heaven, hell, limbo, and purgatory. According to McBrien (1987:443), "some will join God forever in heaven; some may be separated eternally from God in hell; others may find themselves in a state of merely natural happiness in limbo; and others will suffer in purgatory some temporary 'punishment' still required of sins that have already been forgiven."

For the Christian, the teachings of Jesus and the Apostle Paul are the most important sources in arriving at a theology of life after death. Jesus declares to his followers,

> *"I am the resurrection and the life, he who believes in me, though he die, yet shall he live, and whoever lives and believes in me shall never die" (John 11:25 RSV).* (All future quotations from the New Testament are taken from the Revised Standard Version.)

In the fifteenth chapter of the first letter to the Corinthians, the Apostle Paul discusses the significance of Jesus's resurrection for the Christian believer. In this chapter Jesus is portrayed as the "first born from the dead" and as "the one who has destroyed death" (I Cor. 15:26). Paul declares (I Cor. 15:52–58 RSV) that at the end of history,

> *The dead will be raised imperishable, and we shall be changed. For this perishable nature must put on the imperishable, and this mortal nature must put on immortality. When the perishable puts on the imperishable, and the mortal puts on immortality, then shall come to pass the saying that is written:*
> *Death is swallowed up in victory.*
> *O death, where is thy victory?*
> *O death, where is thy sting?*
> *The sting of death is sin, and the power of sin is the law. But thanks be to God, who gives us the victory through our Lord Jesus Christ.*

There are two basic, and somewhat paradoxical, perspectives that are employed by Christian people when facing death. The first has been described above—that through faith in Jesus Christ the Christian has victory over death and gains eternal life with God. The following passage (Rom. 3:31–39 RSV) provides us with an example of this orientation.

> *What then shall we say to this? If God is for us, who is against us? He who did not spare his own Son but gave him up for us all, will he not also give us all things with him? Who shall bring any charge against God's elect? It is God who justifies; who is to condemn? Is it Christ Jesus, who died, yes, who was raised from the dead, who is at the right hand of God, who indeed intercedes for us? Who shall separate us from the love of Christ? Shall tribulation, or distress, or persecution, or famine, or nakedness, or peril, or sword? As it is written,*
> > *"For thy sake we are being killed all the day long; we are regarded as sheep to be slaughtered."*
> *No, in all these things we are more than conquerors through him who loved us. For I am sure that neither death, nor life, nor angels, nor principalities, nor things present, nor things to come, nor powers, nor height, nor depth, nor anything else in all creation, will be able to separate us from the love of God in Christ Jesus our Lord.*

The second approach to death employed by Christians emphasizes the experience of true human loss. This approach is exemplified by Jesus as he responds to the death of his friend Lazarus.

Then Mary, when she came where Jesus was and saw him, fell at his feet, saying to him, "Lord, if you had been here, my brother would not have died." When Jesus saw her weeping, and the Jews who came with her also weeping, he was deeply moved in spirit and troubled; and he said, "Where have you laid him?" They said to him, "Lord, come and see." Jesus wept. So the Jews said, "See how he loved him!" (John 11:32–36 RSV)

C. S. Lewis in his book *A Grief Observed* (1961:24) illustrates how Christians utilize this paradoxical double approach.

What St. Paul says can comfort only those who love God better than the dead, and the dead better than themselves. If a mother is mourning not for what she has lost but for what her dead child has lost, it is a comfort to believe that the child has not lost the end for which it was created. And it is a comfort to believe that she herself, in losing her chief or only natural happiness, has not lost a greater thing, that she may still hope to "glorify God and enjoy Him forever." A comfort to the God-aimed, eternal spirit within her. But not to her motherhood. The specifically maternal happiness must be written off. Never, in any place or time, will she have her son on her knees, or bathe him, or tell him a story, or plan for his future, or see her grandchild.

The Christian funeralization process reflects these themes of victory and loss. The funeral service is primarily a worship service or mass of Christian burial. During the service, hymns are sung and scriptural passages are read that emphasize the resurrection of the dead and provide consolation for the bereaved. Occasionally a eulogy or biographical statement concerning the deceased is read.

In the United States, Christian teaching does not discourage the process of embalming, nor does it prohibit the autopsy, cremation, or any other form of final disposition (as is the case among Jews)—provided that such practices do not indicate a rejection of a belief in the resurrection of the body. American Christian funerals are conducted by members of the clergy and funeral directors in either a church, funeral chapel, and/or cemetery. Memorial services—religious services in which the dead body is not present—are becoming increasingly popular in many Protestant churches.

At the occasion of death, the family of the deceased is expected to disengage from most normal social functioning until after the funeral is completed. Funeral arrangements are typically made with the professional assistance of a funeral director and/or member of the clergy.

For most Roman Catholics and many Protestants, on the day before the funeral, a wake or visitation service will be held in the funeral home. During this time (approximately five hours in duration), friends may view the body and visit with the family of the deceased in order to express their condolences. Roman Catholic families may also have a rosary service and/or prayer service during the wake.

*The Christian funeral attempts to provide a community of
caring to support the bereaved in their loss and remind
them of the hope to be found in Christ's victory over death
in his resurrection.*

The funeral is typically held two to four days after the death. Occasionally, the funeral is delayed if family members are unable to make travel
arrangements on such short notice (this would not be the case for the Jewish
funeral). If final disposition involves cremation, the cremation can take place
either after the funeral or before the memorial service. Burial and entombment dispositions are usually accompanied by rites of committal. On those
occasions where there is no graveside service, words of committal will be
read at the conclusion of the funeral service. At the conclusion of the funeralization process, family members and others who have attended the services
are often invited to share a meal together. This becomes a community rite of
reincorporation.

Islam

As in Christianity, life after death is also an important focus within the Islamic tradition. Earthly life and the realm of the dead are separated by a bridge that souls must cross on the day of judgment. After death, all people face a divine judgment. Then they are assigned eternal dwelling places where they will receive either eternal rewards or punishments determined by the strengths of their faith in God and the moral quality of their earthly lives.

According to the *Qur'an*, there are seven layers of heaven and seven layers of *alnar* ("Fire of Hell"), and each layer is separated from the layer above by receiving fewer rewards or greater punishments (Long, 1987:132). The fundamental reason why persons might be condemned to a life of torment in the Fire of Hell is a lack of belief in God and in the message of his prophet Muhammad. Other reasons include lying, corruption, blasphemy, denial of the advent of the judgment day and the reality of the Fire, lack of charity, and leading a life of luxury (Long, 1987:132).

Like Jews and Christians, followers of Islam believe that God is fundamentally compassionate, but also place a similar emphasis on God as just. Therefore, persons are held accountable for moral integrity at the time of their death. The primary expression of the Islamic concern for justice and accountability is found in the belief in the assigning to paradise or damnation. Accordingly, the Qur'an provides very vivid sketches of both paradise and hell. However, many Islamic theologians also stress that God's judgment is also tempered with mercy, that the angel Gabriel will intercede on behalf of those condemned to punishment, and that they will eventually be pardoned.

The following prayer (the opening of the Surah of the Qur'an) illustrates the Islamic perspective on divine justice and mercy.

> *In the name of God, the Merciful, the Compassionate. Praise belongs to God, the Lord of all Being, the All-merciful, the All-compassionate, the Master of the Day of Doom.*
>
> *Thee only we serve; to Thee alone we pray for succour, Guide us in the straight path, the path of those whom Thou has blessed, not of those against whom Thou art wrathful, nor of those who are astray.*

When death comes to the Muslim, it is expected that he or she will be attended by relatives and close friends. Just prior to death the dying person will recite the following Islamic confession of faith: "There is no god but God, and Muhammad is his messenger." The dying person is also encouraged to request forgiveness from anyone he or she may have offended because, according to the tradition of Islam, "God will not forgive violation of human rights unless those wronged have forgiven" (Rahman, 1987:128).

Islamic tradition forbids embalming and, consequently, it is expected that burial should take place as soon as possible—preferably before sundown. Occasionally, burial is delayed one or two days to provide out-of-town family members an opportunity to attend the burial. In preparation for burial, the family will call into their home or the hospital a person of the same gender as the deceased who knows the prescribed ritual for washing and preparing the body. The eyes and mouth of the deceased will be closed, the arms straightened alongside the body, and the body will be washed and wrapped in a white seamless cloth (shroud) similar to that worn for the pilgrimage to Mecca (Eickelman, 1987:401).

When the body has been fully prepared according to the prescribed ritual, it will be placed in a simple wooden coffin. (Occasionally, Muslims will be covered only by the white shroud when they are buried.) During this preparation, prayers and passages from the Qur'an will be recited by a *hoca*—a lay holy man, not a priest—and care will be taken that the body always face Mecca.

Islamic tradition requires that the funeral service take place without unnecessary delay and that burial rights be simple and austere (Rahman, 1987:128). When it is time for the funeral, the body will be transported from the home or hospital to the mosque on the shoulders of the pallbearers. At the mosque the body will be placed on a stone bier *(musalla)* in the outer courtyard. The funeral service will be a part of one of the five regular daily religious services (usually the noon service). Because Muslims consider burying the dead a good deed, when worshippers leave the mosque and see the coffin in the courtyard, they will participate in the procession to the cemetery even though they were not acquainted with the deceased (Habenstein & Lamers, 1974:162).

The body is now transported from the mosque to the cemetery on the shoulders of those male mourners in the procession. According to Habenstein and Lamers (1974:163),

> It is customary for every man in good health to carry the coffin on his shoulders for seven steps at least, and for passers-by to accompany the procession for at least seven steps. When a new bearer pushes under the coffin, another steps away so that eight or ten people are always under the load. These customs insure that the remains will have an escort, even though the dead person may have no living relatives. At a prearranged spot, hearse and funeral cars await the procession. Where distances to the cemetery are short, the body will be borne to the grave totally on foot.

At the cemetery the body is placed into the grave, and mourners place handfuls of dirt on top of it. The sexton then fills the remainder of the grave using a shovel. At the gravesite, rather than place cut flowers, Muslim mourners plant flowers because they believe that every living plant utters the name of God. During this process prayers are recited and the service concludes with the preaching of a sermon (Habenstein & Lamers, 1974:163).

After returning from the cemetery, all of the participants will partake in a meal that is served at the home of the deceased. Occasionally, some food from this meal is placed over the grave for the first three days after the death. Mourning continues for another three days, while family members receive social support and consolation from friends and members of the community.

While Islamic women are allowed to openly express emotion in the bereavement process, men are encouraged to retain their composure as a sign that they are able to accept the will of Allah. A widow is required by the Qur'an to go into seclusion for four months and ten days before she is allowed to remarry (Eickelman, 1987:401–402).

Hinduism

Unlike the religious traditions we have previously discussed, Hinduism does not have a single religious founder nor a single sacred text. Although the *Vedas* are recognized by almost all Hindus as an authoritative source of spiritual knowledge, Hinduism is not dogmatic. Many different theologies and religious approaches exist within the Hindu tradition. Many gods also exist, with each viewed as an aspect or manifestation of a single ultimate reality, but it is *not* essential to believe in the existence of God in order to be a Hindu (Srinivas & Shah, 1968:358). Essentially, Hinduism is a system of social customs embued with religious significance.

Three key concepts are central to an understanding of Hinduism—*karma, dharma,* and *moksha. Karma* refers to a moral law of causation; it suggests that human actions produce results for which the individual is responsible. *Karma* also refers to the balance of good and bad deeds performed in previous existences. *Dharma* are the religious duties, requirements, and/or prescriptions. The extent to which one fulfills one's *dharma* determines one's *karma.* In turn, *moksha* is the reward for living a saintly life. The main ways of achieving *moksha* are by acquiring true knowledge, performing good deeds, and living a life of love and devotion toward God (Srinivas & Shah, 1968:359).

The central doctrine affecting death-related attitudes and behavior in the Hindu religion is reincarnation and the transmigration of souls *(samsara).* For the Hindu, one's present life is determined by one's actions in a previous life. Furthermore, one's present behavior will shape the future. According to Habenstein and Lamers (1974:116), "The ultimate goal of the soul is liberation from the wheel of rebirth, through reabsorption into or identity with the Oversoul *(Brahma)*—the essence of the universe, immaterial, uncreated, limitless, and timeless."

By way of comparison, while Jews, Christians, and Muslims believe in the immortality of the soul and hope for an afterlife, Hindus hope that their soul will be absorbed at death. For the Hindu, the goal is *not* to experience life after death, but to have one's soul united with the Oversoul. Punishment for the devout Hindu might be to *have* "everlasting spiritual rebirth."

Within the Hindu tradition, death brings two possibilities—liberation and transmigration of the soul. Neither option is inherently fearful, even though separation from one's friends and loved ones may cause sadness and personal loss. Somewhat analogous to the dual perspectives of Christianity, death for the individual brings hope of something better but also the human loss of being separated from a dead loved one.

BOX 4.2 **UNDERSTANDING DEATH IN HINDUISM**

Death and birth are seen by us Hindus as gateways of exit and entry to the stage of this world. This process is described in one of the most striking and famous analogies in the entire *Bhagavadgita*. It is a verse which we movingly recite when the body is being cremated, and it has given comfort and solace to the grieving Hindu heart for centuries.

Just as a person casts off worn-out garments and puts on others that are new, even so does the embodied-soul cast off worn-out bodies and take on others that are new.

This analogy is full of suggestions, but I can only briefly draw your attention to a few of these. First, a suit of clothing is not identical with the wearer. Similarly, the body, which is likened here to worn-out garments, is not the true being or identity of the human person. Second, there is the similarity of a continuity of being. When a worn-out suit of clothing is cast off, the wearer continues to be. Similarly, with the disintegration of the physical body, the indweller, that is, the Self, continues to be. Finally, there is the parallel with the timing of the change. A suit of clothing is changed when it no longer serves the purpose for which it was intended. Similarly, the physical body is cast off when it no longer serves the purpose for which it came into existence.

This does not mean that the Hindu is not saddened by death or does not lament the loss it brings. There is a mysterious element in death which will always sadden and hurt. While we ache and long for the beauty, tenderness, and companionship of a dear one, we are deeply comforted in the knowledge that all that is good and true and real in him or her continues to be. What has passed away is what has always been limited by time.

Since death is a necessary condition for rebirth, Hindus also understand it to be a gateway for fresh opportunities. When we look at death from the limited perspective of a single and short life experience, we often see only its tragic side. We must admit, however, that the perspective is different for God—whose vision spans the boundless past and the unending future. Where we only see end and loss, there will be new beginnings and opportunities for a loved one. We need a selfless faith to trust his wisdom and judgment.

Hinduism conceives of life as a continuous chain of existence. In the Hindu view, the word of life is not restricted to describing the span of time between birth and death. While there are some variations in views among the many traditions of Hinduism, we agree that life is a journey toward God—the reality of all that exists. Life is a quest for that which is true and real in the midst of an existence which is so changeful and finite. For Hindus, God, the true and the real, has the highest value and is the source of all joy. We are all seekers and pilgrims, and the sacred journey of life will continue as long as it takes us to discover this final truth of ourselves and the world. As long as we cling to the finite and changeful, and seek comfort and solace in these, our journeys will be never-ending. The mortal and the finite will never satisfy us. The attainment of God is the fulfillment of our pilgrimage. This is *moksha*, liberation, our home and destination. The longing for it is captured in our daily prayer:

> *Lead us from untruth to truth*
> *From ignorance to knowledge*
> *From death to immortality.*

Anant Rambachan, Department of Religion, St. Olaf College. By permission of the author.

When a death takes place in Hindu society, the body is prepared for viewing by laying it out with the hands across the chest, closing the eyelids, anointing the body with oil, and placing flower garlands around it. This is done by persons of the same gender as the deceased, and this process will be presided over in the home of the deceased by the dead person's successor and heir (Habenstein & Lamers, 1974:119–120).

Because Hindus believe that cremation is an act of sacrifice, whereby one's body is offered to God through the funeral pyre, cremation is the preferred method of body disposal. In preparation for cremation, family members will construct a bier, consisting of a mat of woven coconut fronds stretched between two poles and supported by pieces of bamboo. The uncasketed body of the deceased will be borne on the bier from the deceased's home to the place of cremation by close relatives. This funeral procession will be led by the chief mourner—usually the eldest son—and will include musicians, drum players, and other mourners. The widow of the deceased will always remain behind in the home (Habenstein & Lamers, 1974:121).

The body of this Hindu woman is prepared by female family members and friends in her home.

According to Habenstein and Lamers (1974:121–122), when the body reaches the place of cremation, usually a platform *(ghat)* located on the banks of a sacred river, the body will be removed from the bier and immersed in the holy waters of the river. During this process a priest will perform a brief disposal ceremony. The body will then be smeared liberally with *ghi* (clarified butter) and placed on the pyre for burning. At this point, the chief mourner, who has brought burning coals from the house of the deceased, lights the pyre, and a priest recites an invocation similar to the following:

> *Fire, you were lighted by him, so may he be lighted from you, that he may gain the regions of celestial bliss. May this offering prove auspicious* (Habenstein & Lamers, 1974:123).

After the body has been consumed by the fire and only fragments of bones remain, the mourners will ritually wash themselves in the river in a rite of purification. They will then make offerings to the ancestral spirits of the deceased. Upon completion of this duty they will recite passages from the sacred texts.

Three days after this ritual, a few relatives of the deceased will return to the cremation site in order to gather the bones. A priest will again read from the sacred texts and sprinkle water on the *ghat*, while any remains of the deceased will be placed in a vase and given to the chief mourner. It is then the obligation of the chief mourner to cast these remains in the Ganges or another sacred river (Habenstein & Lamers, 1974:124).

Between 10 and 31 days after the cremation, a *Shraddha* (elaborate ritual feast) is prepared for all mourners and priests who have taken part in the funeral rituals. During the *Shraddha*, gifts are given to the *Guru* (religious teacher), the *Purohita* (officiating priest), and other *Brahmins* (religious functionaries). The social status of the family will determine how elaborate the *Shraddha* will be—for the poor this ritual will last eight to ten hours, and the wealthy may give a *Shraddha* lasting several days. At the close of the *Shraddha*, the mourning period officially ends even though later *Shraddhas* may be given as memorial remembrances (Habenstein & Lamers, 1974:125–126). While it is believed that these ritual meals provide nourishment to the spirit of the deceased in its celestial abode, from a sociological perspective, they serve as rites of family reincorporation and also differentiate the family regarding social status.

According to Habenstein and Lamers (1974:126), next to Hindu wedding ceremonies, funerals are the most important religious ceremonies. While the funeralization process is very costly to families, often resulting in their impoverishment, not providing the *Shraddha* creates more social problems for families than do the financial consequences of these rituals.

Buddhism

There are many types of Buddhism, but the most popular are *Theravada, Mahayana,* and *Tantrayana.* According to Peter Pardue (1968:165), Theravada Buddhism is the dominant religion in Southeast Asia (Burma, Thailand, Laos, Vietnam, Cambodia, and Sri Lanka). Mahayana Buddhism is primarily practiced in Korea, China, Japan, and Nepal. Tantranyana has traditionally been the dominant form of Buddhism in Tibet, Mongolia, and parts of Siberia. While there are differences in each of these sects and in many others found throughout the world, in general, all Buddhists find a common heritage in the life of Siddhartha Gautama ("The Enlightened One" or "Buddha").

Buddha was born in 563 B.C. as a prince in northern India. As a child his thoughts were preoccupied with the finitude of human existence. Unsuccessfully, his family tried to shelter him from human suffering and death. At the age of 29 he left his life of privilege and began to search for personal salvation. After rejecting physical asceticism and abstract philosophy, he attained a state of enlightenment through the process of intense meditation.

For the remaining 50 years of life, he served as a missionary and preached his message of salvation to all people regardless of social position and gender (Pardue, 1968:168).

The Buddhist message of salvation, taught by Buddha in his first sermon, is "The Four Noble Truths." The first truth is that all human existence is characterized by pain and suffering in an endless cycle of death and rebirth. The second truth is that the cause of the agony of the human condition is desire for personal satisfaction, which is impossible to obtain. The third truth is that salvation comes by destroying these desires. By completely destroying ignorance, one experiences enlightenment and the cycle of transmigration of the soul is broken. Finally, in the fourth truth, one can experience perfect peace through the eightfold path to enlightenment. In the words of Pardue (1968:168):

> For this purpose the proper [meditation] is the "eightfold path," an integral combination of ethics (sila) and meditation (samadhi), which jointly purify the motivations and mind. This leads to the attainment of wisdom (prajna), to enlightenment (bodhi), and to the ineffable Nirvana ("blowing out"), the final release from the incarnational cycle and mystical transcendence beyond all conceptualization.

Like the Hindu, the goal for the Buddhist is *not* to experience life after death, but to experience *nirvana*—which has neither the property of existence nor nonexistence. According to Margaret Ayer (1964:52), nirvana is the "state of peace and freedom from the miseries of the constantly changing illusion which is existence."

The location of nirvana is to be found in the image of the flame when a candle is "blown out"—it is in a place beyond human understanding. According to Ayer (1964:53), whenever anyone achieves nirvana "they 'will be seen no more.' It is through loss of desire, selfishness, evil, and illusion that this state of wisdom, holiness, and peace is reached."

Buddhism contends that while physical death causes one to experience life again in a transmigrated form, "death to this world" (via nirvana) provides the gateway for ultimate happiness, peace, and fulfillment. Unlike Hinduism and the other religious traditions we have considered, the ultimate goal of Buddhism is a state of consciousness and *not* a symbolic location for the disembodied soul.

As the religious teachings of Buddha were disseminated throughout Asia, the beliefs and practices were adapted to indigenous cultural traditions dealing with death. Consequently, it is not possible to discuss Buddhist funeral rituals *per se*. Rather, there are Japanese, Korean, Chinese, and Thai funeral customs practiced within a Buddhist context.

In general, there are some similarities in all Buddhist funeral ceremonies. At the Buddhist temple, priests assist families as they engage in this important rite of passage. Prayers of the priests illustrate the "lesson of death"—

that life is vanity. At funerals, Buddhist priests often read the following words from Buddha (cited by Habenstein & Lamers, 1974:97):

The body from which the soul has fled has no worth. Soon it will encumber the earth as a useless thing, like the trunk of a withered tree. Life lasts only for a moment. Birth and death follow one another in inescapable sequence. All that live must die. That man indeed is fortunate who achieves the nothingness of being. All animal creation is dying, or dead, or merits to be dead. All of us are dying. We cannot escape death.

For most Buddhists, cremation is the preferred form of body disposition, but earth burial is also frequently practiced. In Buddhism, unlike Hinduism, there is no "soul"—both the body and the ideas of a soul distract from the proper meditation and attainment of nirvana. Cremation serves the function of promoting the process of liberation of the individual from the illusion of the present world. As a reflection of this orientation, Buddhist priests will recite these words prior to the final disposition of the body (cited by Habenstein & Lamers, 1974:97–98):

O dead one, pursue your destiny. Flee to paradise. You will know rebirth into a better life. Do not linger to haunt those who remain here, and to share this life of invisible darkness which is the lot of the living. Those whom you leave behind reckon accurately your good fortune in your liberation. With happy impatience they await their own turn. You neither want nor need them, and they are happy without you. Now follow your destiny.

During and after the funeral, family members will make offerings through the priest to the spirit of the deceased. They will also give ritual feasts for the priests and other mourners. As in other religious traditions, all of these funeral activities will emphasize the importance of the religious world view, promote community cohesiveness, and reincorporate chief mourners into the routine patterns of social life of the society.

BOX 4.3   RELIGIOUS AND SECULAR ORIENTATIONS

Faith or belief are not the sole privileges of religious people as I once thought. Faith is simply that total commitment of the entire person to an ideal, a way of life, a set of values, to anything or anyone beyond the narrow limitations of myself: God, mankind, the poor, science, human relations, growth and development, anything capable of bringing meaning and purpose to life. . . .

(continued on next page)

The true believer, after I sort out my personal feelings toward the tenets in his creed, reflects to me a sense of inner worth, a spirit of mission and purpose, a confident conviction and a tranquil assurance. Near death the true believer knows why he lived and can face the unfinished tasks of his life with his vision in clear focus. Because true belief brought perspective into life, so will it endow death with a more satisfying point of view. And no matter how wonderful religion may be for many, it is only one of the many ways to gain this stature of true belief.

Robert E. Kavanaugh. 1972. *Facing Death.* Baltimore: Penguin Books, pp. 221 and 224.

TEMPORAL INTERPRETATIONS OF DEATH

Even though the funeral industry and most people in the United States tend to merge religious and death meanings, temporal interpretations of death also provide a means for protecting social order in the face of death. Such interpretations tend to emphasize the empirical, natural, and "this world" view of death.

According to Glenn M. Vernon (1970:33), "when death is given a temporal interpretation and is seen as the loss of consciousness, self-control, and identity, the individual may conclude that he or she can avoid social isolation in eternity by identifying him or herself with specific values, including religious ones." If we define religion as a system of beliefs and practices related to high-intensity value meanings and/or meanings of the supernatural (Vernon, 1970), then it is possible for individuals with temporal orientations to be "religious" in their outlook without affirming an afterlife. Furthermore, since any death has many consequences for the persons on whose life it impinges, we would expect that even religious persons would assign some temporal meanings to death.

Vernon (1970:33) has pointed out that individuals whose interpretations are primarily temporal share the following beliefs and attitudes:

1. They tend to reject or de-emphasize a belief in the afterlife.

2. They tend to believe that death is the end of the individual.

3. They tend to focus upon the needs and concerns of the survivors.

4. They tend to be present-oriented for themselves, but present- and future-oriented for those who will continue after them.

5. Any belief in immortality is related to the activities and accomplishments of the individual during his or her lifetime—including biological off-spring and social relationships the individual has created.

There is a strong temptation to view the person with a temporal orientation as being very different from the person who finds comfort in a religious interpretation of death. In fact, both will attempt to restore the order in their personal lives, and that found in society, by placing death in the context of a "higher" order.

For the individual with religious commitments, protection from anomie and comfort for anxiety are to be found by being in relationship with the supernatural. For the person with a secular or temporal orientation, these same benefits are found in becoming involved with other people, projects, and causes. These involvements, while not pertaining to the supernatural, still provide a frame of reference that transcends the finite individual—a person may die but his or her concerns will continue after they die.

Symbolic Immortality

Symbolic immortality (Lifton & Olson, 1974) refers to the belief that the meaning of the person can continue after he or she has died. For the religious, symbolic immortality is often related to the concept of soul, which either returns to its pre-existent state, goes to an afterlife, is reincarnated in another body, or is united with the Cosmos. For the person whose primary orientation is temporal, symbolic immortality is achieved by being remembered by others, creating something that remains useful or interesting to others, or by being part of a cause or social movement that continues after the individual's death.

BOX 4.4

I am assured of immortality, not by anything I do, but by not dying.

Woody Allen

One of the reasons many parents give for deciding to have children is the need for an heir—someone to carry on the family name. Research has demonstrated that in the United States, families with only female children are more likely to continue having children (in hopes of producing a male offspring) than are families with only male children. For the ancient Hebrews, the cultural institution of the **levirate marriage** required that a relative of the deceased husband have sexual intercourse with his kinsman's widow in order to provide a male heir. If it is possible to pass on something of oneself to one's children, then children are one method to provide symbolic immortality.

Investing oneself in relationships with others also insures that one will be remembered after death. Damon Runyon said as he was dying, "You can keep your things of bronze and stone, just give me one person who will remember me once a year." Some will argue that if we have influenced the lives of others, something of us will continue in their lives after we die.

Organ donations supply a tangible method for providing this type of symbolic immortality. In this way, one can even insure that a part of his or her *physical* self can continue in another person. Currently there is an increasing tendency for individuals to donate their organs and tissues upon death to the living (see Chapter 14). In many urban areas, kidney foundations, eye banks, and transplant centers will supply donor cards and, when death occurs, will arrange for transplants. Currently, there are many kinds of tissues or organs used for transplantation including eye, skin, bone, tendon, bone marrow, kidney, liver, pancreas, blood vessel, lung, and heart.

One of the reasons why people write books, especially death and dying books, is to promote their own symbolic immortality. As long as their books can be read, their influence will outlive their biological body. The same is true for television and motion picture stars. Each year the youthful Judy Garland is resurrected from the dead as *The Wizard of Oz* is shown on television.

Great inventors, political leaders, and athletic "hall of famers" are also given immortality when we use their products, remember their accomplishments, and celebrate their achievements. In the case of medical practitioners and bionic inventors, not only do the living remember their accomplishments, but these efforts extend the lives of those who provide the dead with immortality.

Relative Death Meanings in Society

One of the most feared, distressing, and anxiety-producing deaths is a death that is perceived as being relatively meaningless. A lifetime is spent searching for and creating meaning. The search for meaning is a task that all people share. Furthermore, significant others are involved in the process attempted by individuals in creating meaning for themselves. In many respects, the meaning created turns out to be meaning for the group or society.

As the dying of martyrs dramatically illustrates, a death may be willingly entered into if it is meaningful. Given the right configuration of meaning components (see Chapter 2), *not* to die would be more difficult. For example, dying may be preferable to defining oneself, and being defined by others, as being a coward or a traitor.

Dying is acceptable if it furthers "the cause." People may, in fact, literally work themselves to death in order to obtain a promotion, an artistic achievement, or public recognition. Whatever the specific content, the key factor of concern is the meaning involved. If the meaning is right, dying may be evaluated as a worthwhile thing.

Within a given society there are high-status types of death, as well as low-status types. Giving one's life in defense of family or country is generally conceived as being in the high-status category. In times past, dying in childbirth was considered to be a high-status death for females.

BOX 4.5 **OZYMANDIAS**

PERCY BYSSHE SHELLEY

> I met a traveler from an antique land
> Who said: Two vast and trunkless legs of stone
> Stand in the desert . . . Near them, on the sand,
> Half sunk, a shattered visage lies, whose frown,
> And wrinkled lip, and sneer of cold command,
> Tell that its sculptor well those passions read
> Which yet survive, stamped on these lifeless things,
> The hand that mocked them, and the heart that fed;
> And on the pedestal these words appear:
> "My name is Ozymandias, king of kings:
> Look on my works, ye Mighty, and despair!"
> Nothing beside remains. Round the decay
> Of that colossal wreck, boundless and bare
> The lone and level sands stretch far away.

The person's finite identity is protected by the group's permanence. Just as Standard Oil is the legacy of John D. Rockefeller, John H. Leming and Son's Insurance Agency will remain even after John H. Leming and his sons are dead (providing that the new owners feel that it is in their business interest not to change the name of the company).

The same can be said for people who give themselves to political movements and causes. Marx, Lenin, Stalin, and Mao—as leaders of communism—will be remembered by future communists, despite the efforts by present officials to accomplish the contrary. We even provide infamous immortality to villains, murderers, and traitors. It seems ironic that most of us spend a lifetime working for immortality, when the guns of John Wilkes

Booth, Lee Harvey Oswald, Sirhan Sirhan, and James Earl Ray supply their owners with our everlasting remembrance.

Society's Heroes

The death of an individual brings about a change in influence over the members of his or her group or society. Heroes are more likely to come from the ranks of the dead than the living.

Hero meaning is a symboled-meaning component. One cannot become a hero by oneself. Society bestows the rank of hero only upon certain members, one type of symboled immortality. A death may be part of the process by which heroes are born. When something dies, something else is born or created. The death of a Jesus Christ has had consequences that have expanded in significance over the years. It is likely that Christ's death has had greater impact upon humanity than his life. The Roman Catholic Church only grants sainthood to persons who have been dead for many years. Conversely, a government may grant pardons to convicted persons who died many years ago. Meaning is a flexible, yet powerful thing.

A number of interesting speculative questions arise. If there is an afterlife (in which those who are dead are "alive"), and if all of the heroes will become our contemporaries (assuming we make it, too), what would this do to their hero status? In such a situation, would the hero category be retained? Would this person have to meet new hero qualifications? Would everyone in that "kingdom" be a hero? What would a society of heroes be like? Would the hero category be meaningful?

In conclusion, symbolic immortality is something that only the living can give the dead. Yet, people live with the faith that their survivors will remember them and perpetuate the meaning of their lives after they die. Like religious interpretations of death, temporal meanings enable individuals to protect themselves and their social order from death. One problem remains, however, for those whose immortality depends upon others: What would happen if a nuclear holocaust were to occur and there were no survivors?

BOX 4.6   **THE FADING OF IMMORTALITY**

> In quantitative terms, the twentieth century seems more death ridden than any other. Yet mass death is strangely impersonal; an eighteenth century hanging at Tyburn probably had more immediate impact on the watching crowd than the almost incomprehensible statistics of

modern war and calculated terror have today. In the last century, Byron, Shelley, Keats, and a whole generation of young poets haunted by romanticism and tuberculosis could be "half in love with easeful Death," wooing it as they would woo a woman. Even before World War I, German poet Rainer Maria Rilke could still yearn for "the great death" for which a man prepares himself, rather than the "little" death for which he is unprepared.

In today's literature there are few "great deaths." Tolstoy, Thomas Mann, and Conrad gave death a tragic dimension. Hemingway was among the last to try; his heroes died stoically, with style, like matadors. Nowadays, death tends to be presented as a banal accident in an indifferent universe. Much of the Theater of the Absurd ridicules both death and modern man's inability to cope with it. In Ionesco's *Amedee,* or *How to Get Rid of It,* the plot concerns a corpse that grows and grows until it floats away in the shape of a balloon—a balloon, that is, on the way to nowhere.

"If there is no immortality, I shall hurl myself into the sea," wrote Tennyson. Bismarck was calmer. "Without the hope of an afterlife," he said, "this life is not even worth the effort of getting dressed in the morning." Freud called the belief that death is the door to a better life "the oldest, strongest, and most insistent wish of mankind." But now death is steadily becoming more of a wall and less of a door. . . .

The Christian view of eternity is not merely endless time, and it need not involve the old physical concept of heaven and hell. It does involve the survival of some essence of self and an encounter with God. "Life after death," said theologian Karl Barth, "should not be regarded like a butterfly"—he might have said a balloon—"that flutters away above the grave and is preserved somewhere. Resurrection means not the continuation of life, but life's completion. The Christian hope is the conquest of death, not a flight into the Beyond."

The Fear of Nothingness

Admittedly, this hope so stated is more abstract than the fading pictures of sky-born glory, of hallelujah choruses and throngs of waiting loved ones. "People today could be described as more realistic about death," says one psychiatrist. "But inside I think they are more afraid. Those old religious assurances that there would be a gathering-in some day have largely been discarded, and I see examples all the time of neuroses

(continued on next page)

caused by the fear of death." Harvard theologian Krister Stendahl agrees. "Socrates," he points out, "died in good cheer and in control, unlike the agony of Jesus with his deep human cry of desertion and loneliness. Americans tend to behave as Socrates did. But there is more of what Jesus stands for lurking in our unconsciousness."

Alone with his elemental fear of death, modern man is especially troubled by the prospect of a meaningless death and a meaningless life—the bleak offering of existentialism. "There is but one truly serious philosophical problem," wrote Albert Camus, "and that is suicide." In other words, why stay alive in a meaningless universe? The existentialist replies that man must live for the sake of living, for the things he is free to accomplish. But despite volumes of argumentation, existentialism never seems quite able to justify this conviction on the brink of a death that is only a trap door to nothingness.

There are surrogate forms of immortality: the continuity of history, the permanence of art, the biological force of sex. These can serve well enough to give life a purpose and a sense of fulfillment. But they cannot outwit death, and they are hardly satisfactory substitutes for the still persistent human hope that what happens here in three score years and ten is not the whole story.

AFTERLIFE EXPERIENCES BY THE CLINICALLY DEAD
Empirical Evidence for Afterlife Beliefs?

In the past, one of the assumptions most people made about the field of thanatology was that the real "experts" were not among us—they were dead. With the publication of Raymond Moody's *Life after Life* (1975), many people have stepped forward to challenge this assumption. Having been near death, or having been declared clinically dead by medical authorities, a number of survivors from these experiences have "returned from the dead" to tell us that they now know what it is like to be dead and that they possess empirical evidence to support a rational belief in the afterlife.

The description below, developed by Moody, is a composite of the many accounts by individuals who have survived the experience of being near death or being declared clinically dead. This ideal model was constructed by interviewing more than 150 people who had had these experiences. Moody reports, and other scientists (Noyes & Kletti, 1977; Rawlings, 1978; Ring, 1980) support, the similarity of most of these "life after death" accounts.

BOX 4.7 **LIFE AFTER LIFE**

RAYMOND A. MOODY, JR., M.D., PH.D.

A man is dying and, as he reaches the point of greatest physical distress, he hears himself pronounced dead by his doctor. He begins to hear an uncomfortable noise, a loud ringing or buzzing, and at the same time feels himself moving very rapidly through a long dark tunnel. After this he suddenly finds himself outside of his own physical body, but still in the immediate physical environment, and he sees his own body from a distance, as though he is a spectator. He watches the resuscitation attempt from his unusual vantage point and is in a state of emotional upheaval.

After a while, he collects himself and becomes more accustomed to his body with very different powers from the physical body he has left behind. Soon other things begin to happen. Others come to meet and to help him. He glimpses the spirits of relatives and friends who have already died, and a loving, warm spirit of a kind he has never encountered before—a being of light—appears before him. This being asks him a question, nonverbally, to make him evaluate his life and helps him along by showing him a panoramic, instantaneous playback of the major events of his life. At some point he finds himself approaching some sort of barrier or border, apparently representing the limit between earthly life and the next life. Yet, he finds that he must go back to earth, that the time for his death has not yet come. At this point he resists, for by now he is taken up with his experiences in the afterlife and does not want to return. He is overwhelmed by intense feelings of joy, love, and peace. Despite his attitude, though, he somehow reunites with his physical body and lives.

Later he tries to tell others, but he has trouble doing so. In the first place, he can find no human words adequate to describe these unearthly episodes. He also finds that others scoff, so he stops telling other people. Still, the experience affects his life profoundly, especially his views about death and its relationship to life.

Raymond A. Moody, Jr. 1975. *Life after Life: The Investigation of a Phenomenon—Survival of Bodily Death*. Boston: G. K. Hall, pp. 16–18.

The following questions now become relevant as we contemplate the relationship between these experiences and the other material presented in this chapter:

1. Are these experiences real, and what do they tell us about the dying process and/or being dead?

2. Can afterlife beliefs be empirically supported by these accounts?

3. How do religious beliefs affect the content of near-death or clinical death experiences?

4. What is the impact of near- or clinical death experiences upon death anxiety?

To all of our questions, we must temper our responses by saying that if not real, these experiences are very real to those who have experienced them. Not unlike being in love, returning from the dead is an extremely subjective experience and does not lend itself to verification by others. It is difficult to doubt that the individual has experienced *something*; however, we are unable to prove, or disprove, that the person has died. All we can say scientifically is that the person claims to have had the experience of "being dead."

Returning to our analogy of being in love, all that can be known is that the person says that he or she is in love. Whether or not the person really is cannot be determined empirically. From the perspective of the individual, it does not really matter, because a situation, which has been defined as real, will have very real behavioral consequences.

The same problem arises with regard to a belief in an afterlife. What does **science** say about it? Scientifically, afterlife beliefs cannot be proved, or disproved, with this type of evidence. Science is based upon the principle of **intersubjectivity.** This means that independent observers, with different subjective orientations, must agree that something is "true" based upon their separate investigations. Unfortunately, the opportunity to experience the afterlife (and return) is not uniformly available to all observers. Therefore, while those who have had these experiences may feel rationally justified in their beliefs, the evidence they use is not scientifically based. Science, at this point, can neither verify, nor falsify afterlife beliefs.

In responding to our last two questions, there is some scientific evidence that can provide limited answers. According to Moody (1975) and Canning (1965), the content of afterlife experiences is largely a function of the religious background, training, and beliefs of the individuals involved. Only Roman Catholics see the Virgin Mary and the host of Catholic saints, while encounters with Joseph Smith are reserved for Mormon believers. Like dreams, continuity exists between experiences in "this world" and experiences in the "afterlife." For example, personages in the afterlife are dressed in an attire that would conform to the individual's cultural customs and

TV Guide. November 11, 1978. Used by permission of Henry Martin.

While on the operating table my heart stopped beating and I died. At that moment, Merv, I learned that there was a life after life and a chance for a best selling book based on this discovery, and a hit movie based on the book, and TV guest shots to plug the movie, and commercials generated by TV appearances and . . .

beliefs. Also, relatives appear to be at the same age as they were when they were last seen. In fact, there is so much continuity between this world and the "other world" that persons with afterlife experiences report few, if any, surprises. In response to this evidence, Kathy Charmaz (1980) raises the following question: Is the consciousness reported in these near-death experiences a *reflection* of a shared myth or *evidence* for it?

Concerning the impact of the near-death experience upon death anxiety, there is empirical evidence that fear of death is significantly reduced. However, even though the state of being dead is not distressing to them, anxiety related to the dying process is unchanged. Almost without exception, however, persons who have had these experiences look forward to their eventual deaths.

Finally, there is evidence that individuals (even attempted suicides) do not try to bring about an end to their lives in order to return to the "life beyond." In fact, most individuals find new reasons for living as a result of these experiences.

DEATH ANXIETY AND FEAR

> Lord, If I have to die, Let me die;
> But please, Take away this fear.
>
> KEN WALSH, *SOMETIMES I WEEP*

A point made in this book a number of times is that death *per se* has no meaning other than that which people give it. If this is true, why is it that most of us believe that death is something that intrinsically engenders fear?

Anthropologists would be quick to respond that not all cultures in the world hold that death is necessarily something to be feared (see Chapter 10). However, there seem to be a large number of cultures, including our own, which attach fearful meanings to death and death-related situations. Why is it that so many people have less-than-positive views of death?

In the beginning of this chapter we said that death universally calls into question the order upon which most societies are based. As a marginal experience to everyday life, death not only disrupts normal patterns of interaction, but also challenges the meaningfulness of life. With the exception of those societies where death is a routine event in the lives of the people (e.g., Ethiopia, India, Cambodia, and New Guinea), death in most societies is a stressful event because it brings disorder to those whose lives it touches.

Stress and Change in Everyday Life

Any change in ordinary patterns of social interaction requires that the individual adjust. Most of us prefer the security of situations that are predictable, stable, and routine. The disorder created by changes in everyday life can make for a stressful situation as individuals attempt to adjust to these changes (Holmes & Rahe, 1967).

Death in the United States is viewed as fearful because Americans have been taught systematically to fear it. Horror movies portray death, ghosts, skeletons, goblins, bogeymen, and ghoulish morticians as things to be feared. Sesame Street tries to create for children a more positive view of monsters as children are befriended by Grover, Oscar, and Cookie Monster. With the exception of Casper "the friendly ghost," death-related fantasy figures have not received the same positive images. Instead of providing positive images, our culture has chosen to reinforce fearful meanings of death. Cemeteries are portrayed as eerie, funeral homes are to be avoided, and morgues are scary places where you "wouldn't be caught dead."

One of the reasons death and dying classes incorporate field trips to hospices, funeral homes, crematoria, and cemeteries is to confront negative death meanings and fantasies with first-hand, objective observations. The preparation room at the mortuary is a good example. If you have never been in one, think about the mental image that comes to your mind. For many, the preparation room is a place one approaches with fear and caution—something like Dr. Frankenstein's laboratory, complete with bats, strange lighting, body parts, and naked dead bodies. The great disappointment for most students as they walk through the door is that they find a room that looks like a physician's examination room. "Is that all there is?" is a comment often heard after visiting the preparation room.

Sociologist Erving Goffman (1959) observed that first impressions are unlikely to change and tend to dominate the meanings related to subsequent social interaction patterns and experiences. Some of us want to retain untrue fearful meanings of death, even when confronted by positive images. On a recent field trip to a funeral home, one student refused to enter the preparation room. While other students were hearing a description of embalming procedures, she discovered a bottle labeled "skin texturizer" and became nauseated. Other students had a difficult time understanding her problem because they had had positive experiences.

Another reason for fearful meanings being ascribed to death can be attributed to a traumatic death-related experience. Being a witness to a fatal car accident, discovering someone who has committed suicide, or attending a funeral where emotional outbursts create an uncomfortable environment for mourners can increase death anxiety for individuals. However, such occurrences are rather uncommon for most people and do not account for the prevalence of America's preoccupation with death fears. In a survey of college students, Robert Kavanaugh (1972) found that 78 percent had not seen a dead person up close, and more than 92 percent had yet to witness a death.

In summary, death fears are not instinctive; they exist because our culture has created and perpetuated fearful meanings and ascribed them to death. They are also a function of the fact that death is a nonordinary experience challenging the order of everyday life in society. They are a function of occasional first-hand encounters with deaths so unusual that they become traumatic.

Content of Death Fears

When one speaks of death fear or death anxiety, it is assumed that the concept is unidimensional and that consensus exists relative to its meaning. Such is not the case, however, since two persons may say that they fear death and yet the content of their fears may not be shared. Death anxiety (or death fear) is a multidimensional concept and is based upon the following four concerns:

(1) the death of self; (2) the deaths of significant others; (3) the process of dying; and (4) the state of being dead. This model's more elaborated form (Leming, 1979–1980) shows eight types of death fears that can be applied to the death of self and the death of others:

1. dependency

2. the pain in the dying process

3. the indignity in the dying process

4. the isolation, separation, and rejection that can be part of the dying process

5. leaving loved ones

6. afterlife concerns

7. the finality of death

8. the fate of the body

From Table 4.1 we can see that the content of fear will be influenced by whose death the individual is considering. From a personal death perspective, one may have anxiety over the effect that one's dying (or being dead) will have on others. There might also be private worries about how one might be treated by others—and even by God. From the perspective of the survivor, the individual may be concerned about the financial, emotional, and social problems related to the death of a significant other.

Since there are many factors related to the experience of death and death-related situations that can engender fear, we would expect to find individual differences in type and intensity of death fear, including social circumstance and past experiences. However, with all of the potential sources for differences, repeated administrations of the Leming Death Fear Scale yield consistently high anxiety scores for the fears of dependency and pain related to the process of dying, and relatively low anxiety scores for the fears related to the afterlife and the fate of the body. Approximately 65 percent of the more than 1000 individuals surveyed had high anxiety concerning dependency and pain, and only 15 percent experienced the same level of anxiety relative to concerns about the afterlife and the fate of the body (Leming, 1979–1980). Thus it is the *process of dying*—not the *event of death*—that causes the most concern.

Religion and Death Fears Reconsidered

If we return to the relation between religious commitment and death fear, we might wonder how religious commitment affects the eight types of death

TABLE 4.1

The Eight Dimensions of Death Anxiety As They Relate to the Deaths of Self and Others

Self	Others
PROCESS OF DYING	
1. Fear of dependency	Fear of financial burdens
2. Fear of pain in dying process	Fear of going through the painful experience of others
3. Fear of the indignity in dying process	Fear of being unable to cope with the physical problems of others
4. Fear of loneliness, rejection, and isolation	Fear of being unable to cope emotionally with problems of others
5. Fear of leaving loved ones	Fear of losing loved ones
STATE OF BEING DEAD	
6. Afterlife concerns	Afterlife concerns
Fear of an unknown situation	Fear of the judgment of others—
Fear of divine judgment	"What are they thinking?"
Fear of the spirit world	Fear of ghosts, spirits, devils, etc.
Fear of nothingness	Fear of never seeing the person
7. Fear of the finality of death	again
Fear of not being able to achieve one's goals	Fear of the end of a relationship
	Guilt related to not having done
Fear of the possible end of physical and symbolic identity	enough for the deceased
	Fear of not seeing the person again
Fear of the end of all social relationships	Fear of losing the social relationship
	Fear of death objects
8. Fear of the fate of the body	Fear of dead bodies
Fear of body decomposition	Fear of being in cemeteries
Fear of being buried	Fear of not knowing how to act in
Fear of not being treated with respect	death-related situations

fears discussed earlier. Consistent with what we have seen in Figure 4.1, the theoretical model in this chapter suggests a curvilinear relationship between the two variables—those persons with moderate religious commitment experience the greatest amount of anxiety in each of the eight areas.

In attempting to empirically evaluate this relationship, Leming (1979–1980) found that the theoretical model was supported with only 2 curvilinear trend deviations (see Table 4.2). The deviations were found among people who were the least religious for the fear of dependency in the dying process. It may be that nonreligious individuals are more concerned about being self-sufficient and independent of others, and that they find dependency even more distressing than persons who are more religious. In terms of the fear of

TABLE 4.2

Mean Scores for the Various Types of Death Fears by Level of Religious Commitment

| Type of Death Fear* | LEVEL OF RELIGIOUS COMMITMENT | | | |
	Least Religious 1	2	3	*Most Religious* 4
Fear of dependency in dying process				
Total Mean = 3.9	4.2**	4.1	3.85	3.75
Fear of pain				
Total Mean = 3.7	3.8	4.0	3.65	3.5
Fear of isolation				
Total Mean = 3.0	2.8	3.0	2.95	3.0**
Fear of the finality of death				
Total Mean = 2.9	3.05	3.25	2.8	2.75
Fear of leaving loved ones				
Total Mean = 2.8	3.05	3.25	2.65	2.60
Fear of the indignity in dying process				
Total Mean = 2.75	2.55	2.9	2.85	2.55
Fear of afterlife				
Total Mean = 2.55	2.5	2.95	2.6	2.3
Fear of the fate of the body				
Total Mean = 2.55	2.5	2.7	2.6	2.4
COMBINED LEMING* DEATH FEAR SCORE	24.75	26.45	24.3	22.9
Total Mean = 24.3				

*The possible range for the subscale scores is 1 through 6, with the values of one and six indicating low and high anxiety respectively. For the combined death fear score the potential minimum score is 8 and the highest maximum score is 48.

**Curvilinear Trend Deviation

isolation, there does not seem to be a relationship between death fear and religious commitment.

BOX 4.8 **RELIGION AND DYING**

My conclusion is that religious faith of itself does little to affect man's peace near death. Worry warts are worry warts no matter their theology. It is not the substance or content of a man's creed that brings peace. It is the *firmness* and the quality of his act of believing. Firm believers, true believers, will find more peace on their deathbeds than all others, whatever the religious or secular label we place on their creed. *The believer, not the belief,* brings peace.

Robert E. Kavanaugh. 1972. *Facing Death.* Baltimore: Penguin Books, p. 14.

Upon further investigation, Leming (1979–1980) found that factors of education, age, and even religious preference did not affect the curvilinear relationship. With the exception of the fear of isolation, persons who had the strongest religious commitment were the least fearful with regard to the various areas of death concern. Furthermore, in each of the eight death fear areas the strength of commitment was the most significant variable in explaining the relationship between religion and the fear of death. Robert Kavanaugh (1972:14) seems to have empirical support for his statement, "The believer, not the belief, brings peace."

CONCLUSION

Religion is a system of beliefs and practices related to the sacred—that which is considered to be of ultimate significance. The cultural practice of religion continues because it meets basic social needs of individuals within a given society. A major function of religion, in this regard, is to explain the unexplainable.

For most "primitive," or less complex societies, events are explained by a supernatural rather than rational or empirical means. Thus, an eclipse of the sun or moon was said to be a sign that the gods had a message for humankind. These supernatural explanations were needed, in part, because there were no competing rational or scientific explanations.

Technologically and scientifically advanced societies tend to be less dependent upon supernatural explanations. Yet such explanations are still important, especially when scientific explanations are incomplete. It is not uncommon to hear a physician say, "Medical science is unable to cure this patient; it's now in God's hands." Or, a physician might say, "It's a miracle that the patient survived this illness; I can't explain the recovery." Thus, one might suggest that religion takes over where science and rationality leave off. We depend less on religious or supernatural explanations than nonliterate societies, but nonetheless rely on them when knowledge is incomplete.

Religion plays a significant role in societies by helping individuals cope with extraordinary events—especially death. Not only does religion help restore the normative order challenged by death, but strong religious commitments can enable individuals to cope better with their own dying and the deaths of their loved ones. For others, strong commitments to a temporal orientation may fulfill many of the functions provided by a religious world view.

SUMMARY

1. Religion helps individuals when the order of everyday life is challenged by providing answers to problems of uncertainty, powerlessness, and scarcity created by death.

2. Religious systems provide a means to reestablish the social order challenged by death.

3. When one encounters death, the anxiety experienced is basically socially ascribed.

4. Religion provides individuals with solace when they attempt to cope with death.

5. Temporal interpretations of death provide a means for protecting the social order by emphasizing the empirical, natural, and "this worldly" view of death.

6. Symbolic immortality is evidenced by offspring carrying on the family name, by donating body organs, and by having accomplishments or achievements (positive and negative) remembered by others.

7. Near-death or afterlife experiences are influenced by the individual's religious background, cultural beliefs, and prior social experiences.

8. Death fears exist because cultures create and perpetuate fearful meanings and ascribe them to death.

9. Death anxiety is a multidimensional concept with the *process* of dying rather than the *event* of death causing the most concern.

10. The strength of one's religious commitment is a significant variable in explaining the relationship between religion and the fear of death.

DISCUSSION QUESTIONS

1. How does religion function to provide a restoration of the order challenged by the event of death?

2. What is meant by death fear or death anxiety? Why is this concept multidimensional rather than unidimensional?

3. What types of death fears are the most salient for Americans? How might you explain why these fears are more intense than other fears?

4. What is the relationship between religious commitment and death fear?

5. Explain the following statement: "Religion afflicts the comforted and comforts the afflicted."

6. With regard to death anxiety, why does the believer, not the belief, bring peace?

7. How can symbolic immortality and temporal interpretations of death provide a source of anxiety reduction for those who face death?

8. How can organ donations provide symbolic immortality for donors and their loved ones?

9. Do accounts of near-death experiences provide empirical evidence for afterlife beliefs? Why or why not?

10. What are the similarities and differences in Jewish, Christian, Islamic, Hindu, and Buddhist beliefs about death and funeral practices?

GLOSSARY

Anomie   A condition characterized by the relative absence or confusion of values within a group or society.

Curvilinear   Referring to a type of nonlinear relationship between two variables where at a certain point, associated with the increasing values in the independent variable, the relationship with the dependent variable changes. A scattergram graph of this relationship will either look like a **U** or an inverted **U**.

Death anxiety   A learned emotional response to death-related phenomena that is characterized by extreme apprehension. In this chapter, death anxiety is used synonymously with death fear.

Dysfunctional   Referring to any consequence of a social system that is judged to be a disturbance to the adjustment, stability, or integration of the group or the members of that group.

Etiology   The study of causal relationships that attempts to delineate those factors responsible for a given occurrence.

Intersubjectivity   A property of science whereby two or more scientists, studying the same phenomenon, can reach the same conclusion.

Levirate marriage   An institution typified by the Hebrew requirement that a relative of the deceased husband must have sexual intercourse with his kinsman's widow in order to provide a male heir.

Marginal situations   Unusual events or social circumstances that do not occur in normal patterns of social interaction.

Religion   A system of beliefs and practices related to the sacred, the supernatural, and/or a set of values to which the individual is very committed.

Religiosity   The extent of interest, commitment, or participation in religious values, beliefs, and activities.

Rituals   A set of culturally prescribed actions or behaviors.

Science   A body of knowledge based upon sensory evidence or empirical observations.

Symbolic immortality   The ascription of immortality to the individual by perpetuating the meaning of the person (the self).

Temporal   Referring to a "here and now" or "this worldly" orientation that does not take into account the afterlife or a supernatural existence.

REFERENCES

▬▬▬ Ayer, Margaret. 1964. *Made in Thailand.* New York: Knopf.

Berger, Peter L. 1969. *Sacred Canopy: Elements of a Sociological Theory of Religion.* New York: Doubleday.

Canning, Ray R. 1965. "Mormon Return-from-the-Dead Stories: Fact or Folklore?" *Utah Academy Proceedings, 42,* Pt. I.

Carse, J. 1981. "Death." In Keith Crim, Roger A. Bullard, and Larry D. Shinn (Eds.), *Abingdon Dictionary of Living Religions.* Nashville: Abingdon Press.

Charmaz, Kathy. 1980. *The Social Reality of Death.* Reading, MA: Addison-Wesley.

Durkheim, Emile. 1915. *Elementary Forms of Religious Life.* New York: George Allen & Unwin.

Eickelman, Dale F. 1987. "Rites of Passage: Muslim Rites." In Mircea Eliade (Ed.), *The Encyclopedia of Religion, 12.* New York: Macmillan, pp. 400–403.

Faulkner, Joseph, & Gordon F. DeJong. 1966. "Religiosity in 5-D: An Empirical Analysis." *Social Forces* (45), 246–254.

Glock, Charles, & Rodney Stark. 1966. *Christian Beliefs and Anti-Semitism.* New York: Harper & Row.

Goffman, Erving. 1959. *The Presentation of Self in Everyday Life.* New York: Doubleday.

Habenstein, Robert W., & William M. Lamers. 1974. *Funeral Customs the World Over.* Milwaukee: Bulfin Printers.

Holmes, T. H., & R. H. Rahe. 1967. "The Social Readjustment Rating Scale." *Journal of Psychosomatic Research, 11* (August): Table 3–1, p. 213.

Homans, George C. 1965. "Anxiety and Ritual: The Theories of Malinowski and Radcliffe-Brown." In W. A. Lessa and E. Z. Vogt (Eds.), *Reader in Comparative Religion: An Anthropological Approach.* New York: Harper & Row, pp. 83–88.

Kavanaugh, Robert E. 1972. *Facing Death.* Baltimore: Penguin.

Knobel, Peter S. 1987. "Rites of Passage: Jewish Rites." In Mircea Eliade (Ed.), *The Encyclopedia of Religion, 12.* New York: Macmillan, pp. 396–397.

Leming, Michael R. 1979–1980. "Religion and Death: A Test of Homans' Thesis." *Omega, 10* (4), 347–364.

Lewis, C. S. 1961. *A Grief Observed.* London: Faber and Faber.

Lifton, Robert, & E. Olson. 1974. *Living and Dying.* New York: Praeger.

Long, J. Bruce. 1987. "Underworld." In Mircea Eliade (Ed.), *The Encyclopedia of Religion, 15.* New York: Macmillan, pp. 126–133.

Malinowski, Bronislaw. 1965. "The Role of Magic and Religion." In W. A. Lessa & E. Z. Vogt (Eds.), *Reader in Comparative Religion: An Anthropological Approach,* New York: Harper & Row, pp. 63–72.

McBrien, Richard P. 1987. "Roman Catholicism." In Mircea Eliade (Ed.), *The Encyclopedia of Religion, 12.* New York: Macmillan, pp. 440–441.

Moody, Raymond A., Jr. 1975. *Life after Life: The Investigation of a Phenomenon—Survival of Bodily Death.* Boston: G. K. Hall.

Noyes, Russell, Jr., & Ray Kletti. 1977. "Panoramic Memory." *Omega, 8:*181–193.

O'Dea, Thomas. 1966. *The Sociology of Religion.* Englewood Cliffs, NJ: Prentice-Hall.

Pardue, Peter. 1968. "Buddhism." In *International Encyclopedia of the Social Sciences, 2.* New York: Macmillan, pp. 165–184.

Radcliffe-Brown, A. R. 1965. "Taboo." In W. A. Lessa & E. Z. Vogt (Eds.), *Reader in*

    Comparative Religion: An Anthropological Approach. New York: Harper & Row, pp. 72–83.

Rahman, Fazlur. 1987. *Health and Medicine in the Islamic Tradition.* New York: Crossroad Press.

Rawlings, Maurice. 1978. *Beyond Death's Door.* Nashville: Thomas Nelson.

Ring, Kenneth. 1980. *Life at Death: A Scientific Investigation of the Near-Death Experience.* New York: Coward, McCann and Geoghegan.

Srinivas, M. N., & A. M. Shah. 1968. "Hinduism." In *International Encyclopedia of the Social Sciences,* Volume 6. New York: Macmillan, pp. 358–366.

Vernon, Glenn M. 1970. *Sociology of Death: An Analysis of Death-Related Behavior.* New York: Ronald Press.

Walsh, Ken. 1974. *Sometimes I Weep.* Valley Forge, PA: Judson Press, p. 18.

SUGGESTED READINGS

Berger, Peter L. 1969. *Sacred Canopy: Elements of a Sociological Theory of Religion.* New York: Doubleday.

    Excellent treatment of the role of religious world views as they relate to life crises. Death is discussed as the ultimate marginal situation to normal social functioning that calls forth religious meaning systems.

Eliade, Mircea. 1987. *The Encyclopedia of Religion.* New York: Macmillan.

    Tremendous academic resource on religious rites, beliefs, and traditions. This reference tool is written from an interdisciplinary perspective by international scholars of religion.

Homans, George C. 1965. "Anxiety and Ritual: The Theories of Malinowski and Radcliffe-Brown" in *Reader in Comparative Religion: An Anthropological Approach,* pp. 83–88., ed. by W. A. Lessa and E. Z. Vogt. New York: Harper & Row.

    Leming, Michael R. 1979–1980. "Religion and Death: A Test of Homans' Thesis." *Omega, 10* (4), 347–364.

    Two articles that review the theoretical and empirical evidence regarding the relation between religion and death anxiety.

Kavanaugh, Robert E. 1972. *Facing Death.* Baltimore: Penguin Books.

    As a former Roman Catholic priest, Kavanaugh reflects on his experiences with death in the context of his religious background. He discusses the role of religion in the adjustment process to dying and death.

Moody, Raymond A., Jr. 1975. *Life after Life: The Investigation of a Phenomenon—Survival of Bodily Death.* Boston: G. K. Hall.

    Ring, Kenneth. 1980. *Life at Death: A Scientific Investigation of the Near-Death Experience.* New York: Coward, McCann and Geoghegan.

    Two books that describe and discuss empirical evidence relating to near-death experiences.

THREE

Understanding the
Dying Process

CHAPTER 5

The Dying Process

—

I'm not afraid of dying. I just don't want to be there when it happens.

WOODY ALLEN

5   Of all events in life, dying can be the most stressful. As we saw in the last chapter, people tend to fear the process of dying more than the event of death. Many factors will contribute to and alleviate the stress of the dying process. In this chapter we are concerned primarily with the physical and social factors.

Among other things, dying is a process that happens to the physical body of the individual. Although the determination of the timing of death is problematic, there is a qualitative difference between a live and a dead human being. For the most part, the cause of death is ultimately attributed to physiological factors. However, the biological aspect of dying is less meaningful to us than the events that take place during the dying process.

DEATH MEANINGS AND THEIR EFFECTS ON THE DYING PROCESS

The meaning of our dying will depend to a great extent upon the social context in which it takes place. As discussed in Chapter 2, meanings are the basic component of human behavior because individuals respond to the meanings of phenomena rather than to the phenomena themselves. As the ISAS paradigm states, *individual-level behavior* is in response to *symbols,* relative to the *audience* and to the *situation.* Death-related behavior of the one dying, therefore, and of those who care about that person, is in response to meaning, relative to the audience and to the situation. Meanings are both socially created and socially perpetuated. (For further discussion of death meanings see Leming, Vernon, & Gray, 1977, the source on which much of this material is based).

The major types of meanings to which individuals respond in death-related situations are the following: time meanings, space meanings, norm and role meanings, value meanings, object and self meanings, and meanings of social situations (Vernon, 1972). We will now look at each of these types of meanings and their effects on the dying process.

Time Meanings

As anthropologist Colin Turnbull ("Conversation") once told the author, "Americans want to live forever. If you ask someone how long they wish to live, they will probably say somewhere in the upper 90s because they do not suspect they will reach 100. But if they reach 100, then they will aim for 101, 102, etc." Turnbull says African groups know when it is time to die, and they accept this. Perhaps Richard Pryor sums it up well when he said, "Even if I live for 100 years, I'll be dead a lot longer." Thus, one is dead longer than alive.

In thinking about the dying process, the first thing that comes to awareness is the concept of time. We are confronted with the fact that time, for the terminal patient, is running out. Yet, when does the dying process begin? Are we not all dying, with some reaching the state of being dead before others? From the moment of our births, we are approaching the end of our lives. We assume that terminal patients will experience death before others, but this is not always the case.

BOX 5.1   **GUEST LECTURER**

I invited to class a woman who had been diagnosed as a terminal cancer patient. Deeply impressed by the visitor's positive outlook on the time left to her, one student on the following day noted, "When I came into the session I expected to meet someone who was dying. Instead, I realize that woman is more alive than I am. The discussion wasn't about dying at all, it was about living."

Joan M. Boyle, "Dialectic on Dying." In M. M. Newell, *et al.* (Eds.), *The Role of the Volunteer in the Care of the Terminal Patient and the Family.* New York: The Foundation of Thanatology/Arno Press, pp. 182–189.

Since it is possible to diagnose a disease from which most people die, we can assume that patients with these diseases are more terminal than individuals without them. The terminal patient is very much concerned with the time dimension of his or her physical existence. Many surveys (see Glaser & Strauss, 1965) have demonstrated that as many as 80 percent of patients want to be told if their illness is terminal. Physicians, however, are not always prepared to tell their patients of a terminal diagnosis.

Nonetheless, with more emphasis on consumer rights today, physicians are more likely to tell the patient of his or her diagnosis than was the case in the early 1960s. In a 1961 survey of physicians (Oken, 1961) only 10 percent gave full terminal prognosis disclosure to their patients, while in the 1980s informing the patient has become a widespread tendency (Klenow & Youngs, 1987).

Though many physicians in the past have not favored telling their patients, Elisabeth Kübler-Ross (1969) claims that it is not a question of whether the patient *should* be told, but of *how*. Should patients be told the amount of time they have left? Specifying an amount of time dispels hope and serves no more function than telling the patient that the condition is very serious and life-threatening, advises Kübler-Ross (1969). If the patient

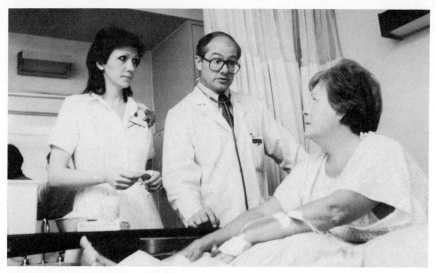

When a patient is told that the disease is terminal, the information must be communicated in a manner that is honest but does not rob the patient of a sense of hopefulness.

presses for time specificity, a range of time should be given such as, "Sixty percent of the patients with your disease live as long as three to five years." This statement provides hope without deluding the patient. Also, it is honest. Medical science cannot say with any certainty that a person will live one year—some die sooner and others live longer (some even outlive the physician!).

BOX 5.2   **SHARING THE EXPERIENCE OF DYING**

Some of the most beautiful human interactions I have witnessed have occurred between dying patients and supportive families. Sometimes the quality of human interactions in the terminal phase far exceeds anything the patient or family experienced prior to diagnosis.

I strongly feel the dying patient should be told as much as he or she wants to know. The family should also be encouraged to share feelings with the patient in an open manner. *Nothing* is worse than dying alone. The terminal patient whose family won't broach the subject, or who is afraid to upset his or her family or doctors with fears and feelings, does die alone.

A physician's comment from a survey of 1093 physicians conducted by Dickinson and Pearson (1980–1981).

Space Meanings

Even when the patient has not been told of a terminal condition, he or she will eventually become aware of it. Frequently, factors related to social space will give the patient such clues. Within the hospital, for example, there are areas where the very ill are treated. When one is placed in the intensive care unit or on an oncology ward, it becomes obvious that all is not well and that death is a real possibility.

Confinement to a health-care institution conveys a tremendous amount of meaning to the patient. For the most part, the patient is alone. Through spatial meanings the individual is "informed" that he or she is removed from those things that give life meaning and purpose—family, friends, and job. For the terminally ill patient this is the first stage of societal **disengagement.**

The following statement (Hale, 1971:1078) demonstrates the significance of space to the dying patient:

> As for the patient himself, he faces his life's ultimate crisis in a foreign place— the hospital. Usually, he dies alone, not in the presence of anyone who cares. Often the family is allowed to visit even the dying only during the hours set by the hospital. And since hospital visits usually lack privacy, they are of little comfort either to the patient or to the relatives who are entering the period of "anticipatory grief." There is little room or opportunity for sharing that most poignant moment of a lifetime—death! There is little opportunity for dignity in those settings.

Though many institutional settings have liberalized their visitation policies somewhat since the early 1970s, unfortunately the above statements by Hale still basically hold.

Within any health-care setting, the patients' very confinements serve to diminish their social and personal power. According to Rodney Coe (1970), three processes occur within the institution to accomplish this: "stripping," control of resources, and restrictions on mobility. The process of *stripping* takes place when the patient is issued a hospital gown and stripped of any valuables for safekeeping; the patient's identity is also stripped. Most factors that differentiate patients with regard to status in the larger society are taken away to create the primary status of patient—all patients look alike. According to Coe (1970:300), "every distinctly personalizing symbol, material or otherwise, is taken away, thus reducing the patient to the status of just one of many." Perhaps this helps explain why physicians are such bad patients— they are forced to relinquish their physician status when they are admitted to the hospital.

The second process that reduces patient autonomy is the *control of resources.* Personal power is the ability to make decisions that determine the direction of one's own life and environment. Without all such information concerning one's situation, it may not be possible to make important decisions. One method used by hospitals to control resources is to deny all patients and their families access to medical charts and records and important information about events in the hospital.

The third process is the *restriction on mobility*. Not being able to leave one's room or bed further reduces the patient's personal power. The patient is put in a position of dependency upon others. Confinement of this type greatly affects the patient's autonomy, and, ironically, permits others to withdraw from the patient.

Social space is very important in the process of patient disengagement. This disengagement can be accomplished by two methods—the patient can withdraw from others and others can withdraw from the patient. If the patient is debilitated by illness, energy may not be abundant enough to continue normal patterns of social interaction. The loss of physical attractiveness can also cause the patient to withdraw. Some patients, knowing that their condition is terminal, may disengage as a coping strategy to avoid having to see all that their death will take from them. Or, they may disengage as a sign of their acceptance of social death—"I'm as good as dead" (anticipatory death).

When significant others withdraw from the patient, patient disengagement will take place. In this situation the process of disengagement is something beyond the patient's control. Family members and friends can refrain from visiting the patient as a sign of their acceptance of social death. The terminal label can stigmatize the patient, and others may treat the individual differently.

Orville Kelly, founder of "Make Each Day Count" (a support group for persons with cancer), tells the story of being invited to a friend's home for dinner. The table was set with the finest china and silverware—with one exception. His place setting consisted of a paper plate and plastic fork, spoon, and knife. He was the guest with cancer.

Randall Wagner, an active volunteer with the American Cancer Society, recalls a situation at a high school football game when his leukemia was in a state of remission. A friend had a thermos of hot chocolate, but had only two cups. The first cup was given to Randall. After he had finished, he returned the cup to be filled for someone else. Nobody would drink out of it, however. He was told to "just keep it."

Many individuals are afraid of "catching cancer." One does not "catch cancer," however. Since many do not know how to relate to persons with cancer and to the terminally ill, they withdraw as a method of coping with their inadequacy.

Norm and Role Meanings

Norms are defined as plans of action or expected behavior patterns felt to be appropriate for a particular situation. **Roles** are plans of action or expected behavior patterns specifying what should be done by persons who occupy particular social positions. Applied to the death-related behavior of the dying patient, norm definitions would involve the general expectation that the dying patient should be brave and accept the fact that life will soon end. The patient is not supposed to cry or become verbal in regard to feelings about his or her death. Nurses often sanction such behavior by giving less attention to patients who deviate from this norm. Elisabeth Kübler-Ross (1969:56–57) gives the following example of one such deviant.

> The patient would stand in front of the nurses' desk and demand attention for herself and other terminally-ill patients, which the nurses resented as interference and inappropriate behavior. Since she was quite sick, they did not confront her with her unacceptable behavior, but expressed their resentment by making shorter visits to her room, by avoiding contact, and by the briefness of their encounters.

Role meanings differ from norm meanings in that they specify, in detailed fashion, what behavior is expected for persons who occupy specific social positions. For example, if a husband/father who is a principal provider in the family is dying, it is expected that he do all he can before death to provide for the financial needs of his family. It would probably be expected that he make arrangements for his funeral, ensure that his bills are paid, finalize his will, and establish a trust fund for his children.

One of the important aspects of norm and role meanings is their relation to the process of societal disengagement, which, as we have seen, occurs when people withdraw from, or no longer seek, the individual's efforts (Atchley, 1977). The individual can also withdraw from societal participation and choose not to perform the roles he or she performed before the terminal diagnosis. This type of disengagement goes beyond withdrawing from interaction patterns with others and refers to a withdrawal from the social structure (e.g., quitting one's job and taking a trip around the world).

Role disengagement has many consequences for the patient and his or her family members. N. J. Gaspard (1970:78) notes the following about a family with traditional gender roles:

> If the father is ill, the mother must generally become the breadwinner, and children who are able often must take over household tasks sooner than they otherwise might. Each person in such a situation may feel both guilt and resentment at such a change whereby they can no longer adequately fulfill the expectations they have had of themselves. Conversely, if the mother is ill, household help may be hired, and problems may arise with regard to the mother's maintaining, in so far as is possible, her self-image in relation to caring for her family.

In addition to the disengagement process, patients are expected to acquire the sick role (Parsons, 1951). They are expected to want to get better and to want to seek more treatment even though everyone realizes that such treatment only prolongs death and not life. This role disengagement can create conflict within the family, especially when the patient has accepted his or her death (and even longs for it), while family members are unwilling to let the patient go. As Kübler-Ross (1969) documents, families many times cannot comprehend that a patient reaches a point when death comes as a great relief, and that patients die easier if they are allowed and helped to detach themselves slowly from all the responsibilities and meaningful relationships in their lives.

Value Meanings

Like all other meaning systems, values (what society has defined as desirable or undesirable) are socially created. They are not inherent in the phenomena, but they are applied by humans to the phenomena. Death *per se* is neither good nor evil. Humans do ascribe value, however, to the different types of deaths. Each of these value meanings has important behavioral consequences.

Most people in our society view death as being intrinsically evil and, therefore, something to fear. We tend to see death as an intruder—the spoiler of our best plans. Thus, in the past, the medical profession has attempted to delay death in favor of life. People are kept on machines to prolong life, even

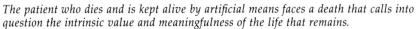

The patient who dies and is kept alive by artificial means faces a death that calls into question the intrinsic value and meaningfulness of the life that remains.

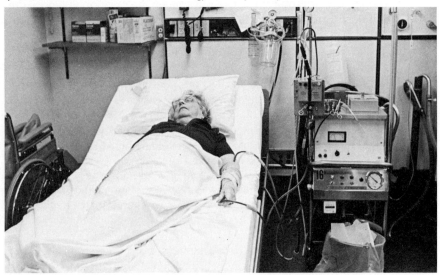

if death is inevitable. We assume that people wishing to die are mentally ill or irrational because death is seen as something to be avoided. Yet, the terminally ill eventually come to view death as a great blessing, when they have finally accepted the fact that they are going to die. This is possible because humans are able to create hierarchies of values where value meanings take on relative meanings. To the terminally ill patient, dignity is more highly valued than is life with pain, indignity, and suffering. Consequently, death may be ascribed positive value by the dying patient who has accepted the inevitability of his or her death.

Object and Self Meanings

The previous discussion focused on meanings that have been applied to an object—the dying patient. From a biological perspective, the person is a living organism—a physical object. From a social–psychological perspective, the patient is a social object—a self.

Many patients defined as having a terminal condition begin to view themselves as being "as good as dead." They have accepted the terminal label, applied it to their understanding of who they are, and have experienced anticipatory death. Families tend to see their loved ones as being in bereavement. This symbolic definition of the patient is reinforced by the role disengagement process, the spatial isolation of the dying patient, and the terminal label placed upon the patient by the physician and other medical personnel. The patient seems to take on a status somewhere between the living and the dead.

BOX 5.3   **DON'T ABANDON THE PATIENT**

> When I say I feel as comfortable with a dying patient as with any other, and that I do not find treating a dying patient unpleasant, I do not mean that I am anaesthetized to the fact that they are dying, and do not have feelings about the patient which are different from my feelings about a patient whom I know will get well. Anaesthesia of feeling is the method which we physicians employ initially in dealing with the pain—ours and theirs—involved in treating a dying patient. But this passes, and when one accepts the patient as part of life, and not someone who is no longer a real part of the world (or a frightening part of the world),
>
> *(continued on next page)*

Box 5.3, continued

then caring for the dying patient becomes (though often sad) neither unpleasant nor something one wishes to avoid. To abandon the dying patient is the worst thing that can be done—both for the patient and the doctor.

A physician's comment from a survey of 1093 physicians by Dickinson and Pearson in 1976.

Elisabeth Kübler-Ross (1969:116) states that the terminally ill have a need to detach themselves from the living to make dying easier. The following example illustrates this point:

She asked to be allowed to die in peace, wished to be left alone—even asked for less involvement on the part of her husband. She said that the only reason that kept her still alive was her husband's inability to accept the fact that she had to die. She was angry at him for not facing it and for so desperately clinging on to something that she was willing and ready to give up. I translated to her that she wished to detach herself from this world, and she nodded gratefully as I left her alone.

When an individual's condition has been defined by self and others as terminal, all other self meanings take on less importance. While a given patient may be an attorney, a Democrat, mother, wife, Presbyterian, and so on, she tends to think of herself primarily as a terminal patient. The terminal label becomes her **master status** because it dominates all other status indicators. Consequently, most of the symbolic meanings previously discussed become incorporated into the individual's self meaning.

Acquiring the terminal label as part of the self definition is not an easy task for the individual. In her best-selling book *On Death and Dying* (1969), Elisabeth Kübler-Ross delineated the following five stages patients go through in accepting their terminal self meaning: denial, anger, bargaining, depression, and acceptance.

In the first stage, *denial,* the patient attempts to deny that his or her condition is fatal. This is a period of shock and disbelief, and the patient wants to believe that a mistake has been made (e.g., that the physician must have read the wrong X-ray). One may seek additional medical advice, hoping that the terminal diagnosis will be proven false. When the diagnosis is verified, the patient may often retreat into self-imposed isolation.

The second stage, *anger,* is a natural reaction for most patients. The patient may vent anger at a number of individuals—at the physician for not doing enough, at relatives for outliving the patient, at other patients for not having a terminal condition, and at God for allowing the patient to die. In other words, a scapegoat is sought—the patient seeks someone or something on which the blame can be placed.

When one has incorporated the terminal label into self meaning, the third stage, *bargaining,* may be reached. The patient may attempt to bargain for a little more time, may include promises to God in exchange for an extension of life, followed by the wish for a few days without pain or physical discomfort. The bargaining always includes an implicit promise that the patient will not ask for more if the one postponement is granted. The promise is rarely kept, notes Kübler-Ross (1969:84).

In the fourth stage, *depression,* the patient begins to realize that a mistake was not made, the X-rays were correctly read, and the prognosis is not good. A realization that meaningful things in life—family, physical appearance, personal accomplishments, and often a sense of dignity—will be lost as death approaches. This is a time to "get one's house in order" and to begin breaking away.

In the fifth stage, *acceptance,* the patient is resigned to death as a sure outcome. While not happy, this acceptance is not terribly sad either. The patient is able to say, "I have said all the words I have to say and am ready to go."

The above stages of dying are not without their critics (see Charmaz, 1980; Garfield, 1978; and Pattison, 1977). Some reject the developmental nature of the sequential stage approach because it lacks universality—not all patients manifest all five types of behaviors. Others have noted that the stages are not mutually exclusive—some patients may bargain, be depressed, and angry at the same time. Finally, others have observed that the order of the stages is more arbitrary than Kübler-Ross would have us believe—dying patients may go from denial to acceptance, followed by depression and anger.

Kathy Charmaz (1980:153) argues that the stages emanate not from the data but rather from preconceived psychiatric categories imposed on the experiences. She notes that what originated as *description* of a reality often becomes *prescription* for reality.

The stages also do not take into consideration adequately the perspective of the patient. Anger, for example, may be vented at others because they have withdrawn from the patient in an attempt to cope with their impending loss. The bargaining behavior of the patient may be motivated not by hope for an extension of time but by a need for moral and social support from caregivers (Gustafson, 1972). Similarly, depression may be a function of the severity of the physical condition of the patient rather than an emotional response to the terminal condition (Charmaz, 1980). As the disease progresses, the strength of the patient will diminish and be evaluated by others as psychological depression. In actuality, the patient may be depressed not by dying, but by the physical effects of the illness.

With regard to the stages of dying, we must conclude that dying behavior is more complex than five universal, mutually exclusive, and linear stages. However, Kübler-Ross has helped us understand that each of the five behaviors is a normal coping strategy employed by dying patients. It may be that it is the social situation that accounts for the similar coping strategies of dying patients, and that in other cultural settings different patterns of behavior will be found.

BOX 5.4   **THE CARE OF THE DYING PATIENT**

No matter how we measure his worth, a dying human being deserves more than efficient care from strangers, more than machines and septic hands, more than a mouth full of pills, arms full of tubes and a rump full of needles. His simple dignity as man should merit more than furtive eyes, reluctant hugs, medical jargon, ritual sacraments or tired Bible quotes, more than all the phony promises for a tomorrow that will never come. Man has become lost in the jungle of ritual surrounding death.

Robert E. Kavanaugh, 1972, *Facing Death*. Baltimore: Penguin Books, p. 6.

Social Situation Meanings

As the dying person comes to grips with a terminal condition, the way in which the social situation is defined will have a tremendous impact upon the process of dying. If the hospital is viewed as a supportive environment, patient coping may be facilitated. However, if the patient feels alone in the place of confinement, and if the hospital is defined as a foreign place, personal adjustment will be hindered.

Like all other meaning systems, the way the individual defines the social situation is an attempt to bring order to the world. Since situational meaning always involves selective perception, the terminal patient will create the meaning for the social environment and will respond to this meaning and not to the environment itself. Each terminal patient will not only experience death in a different environment, but will have a unique interpretation of the social situation. This accounts for the different experiences of dying patients. The hospice movement (see Chapter 6) is an attempt to create a more positive and supportive social situation in which dying can take place.

PHYSICIANS AND THE DYING PATIENT

As noted in Chapter 1, Americans are inadequately and poorly socialized with regard to issues of dying and death. One might expect that the early socialization experiences of physicians would be similar to other members of society. This is exemplified by the following story told to the author by Dr. Charles Huggins, Nobel recipient and professor at the University of Chicago School of Medicine, about his first day as a student in medical school:

> After the gross anatomy professor finished the initial lecture, the class went to the laboratory to begin work on the cadavers. My cadaver was a female. After taking one look at the body (having never seen either a dead woman or a naked woman), I said to myself, "I should have gone to law school after all."

Even though this Nobel recipient entered medical school many decades ago, many first-year students today have had similar experiences and feelings. For many students like Dr. Huggins, the first exposure to death is an impersonal experience in an anatomy laboratory.

In a day in the United States long before Dr. Huggins' time, acquiring a corpse to dissect for medical purposes was apparently not an easy task. Corpse snatching and grave robbing was known to occur with students desiring to learn human anatomy. Medical societies, formed in the late 1700s and early 1800s, became active in attempting to force legislation to permit legal dissection for medical study (Coffin, 1976:194). In 1824 the state of Connecticut passed a law allowing medical schools to take possession of unclaimed corpses from its prisons, and in 1831 a Massachusetts law made human dissection legal. These pioneer acts served as models for other states, and soon there was no reason for grave robbing in the name of science.

Death Education in Medical Schools

Medical education has historically offered only limited assistance to the medical student encountering death for the first time (Dickinson, 1985). From 1975 to 1985 the number of full-term death and dying courses in medical schools in the United States increased from only 7 to 14 (out of a total of 113 and 128 medical schools, respectively). Eighty percent of the medical schools both in 1975 and 1985 offered death education in the form of an occasional lecture or minicourse. The average number of years of these offerings in 1985 was eight. Thus, a death and dying emphasis in medical schools has a brief history and remains somewhat limited today.

The dilemma faced by Dr. Huggins on his first day in gross anatomy lab would have been addressed, however, by the current offering at the University of Massachusetts Medical School. According to S. C. Marks and S. L. Bertman (1980), sessions on death and dying are integrated into the anatomy

course before dissection begins. Some of the objectives are to identify and articulate feelings about death in general and to assist students in identifying and talking about their death and dissection feelings. Unfortunately, this course is unique, and most today are like that experienced by Dr. Huggins decades ago.

Perhaps physicians are expected to be all things to all people. Certainly the death of a patient runs counter to what medicine is all about, since the graduate of medical school takes an oath to "prolong life." From the point of view that the physician is the defender of life, sworn to use his or her best judgment in protecting the patient, death is the enemy, and the dying patient is a lost cause from the beginning.

Historically, the medical training of most physicians seems to be primarily concerned with the patient's physical state rather than social–psychological needs. Some changes are occurring though, as noted by Dartmouth Medical School's interest in "facilitating the medical students' understanding of the patient as a bio–social–psychological being" (Nelson, 1980). The medical students are to learn from the terminally ill patients what it is like to be dying. Thus, the patient becomes teacher. The inclusion of such a humanistic emphasis in death education should help both the dying patients and the medical students.

A survey of over 600 physicians (Dickinson, 1988) in 1986 revealed that the majority (78 percent) agree that more emphasis in medical school should be placed on communication skills with terminally ill patients and their families. Preliminary results from another study of 350 family physicians in South Carolina (Dickinson, 1988) in 1987 reveal that the majority felt their medical education was inadequate in helping them relate to terminally ill patients and their families.

Good rapport with dying patients might be an intrinsic quality of certain medical students that is reinforced by experience, or it might be something in which medical students are given instruction. Though values, ethics, and communication skills may be presented and learned in medical school, there is no guarantee that they will be carried over into clinical practice. Perhaps the results could be known, however, if only the majority of medical schools in the United States offered a course on relating to terminally ill patients and their families. Unfortunately, however, given the current curricula trend since 1975, this is not likely to occur within the near future.

DYING AS DEVIANCE IN THE MEDICAL SETTING

As we have seen, one's treatment of the terminally ill patient may well be a product of socialization into the medical profession. The medical profession's attitudes toward patients, in particular the dying patient, are functional with respect both to the reinforcement of the view of "the physician as healer" and to maintenance of order in the medical subculture.

The dying patient, therefore, is a deviant in the medical subculture because death poses a threat to the image of the "physician as healer." (See Alban L. Wheeler, 1973, for an excellent discussion of dying as deviance—the source from which much of this section was taken.) Death also creates embarrassing and emotionally upsetting disruptions in the scientific objectivity of the medical social system. Thus, the disruption caused by death in the medical social system, if not controlled, could lead to a great deal of conflict.

Situational Adjustment

Students enter the medical profession with certain attitudes and feelings toward patients that will be shaped and continually processed until they comply with those of the medical profession itself. Howard Becker (1964:44–46) refers to this "molding" as "situational adjustment." As one moves in and out of social situations, the requirements for success in each are learned. With a strong desire to deliver the required performance, the individual becomes the kind of person the situation demands. Thus, the medical student is "molded" into the medical profession by learning what is expected and then "doing it." Becker notes that much of the change in an individual is a function of the interpretive response made by the entire group—the consensus the group reaches with respect to its problems.

The process of situational adjustment accounts for changes people undergo, but people also exhibit some consistency as they move from situation to situation. Howard Becker (1964:49–51) refers to this consistent line of activity in a sequence of varied situations as *commitment*. A variety of commitments thus constrains the individual to follow a consistent pattern of behavior in many areas of life.

While situational adjustment refers to one's being molded by the system, a person who drifts away from the expected patterns is likely to be singled out by others. Such a person tends to be labeled as one who does not march to the beat of the drummer.

Labeling Theory

A major school of thought explaining deviance is **labeling theory.** This perspective does not focus on the act or actor, but rather on the audience observing them. When a person is labeled *deviant,* that individual is stigmatized. Erving Goffman (1963) describes the stigmatized individual as a person who is reduced in the minds of others from a "whole and usual" person to a "tainted and discounted" one. Therefore, the key to the identification of deviance is found in the audiences labeling the individual or act as deviant. Thus, in analyzing the dying patient as deviant in the medical subculture, the medical audiences who interact with and participate in the labeling of the patient must be examined.

Regardless of whether or not the individual is responsible for the deviant label, the label-stigmatized individual is still discredited and is treated with less respect than other people. With such labeling, an entire interactional framework is created within which the "normals" relate to the "deviant."

Thus, according to Elliot Freidson (1972:236), when a person is labeled deviant, the stigma interferes with normal interaction. While individuals may not hold the deviant responsible for his or her stigma, they are nonetheless "embarrassed, upset or even revolted by it," says Freidson. Therefore, the assumption can be made that the deviant person elicits certain aversive attitudes from the audience with whom interaction occurs. These aversive attitudes may be so strong as to elicit attempts to manage them and to decrease aversion through avoidance behavior.

Deviance Results in Punishment

In American society, the primary reaction to deviance of any type is punishment of some sort. French sociologist Emile Durkheim (1961) observes that the primary purpose of punishment is not for the deviant himself or herself, but to affirm in the face of the offense the rule the offense would deny. Thus, illness would represent a rejection of the societal value of health and the terminally ill patient to the physician would be the antithesis of the healing and getting-well values taught in medical school.

Characterizing the American deification of physical health, the hospital, and the physician, Robert Kavanaugh (1972:8) makes the following statement:

> Our universal deity, Physical Health, is the major god currently (worshipped). His demands for untold dollars in tribute are incessant. Every day it costs more

to worship at his shrine (the hospital), yet the devout seem only too willing to scrape and to pay. They sit uncomplaining for endless hours in the offices of His high priests (physicians), and will purchase any drug or pill or lotion the priests prescribe, in any combination. In His shrine, the dying are excommunicated, the dead are damned.

The dying person can seldom assume normal role functioning, although he or she also views the illness as undesirable and has tried to cooperate with medical personnel to get well. The dying person, therefore, is permanently cast into a deviant role due to the inability to respond to treatment and get well. According to Box 5.5, however, dying is really a normal state, not a deviant behavior.

BOX 5.5 **DYING AS A NORMAL STATE**

Dying must be considered as a normal state in and of itself. The process of dying is not extraordinarily different from the process of healthy normal living, for they coexist in the same world. It is the world of patienthood which is artificial. Modern medicine with its technology has created industrial complexes called hospitals. That environment is so artificial that creating normalization is essential.

Normalization of the life of the dying person is not the same as is normalization of the life of a patient. To be dying is normal and that is determined by the patient. In attempting normalization for the patient the staff tries to keep the patient from slipping into an exaggerated state of patienthood. In normalization for the dying, the dying person must teach the staff that there is a normal process going on.

Hospitals are places in which dying could be allowed. There are many things patients need at times of their dying to make their time left more tolerable. There is room in hospitals to allow for the dying. Normalization is not really based on ethnic preferences, social patterns, and familial behavior. Normalization targets self-esteem, goal orientation, and abatement of loneliness. It generates a community that allows patients to continue to have full participation in human commerce.

The dying person redefines his or her community. The dying person is the high priest of his or her own temple. It is as if life has a holy of holies where only those initiated into that inner sanctum are allowed. It transcends the human construct of hospital and the secular state of patienthood. Hospitals will only be able to accommodate dying persons if the staff recognizes this transcendent element of the dying process.

(continued on next page)

Box 5.5, *continued*

The current view of the human body as a machine that can be fixed without the spirit leaving the driver's seat makes it difficult to accommodate dying.

Adapted from Jan van Eys, 1988, "In My Opinion . . . Normalization while Dying." *Children's Health Care* (Summer), 17:18–21. For further information about this journal or psychosocial aspects of children's health care, contact: ACCH, 3615 Wisconsin Ave. N.W., Washington, D.C. 20016.

RELATING TO THE DYING PATIENT

Physicians' unwillingness to deal with death and the terminally ill is cited frequently in the literature (see Kane & Hogan, 1986:12). Physicians as a group tend to express more conscious death anxiety than groups of individuals who are physically ill. Anne Kane and John Hogan (1986:20) note that death anxiety is significantly linked with both age and experience for physicians as a whole: The older a physician becomes, the lower the death anxiety. Likewise, the longer one has practiced medicine, the less death anxiety he or she reports. Thus, it is the younger, less-experienced group of physicians reporting higher levels of death anxiety.

In a study of 1012 physicians, Dickinson & Pearson (1979a) concluded that those with a high probability of relating to dying patients (e.g., oncologists) were more open with their patients than physicians who practiced medicine in areas where there was a lower probability of dealing with death (e.g., obstetricians and gynecologists). Since this study suggests that differences exist among medical specialties in relating to dying patients, it is possible that one factor influencing the selection of a medical specialty is the medical student's personal understanding and feelings concerning dying and death issues.

In this same study of physicians, Dickinson & Pearson (1979b) found that female physicians related better to dying patients and their families than did male physicians. Perhaps the women's traditionally rewarded "feminine" characteristics of gentleness, empathy, expressiveness, responsiveness, and kindness help to explain these differences. If more physicians and other medical personnel were to display these human qualities with a greater frequency, patients might receive more help and support in their dying.

Gender Versus Professional Role

Physicians and nurses are intricately entwined in dealing with dying patients (Pine, 1975). It is the physician who defines when the patient is "dying" and is "dead," and the nurse who must wait for an "official message" from the physician. The patient may then be treated as if there were little chance for recovery. This alteration in treatment is predicated by the physician's decision but is not carried out until he or she communicates it.

BOX 5.6   **AM I DEAD?**

> Once upon a time, a patient died and went to heaven, but was uncertain where he was. Puzzled, he asked a nurse standing nearby, "Nurse, am I dead?"
> "Have you asked your doctor?" she said.
>
> Anonymous, Circa 1961.

In a study by Thomas Campbell and his colleagues (Campbell, Abernathy, & Waterhouse, 1984) comparing the attitudes of physicians and nurses toward death, differences were found that were tied to professional roles, not to gender. Nurses tended to see a more positive meaning in death than did physicians—death represented rebirth rather than abandonment, and tranquility rather than fearfulness. Since physicians make the crucial decisions while nurses carry out the orders, the implication of patient death as professional failure is reduced for nurses.

What about female nurses versus female physicians? Howard Becker's stress on situational adjustment (1964), followed by a consistent commitment, seems to suggest that socialization to occupational role overcomes earlier gender role socialization to explain the different attitudes of female nurses and female physicians regarding dying patients in a study by Dickinson & Ashley-Cameron (1986). Even if women have traditionally been socialized to be the more nurturant gender, more sensitive and responsive to the needs of others, the expression of sensitivity and responsiveness differs between female physicians and nurses. Thus, the differences between physicians and nurses regarding death and terminally ill patients tend to be more a function of the role expectations of the particular medical occupation than of gender (Dickinson & Ashley-Cameron, 1986).

Jack Kamerman (1988:62) cautions, however, that as nurses are given greater responsibility in diagnosis and treatment, their attitudes toward death may move closer to those of physicians. In addition, as nurses become more susceptible to the strains that physicians experience at patient death, it is possible that they will retreat farther behind the shield of professional detachment—particularly if nursing follows the medical model of professional status.

Awareness Contexts of Dying

Whether male or female, nurse or physician, communication with terminally ill patients is of utmost importance. Glaser & Strauss (1965) present four awareness contexts in interacting with a dying patient. They define the awareness context according to what each interacting person knows of the patient's defined status, along with the recognition of the others' awareness of his or her own definition. The four awareness contexts are closed, suspicion, mutual pretense, and open.

Closed awareness is usually the first context. In order to maintain the patient's trust, and yet keep him or her unaware of the terminal condition, the staff may construct a fictional future biography. If the patient has not been told "the truth," or has been "told" but did not want to hear, this often places an additional burden on the nursing staff. Since most patients are able to recognize death-related situational and spatial clues, this context tends to be unstable, and the patient usually moves to suspicion or full awareness context.

Suspicion awareness is a contest for control between the patient and medical staff. The patient suspects that he or she is dying but receives no verification from the staff. Nurses must use teamwork to refute this challenge.

Mutual pretense often follows and requires subtle interaction with both patient and staff "acting correctly" to maintain the pretense that the patient is not approaching death. A game continues to be played whereby everyone acts as if they know nothing about the terminal condition of the patient.

If mutual pretense is not sustained, *open awareness* follows with many ambiguities. The patient is obligated to not commit suicide and to die "properly." If the patient is dying in an unacceptable manner, he or she faces difficulties when trying to negotiate for things from the staff. Dying "properly" is difficult, however, since the hospital staff expects "proper" dying, but the patient has no model to follow, notes Robert Blauner (1966).

Though there is no good role model to follow in dying, perhaps the late Senator Hubert H. Humphrey of Minnesota comes close. Even in his dying, he kept a positive attitude and frequently made telephone calls to individuals to wish them well and to greet them. Calling former President Richard M. Nixon, for whom many in Humphrey's position would have had limited affection, to wish him a happy birthday epitomizes Humphrey's behavior during the final days of his illness.

Nurses with more experience with dying patients were more likely to avoid the dying than nurses with less experience, according to a study by Pearlman, Stotsky, & Dominick (1969). Since the physician often directs the medical team, nurses are often forced to work in a closed awareness context regardless of their own view. Ashley-Cameron & Dickinson (1979) found that nurses working with dying patients seem to be comfortable in a closed awareness context. Since they spend more time with patients in the hospital than do physicians, a closed awareness context may produce a more comfortable setting for the nurse.

Whether attempted by a nurse or a physician, coping with terminally ill patients does not come easily. Society has not prepared the health-care professional for such interaction. Some obviously react better than others. The key to good relations with dying patients is personally coming to grips with death. One should also have good communication skills. If only the dying patient could be viewed as a person, not the "lung cancer in Room 314," and treated as a human being, certainly the trauma of the dying process could be eased. In the end medical personnel, the patient, and the family would benefit.

THE AUTOPSY

A dissection and examination of a just-deceased patient is an **autopsy** (Clark & Springen, 1986). The pathologist performing the autopsy assumes a mechanical, physical cause for the death. A *complete autopsy* refers to an examination of the organs of the three major cavities of the body—the abdomen, chest, and the head. The pathologist makes a Y-shaped incision extending from each armpit to the center of the lower abdomen. Various internal organs are removed and weighed; blood, urine, and other fluids are sampled. Much can be told from the size, color, and feel of various body parts. For example, an alcoholic's liver may be pale and shriveled, and a diseased heart is likely to be flabby and grossly enlarged.

An autopsy is at the discretion of the next of kin, unless the death is a medical examiner's (coroner) case. Then it is performed as a matter of law (Korndorffer, 1978). Family members should understand that as with organ donations, which can be done concurrently, the autopsy represents an opportunity for good to come from a sad occasion, and in that sense represents a contribution by the deceased (Webster, Kopin, Glassroth & Patterson, 1989: 326).

The purposes of an autopsy are noted by W. C. Roberts (1978):

1. Serves as a check on the accuracy of the clinical diagnoses and historical data

2. Can be a check on the appropriateness of medical and surgical therapy

3. Helps gather data on new and old diseases and surgical procedures

4. Obtains information beneficial to the deceased's family

5. Clarifies real or potential medicolegal deaths

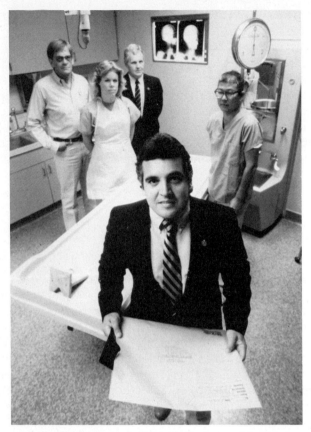

An autopsy is performed whenever the cause of death is uncertain. While the process is a mechanical procedure, the dignity of the patient should always be respected.

The autopsy has ancient roots and has produced countless medical advances over time (Clark & Springen, 1986). The cumulative data gathered through autopsies have enabled physicians to treat or prevent a number of diseases. Postmortems have confirmed the link between cigarette smoking and lung cancer. They helped reveal abnormalities involved in congenital heart defects, multiple sclerosis, Alzheimer's disease, and viral infections in the brain that may cause dementia (shown by some victims of AIDS). Perhaps the purpose of an autopsy is best summed up by the statement on the entrance to the autopsy room at the Medical University of South Carolina: "This place is where death rejoices to come to the aid of life."

Despite the usefulness of autopsies, their number has sharply declined in the United States in recent years (Altman, 1988). In the mid-1940s half the patients who died in a hospital were dissected, while today only 13 percent are subjected to postmortems (Clark & Springen, 1986). Autopsy findings are believed to increase the reliability of death certificate data and, therefore, provide an essential check on the accuracy of diagnoses–although there may be legitimate disagreement between the attending physician and pathologist as to precisely what killed the patient.

Physicians, hospital administrators, and families of the deceased have shown reduced interest in autopsies. Physicians in particular fear that an autopsy will uncover an error and thus spur malpractice suits (Clark & Springen, 1986). High-tech methods of diagnosis such as CAT scans have made some believe that postmortems are not necessary. Autopsies also cost hospitals $1,000 to $3,000 each and must be subsidized by general charges, since they are not directly covered by health insurance. In addition, physicians are reluctant to ask bereaved next of kin for permission to perform a procedure that many regard as upsetting and an invasion of privacy.

BOX 5.7

> "Doctor," complained the patient, "all the other physicians I've consulted with seem to disagree with your diagnosis."
> "Yes, I know they do," said the doctor, "but the autopsy will prove I'm right."

In Box 5.8, a college student discusses her observations of an autopsy and her emotional reactions to it. While it is difficult to generalize from one experience, it is possible that her first encounter with the autopsy is like that of many first-year medical students.

BOX 5.8   **AN AUTOPSY OBSERVED AND EXPERIENCED**

> We stepped into the autopsy room wondering what to expect. I was nervous, for we had just been told that we might feel sick, and if we did, we should leave the room so we would not faint and hurt ourselves. The sights and smells overwhelmed my senses. The mixed odors were of formaldehyde and old blood, and the air was thick with that scent. I was wondering how long I would last in this environment when
>
> *(continued on next page)*

we were offered surgical masks to wear. "I nearly fainted from the smell when I watched my first autopsy. Those masks help a little," said the resident who was working on the case. She was right about that.

The room was lined with stainless steel shelves and drawers. These contained countless preserved specimens from "interesting or unusual cases" to be studied in the future or used as references for curious medical students. Two large, rectangular, steel tables were in the center of the room. Each table had a gutter and tilted into a draining area leading to a sink. The water was always running to wash down the blood.

If what I've described so far is all there was, the room itself would not have been too bad. But there was more to the scene. On the top of one of the steel tables lay a large, naked, old, male body. That was my second shock (after the smell) and the major cause for my alarm. Fearing that I would pass out, I stood as far away from the tables and other people as I could. I took deep breaths and I stood with my legs spread apart for better balance, but I did not faint.

This man on the table seemed so vulnerable. I tried to think of him only as a body. Despite my efforts I began imagining myself in his position—a resident, a medical student, and an autopsy specialist cutting, probing, and making comments about my physical condition; other interested people coming into the room now and then to check out the progress; and six more students curiously watching the whole procedure. I did not like this situation, and I felt sympathy for the autopsy victim. Yet I was curious enough to stay and try to survive the whole autopsy.

When we had become accustomed to our surroundings, the resident told us about the "patient." This fifty-five-year-old white male had come to the hospital to get his foot treated. He had an ulcer (an open sore common to diabetics like himself) on his foot. "He was very lucky to have come in when he did, his foot ulcer was getting bad and it could have led to gangrene," said the resident. His accident happened as he was dressing to leave the hospital after getting treatment for the ulcer. He fell and broke his hip. His surgeon operated, making a large incision from the upper thigh to his waist. He replaced the joint and sent him into recovery. The surgeons thought he was doing well, but he died the next day. (Hip operations are not usually life-threatening.)

This man had a good heart and did not smoke. He was not fat and he seemed to be in good health. What went wrong? The autopsy team was instructed to look for possible blood clots or other problems in the internal organ system.

When we began observing, the autopsy specialist was finishing the job of resuturing the long incision in the victim's hip. A blood clot the size of a big potato had been extracted. It was soft and Jello-like and looked like a raw liver. When I asked, they told me that it was a small clot and that it was not the main reason for this poor man's death.

The next part of the autopsy process again unnerved me—and again I did not faint though I thought I would. The autopsy specialist made a huge Y-shaped incision from the lower abdomen to the lower chest branching out to the shoulders. The layer just below his skin was yellow and fatty, and the strong muscle layer was dark red. The upper layer peeled away from the muscle, but the muscle stuck tight to the ribs. The specialist then hacked through the muscle and ribs around the outside of the chest cavity with a curved pruning shears that had long handles for good leverage. Then he pulled away that layer to expose the heart and lungs.

The centrally located heart was at least as big as two of my fists. The lungs were located high in the chest region, starting at the top of the shoulders and going down only halfway to the lower ribs. They were pink and porous, and I wondered how such small organs could take in enough air for a man his size.

The heart, lungs, liver, and the rest of the smaller organs were then removed and put aside to be studied by the resident medical student, Kris. While Kris "breadsliced" (cut lengthwise at one-inch intervals to study the inside of the organ) the liver, lungs, and digestive system, the autopsy specialist started his electric saw; I wondered what he was planning to do with it. The noise was alarming. He cut a one-foot segment of the backbone out of the man's back and then cut that lengthwise down the middle. Then he extracted the spinal cord and laid it on the table for us to see. I touched it. The finger-thick cord was made up of hundreds of tiny nerves. To see and touch all of these incredible impulse messengers awed me.

The specialist was not done with the saw. While we were watching the dissection of the organs, the patient's scalp lay inside out over his face. I was glad that I could not see his face. The saw started again and cut away a portion of his skull at the back of his head. I looked inside the hole at the body's mastermind—the brain. The resident told me that the brain was too soft to cut right then, so they would store it in formaldehyde for several days until it "firmed up."

As we were examining the organs on another table, two more male medical students arrived. They planned to practice inserting a vein

(continued on next page)

Box 5.8, continued

catheter. To practice they used our patient's leg veins. They worked at cutting a small hole and inserting the catheter tube (which drains out blood). They saw that there were some young, female observers in our group so they wanted to be noticed. They joked about how they were going to save him now. I was appalled at this crude behavior. I wondered how anyone could joke in a situation like this one. I tried to remind myself that it was a horrible place to work and that these students used humor to relieve their tensions and make their work more manageable.

We had to leave soon after that incident. We thanked the resident and autopsy specialist and left the room. It was nice to take off the gloves, masks, and aprons we had been wearing. Fresh air was welcome, too. But I began thinking about what I had seen that morning. I was upset by the whole situation: an innocent, older man suddenly dies, and with the loss of his life, he loses his identity and dignity. He was just a body for anatomical study. He was not a person, though he was still wearing his wedding ring.

As I contemplated this paradox, I thought again of the whole autopsy process, and was dismayed again. It had been so brutal. It was nothing like the delicate surgery I had expected. Since an autopsy must show every detail, huge incisions must be made. Nothing needs replacement, so little care is taken to keep the parts intact. This carelessness upset me.

I tried to sort everything out in my mind—the patient, the tragic accident, the brutal procedure, the stoic autopsy specialist, the helpful and concerned medical student (Kris), and the joking male medical students. All of this was too much for me to comprehend.

All that day and night, I kept smelling the autopsy odor in various places I went; I could not escape it! The next morning I wrote down my feelings in my journal concerning what I had seen and felt. I also talked with people about my frustrated emotions for several weeks. With the passing of time I can now talk about it, but sometimes I think about that old man.

Written by Elizabeth Maxwell, a college sophomore at St. Olaf College, after visiting a medical center during a health science internship experience in 1984. Used by permission of the author.

CONCLUSION

Since the thought of dying is stressful, it seems appropriate that we be aware of dying and death. We would hope that more awareness will result in a greater acceptance of dying and death. Through a better understanding of death meanings, our coping with dying and death should be enhanced. It is difficult to relate to the dying if we ourselves have not been sensitized to our own death.

Traditionally, medical schools have had very limited offerings in death education. On-the-job training may only reinforce one's anxieties about the dying. It is encouraging that medical schools seem more concerned about the social and psychological aspects of their patients today. While death education does not constitute a significant place in current medical curricula, the situation is nonetheless improving.

With dying patients being viewed as deviants in the medical subculture, the treatment of the dying is not always the most humane. After all, death is counter to what physicians learn in medical school. They take an oath to prolong life and relieve suffering—sometimes contradictory situations. To lose a patient is a failure.

We often play games in communicating with a dying patient. We know, the physician and nurse know, and the patient knows (whether told or not) when the condition is terminal, but we often exist in a closed awareness context. No one lets the other know that he or she knows. Death talk remains taboo.

SUMMARY

1. The meaning of dying is dependent on the social context in which it takes place.

2. Time, space, norm, role, value, self, and situational meanings are important components of the meaning of our dying.

3. One may go through stages in accepting his or her terminal self meaning.

4. Physicians have limited education concerning issues of dying and death.

5. The dying patient is *viewed* as a deviant in the medical setting; thus, the dying patient is *treated* accordingly.

6. Different awareness contexts exist between medical personnel, patients, and the patients' families.

7. After death, autopsies are sometimes performed to aid in determining the cause of death.

DISCUSSION QUESTIONS

1. What does it mean to you to say that the meaning of dying will depend on the social context in which it takes place?

2. Would you prefer to live with a person with a terminal disease or a person who is chemically dependent? Discuss the advantages and disadvantages of each.

3. How could steps be taken to overcome the diminished social and personal power of the hospital patient? Are such limitations on patients necessary for an orderly hospital?

4. Discuss the statement: The terminally ill eventually come to view death as a blessing.

5. You have just been told that you have inoperable cancer. Discuss how you think you would react. In what ways would you change your life?

6. If a patient's death represents a failure to a physician, how can medical schools assist in creating an attitude of acceptance of death as the final stage of growth?

7. List as many types of deviant individuals as you can. Do you include the dying patient as deviant? Why or why not?

8. Deviance may vary with time and place. What is meant by this statement?

9. Discuss Glaser & Strauss's four awareness contexts. Which do you think most often exists in a medical setting with a dying patient?

GLOSSARY

Autopsy   A pathologist's medical examination of the organs of the body after death to determine the cause of death.

Awareness context   The knowledge of each interacting person of the others' defined status and the recognition of the others' awareness of his or her own definition.

Disengagement   The process by which either an individual withdraws from society or society withdraws from or no longer seeks the individual's efforts.

Labeling theory   An approach to behavior which states that in focusing on the significance of how an act is viewed, emphasis is placed on the audience observing rather than on the act itself or the actor.

Master status   The status (position) that dominates all other statuses in the mind of an individual.

Norm   A plan of action or expected behavior pattern thought to be appropriate for a particular situation.

Role   Specified behavior expected for persons occupying specific social positions.

REFERENCES

Altman, Lawrence K. 1988. "U.S. Moves to Improve Death Certificates." *The New York Times,* October 18, p. 25.

Ashley-Cameron, Sylvia, & George E. Dickinson. 1979. "Nurses' Attitudes toward Working with Dying Patients." Unpublished paper presented at the Alpha Kappa Delta Research Symposium, Richmond, VA (February).

Atchley, Robert C. 1977. *The Social Forces in Later Life,* Second Ed. Belmont, CA: Wadsworth.

Becker, Howard. 1964. "Personal Change in Adult Life." *Sociometry* (March), 27:40–53.

Blauner, Robert. 1966. "Death and Social Structure." *Psychiatry, 29:*378–394.

Campbell, Thomas W., Virginia Abernethy, & Gloria J. Waterhouse. 1984. "Do Death Attitudes of Nurses and Physicians Differ?" *Omega, 14:*43–49.

Charmaz, Kathy. 1980. *The Social Reality of Death.* Reading, MA: Addison-Wesley.

Clark, Matt, & Karen Springen. 1986. "The Demise of Autopsies." *Newsweek,* November 17, p. 61.

Coe, Rodney M. 1970. *Sociology of Medicine.* New York: McGraw-Hill.

Coffin, Margaret M. 1976. *Death in Early America.* New York: Elsevier/Nelson Books.

"Conversation with Dr. Charles Huggins," January 15, 1973.

"Conversation with Colin M. Turnbull," April 24, 1975.

Dickinson, George E. 1985. "Changes in Death Education in U.S. Medical Schools during 1975–1985." *Journal of Medical Education* (December), 60:942–943.

Dickinson, George E. 1988. "Death Education for Physicians." *Journal of Medical Education* (January), *63:*412.

Dickinson, George E., & Sylvia Ashley-Cameron. 1986. "Sex Role Socialization Versus Occupational Role Socialization: A Comparison of Female Physicians' and Female Nurses' Attitudes toward Dying Patients." Unpublished paper presented at the Eastern Sociological Society's Annual Meeting in New York, NY, April 4–6.

Dickinson, George E., & Algene A. Pearson. 1979a. "Differences in Attitudes toward Terminal Patients among Selected Medical Specialties of Physicians." *Medical Care, 17:*682–685.

Dickinson, George E., & Algene A. Pearson. 1979b. "Sex Differences of Physicians in Relating to Dying Patients." *Journal of the American Medical Women's Association, 34:*45–47.

Dickinson, George E., & Algene A. Pearson. 1980–1981. "Death Education and Physicians' Attitudes toward Dying Patients." *Omega, 11:*167–174.

Durkheim, Emile. 1961. *Moral Education.* Glencoe, IL: The Free Press.

Freidson, Elliot. 1972. *Profession of Medicine.* New York: Dodd Mead.

Garfield, Charles A. 1978. *Psychosocial Care of the Dying Patient.* New York: McGraw-Hill.

Gaspard, N. J. 1970. "The Family of the Patient with Long-Term Illness." *Nursing Clinics of North America, 5:*77–84.

Glaser, Barney, & Anselm Strauss. 1965. *Awareness of Dying.* Chicago: Aldine.

Goffman, Erving. 1963. *Stigma.* Englewood Cliffs, NJ: Prentice-Hall.

Gustafson, Elizabeth. 1972. "Dying: The Career of the Nursing Home Patient." *Journal of Health and Social Behavior, 13:*226–235.

Hale, R. 1971. "Some Lessons on Dying." *Christian Century* (September):1076–1079.

Kamerman, Jack B. 1988. *Death in the Midst of Life: Social and Cultural Influences on Death, Grief and Mourning.* Englewood Cliffs, NJ: Prentice-Hall.

Kane, Anne C., & John D. Hogan. 1986. "Death Anxiety in Physicians: Defensive Style, Medical Specialty, and Exposure to Death." *Omega,* 16:11–22.

Kavanaugh, Robert E. 1972. *Facing Death.* Baltimore: Penguin.

Klenow, D. J., & G. A. Youngs. 1987. "Changes in Doctor/Patient Communication of a Terminal Prognosis: A Selective Review and Critique." *Death Studies,* 11:263–277.

Korndorffer, W. E. 1978. "Medical Examiner's Office." In R. G. Benton, *Death and Dying: Principles and Practices in Patient Care.* New York: D. Van Nostrand, pp. 288–303.

Kübler-Ross, Elisabeth. 1969. *On Death and Dying.* New York: Macmillan.

Leming, Michael R., Glenn M. Vernon, & Robert M. Gray. 1977. "The Dying Patient: A Symbolic Analysis." *International Journal of Symbology* (July) 8:77–86.

Marks, S. C., & S. L. Bertman. 1980. "Experiences with Learning about Death and Dying in the Undergraduate Anatomy Curriculum." *Journal of Medical Education,* 55:844–850.

Nelson, W. A. 1980. "Clinical Teaching of Care for Terminally Ill in a Psychiatry Clerkship." *Journal of Medical Education,* 55:610–615.

Oken, D. 1961. "What to Tell Cancer Patients." *Journal of the American Medical Association,* 175:1120–1128.

Parsons, Talcott. 1951. *The Social System.* New York: The Free Press.

Pattison, E. M. 1977. *The Experience of Dying.* Englewood Cliffs, NJ: Prentice-Hall.

Pearlman, J., B. A. Slotsky, & J. R. Dominick. 1969. "Attitudes toward Death among Nursing Home Personnel." *Journal of Genetic Psychology,* 114:63–75.

Pine, Vanderlynn. 1975. "Institutionalized Communication about Death and Dying." *Journal of Thanatology,* 3:1–12.

Roberts, W. C. 1978. "The Autopsy: Its Decline and a Suggestion for its Revival." *The New England Journal of Medicine,* (August 17) 299:332–338.

Vernon, Glenn M. 1972. *Human Interaction.* New York: Ronald Press.

Webster, J. R., D. Derman, J. Kopin, J. Glassroth, & R. Patterson. 1989. "Obtaining Permission for an Autopsy: Its Importance for Patients and Physicians." *The American Journal of Medicine* (March), 86:325–326.

Wheeler, Alban L. 1973. "The Dying Person: A Deviant in the Medical Subculture." Unpublished paper presented at the Southern Sociological Society Annual Meeting, Atlanta, GA (April).

SUGGESTED READINGS

Glaser, Barney, & Anselm Strauss. 1965. *Awareness of Dying.* Chicago: Aldine.
Uses the approach of awareness to deal with the practical and theoretical aspects of interaction among terminal patients, their families, and hospital personnel.

Kamerman, Jack B. 1988. *Death in the Midst of Life.* Englewood Cliffs, NJ: Prentice-Hall.
A sociological approach to social and cultural influences on death.

Kavanaugh, Robert E. 1972. *Facing Death*. Baltimore: Penguin Books.

Dying and death from the perspective of a psychologist and former priest.

Neale, Robert E. 1971. *The Art of Dying*. New York: Harper & Row.

Presents problems of dying by placing the reader in the role of the dying person.

Schoenberg, Bernard (Ed.). 1981. *Education of the Medical Student in Thanatology*. New York: Arno Press.

An anthology on the socialization of students into the medical profession.

Sudnow, David. 1967. *Passing On: The Social Organization of Dying*. Englewood Cliffs, NJ: Prentice-Hall.

Explores the sociological structure of certain aspects of death in hospital settings, both private and public.

Yalof, Ina. 1988. *Life and Death: The Story of a Hospital*. New York: Random House.

The author interviews employees of an inner-city hospital and reports on what they do and how they feel about their jobs. Topics included in the book are the emergency room, heart transplants, the delivery room, the operating room, medical school, and pediatrics.

CHAPTER 6

The Hospice Approach

Alternative Care for the Dying

———

Does dying frighten you? Frequent responses
to this question are the following:

*"I'm afraid of the pain." "I don't want to be alone when I'm
dying." "I'm afraid of a long, protracted period of suffering." "I
don't want to die in a hospital. Let me die at home." "I'm not
afraid for myself, but I am worried about the effect of my death
on those I love."*

6 In Chapter 4 we discovered that of the eight different types of death fears, the three areas of highest anxiety are the fear of dependency, the fear of pain, and the fear of isolation (Leming, 1979–1980). As the comments above reflect, it is the *process* of dying and not the *event* of death that causes the most concern for people in this country. This chapter is about the worldwide hospice movement that has developed as a response to fears related to the dying process and institutionalized ways in which death is typically handled in institutional settings.

THE HISTORY OF THE HOSPICE MOVEMENT

In medieval times the word **hospice** referred to a way-station for travelers. The word itself is rooted in the Latin word *hospitium,* meaning hospitality, inn, or lodging. It is also derived from the word *hospes,* which means host or guest. Sandol Stoddard (1978) describes some of the early hospices in her book *The Hospice Movement.* Probably the most famous hospice in the world is the Hospice of Great Saint Bernard in the Alps. This hospice trains dogs to rescue travelers lost on the Alpine slopes. With the passing of time, the word came to encompass houses maintained for the sick as well as the traveler.

St. Christopher's Hospice in London, England, played a pivotal role in the development of the modern hospice movement. Opened in 1967, it was founded by Dr. Cicely Saunders, who began her career as a nurse and subsequently became a social worker. It was not until Dr. Saunders became a physician, however, that she was able to influence the course of health care for people dying of a terminal illness. Her achievements were recognized by Queen Elizabeth II in 1981 when she granted her the status of dame.

The first modern hospice program in the United States was the Connecticut Hospice, whose origin was directly related to that of St. Christopher's in London. In 1963, Dr. Cicely Saunders was invited to lecture in New Haven at the Yale University School of Medicine. Over the next several years, contacts between Dr. Saunders and personnel from the Yale Nursing and Medical Schools were frequent. Local leaders from various disciplines became involved in the development of a hospice in Connecticut, and their planning resulted in the establishment in 1971 of Hospice Incorporated, later changed to The Connecticut Hospice.

The original intent of the planning group was to build an inpatient facility similar to St. Christopher's. Funding proved to be a problem, however, and the group decided to inaugurate its home care program in 1974. To test the viability of home care, the National Cancer Institute provided funds for a three-year demonstration project. As a result, an inpatient facility was eventually built with the help of both federal and state funds, and opened in 1980.

After the inpatient facility was completed, The Connecticut Hospice, with the help of a foundation grant, organized a separate corporation—The Connecticut Hospice Institute for Education, Training, and Research, Incorporated. The institute offered special help to health-care leaders desiring to improve the quality of care to the terminally ill and their families. In 1981, the institute was merged with its founder and continues its educational work as a department of The Connecticut Hospice.

Since that beginning, the number of hospice programs throughout the United States has increased to over 1700 programs. In 1978, the National Hospice Organization (NHO) was formed to provide for coordination of hospice activities and to assure that quality standards of care would always be demonstrated by any program calling itself a hospice. Instrumental in working toward the development of an accreditation procedure, the NHO also provides educational programs, technical assistance, publications, advocacy, and referral services to the general public. While it serves most of the nation's hospices and over 1800 professional members (National Hospice Organization, 1989), every state now also has its own hospice organization to promote education and standards of quality.

THE NATURE OF THE CONTEMPORARY HOSPICE

While different types of hospice institutions exist, all hospice programs are unified by the general philosophy of patient care. Hospice is a specialized health-care program that serves patients with life-threatening illnesses—approximately 95 percent of hospice patients in the United States have cancer. Nationally, the average number of days a hospice patient spends in hospice care is approximately 50—slightly less than two months (Bass, Garland, & Otto, 1985–1986). The majority of hospice services are delivered in the home, with inpatient care available as needed. In hospice, the *patient-family* is the unit of care. The primary goals of hospice care are to promote patient-family autonomy, assist patients in obtaining pain control and real quality of life before they die, and enable families of patients to receive supportive help during the dying process and in the bereavement period.

Pain Management

A hospice program is basically a medical program with physician direction and nurse coordination. Hospice leaders have discovered that patients cannot achieve quality of life unless physical pain and symptoms such as nausea, vomiting, dizziness, constipation, and shortness of breath are under control. A major emphasis of hospice, therefore, is pain and symptom management.

Traditional medical care is often based upon a "P.R.N." (Latin for *pro re nata*) approach, which means that medication is given "as the situation demands." In practice, this means that often a person must first hurt and ask for relief before the pain can be stopped. This procedure is responsible for much suffering among the terminally ill. Hospice physicians believe that a patient should not hurt at all. Regular medication is, therefore, given in advance before the pain begins. The aim is to erase the memory of the pain that has been experienced and to deal with the fear of pain in the future. Pain medications are standardized to the needs of the patient. The aim is to control the pain and other symptoms without sedating the patient. Every symptom is treated as a separate illness, for only when each symptom is under control can a patient begin to find fullness and quality of life.

The hospice concept includes both home care and inpatient care. Ideally, hospice care represents a continuum that includes both forms of care when each is necessary. However, the major emphasis of hospice treatment is upon home care.

Home and Inpatient Care

Inpatient care usually becomes necessary for one of three reasons. The first is that in order to bring the patient's pain and symptoms under control, a stay of a few days in an inpatient facility may be necessary or helpful. The second is that the family taking care of the patient at home may become exhausted and need a few days rest while the patient is cared for elsewhere. The third reason is that home care is inappropriate at a given stage of the illness due to the patient's condition or home situation. It is hoped that upon admission to an inpatient facility, patients will be able to move back and forth from home care to inpatient care at various stages of the illness.

The Hospice Team

Hospice care is provided by an interdisciplinary team, with each discipline having something to contribute to the whole. All disciplines work together, each in its own area of expertise, and each interdisciplinary team includes several layers or levels of care. At the center of the team is the *patient and his or her family*. The hospice movement emphasizes the need for people to make their own decisions with the supportive help of health-care professionals and other trained persons. A vital part of the process is the *patient's own physician*—the professional who will continue to be in charge of the care of the patient and write medical orders when necessary.

The next layer of the team includes the hospice's professional caregiving staff. This consists first of *physicians*, required to direct medical care. *Nurses* comprise the next category. Registered nurses are responsible for coordinating the patient's care. Licensed practical nurses and nurses' aides are also included—especially in inpatient settings.

The *hospice social worker* constitutes an important part of the team. The social worker spends considerable time working with families, thus enabling family members to communicate with each other. While family members may be aware that the patient is dying, they may never have discussed it with each other or with the patient. The social worker also spends time in dealing with social problems, such as alcoholism and marriage problems, and in working with the children or grandchildren of patients. In modern society all too often children have been shielded from participation in events centering on the death of a family member.

Pastoral care is also a basic part of the team. A larger hospice may employ a *chaplain*, who will direct pastoral care to patients and their families, counsel other members of the caregiving team on spiritual issues, and try to involve clergy of the community in the care of their own people. In smaller hospice programs all of the care may be provided by local clergy who work closely with the hospice staff.

Financial counseling is a significant aspect of the hospice team. Because patients and families have often exhausted their financial resources at the time of care, attention is given to forms of third-party reimbursement, such as those provided by Medicare or private insurance companies, and to seeking other programs for which the patient may be eligible.

The next layer of the hospice team involves a variety of health-care professionals or other key leaders in the community whose help may be called upon during the illness. A *psychiatrist* or *psychologist* may be needed to provide expert counseling help. *Nurses, home health aides,* and *homemakers* employed by public health nursing agencies—such as visiting nurse associations—may be needed to provide special continuing health care or to share in the provision of patient care. *Physical* and/or *occupational therapists* may be needed to work with the patient to insure maximum daily functioning. Finally, the services of a *lawyer* and/or *funeral director* may be required to help the patient settle personal affairs and provide for the needs of survivors after the death.

Artists are increasingly recognized as important members of the hospice team. The Connecticut Hospice pioneered the development of an arts program that considers the arts as a means to help patients find meaningful fulfillment during their last days. In many programs artists in such areas as metalwork, photography, pottery, drama, dance, and music work with patients interested in such self-expression.

Trained *volunteers* comprise an essential part of the hospice team. Medicare reimbursement is predicated on the requirement that volunteer time represent 5 percent of all patient care—no hospice can exist for long without a strong volunteer component. According to Chwee Lye Chng & Michael Ramsey (1984–1985:240), hospice volunteers are recruited from many groups: housewives, students, retired persons, and professionals such as social workers, psychologists, teachers, gerontologists, members of the clergy, and architects. Many volunteers have lost loved ones and find that this experience provides them with an opportunity to serve others. Some volunteers are retired health-care professionals such as physicians or nurses. Others are nonprofessionals who are deeply interested in the needs of dying patients and their families. Each volunteer brings with him or her skills and experiences that can greatly enhance the life of the terminal patient (Chng & Ramsey, 1984–1985:240).

Before volunteers begin a hospice program's extensive training program they are interviewed by the volunteer coordinator and may be asked to complete specially designed questionnaires that assess their feelings and sensitivity toward dying persons. Every hospice program has an initial volunteer training program and regular inservice training to maintain and update the volunteers' skills (National Hospice Organization, 1988).

Some volunteers work in patient-care tasks such as providing transportation, sitting with a patient to free family members to get out of the house for a while, carrying equipment, or providing bereavement counseling for family members after the death of the patient. However, according to Chng & Ramsey (1984–1985:239), hospice volunteers perform primarily three roles—companion/friend, advocate, and educator.

The unpaid volunteer has the double benefit of being identified by the patient and family as being knowledgeable but without having the professional status that can create a social distance. In the hospice program where I volunteer, we refer to the companion/friend role as being a "competent presence" or "safe place." In being a stranger who provides a "listening ear," without emotional involvements or professional entanglements, the volunteer can support the patient and family members like no other participant in the social network of dying.

The volunteer also functions in an advocate role by acting on behalf of the dying patient and family. Sometimes patients and their loved ones are afraid to challenge or ask questions of physicians and other medical personnel. The volunteer, who has become a trusted friend and confidant, can often speak up for patients and their families and make their needs known to those responsible for their care. Presently, I am the primary volunteer with a male patient who was undermedicated. When the patient complained to his nurse regarding his pain, he was told to "brave it out." Knowing the medical system, I was able to contact the appropriate individuals, who were, indeed, able to have his pain medications reevaluated. The words of Chng & Ramsey (1984–1985:240) are good advice at this point:

> To be truly effective, the suggestions of the volunteer have to stem from knowledge and understanding of the intricate patient–family–institutional configura-

tions. Under the careful guidance of professionals, the volunteer can serve a significant role as ancillary to professionals.

The final role served by volunteers is that of educator. Most individuals in our society have not had many personal experiences with death. The hospice volunteer can learn from each experience in working with dying patients and pass on insights that may be helpful to patients and families. The volunteer can help the dying and their loved ones understand that the dying process is usually complex, stressful, and disordered. In addition, most patients and families have a strong need to have their feelings and experiences validated. Patients and families who have a difficult time understanding their feelings, emotions, and experiences during the dying process should be assured that they are "quite normal."

Within the community at large, there are a number of influences at work that either assist with patient care or help to make it possible. *Family members* or *friends* are urged to participate in the patient's care as much as possible. When family members cannot provide as much care as may be needed at certain times, hospice personnel will try to meet the patient's needs by exploring all possible options to do so (National Hospice Organization, 1988). The patient-family support system is the most significant factor in the dying process for many patients, but elements of the system will also include numerous close or distant relatives, friends, neighbors, members of local churches, and/or other civic groups.

Hospice programs are dependent on a high degree of community interest and support. Bringing this about requires a planned program of public information. The concept of hospice must be sold to the medical community and to other members of the larger community. Specific activities require not only financial support (especially while the hospice program is developing), but a willingness to testify before regulatory agencies about the granting of hospice accreditation, Medicare certification, and/or approval to begin offering services to the people of the area.

Patient-Centered Care

One of the distinguishing features of the hospice concept of care is that, whenever possible, hospice enables patients to make decisions about how and where they want to live their lives. Patient-centered care is nonjudgmental, unconditional, and empowering.

One of the patients of the hospice program where I volunteer provides an example of this philosophy of care. This patient had adult children in town but lived as a single person. He had lung cancer and desired to die at home alone. He was also a smoker and heavy alcohol drinker.

Our hospice program agreed to honor the patient's desires whenever it was possible. Therefore, a hospice nurse visited his house every four hours,

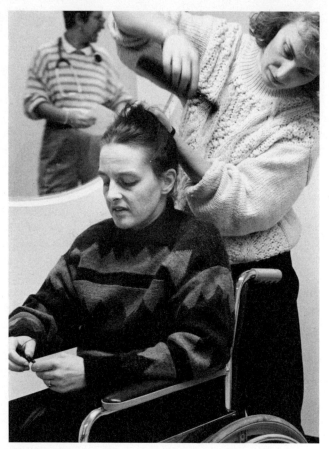

For many hospice patients, just having a volunteer attend to their physical appearance is an important aspect of patient-centered care.

and members of the police department checked in on the patient every hour from 10 P.M. to 7 A.M. The patient's pain was kept under control without sedation taking place. A hospice volunteer (who also happened to be a licensed vocational nurse) visited the patient two to three times each day, and she, along with friends and family members, met the patient's requests for liquor and cigarettes. Visits from all members of the hospice team never lasted longer than ten minutes. The patient died as he wanted—in his home, free from pain, and in control of his own care.

While not every member of the hospice team, or the patient's family, would have chosen to die as this patient did, everyone respected the patient's right to make decisions regarding his care. The hospice philosophy states that patients and their families have the right to participate in decisions concerning their care, and that they should not be judged because their decisions are contrary to the beliefs of their caregivers.

BOX 6.1 **THE DYING PERSON'S BILL OF RIGHTS**

I have the right to be treated as a living human being until I die.

I have the right to maintain a sense of hopefulness, however changing its focus may be.

I have the right to be cared for by those who can maintain a sense of hopefulness, however changing this might be.

I have the right to express my feelings and emotions about my approaching death in my own way.

I have the right to participate in decisions concerning my care.

I have the right to expect continuing medical and nursing attention even though "cure" goals must be changed to "comfort" goals.

I have the right not to die alone.

I have the right to be free from pain.

I have the right to have my questions answered honestly.

I have the right not to be deceived.

I have the right to have help from and for my family in accepting my death.

I have the right to die in peace and dignity.

I have the right to retain my individuality and not be judged for my decisions which may be contrary to the beliefs of others.

I have the right to expect that the sanctity of the human body will be respected after my death.

I have the right to be cared for by caring, sensitive, and knowledgeable people who will attempt to understand my needs and will be able to gain some satisfaction in helping me face my death.

Marilee Donovan & Sandra Pierce. 1976. *Cancer Care Nursing*. New York: Appleton Century Crofts, p. 33.

Bereavement Care

Since the family is part of the unit of care, the responsibility of the caregiving organization cannot arbitrarily stop when the patient dies. Hospice programs offer continuing bereavement follow-up to members of the patient's family for as long as may be appropriate. Some hospices have a **bereavement team,** consisting primarily of interdisciplinary volunteers, which follows up on all the families after the patient dies or on those family members for whom there is felt to be a major risk of serious problems developing later.

The bereavement team of The Connecticut Hospice illustrates this continued follow-up. The team consists of a number of persons who have previously served as volunteers within the organization. A considerable amount of time was spent by the team studying grief and how they could best aid people in the grieving process. When members feel that bereavement follow-up would be helpful to a family, a referral is made to the team. The team has found that many family members appreciate and need the opportunity to tell the story of the patient's illness to someone who has not previously heard it. Occasionally, a bereavement team member enters the picture while the patient is still alive.

Once the referral has been made, the team works out a care plan for the family, and a team member accepts the family as his or her own responsibility. The objective of bereavement care is to encourage the family to carry on its grieving process in an open and helpful manner. Hospice bereavement care has several goals (Boulder County Hospice, 1985):

1.   To assess the normal grief response

2.   To assess individual coping mechanisms and stress levels

3.   To assess support systems

4.   To set up additional support (groups, individual therapy, visits by team members) when needed

5.   To identify individuals at high risk and make appropriate interventions

6.   To make referrals for financial problems and medical care.

Here, too, as in other aspects of hospice care, the art of listening is emphasized. Family members need someone willing to listen while they discuss their feelings. Bereavement team support may last for a year or more, although the team tries to encourage family members to stand on their own feet as soon as possible.

Persons Served by the Hospice

Hospice care knows no age restrictions, though one-half to two-thirds of the patients tend to be persons over 60 years of age. Most hospices provide care for patients suffering from any illness with a time-limited prognosis. According to David Bass, Neal Garland, & Melinda Otto (1985–1986:67):

> The "average" hospice patient is white, in his or her middle sixties, . . . is afflicted with a form of cancer and . . . is being taken care of by his or her spouse. The patients remain in the program for an average (mean) of forty-seven days.
>
> The profile of the "average" patient, while helpful in a number of ways, also conceals as much as it reveals. For example, while it is true that the average hospice patient is sixty-two years of age, there is a substantial segment of patients who are either much younger or older than this average. Further, evidence presented in our research suggests that younger-than-average patients have different experiences with hospice care (i.e., they remain in the program for a shorter period, receive fewer staff visits, and are more likely to die in a facility).

Patient eligibility criteria usually include a diagnosis of a terminal illness, a prognosis of six months or less, consent and cooperation of the patient's own physician, and a willingness to deal with the dying process in an open awareness context. Home care is often more viable when there is a relative (or friend) who can be a primary caregiver in the home, and can assume responsibility for patient care when the latter is unable to provide care for himself or herself. Inpatient care usually requires that help is needed with pain or symptom control.

Special Aspects of Home Care

Since 65 percent of American hospice patients die at home (Lack & Buckingham, 1978), one of the questions frequently raised by family members is what to do if an emergency develops in the middle of the night or on a holiday. While many physicians and other health-care professionals do not make house calls, hospice personnel do. Home care for hospice patients is made viable by the fact that a physician and a nurse are on call 24 hours a day, seven days a week. This gives patients and families confidence that they can manage at home.

Community physicians continue to be involved in the care of their patients, and usually remain primary caregivers, while the patient is receiving home care. Such community involvement relates the hospice program to the area in which it is located and tends to give hospice care greater visibility than is sometimes true of health-care programs.

In **inpatient care** the patient's own physician turns over the care of the patient to a hospice physician but must be willing to resume care if the patient is able to return home. Whereas traditional medical care in recent years has tended to concentrate care in specialized hospitals or in nursing homes, hospice care returns the focus to the family.

BOX 6.2 **SIGNS OF APPROACHING DEATH AND WHAT TO DO TO ADD COMFORT**

Hospice exists to support the family's desire to aid a loved one in dying in familiar surroundings. This time period is a very difficult one for families. The following was devised to help ease this time by alleviating some of the fears of the unknown. The information may help caregivers prepare for, anticipate, and understand symptoms as a patient approaches the final stages of life. It is important to note that some symptoms may appear at the same time and some may never appear.

Symptom: The hospice patient will tend to sleep more and more and may be difficult to awaken.
Action: Plan activities and communication at times when he or she seems more alert.

Symptom: You may notice your loved one having confusion about time, place, and identity of people.
Action: Remind your family member of the time, day, and who is with him or her.

Symptom: Loss of control of bowel and bladder may occur as death approaches, as the nervous system changes.
Action: Ask the hospice nurse for pads to place under the patient and for information on skin hygiene. Explore the possibility of a catheter for urine drainage.

Symptom: Arms and legs may become cool to touch and the underside of the body may become darker as circulation slows down.
Action: Use warm blankets to protect the patient from feeling cold. Do not use electric blankets, since tissue integrity is changing and there is danger of burns.

Symptom: Due to a decrease in oral intake, your loved one may not be able to cough up secretions. These secretions may collect in the back of the throat causing noisy breathing. This has been referred to as the "death rattle."
Action: Elevate the head of the bed (if using a hospital bed) or add extra pillows. Ice chips (if the patient can swallow) or a cool, moist washcloth to the mouth can relieve feeling of thirst. Positioning on a side may help.

Symptom: Hearing and vision responses may lessen as the nervous system slows.

(continued on next page)

Action: NEVER assume the patient cannot hear you. ALWAYS talk to the patient as if he or she could hear you.

Symptom: There may be restlessness, pulling at bed linens, having visions you cannot see.
Action: Stay calm, speak slowly and assuredly. Do not agree with inaccuracy to reality, but comfort with gentle reminders to time, place, and person.

Symptom: Your loved one will not take foods or fluids as the need for these decreases.
Action: Moisten mouth with a moist cloth. Clean oral cavity frequently. Keep lips wet with a lip moisturizer.

Symptom: You may notice irregular breathing patterns and there may be spaces of time of no breathing.
Action: Elevate the head by raising the bed or using pillows.

Symptom: If your loved one has a bladder catheter in place, you may notice a decreased amount of urine as kidney function slows.
Action: You may need to irrigate the tube to prevent blockage. If you have not been taught to do this, contact a hospice nurse.

Hospice In The Home Program—Visiting Nurse Association of Los Angeles, Inc.

Special Aspects of Inpatient Care

Because the family is the unit of care within the inpatient hospice facility, sufficient space must exist for a large number of family members to congregate. In addition, such care requires a homelike environment—the aim is to make the facility as much like a home away from home as is possible. Patients are encouraged to bring with them favorite possessions such as pictures, a favorite chair, or plants.

No arbitrary visiting restrictions are placed on those wishing to see hospice patients. One may visit at any time of day or night. Visitors of any age, including young children, are not restricted in their visitation. Furthermore, family pets, such as dogs or cats, may come as well.

The inpatient facility of The Connecticut Hospice in Branford illustrates the above principles. The family room is off-limits to staff and solely provided for the comfort of family members. Kitchens containing a refrigerator, a microwave oven, a stove, and a sink are available for use by families. Washing machines are maintained for their use. Large living rooms with fire-

The goal of an in-patient hospice facility is to provide a home-like environment where the patient and his or her family can appreciate the joys of social relationships.

places are also available. Ten four-bedded rooms for patients help to develop social support systems among family groups. There are also four single bedrooms. Spacious corridors next to patient rooms contain plants and areas for family gatherings. Beds may be moved around as desired—on a nice day these beds are often outside on patios. A commons room and chapel are used not only for religious services but for presentations by various kinds of artists. Operated by volunteers, a beauty parlor is available to help patients feel better about themselves. A preschool exists for three- and four-year-old children of staff, volunteers, and people in the community. When the patient dies, he or she is taken to a viewing room for the family members.

Hospice care places considerable emphasis on the tastiness, attractiveness, and nutritional value of food prepared for patients. The Connecticut Hospice employs a gourmet chef with training in Paris to supervise its food preparation.

BOX 6.3 **A VERY SPECIAL KIND OF CARING**

DOROTHY STORCK

> David is sitting cross-legged on his bed in his striped pajamas as the three of us came into the room—his mother, Toviah Freedman, who is his family counselor, and I.

It is dim because David's medication is making his eyes water and the light bothers him. But there is nothing of gloom in the room.

Four brightly colored balloons hang over David's head, suspended by a string from the ceiling. On each one is printed: "Get Well."

There is little chance that David will get well.

David is 24 and for a year now he has known that he has leukemia. A bone marrow transplant operation could buy him some time, if he survives it. Without it he will almost certainly die within months. In April his disease went into remission and they sent him to Johns Hopkins hospital in Baltimore for the bone marrow transplant. Before the specialists could begin the grueling procedure, his condition changed. He came out of remission. They sent him back to Philadelphia.

"Hi, Mom," David says cheerfully. "Hi, Toviah," to the palliative care counselor who has been like a member of his family for a year. And "Hi" to me, the stranger he allows briefly into his life to ask questions about his dying.

He holds out his hand. We have not met before. His grip is strong. He smiles and makes apologies for the twilight of the room. I am nervous; he is not. David has put behind him in this year the inconsequential worries of social intercourse. His mother, a small, dark-haired woman with lovely eyes, waves a paper bag at him.

"Apple strudel," she says, and he applauds. She puts it on a table.

In the last year, David has been in and out of the seventh floor oncology (cancer) unit at the Hospital of the University of Pennsylvania (HUP) several times. He was forced, finally, to give up his job as a medical orderly in a small New Jersey hospital. He keeps his apartment while he waits for a remission that may not come.

He has some pain while he waits. He says he has reached a point in his mind where he can control much of it. The drugs help with the rest. The specially trained team that is caring for him will give him whatever pain-killing drugs he needs, at any time, 24 hours of the day or night. He is on palliative care for the terminally ill. He is in hospice.

David is one of 42 patients who are now in this care program at HUP. All but six of them are living at home. They will continue to do this as long as they are able.

"Palliative care" means patient comfort, not only of a physical kind. It includes emotional care for the dying, and for their families. It is an offshoot of the hospice movement that began in England.

"Our job is to make the patient's remaining life as pleasant as it can be," says Dr. Barrie Cassieth, the psychologist who started the hospice

(continued on next page)

program at HUP a year ago. "Hospitals are geared to treat disease. There comes a point where you can't do that any longer. Then you treat the patient. . . . The family is part of that."

A trained counselor, a member of the team, visits both the patient and the family regularly. He or she is there whenever needed, night or day, and will help with whatever problems come up, whether it's as simple as the transfer of a car title from the patient to his wife, or as complicated as the transfer of guilt from the sick to the well. There is bereavement counseling for family members after the death.

"When we were in Maryland," David's mother is saying, "and we found out the operation was cancelled, I was sitting in that motel room that night and I couldn't stop crying. I needed to call someone, but I couldn't call anyone who didn't understand. I called Toviah."

David nods, remembering.

"I used to be hostile, angry," he says. "I'd say terrible things to my mom . . . It was difficult to face up to reality, to say, 'Look, Mom, we'll have to make plans about when I die.' It was hard enough to accept it myself . . . Then I saw my relationship changing with my friends, my brother, my parents. I was losing contact."

There is silence for a moment in the room. Not grief, but a fullness.

"My husband and I, we were feeling cut off," David's mother says after a while. "I had to reach out and say, 'Hey, if you don't want to talk, OK. But don't ignore us.' It was a risk."

"We were trying to protect each other," David says softly. "I was trying to be the strong one."

His mother looks at him. The understanding between them is a long, shimmering cord. "So was I," David's mother says.

MODELS OF INPATIENT HOSPICE CARE

Three models of inpatient hospice care exist: freestanding, hospital-based, and nursing home-based. A *freestanding hospice* is entirely independent—it works closely with other components of the health care system, but employs its own staff and raises its own funds. The Connecticut Hospice, for example, is a 44-bed, freestanding inpatient facility and home-care program. The second model is a *hospital-based hospice* that provides a unit for inpatient care within its physical plant. It provides for home care through the hospital's own home-care department by arrangements made with a local public health nursing agency or by its own staff employed for that purpose. The Northfield City Hospital (Minnesota), where I serve as a volunteer, is an example of a hospital-based program. The third model is the *nursing home-based hospice* that also provides inpatient care when needed and arranges for home care in various ways.

Hospice planning groups exist in virtually every major, and many smaller, cities across the United States. They range from discussion groups of interested citizens to fully developed freestanding hospice programs. Presently, there are more than 1700 hospice programs in the United States.

BOX 6.4   **TWO HOSPICE PROGRAMS IN NEW YORK CITY**

Paul M. DuBois (1980) describes several hospice programs. Calvary Hospital is classified as a chronic disease hospital with one-third of all deaths from cancer in New York City occurring there. Patients are admitted with a minimum of three weeks of life remaining and a maximum of around six weeks. Daily care at Calvary costs half that of a well-known, acute-care hospital for cancer patients nearby, but is approximately the same cost as some other less renowned nearby hospitals not focusing on dying patients. One primary physician is assigned to each patient. A well-organized recreation program includes trips for patients to nearby special events such as operas and plays. While the patients sleep in two constant-care units with 24 beds, day rooms are also provided for patient use.

Hospice-type features are found at St. Luke's Hospital in Manhattan, notes DuBois (1980). The program began there in 1975, with a special hospice team working with five to ten patients scattered throughout the hospital. Patients are told they are hospice patients. They receive special privileges and extra attention from hospice staff (coordinator, two half-time nurses, half-time physician, half-time social worker, and additional assistance from chaplains and volunteers). Special privileges include extra visitors outside normal visiting hours, visits by children and even pets, and an apartment to enable visitors to stay overnight. Alcoholic beverages are allowed as determined by the primary physician.

HOSPICE ISSUES

Some have called the development of hospices a "people's movement." If the existing health-care programs in the community had been meeting the needs of the dying and supporting their families throughout the period of the illness and bereavement, hospices would not have been necessary. They originated in local communities, however, as the result of the desire of health-care professionals and civic leaders to provide better care. Many hospice leaders have seen their role as eventually working themselves out of their jobs as the principles of hospice care are absorbed by the health-care system. In the meantime, however, hospices pose a number of critical issues for health care in America. We will now examine some of them: the quality of life, the patient-family as the unit of care, cost, the training of professionals, and public attitudes.

Quality of Life

The hospice movement proclaims that every human being has an inherent right to live as fully and completely as possible up to the moment of death. Some traditional health care, emphasizing the curing of the patient at any cost, has ignored that right.

Many physicians have been trained, for example, to emphasize restoring the patient to health. Accordingly, many patients are subjected to a series of operations designed to prolong life, even though a cure is sometimes impossible, as in the case of a rapidly progressing cancer. Most hospice patients have had some surgery, chemotherapy, or radiation treatments. Some continue these even while they are hospice patients because of the pain-relieving nature of the treatments (radiation may reduce the size of a tumor and, therefore, reduce the discomfort). There comes a point, however, if quality of life is a goal, that one should refuse further surgery, seek ease of pain without curing, and attempt to live qualitatively rather than quantitatively. In hospice, cure goals for patients are changed to comfort goals, and every patient has a significant role in all health-care decisions.

Because of the emphasis on quality of life, hospices pay attention to many different facets of pain reduction, including but not limited to physical pain. Hospice medical professionals have spent considerable time in developing a variety of methods of pain control that subdue, not only what the patient describes as pain, but also the symptoms related to the illness.

Much of this emphasis upon pain control has developed despite the practice by some professionals of sedating patients in pain. Quality of life cannot be achieved if the patient is "knocked out" or has become a "zombie." Physicians try to find the point at which the pain is managed, but before sedation occurs. Such pain management has necessitated considerable retraining of health-care leaders.

BOX 6.5 **THE MEANING OF PAIN**

> Anxiety and depression are part of the chronic nature of pain. The patient is anxious about the pain returning; he or she is anxious because of the meaning of the pain. This is not the acute pain doctors

Box 6.5, *continued*

are trained to deal with. It is not like the pain of a toothache or child-birth or appendicitis—pains which have a foreseeable end. Acute pain may serve a purpose by warning of a malfunction. Pain for the cancer patient has a sinister meaning. If I wake up in the morning with a stiff neck I assume I slept in a draft. The cancer patient wakes up in the morning with a stiff neck and assumes she has metastases. The degree of perceived pain is totally different in these two situations. One must take into account the anxiety that these patients are suffering, along with the chronic depression caused by chronic pain.

Sylvia A. Lack, 1979, "Hospice: A Concept of Care in the Final Stage of Life." *Connecticut Medicine,* 43 (6):369–370.

Hospice people also deal with social, psychological, financial, and spiritual pain. Terminally ill patients may experience social abandonment or personal isolation that comes when friends and acquaintances stop visiting them because of an inability to cope with issues of death, a lack of knowledge about what to say or do, or simply a lack of awareness of what the patients are experiencing. According to Chng & Ramsey (1984–1985), "in too many cases family members may inadvertently 'reject' the patient when confronted with the reality of death, while the professional staff may distance itself to avoid becoming too emotionally involved." It is ironic that the dying patient's need for social support and companionship is at a time when he or she may often be more alienated than at any other time in life.

Financial problems are also experienced by patients and their families, who face large hospital and medical bills at a time when family income may also be diminished. Finally, there is a spiritual pain that people experience when they seek answers to existential questions and ultimate meaning and purpose in the face of suffering. "Why did God allow this to happen to me?" and "Why do bad things happen to good people?" are questions frequently asked by patients and their families.

Hospice care makes the meeting of social, psychological, financial, and spiritual needs a major priority in patient care. By doing this, hospice provides an alternative to the health care found in most medical treatment centers. However, none of the social, psychological, financial, or spiritual needs of patients (or their families) can be met until all health-care professionals are comfortable with discussing death-related issues. If a physician, for example, is afraid of death or chooses to ignore it, it will be difficult for him or her to enable the patient to deal with the issues involved.

On another scale, the hospice movement emphasizes the importance of the environment in which quality of life can be experienced. The term *envi-*

ronment refers to the home setting where provisions are made for the patient's needs. Much of the architecture, decor, and furnishings of most health-care facilities has been provided for the convenience of staff rather than for the needs of patients.

A critical question is what constitutes quality of life? What do people most want to accomplish before they die? What do they most want to do? When one of my hospice patients in Northfield, Minnesota, was asked that question, he said that he had always wanted to take a helicopter ride. With the help of the local NBC television station, we made this dream a reality. Like this patient, almost everyone has unfinished business in life. Some may wish to renew relationships with friends or family members. Others may desire to put their own affairs in order, to write their memoirs, to plant a garden, to watch the sunset, or to plan their own funeral service.

Robert Kavanaugh (1972) tells the story of Elaine, who, in her last months of life, studied for her real estate license examination, passed the test, and with the help of her husband sold two houses. Thus, at age 37, Elaine found her first job while dying.

The Patient-Family As the Unit of Care

Traditional health care has concentrated on the patient and ignored the family. Perhaps many health-care workers would say, if given an opportunity to state their opinions confidentially, that they would prefer family members to stay away. Traditional ratios of physicians, nurses, social workers, or chaplains to those needing care have been based on an assumption that only the patients need attention. While hospice staff, to be sure, are not given the responsibility to meet physical needs of family members, they do have tremendous concern for the social, psychological, and spiritual needs of the family.

Hospices challenge the health-care system to provide an adequate ratio of professional staff members to patients. For example, in the state of Connecticut the public health code, in its regulations for hospice licensure, stipulates that at all hours of the day or night there must be at least one registered nurse for every six patients, and at least one nursing staff member (licensed practical nurse or nurse's aide and a registered nurse) for every three patients.

Family care, however, involves much more than numbers of staff. It requires that health-care workers know how to cope with the fears, worries, tears, and turmoil of family members; and when to speak, when not to speak, and what to say. It requires that they take time to listen, to determine how they may be most helpful.

Hospice care is costly care due to the number of staff people involved. It challenges society as a whole to give priority to such care because of the right of the dying to quality of life. A harried nurse in a traditional hospital setting, trying to meet the needs of perhaps a floor of patients at night, is not being granted the time required to sit with a dying patient for whom night is especially fearful. Neither does this nurse have the time to be of assistance to husbands, wives, or children struggling with grief.

The interdisciplinary team supports the staff person within each discipline by enabling resources of the entire team to come into play in meeting family needs. For example, a night-shift nurse asked questions relating to spiritual care might wish to give an answer at the time the question is asked. This nurse will, however, also have the resources of the chaplain to determine the best methods to meet patient needs. In hospice care the patient-family unit is involved in decision making. This poses crucial questions to caregivers who may be accustomed to making decisions and having everyone go along with what they have decided.

BOX 6.6 **HOW TO LIVE WITH A LIFE-THREATENING ILLNESS**

With the help of hospice you can:

1. Talk about the illness. If it is cancer, call it cancer. You can't make life normal again by trying to hide what is wrong.

2. Accept death as a part of life. It is.

3. Consider each day as another day of life, a gift from God to be enjoyed as fully as possible.

4. Realize that life never is going to be perfect. It wasn't before, and it won't be now.

5. Pray, if you wish. It isn't a sign of weakness, it is your strength.

6. Learn to live with your illness instead of considering yourself dying from it. We are all dying in some manner.

7. Put your friends and relatives at ease. If you don't want pity don't ask for it.

8. Make all practical arrangements for funeral, will, etc., and make certain your family understands them.

9. Set new goals; realize your limitations. Sometimes the simple things of life become the most enjoyable.

10. Discuss your problems with your family, including your children if possible. After all, your problems are not individual ones.

Orville Kelly, *Make Each Day Count Newletter.*

The Costs of Care

No prospective hospice patient may be turned away because of lack of money. Hospice care is insured by the Medicare Hospice Benefit enacted in 1982, provided the hospice is Medicare Certified. A hospice program must undergo a vigorous evaluation of the services it provides to become Medicare Certified and agree to directly provide the following services: nursing care, medical social services, physician services, counseling, volunteer services. As of January 1, 1989, over 625 hospices were Medicare Certified (National Hospice Organization, 1989). According to the National Hospice Organization (1989), the daily, per-patient payment rates made to Medicare Certified hospices (before adjustment for local wage adjustments) are:

Routine home care	$ 63.17
Continuous home care	$368.67
Inpatient respite care	$ 65.33
General inpatient care	$281.00

To the above payments there is a $8304 annual per patient program cap (this cap is computed on an aggregate basis for all Medicare patients in the hospice program). Furthermore, Medicare specifies that at least 80 percent of hospice care provided by a Certified Hospice Program must be provided in the home (National Hospice Organization, 1989). Additionally, hospice became an optional benefit under state Medicaid in 1986.

The General Electric Company was the first major employer in the United States to provide a hospice benefit for its employees. In 1989, a survey of 1500 corporations determined that 64 percent provide some form of hospice benefit for their employees (National Hospice Organization, 1989). Furthermore, the majority of private insurance companies offer a comprehensive hospice care benefit plan (National Hospice Organization, 1989), and major medical insurance policies, provided through insurance companies and offered to employees as part of a benefit package, also underwrite hospice coverage in some instances. However, many hospice programs rely heavily, if not entirely, on grants, donations, and memorials to meet the needs of their patients and families (National Hospice Organization, 1988).

Thus far, however, the problem has been that provisions are not made for all hospice services. This is true because the laws and regulations governing programs such as Medicare were written on the assumption that the patient was the unit of care and that she or he would recover.

Hospice leaders hope to make it possible for any person of any age suffering from a terminal illness to be eligible for Medicare payments for the costs of hospice care. They are also firm in their conviction that such care saves considerable money in the long run. Many patients currently hospitalized would not need hospitalization if home-care services were available for patients and families. A basic societal question is whether as Americans we believe enough in quality of life for the dying to be willing to make it possible.

Though hospice care requires a higher ratio of staff to patients than that usually provided in health-care programs, the cost is nonetheless lower than other forms of care. Because the majority of hospice patients are able to remain at home for much if not all of the illness, the costs of patient home care, when compared with any forms of inpatient care, are proportionately low. Due to the level of services provided, hospice inpatient care, however, will normally be higher than that provided in a nursing home, but lower than inpatient care in a general hospital setting.

BOX 6.7 **THE LAST DAYS OF MARY BALL**

JUDY SKLAR RASMINSKY

It was in May 1978 that 30-year-old Mary Ball, a vivacious practical nurse, learned she was probably going to die. That month she had undergone four operations: the diagnosis was widespread cancer. Unprepared, panic-stricken, Mary became deeply depressed. The fact that her mother had died of cancer when Mary was 16 magnified her dread. Then one day her mother-in-law yelled at her, "You're not trying!" Mary realized that she wanted to make the most of her remaining time with her 32-year-old husband, Karl, and their two children.

Through 17 months of chemotherapy, she and Karl leaned on each other. Their hopes soared when Mary regained enough weight and strength to return to work. Then, in 1980, there was more surgery, followed by more chemotherapy. The prognosis was not good. This is the story of Mary Ball's dying—and of how a remarkable program helped to ease her last four months with grace and dignity.

November 12, 1980. In bed in their trim little house in rural Northford (Connecticut), Mary and Karl cling together, crying. Earlier that day they have learned from Mary's doctor, Bruce Lundberg, that cancer has spread throughout her bones. No treatment will make her well. Dr. Lundberg has suggested a different kind of help—the Connecticut Hospice, a Branford-based team that, since 1974, has cared for more than 1800 dying patients and their families.

November 13, 1980. A hospice nurse telephones to ask if she can visit that night. Mary and Karl say no. Mary has just had radiation treatment

(continued on next page)

for her pain, and she is tired. Besides, they are uncertain, apprehensive. What are they getting into? They must know more before they involve the children, Karl, Jr., 15, and Matthew, 6.

November 17, 1980. The hospice nurse calls again. The Balls take the outstretched hand. Home-care nurse Florence Larson arrives. Forthright, lively and gray-haired, she has been a nurse for over 30 years. She tells them that the hospice team can assist with pain management, nursing care, household help, money problems, counseling for the children: "We will support you in whatever *you* want to do to make Mary's life as happy and normal as possible."

Mary would like to remain with her family as long as she can. Winter is the slack time for a painting contractor, and Karl will stay home to care for her. Florence says she will visit regularly. The hospice team will be available day or night, seven days a week.

Mary has one urgent question: Can her pain be controlled? Dr. Lundberg has suggested morphine, but she is scared of it. Florence gently explains that morphine is an excellent painkiller and the correct dose "won't bomb you out."

"Who will pay for all these services?" Karl asks. "Your insurance," Florence answers. "But you'll never see a bill. We'll handle the paper work."

When Florence leaves 90 minutes later, the Balls feel as if a weight has been lifted from their shoulders. But they do not want counseling for the children. "I want to deal with them in my own way," says Karl. Leery of interference in their lives, they ask Florence to come just once every two weeks.

November 24, 1980. Mary visits Dr. Lundberg. Her pain persists, and having mulled over Florence's explanation, she is willing to try morphine. Dr. Lundberg prescribes a dose to be taken orally every four hours.

November 27, 1980. Karl's brother and sister-in-law are at the house for Thanksgiving Day. Suddenly, Mary's pain becomes unbearable. Anxious not to spoil the holiday, she takes more morphine and huddles on the sofa in the den trying to hide her agony. Karl telephones Florence. She calls Dr. Lundberg, who doubles the dose of liquid morphine and prescribes a booster shot. Florence picks up the medicine at the hospice in-patient building. About an hour after Karl's call she is giving Mary a shot of morphine. A half-hour later, Mary's torment over, Florence leaves and the party goes on.

December 11, 1980. Dr. Lundberg and Mary discuss the prospect of more chemotherapy. They conclude that the risks outweigh the potential benefits at this stage. To Florence, Mary says, "I don't want to feel sick. I want to use the time I have left to enjoy and be part of my family." Florence says, "I think that's up to you and your doctor, and I support you in that decision."

Christmas, 1980. Mary makes three shopping trips to buy the family's presents. She tires easily, so Karl pushes her up and down the store aisles in a wheelchair that Florence had ordered. She attends a church pageant Matt is in and supervises the trimming of their tree. In good spirits, Mary refuses a visit from Florence.

December 31, 1980. Mary is constipated. Florence comes to her aid. Natural fruit juices finally do the trick. "Florence is my security blanket," says Mary. "It's a relief just to hear her voice." Florence always seems to have time for a chat, a cup of coffee, a back rub for Mary.

January 2, 1981. Unable to keep her liquid morphine down, Mary needs a booster shot. Noreen Peccini, another member of the hospice home-care team, teaches Karl to give the injections to relieve him of the helplessness he hates. "Five years ago I couldn't even show him an I.V. bottle," grins Mary. "Now he does everything."

January 22, 1981. Mary is in greater pain, and Dr. Lundberg increases her morphine. She is eating less and sleeping more, but she is awake when the boys come home from school. Reserved and self-sufficient like his father, Karl, Jr., says little when he comes in to see her. Matt, ebullient and gregarious like his mother, hops into bed for a cuddle. Karl, Jr., still brings home top marks and plays football after school; Matt still asks Mary's permission to have friends over and she still reminds him to change his clothes. "We just take one day at a time," Karl says. "I answer the kids' questions and try to tell them things at the right time. I told Karl, Jr., that his mother might have to go into the hospice in-patient facility, and he is aware of the eventuality and that is enough."

January 28, 1981. At 6:30 p.m., Florence receives a call from a terrified Karl. Mary's face is puffed up like a balloon. When Florence arrives at seven, Mary is so scared she has vomited. Florence establishes that the swelling isn't life-threatening. While she is alone with Florence, Mary's eyes fill with tears. "I am getting so discouraged," she says. "Sometimes I hate to tell Karl how much I hurt, because he goes crazy—not that crying is crazy—wishing he could do more for me." Florence sits with her a long time, talking quietly.

(continued on next page)

January 29, 1981. Hospice physician Will Norton visits to check on Mary's swelling. He notices her bed sores and orders a hospital bed with an automatic inflating and deflating mattress to relieve the pressure on her back. The bed, delivered the next day, makes Mary "at least 100 percent more comfortable."

February 10, 1981. Mary wakes up disoriented. For a moment she doesn't even recognize Karl. After he moves her about in the bed and gives her some apple juice, she is herself again. But she is no longer able to walk to the bathroom alone, and Karl wakes every three hours to give her morphine and turn her in bed.

February 28, 1981. Mary's pain is increasing, her breathing is shallow, her pulse rapid. At times she is confused. "I'm taking a turn for the worse," she tells Karl.

Mary is worse. Her dying is down to a matter of days. She is relieved and ready, but suddenly desperately afraid of becoming a burden. Should she go to the in-patient facility? Florence consults with Karl, who assures Mary he can handle the situation. To take some of the pressure off Karl during the day, Florence arranges for eight-hour-a-day help.

Evening. Mary perks up when Charles Rodriguez, their minister, comes in. "You know, Charles, I'm dying," she says, "and I'm not frightened." Karl is immensely comforted to hear this.

March 3, 1981. On behalf of the children of the church, a boy presents Mary with a card and a dozen roses. As Karl arranges the flowers in the kitchen, Matt asks for one. Later he gives his mother the rose and a card. On it he has drawn himself with arms spread wide, the way he did when he was very small, saying, "I love you, Mom, this much."

March 5, 1981. Mary's pain is excruciating. Karl calls the hospice for the go-ahead to give Mary a shot of morphine. Later Florence offers to stop by, but Karl says, "Gee, Florence, I don't think you need to. Everything is fine." Florence doesn't insist. "Mary is dying, and they're handling it," she says.

March 8, 1981. Mary has a 105-degree fever and is often delirious. Her family—sister, brother, father, aunt—come to say good-by.

March 9, 1981. Karl is worried that the children might be frightened by their mother's dying at home. He considers moving Mary to the hospice building. Yet he believes she still wishes to stay at home. Mary is in a dreamlike state, unresponsive; but, while Karl is talking with hospice nurse Ruth Mulhern, she becomes alert. The time has come for her to go into the hospice, she says. She thanks Karl for all he has done for her and tells him she loves him.

That afternoon, Florence helps to settle Mary into her new surroundings—a cheerful, plant-filled room at the hospice building.

March 10, 1981. Evening. Mary is in a dream world, but when Florence touches her she responds, "Florence, I'm so glad to see you." It is so like Mary to be thinking positively. Then she drifts away, and as Florence and Mary's aunt stand at her bedside, she quietly stops breathing.

Karl is walking out of his front door when the phone rings. The boys are already on the way to the car to go to the hospice. He calls them back and sits them down on the living room couch. As he puts an arm around each, he tells them that their mother has just died. Crying, he says, "Except for her love, you two are the greatest gift your mother ever gave me."

March 13, 1981. At Mary's wake, flowers overflow the room. Karl, Jr., stands beside his father. When Florence approaches, the shy, quiet boy, who never reaches out to people, embraces her.

March 14, 1981. The church is packed for Mary's funeral. At the close of the service, the congregation sings her favorite hymn, "All Things Bright and Beautiful," in celebration of her life.

March 24, 1981. Florence visits Karl. The boys have gone back to school. He is preparing to return to work. Karl's father, who came from Florida for Mary's funeral, will stay as long as he is needed. Florence tells Karl the hospice has volunteers trained to help families with their grieving. He declines more help, but thanks her for everything. "Without your assistance we couldn't have lived Mary's last months the way we wanted to," he says. Back at the hospice, Florence has a sense of completion. She shrugs off her colleagues' praise. "We're here to guide, not take over," she says. "From the day I walked in, I was amazed at the way Mary and Karl related to each other and to me. They never drained me; they gave. I always left there a little wiser."

The Training of Professionals

Most physicians, nurses, social workers, and clergy were trained in their respective fields of work without special attention to the needs of the dying. To rectify this problem, hospice programs in most states provide seminars and workshops that deal with the basic principles of hospice care. These programs not only train hospice leaders and volunteers in the specifics of hospice care, but also provide other health-care workers with the knowledge and skills to do a better job in their own settings regardless of whether or not they work in a hospice program.

Health-care decision-makers need to be encouraged to invest the time and money required for their staffs to better cope with the terminally ill and their families. Likewise, the curricula of schools of medicine, nursing, social work, and theology need to be revised in order to provide specialized training along the lines outlined in this chapter.

Public Attitudes

The hospice movement began at a time when public consciousness of death and dying issues had reached an all-time high. It afforded an opportunity to do something tangible for other people, and many took advantage of the chance to volunteer for an active role. At the same time, increasing public awareness of death and dying gave rise to considerable publicity in the media. This helped provide public support when hearings were held by regulatory agencies relative to the granting of approval for hospice services.

Public attitudes toward care of the terminally ill and their families will play an increasingly important role in the future. These attitudes will help to determine whether health-care professionals will, in fact, broaden the scope of care to encompass the family and strengthen their skills in dealing with dying patients. Patients and families are, after all, consumers. In this age of consumer awareness it is becoming increasingly evident that those who purchase services can control to some extent the types of services available. Health-care professionals are increasingly responsible to desires of their clients. The most important factors causing caregivers to seek improvement of skills will be the desires of those they serve. At the same time, especially in areas of competition among hospitals, consumer awareness will play an important part in encouraging such institutions to humanize the care they give.

Many physicians, nurses, social workers, clergy, and other personnel at hospitals and nursing homes have heard about hospice care and have taken the initiative to secure specialized training and to incorporate the hospice philosophy into routine treatment of their patients. When any people's movement arises, an immediate question is whether it will become institutionalized to such an extent that the original spirit will be lost as it adjusts to the reality of regulation, control, and payments of costs. The hospice movement is currently at that juncture. There is every cause for encouragement that one of two things will happen: Either hospices will continue to provide the specialized care for dying patients, or the health-care system itself will change to incorporate many of the improvements represented by the hospice movement. Either outcome should result in the betterment of medical care for patients and their families.

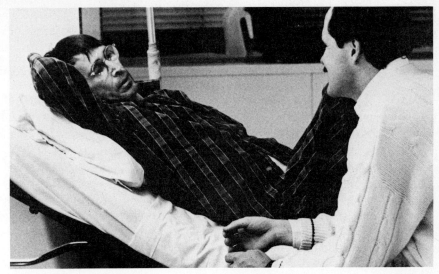

One key to the success of the hospice movement is the level of volunteer involvement in patient care. In this photograph, a hospice volunteer offers the patient friendship, companionship, and the competent presence of a non-judgmental listener.

EVALUATION OF HOSPICE PROGRAMS

While evaluations of hospice programs have not flooded the literature, some studies have taken a look at the hospice approach. In an inhouse evaluation of The Connecticut Hospice, Lack & Buckingham (1978) reported less depression, anxiety, and hostility among terminally ill patients receiving home care as compared to others without these services. In addition, it was found that the overall social adjustment of family members was improved— individuals were better able to express thoughts and feelings with less distress.

Colin M. Parkes (1978) reports that only 8 percent of those who died at St. Christopher's Hospice in London suffered unrelieved pain; this compares with 20 percent who died in hospitals and 28 percent who died at home. John Hinton (1979), in comparing the attitudes of terminally ill patients at a British hospice to those in hospital wards, noted that hospice patients appeared less depressed and anxious while preferring the more open type of communication environment available to them.

Janet Labus & Faye Dambrot (1985–1986) compared the experience of 28 cancer patients who died in an independent, voluntary, community-based hospice program with 29 nonhospice cancer patients who were treated in a small community hospital in Northeastern Ohio. While all of the nonhospice patients died in the hospital, 50 percent of the hospice patients died at home.

Furthermore, hospice patients at the time of admission were less likely to be ambulatory than hospital patients. According to Labus & Dambrot (1985–1986:227),

> The hospice group was younger, had more people living with them, and had been ill for a shorter period of time prior to hospice admission than the hospital group. Hospice patients spent more time in the hospice program after admission prior to death. The hospital patients spent fewer days in the hospital prior to death. Hospice patients were referred to other agencies significantly less frequently than hospital patients.

Janet Labus & Faye Dambrot (1985–1986:230–231) concluded that this hospice program was succeeding in fulfilling the needs of their patients and in containing health-care costs through the multi-disciplinary team—only one outside referral had had to be made, and 50 percent of the patients died at home. They argue that since the hospice group was on average seven years younger (due to the requirement that a primary caregiver be available in the home), the hospice movement ought to consider ways in which their programs might be extended to groups presently excluded—the elderly and single terminal patients.

BOX 6.8 **A FEW RESERVATIONS CONCERNING THE HOSPICE MOVEMENT**

Some American doctors are cautious about the hospice idea. John C. Hisserich of the Cancer Center at the University of Southern California is eager to see the idea tried, but he warns that no scientific evaluation has been made of hospice care and that evidence of success is largely anecdotal. He also believes that hospice enthusiasts sometimes exhibit "a certain zealotry about the thing that may be necessary but that has the effect of turning off physicians who might otherwise be interested. . . ."

Perhaps the most serious reservations about efforts to sprout hospices in America come from Mel Krant, director of cancer programs at the new University of Massachusetts School of Medicine in Worcester. "My first reaction," he says, "is it's going to fail as an American idea. It will get into operation, but its intent will fail." The reason, he feels, is that hospices will simply add to the excessive fragmentation, overspecialization, and discontinuity in American medicine. A hospice will be the incarnation of yet another specialty—care of the dying—and will become "another discontinuous phenomenon" when what is needed is integration. Krant has high regard for the English hospices, but he fears

Box 6.8, continued

that without the spirit of voluntarism and community feeling that exists in England, and without leaders as "utterly devoted" as Cicely Saunders, hospices will turn out looking like nursing homes. He also thinks hospices would help relieve hospitals and physicians of their true responsibilities, which should include more community involvement. Krant thinks it better that Americans develop their own indigenous models for incorporating hospice concepts.

Constance Holden. *Science,* July 1976, Vol. 193

In the evaluation of hospice programs, another important concern is the effect of these programs upon professional caregivers. A study of hospice nurses conducted by Pamela Gray-Toft & James Anderson (1986–1987) sought to explain burnout and rapid turnover in the nursing staff. They found that hospice caregiving is significantly more stressful for nurses for the following reasons:

1. Traditional nurses often resent the special roles and treatment received by hospice nurses within institutional settings. Many hospital-based hospice nurses report feeling socially isolated from other hospital nurses.

2. Hospice nurses are often regarded by others as being "weird" or "different" because they choose to work with the dying.

3. The hospice concept of care creates increased (and often unrealistic) patient expectations; consequently, hospice nurses experience inordinate demands placed upon them by the patients and families with which they work.

4. Because hospice often creates long-term relationships between dying patients, families, and nurses, nurses often experience strong feelings of loss and grief after the death of their patients. Many times hospice nurses are not provided an opportunity to grieve after a patient's death because of the demands of their other duties.

5. Hospice nurses are overexposed to death, which can sometimes contribute to a morbid view of life.

As a result of these findings Gray-Toft & Anderson (1986–1987) created an experimental staff-support program for hospice nurses. Based on the initial success of this experiment, the group-support program has now expanded to include the professional contributions of a chaplain and medical social worker.

A prominent figure in the thanatology movement, Robert Kastenbaum (1981) notes that while hospice program evaluations tend to be encouraging, methodological flaws and limitations exist that are difficult to avoid. He notes three primary limitations to such evaluations: (1) High-quality research is difficult to conduct in such settings where the sensitivities of so many people must be considered; (2) techniques for effective research into care of the terminally ill are at an infant stage of development; (3) research and evaluation priorities generally fall way down on the list—improved care is the primary objective.

While Kastenbaum (1981) notes that many emerging reports on hospice are emphasizing the relative cost of hospice care as compared with traditional hospitalization, he hopes that the question of cost does not gain undue prominence. He is concerned that financial issues may warp our expectations and affect our ability to concentrate on the caring process itself.

It is the conclusion of Edward Crowther (1980) that the United States is not ready for the hospice. He notes that it is not a question of training or funding, but more of a problem of being unable or unwilling to change our attitudes toward proper care for a dying patient.

Crowther (1980) cites typical hospice development committee problems as power struggles, personal conflicts, and different opinions on approaches to take. The biggest stumbling block, however, seems to be attitudinal. He notes that the medical community remains to be convinced that current methods of treating the terminally ill must be changed. The dying cannot be treated in the same way as those who can expect to be cured. Physicians must learn the difference between the hospice goal of "care" and the traditional goal of "cure." The care concept admits that the patient is dying. Medical personnel must put their knowledge and efforts into relief of distressing symptoms and into human understanding. If this change in attitude does occur, Crowther believes that terminal care consistent with the ideals of the hospice movement can be provided in the United States.

CONCLUSION

As the American way of life has changed from a primary group orientation to a more secondary, impersonalized style, so has dying shifted from the home to the hospital or nursing home setting—away from kin and friends to a bureaucratized setting. The birth of the hospice movement in the United States might be considered a countermovement away from this trend. As we seek out primary group relations in our secondary-oriented society, we seek to die in the setting of a familiar home rather than in the sterile environment of a hospital. Perhaps we are evidencing a return to a concern for each other—a dignity to dying may be on the horizon.

Hospice is a return to showing care and compassion. It is a revival of neighbors helping neighbors—a concept so often lost in our urbanized society. Hospice consists of professionals literally going the extra mile and coming to one's home when needed—medical personnel actually making house calls. Hospice, for example, encourages children under fourteen to be present with the terminally ill person rather than making them wait in the hospital lobby. Hospice is a grass-roots movement springing up in small communities, as well as larger urban settings, to provide better health care. To paraphrase the words of Robert Kavanaugh (1972:19), the hospice concept of care assists us to unearth, face, understand, and accept our true feelings about death and provide us with the opportunity for joyful living and dying as we choose. In short, hospice is a movement in America that transforms our impropriety at death into a celebration of life.

With federal money now covering some hospice expenses and with rigid government requirements for approval of hospice programs, it is important that every effort be made to prevent hospice programs from being strangled by the bureaucracy that financially assists patients—the bureaucracy that gives them little choice from dying in traditional hospital and nursing-home settings. Furthermore, hospice programs must continue to make the patient-family unit the central focus of its care and treat these clients in a nonjudgmental and unconditional manner, thus empowering them as autonomous human beings.

SUMMARY

1. Hospice is a specialized health-care program that serves patients with illnesses such as cancer during the last days of their lives.

2. Hospice care includes both home care and inpatient care.

3. The hospice interdisciplinary team includes the patient, family, physician, nurse, social worker, chaplain, trained volunteer, psychologist, physical therapist, and lawyer.

4. A homelike environment is provided for hospice inpatient care.

5. The first hospice program in the United States was The Connecticut Hospice, modeled after St. Christopher's in London.

6. The hospice movement demonstrates that every human being has an inherent right to live as fully and completely as possible up to the moment of death.

7. Hospice care emphasizes relief from physical, social, psychological, and spiritual pain.

8. While much of the cost of hospice care is covered by third-party reimbursements, Medicare, and/or Medicaid, no prospective hospice patient is turned away because of lack of money.

DISCUSSION QUESTIONS

1. What is hospice care? How does it differ from the treatment given by most acute care hospitals? Identify the major functions of a hospice program.

2. Trace the history of the hospice movement in the United States.

3. Discuss issues related to the family as a unit of care in hospice programs. How do hospices try to achieve quality of life for each of the "patients" they serve? How does the interdisciplinary hospice team concept help accomplish this?

4. What are some of the special aspects of inpatient and home care in hospice programs? What are some of the advantages of each of these approaches?

5. What, in your opinion, are the negative aspects of hospice care? How would you suggest they be rectified?

6. Do you feel that bereavement care should be offered to the families of the terminally ill even after their loved ones have died? Justify your answer in terms of medical, emotional, and financial considerations.

7. If you were terminally ill, would you consider entering a hospice? Explain your answer, and refer to specific reasons such as cost, family burden, and imminent death.

GLOSSARY

Bereavement team An interdisciplinary group made up primarily of volunteers who follow up on families after the patient dies in order to encourage healthy grieving.

Hospice A specialized health-care program that serves patients with illnesses such as cancer during the last days of their lives.

Inpatient care The type of institutionalized help required, for example, as the illness progresses and which may be provided in a hospice facility.

REFERENCES

Bass, David M., T. Neal Garland, & Melinda E. Otto. 1985–1986. "Characteristics of Hospice Patients and their Caregivers." *Omega, 16* (1): pp. 51–68.

Boulder County Hospice. 1985. *Bereavement Care Manual.* Boulder, CO: Boulder County Hospice, Inc.

Chng, Chwee Lye, & Michael Kirby Ramsey. 1984–1985. "Volunteers and the Care of the Terminal Patient." *Omega, 15* (3): pp. 237–244.

Crowther, C. Edward. 1980. "The Stalled Hospice Movement." *The New Physician,* pp. 26–28.

DuBois, Paul M. 1980. *The Hospice Way of Death.* New York: Human Sciences Press.

Gray-Toft, Pamela A. & James G. Anderson. 1986–1987. "Sources of Stress in Nursing Terminal Patients in a Hospice." *Omega, 17* (1): pp. 27–38.

Hinton, J. 1979. "Comparison of Places and Policies for Terminal Care." *Lancet,* pp. 29–32.

Holden, Constance. 1976. "Hospices: For the Dying, Relief from Pain and Fear." *Science, 193* (4): p. 391.

Kastenbaum, Robert J. 1981. *Death, Society, and Human Experience,* Second Ed. St. Louis: Mosby.

Kavanaugh, Robert E. 1972. *Facing Death.* Baltimore: Penguin Books.

Labus, Janet G. & Faye H. Dambrot. 1985–1986, "A Comparative Study of Terminally Ill Hospice and Hospital Patients." *Omega, 16* (3): pp. 225–232.

Lack, Sylvia A. 1979. "Hospice: A Concept of Care in the Final Stage of Life." *Connecticut Medicine, 43* (6): pp. 369–370.

Lack, Sylvia A., & R. Buckingham. 1978. *First American Hospice: Three Years of Care.* New Haven: Hospice, Inc.

Leming, Michael R. 1979–1980. "Religion and Death: A Test of Homan's Thesis." *Omega, 10* (4): pp. 347-364.

National Hospice Organization. 1988. "The Basics of Hospice." Arlington, VA: National Hospice Organization.

National Hospice Organization. 1989. "Hospice Fact Sheet." Arlington, VA: National Hospice Organization.

Parkes, Colin M. 1978. "Home or Hospital? Terminal Care As Seen by Surviving Spouses." *Journal of the Royal College of General Practice, 28:* 19–30.

Rasminsky, Judy Sklar. 1981. "The Last Days of Mary Ball." 1979. Reader's Digest, *119* (October 1981).

Sorenson, Karen C., & Joan Luckmann. *Basic Nursing: A Psychophysiological Approach.* Philadelphia: W. B. Saunders.

Stoddard, Sandol. 1978. *The Hospice Movement: A Better Way of Caring for the Dying.* New York: Vintage.

Storck, Dorothy. 1981. "A Very Special Kind of Caring." *The Philadelphia Inquirer* (October).

SUGGESTED READINGS

Death Education, 2 (1, 2), 1978.
> Special issues on the hospice movement covering six models of hospice care found in the United States, England, and Canada.

DuBois, Paul M. 1980. *The Hospice Way of Death*. New York: Human Sciences Press.
> An overview of the hospice movement highlighting case studies of three hospices as well as the federal government's involvement.

Koff, Theodore H. 1980. *Hospice: A Caring Community*. Cambridge, MA: Winthrop Publishers.
> Delineates the practical and theoretical principles of the hospice, and provides information on the administrative, developmental, and personal elements of hospice care.

Lamberton, Robert. 1973. *Care of the Dying*. London: Priory Press, Ltd.

Saunders, Cicely. 1959. *Care of the Dying*. London: Macmillan.
> Two early, influential works that explain the hospice philosophy and care for dying patients and their families.

Martocchio, Benita C., & Karin Dufault. 1985. "Symposia on Hospice and Compassionate Care and the Dying Experience." *The Nursing Clinics of North America*, 20 (2), June. Philadelphia: Saunders.
> The entire issue of this journal is dedicated to the hospice concept of care for dying patients. Sixteen essays cover a broad range of topics.

National Hospice Organization. 1989. "Hospice Fact Sheet." National Hospice Organization. 1988. "The Basics of Hospice." Arlington, VA: National Hospice Organization.
> These pamphlets along with other information regarding the hospice concept of care are valuable resources that can be obtained without charge by contacting the National Hospice Organization, 1901 North Moore Street, Suite 901, Arlington, VA 22209, or calling (703) 243–5900.

Stoddard, Sandol. 1978. *The Hospice Movement: A Better Way of Caring for the Dying*. New York: Vintage.
> A vivid description of the workings of the hospice program, emphasizing how the patients and their families begin to help others.

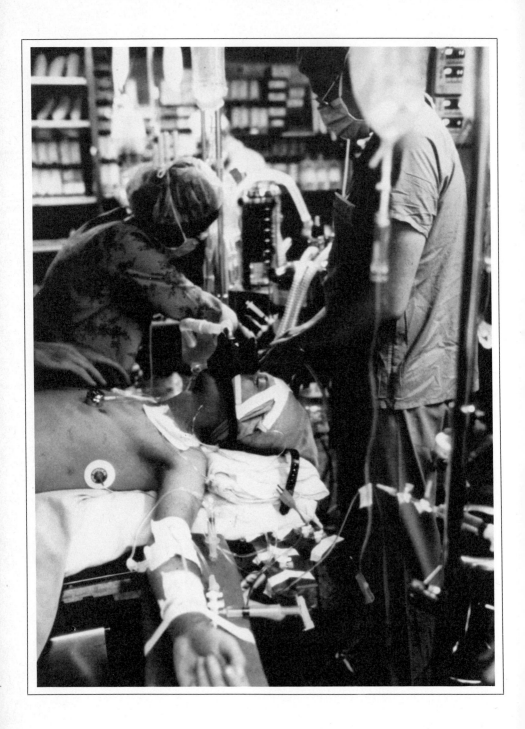

CHAPTER 7

Euthanasia and Biomedical Issues

—

It is silliness to live when to live is torment; And then have we a prescription to die when death is our physician?

WILLIAM SHAKESPEARE, *Othello*

All substances are poisons; there is none which is not a poison. The right dose differentiates a poison and a remedy.

PARACELSUS*

Sieben Defensiones. Verantwortung über etliche Verunglimpfungen seiner Missgönner. In Paracelsus: Selected Writings. *Norbert Guterman, trans. New York: Pantheon, 1958.*

7 What is **euthanasia?** For many it means mercy killing; for others it means natural death without the so-called benefit of technologies related to *life-extending, death-prolonging* medical interventions. However, the etymology of the term reveals that euthanasia literally means "good death." Both definitions above, then, may qualify.

SANCTITY AND QUALITY OF LIFE

When most people think about a "good death," they usually do so within the context of their understanding of the meaning of life. What is life? When does life begin? When does life end? Is there a difference between biological life and human life as socially defined?

Occasionally you may read of a serious automobile accident whose survivor is said to be in a vegetative state. Has the patient died? Is the patient no longer human? Now consider the situation in which an individual is assaulted and put into an irreversible coma. Has the assailant committed murder or assault and battery? If this same patient is disconnected from life support or **intubation** (tube feeding) and dies, who caused the death—the person who committed the crime or the medical personnel who withdrew the life support or feeding device?

BOX 7.1 **BOY IN COMA UNHOOKED FROM LIFE SUPPORT; DOUBT CAST ON ASSAULT CASE**

Doctors disconnected a life-support machine and let Craig Sieck, 15, die Tuesday despite doubt about what effect it will have on criminal charges against the youth accused of beating him.

Sieck had been in a coma since he was beaten and kicked in the head a week ago. James Sticka, 17, was charged with aggravated battery in connection with the beating. After tests on Sieck showed no brain activity, doctors said he had suffered "brain death."

"With another party involved, it could be a legal matter as to whether this party or the hospital was responsible for the death. The law in Illinois is not clear," hospital administrator John Imirie said.

Minneapolis Star and Tribune (UPI), March 15, 1978. Reprinted with permission of the Star Tribune.

In general, people respond to such questions about medical conditions from one of two orientations concerning the meaning of life. The first perspective would emphasize the **sanctity-of-life,** while the second emphasizes a **quality of life.** Euthanasia from a sanctity of life perspective would contend that all *"natural"* life has intrinsic meaning and should be appreciated as a divine gift. As a consequence, human beings have the obligation to enhance the quality of life as it may exist.

Hessel Bouma et al. (Bouma, Diekema, Langerak, Rottman, & Verhey, 1989:267) note that the Hippocratic tradition in the medical profession recognizes that physicians' responsibility to terminally ill patients is to simply "mitigate their suffering while allowing them to die." Furthermore, the Hippocratic Oath, reacting against an earlier practice of actively and intentionally hastening the death of a terminal patient, forbids the giving of "a deadly drug" to dying patients (Bouma et al., 1989:267–268).

The following two quotations illustrate the sanctity-of-life perspective.

> The sanctity of life approach is concerned about the quality of human life. The quality of all our lives suffers, it insists, unless every human life is considered inviolable because of the very fact of its existence. A dying patient's relationship to those about him symbolizes the relationship of all men to one another. To practice direct euthanasia, even at the request of the patient, is to weaken the claim of each one of us to the right to have others respect and not violate us (Weber, 1981:49).

> No horror against life is impossible once we have allowed anyone but the Creator to usurp sovereignty over life. Whom the gods would destroy they first make mad. Legalized euthanasia (mercy killing) is such madness (Morriss, 1987:149).

The quality-of-life perspective would hold that when life no longer has quality or meaning, death is preferable to life. The following statements by Claire Harrison, the central character in Brian Clark's play (1981:73–74) *Whose Life Is It Anyway?*, illustrate this perspective.

> Any reasonable definition of life must include the idea of its being self-supporting. I will spend the rest of my life in a hospital, but that while I am there, everything is geared just to keeping my brain active, with no possibility of it ever being able to direct anything. As far as I can see, that is an act of deliberate cruelty. . . .
> The best part of my life was, I suppose, my work. The most valuable asset that I had for that was my imagination. It's just a shame that my mind wasn't paralyzed along with my body. Because my imagination—which was my most precious possession, has become my enemy. And it tortures me with thoughts of what might have been and of what might be to come. I can feel my mind slowly breaking up. . . .
> I am filled with absolute outrage that you, who have no connection with me whatever, have the right to condemn me to a life of torment because you can't see the pain. There's no blood and there's no screaming so you can't see it. But if you saw a mutilated animal on the side of the road, you'd shoot it. Well, I'm

only asking that you show me the same mercy you'd show an animal. But I'm not asking you to commit an act of violence, just take me somewhere and leave me. And if you don't, then, you come back here in five years and see what a piece of work you did today. . . .

Both sanctity-of-life and quality-of-life perspectives introduce ambiguous terms for those who must decide appropriate criteria for a "good death." Those who take a sanctity-of-life perspective must adequately define "natural" life. Should biological life, sustained by a respirator, be considered "natural"? How about life sustained by a feeding tube or intravenous glucose solution? When is it appropriate to reject medical intervention, and how can we determine when a "natural" death has taken place?

Ivan Illich (1976:207–208) illustrates this problem.

> Today, the man best protected against setting the stage for his own dying is the sick person in critical condition. Society, acting through the medical system, decides when and after what indignities and mutilations he shall die. The medicalization of society has brought the epoch of natural death to an end. Western man has lost the right to preside at his act of dying. Health, or the autonomous power to cope, has been expropriated down to the last breath. Technical death has won its victory over dying. Mechanical death has conquered and destroyed all other deaths.

From a quality-of-life perspective, the concept of "quality" is even more difficult to define. Who should decide when life has quality? Quality is a relative term and its meaning often changes over the life cycle and as a result of social circumstance. I have little doubt that the quality of my life would diminish if I became paralyzed, blind, and/or deaf. However, many people with these disabilities experience a life of quality filled with purpose and meaning.

PASSIVE AND ACTIVE EUTHANASIA

There are two methods by which individuals try to facilitate a "good death"—passive and active euthanasia. **Passive euthanasia** involves a protocol whereby no action or medical intervention hastens death. Usually involving the removal of medical technology or the withholding of medical intervention, it is supported by people who affirm both sanctity-of-life and quality-of-life perspectives. In a 1985 Harris Poll, 85 percent of respondents endorsed a terminally ill patient's right to tell the doctor to stop trying to extend life. While not legally binding, living wills provide a vehicle by which individuals make their intentions known concerning the withholding of medical treatment. (Chapter 14 discusses the legal steps involved in the creation of living wills that assist family members to make decisions regarding the medical treatment of terminally ill patients.)

BOX 7.2 # ROUTINE CPR CAN ABUSE THE OLD AND SICK

Since cardiopulmonary resuscitation was introduced in 1960, it has saved countless lives. But we are in danger today of abusing this procedure. At some point, we must stop adding to the suffering of dying patients by pounding on their chests, possibly breaking bones, just to extend their lives by a few days or weeks.

CPR is performed routinely in hospitals, without regard to patients' chances of recovering to lead normal lives. Why try to revive with CPR a patient who has been sick for years with diabetes, hypertension, heart disease and kidney failure, and who has just had an operation for a perforated intestine? Why batter the sternum of a drastically debilitated, 85-year-old woman who is suffering from pneumonia?

In terminal cases like these, the idea of beating on the chest of an old and sick person is morally and physically repugnant. Yet, for the lack of prior understandings between patients, families, and physicians, the procedure continues to be used indiscriminately.

Although some people will refuse as long as possible to let a loved one die, most families will abide by the medical decision on CPR. Trouble arises, however, when neither the terminal patient nor the doctor raises the subject of CPR soon enough. There is a vague hope that the problem may not have to be faced soon. Then, under the duress of the moment, it is hard for families to make a quick decision. So, the physician simply follows the routine of CPR.

What can we do to avoid this predicament?

First, we have to educate the public and professionals. An increasing number of patients are asking for a peaceful death. In time, I hope that this demand will become universal. Medical and nursing schools need to teach more about accepting death and dying.

Second, patients should sign living wills. Many states have enacted laws that recognize the terminally ill patient's right to refuse life-sustaining treatment. By court decisions, 12 states have acknowledged such a right.

Third, patients with incurable diseases should be tactfully approached by their families and physicians about the use of aggressive measures. While discussing the subject, one should not convey hopelessness; hope is an important part of medical care.

If the patient is opposed to resuscitation, the primary physician must write clearly on a patient's chart, "No CPR." Simply having an understanding with the nurses on the floor will not work. When a CPR code is activated by hospital monitors, doctors and nurses will rush to the

(continued on next page)

victim. If the attending physician is not around and there are no instructions on the patient's record, confusion arises about what to do.

In our lawyer-dominated society, hospitals have been forced to devise bureaucratic rules that may not have the patients' welfare foremost in mind. Moreover, once a patient is on the life-support system it is not easy to "pull the plug." Legal complexities will override ethical justifications. Thus, it is all the more important to decide ahead of time what steps are appropriate to revive incurable patients.

Fazlur Rahman. *Minneapolis Star and Tribune*. February 27, 1989, p. 9A. (Originally written for *The New York Times*.) Copyright © 1989 by The New York Times Company. Reprinted by permission.

Some people have received the *false* impression that passive euthanasia is incompatible with a belief in the sanctity of life. The following statement by Pope Pius XII (1977: 283–284, 286) illustrates the Roman Catholic Church's belief in maintaining sanctity of life while affirming passive euthanasia.

> Natural reason and Christian morals say that man (and whoever is entrusted with the task of taking care of his fellowman) has the right and the duty in case of serious illness to take the necessary treatment for the preservation of life and health. This duty that one has toward himself, toward God, toward the human community, and in most cases toward certain determined persons, derives from well ordered charity, from strict justice, as well as from devotion toward one's family.
>
> But normally one is held to use only *ordinary means*—according to circumstances of persons, places, times, and culture—that is to say, means that do not involve any grave burden for oneself or another. A more strict obligation would be too burdensome for most men and would render the attainment of the higher, more important good too difficult. Life, health, all temporal activities are in fact subordinated to spiritual ends.
>
> Consequently, if it appears that the attempt to resuscitation constitutes in reality such a burden for the family that one cannot in all conscience impose it upon them, they can lawfully insist that the doctor should discontinue these attempts, and the doctor can lawfully comply.

In this statement it is clear that the use of extraordinary measures is not required of terminal patients, members of their family, or attending physicians. However, differentiating between ordinary and extraordinary treatment is not an easy task. Gerald Kelly (cited by Bouma et al., 1989:274–275) defines these terms in the following manner:

Ordinary means of preserving life are all medicines, treatments, and operations, which offer a reasonable hope of benefit for the patient and which can be obtained and used without excessive expense, pain, and other inconveniences.

Extraordinary means of preserving life are all those medicines, treatments, and operations which cannot be obtained without excessive expense, pain, or other inconvenience, or which, if used would not offer a reasonable hope of benefit.

These definitions introduce other ambiguous terms—"reasonable hope," "excessive expense," "excessive pain," and "excessive inconvenience." What is reasonable and excessive? Who among us can make decisions employing these highly relative concepts? Which of the following should society hold responsible to determine these matters: politicians, physicians, lawyers and judges, members of the community at large, and/or patients and their families?

Many within the medical community have operationalized **ordinary measures** to be any procedure that is "usual and customary" medical practice, and **extraordinary measures** to be those procedures that are exotic, innovative, and medically experimental. However, it is clear that this distinction provides us with little help because (1) technology has a way of imposing itself upon modern society in an amoral fashion and (2) what has been considered innovative and experimental becomes usual and customary with time. Consider the situation in which a Down's Syndrome infant starves to death because parents will not permit a physician to perform a simple operation that would allow food to be digested by the child.

The fate of this Down's Syndrome infant is a classic example of what sociologists call **cultural lag**—a condition created by rapid medical technological development and relatively static definitions of biological life and death. Medical practice today can prolong life (or postpone death) without having precise definitions of a point at which meaningful living has stopped and death has occurred. This condition would be of little significance if medical science were unable to maintain some biological functioning of the individual with artificial means, but such is not the case. As Joseph Fletcher (1977:355) says, when the terminal patient "contemplates modern medicine's ability to prolong life, death itself is welcomed compared to the terrors of senility and protracted terminal treatment."

Furthermore, even if one were able to distinguish between ordinary and extraordinary treatments, would it be acceptable for patients (or someone acting on their behalf) to request the withdrawal of ordinary life support such as food and water? This is an issue that tends to divide persons who affirm a sanctity-of-life perspective and favor passive euthanasia.

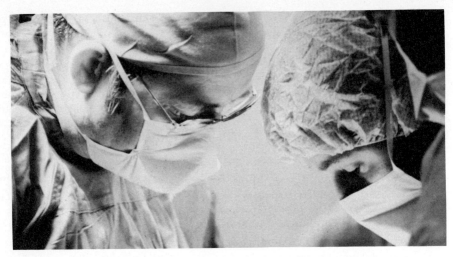

Modern medicine has provided us with technological advances that blur the distinctions between ordinary and extraordinary treatments for the terminally ill patient.

If one can accept the legitimacy of passive euthanasia, Lowell Erdahl (1987:143) raises the following questions:

> There are circumstances in which active euthanasia is more compassionate than passive. Is it, for example, more kind to cause death by dehydration and starvation than it is to kill the patient by lethal injection? In both cases the motive and effect are exactly the same; only the method is different. Is it possible that in some cases the sin of omission (permitting death by dehydration and starvation) may be greater than the sin of commission (causing death by lethal injection)?

Active euthanasia requires a direct action to bring about death. There are two types of active euthanasia: **suicide** and **mercy killing.** Suicide is the voluntary act of taking one's own life. Those who favor active euthanasia prefer to use the term **self-deliverance** when a life of a terminally ill patient is terminated. However, they would reject the legitimacy of suicide for persons with clinical depression or other forms of psychological pain.

In the United States, the Hemlock Society assists terminally ill individuals in the act of self-deliverance. In 1981 the Hemlock Society—published a book written by its founder and director, Derek Humphry, entitled *Let Me Die Before I Wake: Hemlock's Book of Self-Deliverance for the Dying.* The first 10 chapters of this book provide detailed case studies of individuals (often with the assistance of family members and friends) who chose self-deliverance as an alternative to passive euthanasia. The remainder of the book provides a bibliography and an extended discussion of personal and legal issues related to the decision to take one's life.

A year earlier, the English counterpart of the Hemlock Society—EXIT (founded in 1935 as the British Voluntary Euthanasia Society)—published *A Guide to Self-Deliverance* (1980). This book is unique because it provides the reader with detailed instructions to successfully and painlessly commit suicide. In the United States this book would have been construed as an attempt to intentionally aid and/or solicit another to commit suicide—a felony in most states. For that reason, the Hemlock Society has not been explicit in providing such information to its members.

The Hemlock Society has been careful to differentiate suicide from self-deliverance, and self-deliverance from mercy killing. Suicide is often condemned socially and religiously as a selfish act or as an "overreaction of a disturbed mind." Suicide is considered by many as an irrational act that is a permanent solution to what is often a temporary problem. In contrast, self-deliverance should be considered a positive action taken to provide a permanent solution to the long-term pain and suffering for the individual and his or her loved ones faced with a terminal condition. (Chapter 8 provides an extended treatment of suicide unrelated to terminal illness.)

Self-deliverance is a completely voluntary act on the part of the patient, while mercy killing involves other people's behavior that may or may not be sanctioned by the patient. In a 1985 Harris poll 61 percent of the respondents favored the patient's right to ask the doctor actually to "put him out of his misery." However, at the present time both suicide (self-deliverance) and mercy killing are illegal in the United States. Furthermore, U.S. laws do not distinguish between murder and mercy killing, and therefore mercy killing is always treated as a criminal offense regardless of the motivations of individuals involved.

The Hemlock Society and EXIT wish to eliminate the stigma attached to self-killing and to extend to all individuals the right of active, rational, and voluntary euthanasia whenever the dying process only promises unrelieved pain and a life devoid of dignity, meaning, and purpose. The Hemlock Society has endorsed the 1990 Oregon Death with Dignity Act as a legal proposal to guarantee these rights.

BOX 7.3   **DIRECTIVE TO PHYSICIANS**

This directive is made this _____ day of _____ (month) _____ (year).
I, _____ being of sound mind, willfully and voluntarily make known my desire

(a) ☐ **That my life shall not be artificially prolonged** and
(b) ☐ **That my life shall be ended with the aid of a physician under the circumstances set forth below, and do hereby declare:**
   (You must initial (a) or (b), or both.)

(continued on next page)

1. If at any time I should have a terminal condition or illness certified to be terminal by two physicians, and they determine that my death will occur within six months,

    (a) ☐ **I direct that life-sustaining procedures be withheld or withdrawn,** and

    (b) ☐ **I direct that my physician administer aid-in-dying in a humane and dignified manner.** (You must initial (a) or (b), or both.)

    (c) ☐ **I have attached Special Instructions on a separate page to the directive.** (Initial if you have attached a separate page.)

The action taken under this paragraph shall be at the time of my own choosing if I am competent.

2. In the absence of my ability to give directions regarding the termination of my life, it is my intention that this directive shall be honored by my family, agent (described in paragraph 5), and physician(s) as the final expression of my legal right to

    (a) ☐ **Refuse medical or surgical treatment,** and

    (b) ☐ **To choose to die in a humane and dignified manner.** (You must initial (a) or (b), or both and you must initial one box below.)

        ☐ If I am unable to give directions, I *do not* want my attorney-in-fact to request aid-in-dying.

        ☐ If I am unable to give directions, I *do* want my attorney-in-fact to ask my physician for aid-in-dying.

3. I understand that a terminal condition is one in which I am not likely to live for more than six months.

4. a. I, _____

    do hereby designate and appoint _____
as my attorney-in-fact (agent) to make health-care decisions for me if I am in a coma or otherwise unable to decide for myself as authorized in this document. For the purpose of this document, "health-care decision" means consent, refusal of consent, or withdrawal of consent to any care, treatment, service, or procedure to maintain, diagnose, or treat an individual's physical or mental condition, or to administer aid-in-dying.

    b. By this document I intend to create a Durable Power of Attorney for Health Care under The Oregon Death With Dignity Act and ORS Section 126.407. This power of attorney shall not be affected by my subsequent incapacity, except by revocation.

    c. Subject to any limitations in this document, I hereby grant to my agent full power and authority to make health-care decisions for me to the same extent that I could make these decisions for myself if I had the capacity to do so. In exercising this authority, my agent shall make health-care decisions that are consistent with my desires as stated in this document or otherwise made known to my agent, including, but not limited to, my desires concerning obtaining, refusing, or withdrawing life-prolonging care, treatment, services and procedures, and administration of aid-in-dying.

5. This directive shall have no force or effect seven years from the date filled in above, unless I am incompetent to act on my own behalf and then it shall remain valid until my competency is restored.

6. I recognize that a physician's judgment is not always certain, and that medical science continues to make progress in extending life, but in spite of these facts, I nevertheless wish aid-in-dying rather than letting my terminal condition take its natural course.

7. My family has been informed of my request to die, their opinions have been taken into consideration, but the final decision remains mine, so long as I am competent.

8. The exact time of my death will be determined by me and my physician with my desire or my attorney-in-fact's instructions paramount.

I have given full consideration and understand the full import of this directive, and I am emotionally and mentally competent to make this directive. I accept the moral and legal responsibility for receiving aid-in-dying.

This directive will not be valid unless it is signed by two qualified witnesses who are present when you sign or acknowledge your signature. The witnesses must not be related to you by blood, marriage, or adoption; they must not be entitled to any part of your estate; and they must not include a physician or other person responsible for, or employed by anyone responsible for, your health care. If you have attached any additional pages to this form, you must date and sign each of the additional pages at the same time you date and sign this power of attorney.

Signed: _____

_____
City, County, and State of Residence

(This document must be witnessed by two qualified adult witnesses. None of the following may be used as witnesses: (1) a health care provider who is involved in any way with the treatment of the declarant, (2) an employee of a health care provider who is involved in any way with the treatment of the declarant, (3) the operator of a community care facility where the declarant resides, (4) an employee of an operator of a community care facility who is involved in any way with the treatment of the declarant.

The Oregon Death With Dignity Act, Oregon Revised Statutes, Chapter 97, 1990.

The Legalization of Mercy Killing: The Dutch Experiment

In the Netherlands, physicians are allowed to perform mercy killing through lethal injections if the doctors follow a strict procedure established by the Dutch medical profession and sanctioned by the courts. In this procedure, the following conditions must be met (Diekstra, 1987:56):

1. The choice of suicide must be a free-will decision of the person and not made under pressure by others.

2. The wish to die can be an enduring one.

3. The person must be experiencing unbearable physical and/or emotional pain, and the improvement of this condition cannot reasonably be expected.

4. The person must not be mentally disturbed at the time of the decision to commit suicide.

5. The suicide should be carried out in such a way that harm is not caused to others.

6. The person who assists the suicide should be a qualified health professional, and only a medical doctor is allowed to administer the lethal drug.

7. The helper should never handle such cases entirely on his or her own, but should ask for professional consultation from colleagues (e.g., other medical colleagues and/or members of the clergy).

8. The assisted suicide would be fully documented, and the documents should be made available to the appropriate legal authorities.

Though this procedure is not technically legal, since 1972 the Dutch courts have enacted legal precedents that have made physician-assisted suicide fairly common. According to Paul Montgomery (1987), annually more than 6000 people in Holland commit suicide with medical assistance from physicians. Furthermore, the majority of Holland's AIDS (Acquired Immune Deficiency Syndrome) patients end their lives prematurely through medical intervention. Clearly, mercy killing has become socially sanctioned in a modern industrial nation. What are the effects of this precedent upon other European nations and the United States?

BOX 7.4   **FATHER CAUSES SON'S DEATH**

A father unhooked his comatose baby son's life-support system early Wednesday, then took him into his arms and kept hospital workers at gunpoint until the child was dead.

"I'm not here to hurt anyone. I'll only hurt you if you try to plug my baby back in," police quoted Rudy Linares as saying.

"You can understand the motivation," police Sgt. William Rooney said. "I guess he didn't want his child to continue living under those conditions."

A hospital spokeswoman said Linares' 16-month-old son, Samuel, was taken to Rush-Presbyterian by ambulance last August with a blocked windpipe after he swallowed an object, believed to be either a balloon or a small piece of aluminum foil.

Oxygen deprivation left him partially brain dead, according to Rush-Presbyterian–St. Luke's Medical Center spokeswoman Carolyn Reed, and Samuel had been in a coma since his arrival. The child's mother, Tamara Linares, said doctors worked 12 hours to resuscitate her son in August, despite their pleas to the contrary.

Doctors had notified the parents Tuesday that the child was to be transferred to a long-term care unit, Reed said. Police said Linares and his wife walked into the hospital about 1 a.m. and were escorted to the pediatric intensive care unit, where their son's breathing had been sustained by a ventilator since the accident. About 20 minutes later, after his wife left the room for a drink of water, Linares pulled out a handgun, ordered hospital staff out of the unit, unhooked the infant from the life support system and sat with his son in his arms.

One nurse disregarded Linares' order and attempted to reconnect the system, but left the room when he cocked the hammer of the handgun, police said. After 30 minutes the Linares child died.

"He never pointed the gun at anyone other than the child," said Rooney. "He sat there in a chair until the baby had expired, then turned the gun over to the officers." Detective Gary Bulava said Linares was "calm at times. . . . he did a lot of crying."

Linares, 23, a painter from west suburban Cicero, was charged with murder, said a spokeswoman for the Cook County state's attorney's office. At an evening court hearing, however, he was released on a $75,000 recognizance bond, which means he is free and does not have to post money unless he fails to appear at future hearings. Judge Marvin Ruttenberg told Linares to appear in court again today.

About 25 people turned out to support him, including his wife, mother, father, and brother. His wife, who said the couple had planned to see a lawyer Friday about having the child's life-support system disconnected, was not charged.

"This is the best thing," she told radio station WBBM-AM earlier. "Sammy is out of his misery." The couple have two other children, both under 5.

Associated Press. *Minneapolis Star and Tribune*, April 27, 1989, pp. 1A and 12A.

The Slippery-Slope Argument

Persons who oppose active euthanasia often do so on the grounds of what they call the **slippery-slope-to-Auschwitz argument.** They would allege

"Stop saying, 'No heroics,' Mrs. Baylor. He only
has a head cold."
Reprinted with permission of Universal Press Syndicate.

that the justification for withholding some treatments also justifies withholding any and all treatments from those whom society considers unworthy. It is further argued that if a society wishes to extend to any of its members the right to active euthanasia, none of its members is protected from being killed. Such was the case under Hitler when German society's "unproductive," "defective," and "morally and mentally unfit"—Jews, homosexuals, and handicapped—were sent to Auschwitz and other places of confinement to be "euthanasized" (murdered).

The slippery-slope argument asserts that society moves toward a disregard for human life in predictable steps. The first step is the acceptance of passive euthanasia when medical technology and surgical procedures are withheld from (or rejected by) chronically and/or terminally ill patients. The second step occurs when ordinary or customary procedures are withdrawn—such procedures would include food and water. We arrive at the third step when society accepts the legitimacy of suicide (self-deliverance). The fourth step is when these "rights" are extended to nonterminal patients such as quadriplegics. In the fifth step, the medical system will assist patients in self-deliverance or active euthanasia (as is presently the situation in Holland), believing that the incurably ill deserve the same "humane" treatment as that accorded to a beloved animal that is "put to sleep." All of these provisions are extended to the nonterminally ill and/or persons acting on their behalf in the sixth step. Finally, we arrive at the seventh step—"Auschwitz"—

when society is willing to accord these "privileges" to the unwilling, incompetent, and/or undesirable.

While one might disagree with the inevitability of these steps to lead toward a rejection of the sanctity of human life, we may acknowledge that the noble intentions of those who favor active euthanasia do not in themselves justify a public policy allowing mercy killing, nor will they counteract the potential abuse to which euthanasia can be put by those whose motives may be self-serving (Bouma et al., 1989:301).

Without a doubt, even so-called "voluntary" actions can be unduly influenced by social pressures. Consider the case of an elderly nursing home resident who realizes that the cost of her care depletes financial resources that might be used to support an able-bodied spouse or to bequeath to other family members. When one defines oneself as a burden to society, is euthanasia (even self-deliverance) truly a voluntary choice? In the words of Erdahl (1987:145),

> As costs of care increase, individuals in specific circumstances and society as a whole will be strongly tempted to sell out both compassion and responsible reverence for life in exchange for economic considerations. If the day comes when euthanasia is established as an economic policy, we will have ceased to be either fully moral or fully human.

BOX 7.5 **WHERE DEATH COMES NORMALLY**

The scenery from the taxi window fits perfectly onto the familiar London palette: A gray, green, and brown cityscape marks the route to the collection of medical buildings known as St. Christopher's.

St. Christopher's was the first modern hospice. It was opened 21 years ago to give more than tender, loving care to the dying; it promised to give medically skillful loving care.

I have come here because we read and hear so much about two alternatives for the terminally ill: suffering and suicide, merciless medicine and mercy killing. Many in America now believe that medicine is more concerned with prolonging life than preventing pain.

The beacon of the modern hospice movement offers a very different mode. A place where medicine and humanity can ease the way to death without technological heroism or its horror stories. A place where death is allowed its normalcy.

The hospice doesn't artificially prolong life, nor does it shorten life. Indeed, Dr. Tom West, director of St. Christopher's, makes clear dis-

(continued on next page)

tinctions between the hospice and euthanasia movements. "The pro-euthanasia community feels that if you can't cure a patient with cancer and can't control the symptoms, you should offer the patient a chance of opting out of life. Hospice is saying you *can* control symptoms and, having controlled symptoms, it is amazing to see how much use patients and families make of that extra time. I have seen so many situations that it makes me sweat to think I might have cut the life short."

West adds his own beliefs into the equation carefully: "I happen to think we are not meant to shorten our time. I also happen to think we are not meant to suffer." The widespread perception of these as the only choices comes, he believes, out of mainstream medicine's ignorance about pain-killing drugs and from the reluctance of doctors to use them.

"Every patient that every doctor has is going to die. But if you look at the curriculum of medical schools, symptom control is just not there." If he has a goal, it would be to carry the message of hospice, particularly about the control of pain, back into the world of mainstream medicine. To see the line between hospice medicine and traditional medicine blurred.

Unfortunately, today the glare of publicity is regularly focused on a patient who faced a choice between prolonging suffering and cutting life short. It's focused on a husband or wife who faced the options of merciless medicine or mercy killing. But hospice has been learning and teaching that there's a third and a better way.

PUBLIC POLICY

Until this section we have primarily taken a social exchange perspective on biomedical issues. We have analyzed euthanasia from a cost–benefit point of view and assumed that the individual (or small group of people) is the appropriate unit of analysis. In the remainder of this chapter we will analyze American public policy in dealing with the health needs of critically ill persons.

Many Americans assume that health care should be a guaranteed right of all citizens who desire and can afford to pay for it. For those unable to pay, the government provides basic health care through Medicaid, federally assisted payments to the poor. While passive euthanasia would affirm the right of those who choose to reject medical intervention, many believe that

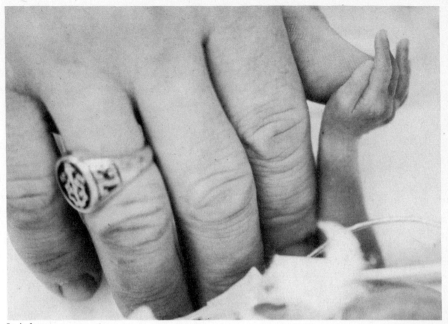

Is it better to spend money to save the life of one premature infant or provide prenatal care for 10,000 women?

those who wish to live have a legitimate claim on the resources of society in providing the medical assistance necessary for living.

With annual medical care costing more than $600 billion and with heightened concerns for fiscal responsibility and cost containment, Americans are beginning to question universal access to health care for all citizens. This re-evaluation of health-care public policy is motivated by a utilitarian concern for distributive justice.

Utilitarianism is the belief that social policy should be directed at providing the greatest good (maximum benefits) for the greatest number of people. If it costs more than a million dollars to provide an artificial heart for one patient to live three months in a hospital, it is believed that the same amount of money might be more appropriately spent on prenatal care for 10,000 women. Furthermore, in the United States approximately 50 percent of the medical expenditures that an individual will incur during his or her lifetime will be for medical services delivered in the final six months of life. Since all of us are involved to some extent in paying for these medical costs (either through government subsidy or health insurance premiums), it is easy to question whether or not these expenditures are a worthwhile investment for such a limited return.

These types of cost–benefit analysis de-emphasize the health needs of particular individuals in favor of the health needs of the entire society. Garrett Hardin (1985:21), professor of ecology at the University of California at Santa Barbara, presents this argument with the following statement: "Easy access to health care is exhausting America's medical resources." According to Hardin, whenever meeting medical needs becomes an obligation of the entire community, utilization will always benefit individuals, while costs will be shared by all members of the system. Therefore, individuals can never be expected to limit their use, and health-care costs will naturally rise to a place were the system will collapse—the end of health care to all.

Hardin (1989:21–22, 25) asks:

> Should the artificial heart be considered an inalienable right of any needy patient? Should the public at large pay the extra cost of saving premature babies? What is to be gained by extending the lives of comatose patients a few more years? It is clear that our society faces a grave danger: as medical technology advances and we spend more and more for less and less, we edge ever closer to what might be called the tragedy of the medical commons. . . .
> A tragic end can be prevented only by saying NO! But what should we limit? The kinds of defects and malfunctions eligible for treatment? The age beyond which a patient may not be treated with heroic medicine? These are good candidates. Every point in our medical and legal systems seems to be biased in favor of compassion. At some point compassion must yield to principle.

Former Governor Richard Lamm raised this same type of life-boat ethic philosophy in considering the health needs of Colorado's poor. According to Dr. John Kitzhaber (cited by Robinson, 1989:4–5), a physician and the president of the Oregon State Senate,

> We spend over $50 billion a year on people in the last six months of their lives, while closing pediatric clinics. We spend over $3 billion a year on intensive care for newborn babies, while denying prenatal care to hundreds of thousands of expectant women. Every dollar spent on health care is one that can't be spent on schools, roads, or a cleaner environment.

In the last ten years many states have changed eligibility requirements that have removed more than 800,000 American women and children from Medicaid. Presently Medicaid covers only 38 percent of the nation's poor, while ten years ago it provided benefits for 64 percent (Robinson, 1989:5).

Dr. Daniel Callahan, director of the Hastings Center, has advocated that persons over 80 be ineligible for Medicare reimbursements for cancer surgery, intensive-care, and heart bypass surgery. Callahan (cited by Robinson, 1989:5) says:

> As a nation, we must set a hard line against the endless prolongation of life. We must direct our medical energies only to the relief of pain and suffering in the elderly, and to help them prepare for a graceful death after a full life.

CONCLUSION

━━━ We have obviously come to a point where very tough health-care decisions must be made. Many of these are personal and family decisions—how long do we wish to extend the dying process for ourselves and those we love? Other decisions will involve the welfare of the entire society and will require us to make choices between extending terminal care to those whose time is diminished and investing resources to prevent the more able-bodied from becoming ill. From a personal perspective, we will always find it difficult to withhold treatment from anyone. From a national perspective, we must always support health-care policies that will benefit most of our citizens without inflicting pain and suffering on any.

SUMMARY

━━━ 1. Euthanasia, or "good death," must be defined within the context of one's understanding of the meaning of life.

2. Euthanasia from a sanctity-of-life perspective would contend that all "natural" life has intrinsic meaning and should be appreciated as a divine gift. As a consequence, human beings have the obligation to enhance the quality of life as it may exist.

3. Euthanasia from a quality-of-life perspective would hold that when life no longer has "quality," death is preferable to living a life devoid of meaning.

4. There are two methods by which individuals try to facilitate a "good death"—passive and active euthanasia. Passive euthanasia involves a protocol whereby no action or medical intervention hastens death. Passive euthanasia usually involves the removal of medical technology or the refusal of medical intervention. Passive euthanasia is supported by people who affirm both sanctity of life and quality of life perspectives.

5. Active euthanasia requires a direct action to bring about death. There are two types of active euthanasia: *suicide* and *mercy killing*.

6. Suicide is the voluntary act of taking one's own life. Those who favor active euthanasia prefer to use the term "self-deliverance" when a life of a terminally ill patient is terminated. Self-deliverance should be considered a positive action taken to provide a permanent solution to the long-term pain and suffering for the individual and his or her loved ones faced with a terminal condition.

7. Self-deliverance is a completely voluntary act on the part of the patient; mercy killing involves other people's behavior, which may or may not be sanctioned by the patient. At the present time both suicide (self-deliverance) and mercy killing are illegal in the United States.

8. Courts in the Netherlands have enacted legal precedents which have made physician-assisted suicide fairly common.

9. Persons opposing active euthanasia often do so with the "slippery-slope-to-Auschwitz" argument. They allege that the justification for withholding some treatments also justifies withholding any and all treatments from those whom society considers unworthy. The slippery slope argument asserts that society moves towards a disregard for human life in predictable steps.

DISCUSSION QUESTIONS

1. Compare and contrast sanctity-of-life and quality-of-life perspectives on euthanasia. What are the limitations of each perspective?

2. Compare and contrast passive and active euthanasia. What are the difficulties of implementing each of these approaches for current social policy dealing with health care for the terminally ill?

3. What are the difficulties in defining the following terms:
   a. Natural death
   b. Quality of life
   c. Ordinary and extraordinary medical interventions
   d. Usual and customary medical procedures
   e. Excessive expense and reasonable benefit

4. If your parent were dying from an extremely painful and incurable form of cancer and decided that life was not worth living, what role would you be willing to play in assisting him or her in self-deliverance? Would you be unwilling to assist your parent? If not, what actions would you take in discouraging your parent's action?

5. Provide arguments for and against the removal of food and water from a terminal patient in a coma.

6. Provide arguments favoring and disagreeing with national legislation legitimizing mercy killing.

GLOSSARY

▬▬▬ **Active euthanasia** A direct action that causes death in accordance with the stated or implied wishes of the terminal patient. There are two types of active euthanasia: *suicide* and *mercy killing*.

Cultural lag A situation in which some parts of culture change more slowly than others. A typical situation is that technology changes faster than the values of the culture.

Euthanasia A "good" death.

EXIT The British society that promotes euthanasia.

Extraordinary measures All those medicines, treatments, and operations that cannot be obtained without excessive expense, pain, or other inconvenience, or which, if used, would not offer a reasonable hope of benefit.

Intubation A procedure whereby the patient is fed through a tube placed in the stomach.

Mercy killing Ending the life of a terminal patient in accordance with that person's stated or implied wishes.

Ordinary measures All medicines, treatments, and operations that offer a reasonable hope of benefit for the patient and which can be obtained and used without excessive expense, pain, or other inconvenience.

Passive euthanasia The withholding of treatment, which, in effect, hastens death.

Quality of life The perspective that when life no longer has *quality,* death is preferable to living a life devoid of meaning.

Sanctity of life The perspective that all *natural* life has intrinsic meaning and should be appreciated as a divine gift. As a consequence, human beings have the obligation to enhance the quality of life as it may exist.

Self-deliverance A rational and voluntary act of taking one's life; an alternative to the terms *suicide* and *mercy killing*.

Slippery-slope-to-Auschwitz argument The belief that if a society wishes to extend to any of its members the right to active euthanasia, none of its members is protected from being killed. Auschwitz was the German concentration camp where people were killed during World War II.

Suicide A voluntary act of taking one's life.

Utilitarianism The principle of evaluation based upon the goal of providing the greatest good (maximum benefits) for the greatest number of people.

REFERENCES

▬▬▬ Bouma, Hessel, Douglas Diekema, Edward Langerak, Theodore Rottman, & Allen Verhey. 1989. *Christian Faith, Health, and Medical Practice.* Grand Rapids, MI: Eerdmans.

Clark, Brian. 1981. *Whose Life Is It Anyway?* Chicago: The Dramatic Publishing Company.

Diekstra, Rene F. W. 1987. "Suicide Should Not Always Be Prevented." In Janelle Rohr (Ed.), *Death and Dying: Opposing Viewpoints.* St. Paul, MN: Greenhaven Press.

Erdahl, Lowell. 1987. "Euthanasia Is Sometimes Justified." In Janelle Rohr (Ed.), *Death and Dying: Opposing Viewpoints.* St. Paul, MN: Greenhaven Press.

EXIT. 1980. *A Guide to Self-Deliverance.* London: EXIT.

Fletcher, Joseph. 1977. "Ethics and Euthanasia." In Dennis J. Horan and David Mall (Eds.), *Death, Dying, and Euthanasia.* Washington, DC: University Publications of America.

Goodman, Ellen. 1988. "Where Death Comes Normally." *The Boston Globe.*

Hardin, Garrett. 1985. "Crisis on the Commons." *The Sciences,* September–October, pp. 21–25.

Hemlock Society. 1981. "The Hemlock Manifesto." Los Angeles, CA: The Hemlock Society.

Humphry, Derek. 1982. *Let Me Die Before I Wake: Hemlock's Book of Self-Deliverance for the Dying.* Los Angeles, CA: The Hemlock Society.

Illich, Ivan. 1976. *Medical Nemesis: The Expropriation of Health.* New York: Pantheon.

Minneapolis Star and Tribune. 1989. "Father Causes Son's Death." April 27.

Montgomery, Paul. 1987. "In Holland, the Promise of an Easy Death ." *Minneapolis Star and Tribune.* September 2, p. 15A.

Morriss, Frank. 1987. "Euthanasia Is Never Justified." In Janelle Rohr (Ed.), *Death and Dying: Opposing Viewpoints.* St. Paul, MN: Greenhaven Press.

Pope Pius XII. 1977. "The Prolongation of Life: An Address of Pope Pius XII to an International Congress of Anesthesiologists." In Dennis J. Horan & David Mall (Eds.), *Death, Dying, and Euthanasia.* Washington, DC: University Publications of America.

Rahman, Fazlur. 1989. "Routine CPR Can Abuse the Old and Sick." *The New York Times.* February 20.

Robinson, Donald. 1989. "Who Should Receive Medical Aid?" *Parade Magazine,* May 28, pp. 4–5.

UPI. 1978. "Boy in Coma Unhooked from Life Support; Doubt Cast on Assault Case." March 15.

Weber, Leonard J. 1981. "The Case against Euthanasia." In David Bender (Ed.), *Problems of Death: Opposing Viewpoints.* St. Paul, MN: Greenhaven Press.

SUGGESTED READINGS

Bouma, Hessel, Douglas Diekema, Edward Langerak, Theodore Rottman, & Allen Verhey. 1989. *Christian Faith, Health, and Medical Practice.* Grand Rapids, MI: Eerdmans.
This book deals with biomedical issues from multidisciplinary and Christian points of view.

Callahan, Daniel. 1987. *Setting Limits: Medical Goals in an Aging Society*. New York: Simon and Schuster.

Interesting food for thought about decisions regarding the elderly when financial resources are limited.

Horan, Dennis J., & David Mall (Eds.). 1977. *Death, Dying, and Euthanasia*. Washington, DC: University Publications of America.

Rohr, Janelle (Ed.). 1987. *Death and Dying: Opposing Viewpoints*. St. Paul, MN: Greenhaven Press.

Weir, Robert F. (Ed.). 1986. *Ethical Issues in Death and Dying*. New York: Columbia University Press.

Three excellent anthologies on biomedical issues.

Humphry, Derek. 1981. *Let Me Die Before I Wake: Hemlock's Book of Self-Deliverance for the Dying*. Los Angeles: The Hemlock Society.

This book presents a number of case studies of terminally ill individuals (often with the assistance of family members and friends) who choose self-deliverance as an alternative to passive euthanasia. It also provides a bibliography and an extended discussion of personal and legal issues related to the decision to take one's life.

CHAPTER 8

Suicide

———

There are times in life when we would like to die temporarily.

MARK TWAIN

Suicide is a permanent answer to a temporary set of problems.

NBC EVENING NEWS, MARCH 12, 1987

8 Though suicide has been around for as long as recorded history, the word *suicide* is of relatively recent origin. It is not in the Bible, for example, or in the pamphlet by John Donne (1644/1930) on self-homicide. The *Oxford Dictionary* states that suicide was first used in English in 1651, and is derived from the modern Latin "suicidium" ("self" and "to kill") (Farberow, 1975). Probably one of the more famous suicides was Socrates' drinking of hemlock.

Early societies sometimes forced certain members into committing suicide for ritual purposes. Occasionally expected of the wives and slaves of husbands or masters who had died, it was an expression of fidelity and duty. Modern Judaism, which officially regards suicide as a sin, rests upon a long tradition, however, that honors heroic suicides to avoid slavery or rape, or the danger of being forced into idol worship (Curran, 1987). The Old Testament mentions four individuals taking their own lives (Samson, Saul, Abimilech, and Achitophel), and the New Testament records only the suicide of Judas Iscariot, but in no case are their acts condemned in the scriptures (Alvarez, 1971). For Japanese kamikaze pilots in World War II, suicide represented the "great death."

Attitudes toward suicide changed radically when St. Augustine, drawing heavily from the philosophy of Plato and Aristotle, laid down rules against suicide that became the basis for Christian doctrine throughout the succeeding centuries. Societal opposition to suicide in Christian communities continued throughout the Middle Ages, until the Renaissance broadened thinking on the subject. Public and private opinion, however, remained far from unanimous. Even today in the United States, attempted suicide is considered a felony in nine states: Alabama, Kentucky, New Jersey, North and South Carolina, North and South Dakota, Oklahoma, and Washington (Curran, 1987).

The meaning of suicide continues to be problematic. If we accept the definition of suicide as "any death resulting either from a deliberate act of self-destruction or from inaction when it is known that inaction will have fatal consequences" (Theodorson & Theodorson, 1969:427), we could possibly classify the following persons as engaging in suicidal behavior:

1. one who smokes cigarettes, knowing that the Surgeon General has determined that smoking is an important cause of lung cancer

2. a race car driver who drives even though he or she knows that in any given race there is a good chance that someone will be killed

3. one who takes a bottle of sleeping pills, hoping to call attention to oneself as having personal needs that are not being met

4. someone who continues to eat fatty foods after having suffered a heart attack

Doonesbury

BY GARRY TRUDEAU

5. someone in the advanced stages of cancer who refuses chemotherapy or surgery

6. someone who overeats (or undereats) to the extreme that his or her health is directly affected

7. someone with high blood pressure who refuses to take medication to control it or fails to control food intake or to exercise

8. someone who mixes alcohol and drugs

Most of us probably would not consider the above actions as suicidal behaviors, but, rather, we would be concerned with the intent of the person. In classifying deaths as suicides, however, it is difficult to determine the motivations of a person no longer living.

A qualitative difference exists between a suicide gesture and a completed suicide. Suicide gestures are motivated by a need for support from others, while completed suicides are acts of resignation. At this point, we have a problem of tautology—suicide gestures that mistakenly end in death are classified as intentional suicides, and unsuccessful suicide attempts are considered suicide gestures. In addition, suicides are sometimes classified as accidents or natural deaths as a favor to family members or as a method of "providing a more positive view" of the deceased. Thus, there are deaths resulting from intentional acts of self-destruction recorded as "natural deaths," and there are suicidal gestures accidentally ending in death being classified as suicide. Clearly, problems exist in compiling suicide statistics.

In recent years suicide has attracted increasing interest as a large-scale social phenomenon (Battin, 1982). Awareness of the problem has caused both increased scrutiny by sociologists, psychologists, and researchers in other disciplines, and increased efforts to reduce its incidence by physicians, counselors, social workers, and the police. Efforts to seek causes and to reduce the frequency of suicide work together. In recent years, suicide research centers and suicide-prevention services have developed, and the literature on suicide has increased significantly. Even a suicide "cookbook," entitled *Suicide, Its Use, History, Technique and Current Interest* by Claude Guillon and Yves LeBonniec, was published in France in 1982 and soon worked its way to the United States. Box 8.1 discusses the staggering cost of suicide in the United States today.

BOX 8.1   **HUMAN COST FIGURED FOR HOMICIDE, SUICIDE**

Suicide and homicide result in more premature loss of life for Americans each year than anything but accidents, AIDS, cancer, and heart disease. The United States reported 19,796 homicides and 29,286 suicides in 1984. Those intentional killings took from their victims more than 1.2 million "years of potential life" they would have had if they had lived to be 65, according to the National Centers for Disease Control (CDC).

The average suicide occurred at age 43; the average homicide killed a 34-year-old. White males had the highest rate of life lost to suicide, followed by males of other non-black minorities, then black males and white females. Black men, however, had the highest rate of life lost to homicide, followed by black women, non-white males of other minorities and white males.

The Atlanta-based CDC said the statistics "emphasize the urgent need for efforts to prevent premature mortality from suicide among white males and from homicide among black males." Firearms accounted for most of the life lost to both suicide (57 percent) and homicide (61 percent). The CDC called for programs to prevent injuries and deaths from guns.

The CDC studies the loss of "potential life" to gauge the most serious causes of premature death in the United States. Age 65 is used merely as a statistical benchmark; the national life expectancy is actually higher than that. Accidents, the leading cause of premature death, account for about 2.2 million years of potential life lost in the United States each year.

Associated Press. Adapted from *News and Courier,* Charleston, South Carolina, August 21, 1987, p. 13A.

In the United States, more than 28,000 individuals commit suicide each year—one person every twenty minutes (Mayo Clinic, 1985). The number of reported suicides represents only 10 to 15 percent of the people attempting suicide. Thus, suicide is a major concern in the United States today.

THEORETICAL PERSPECTIVES

Sociological Perspective

The most significant contribution on suicide by sociologists has been the sociological perspective itself—the insistence on seeing suicidal actions as in some way the result of social factors (Douglas, 1967:158). Suicidal persons construct meanings of suicide and motivations for committing it out of collective values on which the social structure rests. What constitutes suicide and the reasons for it are both understood through the meanings conferred on it by various persons. Thus, meanings of suicide arise out of what people think, feel, and do about it rather than what occurs in the act. What people think, feel, and do about acts defined as suicide is intertwined with larger social values and meanings (Charmaz, 1980:234).

A comprehensive sociological theory of self-destruction was proposed in 1897 by the noted French sociologist Emile Durkheim entitled *Suicide: A Study in Sociology* (1897/1951). The most frequent interpretation of Durkheim's *Suicide* by American sociologists involves the following propositions (Douglas, 1967:39–40):

1. The structural factors cause certain degrees and certain patterns of social interaction.

2. The degrees and patterns of social interaction then cause a certain degree of "social integration."

3. "Social integration," defined as either states of individuals or as a state of the society, is then defined as the "strength of the individual's ties to society."

4. The "strength of ties" is then defined either in terms of egoism, altruism, and anomie or else the "strength of ties" is hypothesized to be the cause of the given degrees of egoism, altruism, and anomie.

5. Egoism is defined as a relative lack of social or collective activity that gives meaning and object to life; altruism is defined as a relatively great amount of social activity; and anomie is defined as a relative lack of social activity that acts to constrain the individual's passions which, without constraint, increase "infinitely."

6. And, finally, the given balance of the degrees of egoism, altruism, and anomie is hypothesized to be the cause of the given suicide rate of the given society.

Thus, the three types of Durkheim's suicide noted above are related to his conception of social integration. **Egoistic suicide** occurs when the person is inadequately integrated into society, such as the intellectual or the person whose talent or station in life places him or her in a special category (a celebrity or star, for example); such a person is, therefore, less likely to be linked to society in conventional ways. **Altruistic suicide** occurs when the individual is overly integrated into society, has an exaggerated concern for it, and is willing to die for the group; the kamikaze pilots of World War II and the terrorists of today are examples. **Anomic suicide** results from the lack of regulation of the individual, when the norms governing existence no longer control that individual; such a suicide feels betrayed by the failure of social institutions, for example, the person committing suicide after a stock market crash or the loss of a job.

As renowned sociologist Talcott Parsons (1949) interpreted the book (Durkheim, 1897), Durkheim considered altruistic suicide to be largely the result of the external forces of group structure, whereas egoistic suicide was more a result of the internal forces of the "collective conscience"; anomic suicide was seen as almost entirely the result of the internal forces of the "collective conscience."

A fourth type, called **fatalistic suicide,** was also introduced by Durkheim (1897/1951) and has recently received more attention. This type suggests that one may receive too much control by society and feel oppressed under extremely strict rules. In fatalistic suicide, one dies in despair of being able to make it in a society that allows little opportunity for satisfaction or individual fulfillment. Both the altruistic and the fatalistic suicide involve excessive control of the individual by society (Kastenbaum, 1986:205–206).

Dramaturgical Perspective

Derived from the general approach of symbolic interactionism, the **dramaturgical perspective** uses the metaphor of the drama to explain behavior. Rather than inquire into the definition of the situation, the dramaturgical analyst emphasizes the situation that is visible to the observer. When someone commits suicide, for example, the analyst would look at family members' behavior and would assess the meaning of the death to the family as it shows in their actions, rather than words. This approach takes nonverbal behavior into account.

A dramaturgical approach does not accept the social determinist view that social forces motivate the individual to act, but states that motives are invoked after the fact by social actors to explain for past actions (Charmaz, 1980:26–31). Behavior is analyzed from the standpoint of the observer (etic approach) rather than the subject (emic approach). While the dramaturgical analyst emphasizes action, the symbolic interactionist emphasizes intention. Both perspectives lead to an examination of meanings derived from interaction.

A good example of the dramaturgical approach is illustrated by the film entitled "But Jack Was a Good Driver." In this film Jack, a high school student, has died in a single-car accident. As his two friends walk away from the cemetery, they begin to recall recent events involving Jack. As they describe Jack's actions in the preceding weeks, he had flunked a chemistry exam, broken up with his girlfriend, given his record collection away, and acted in unusual ways. They conclude that Jack's "accident" was more likely a suicide, since his recent actions had shown some signs of suicide. The observers (Jack's friends) viewed the actions of the actor (Jack)—the dramaturgical approach.

Existentialist Perspective

Existentialist philosophy acknowledges that human existence is finite and that we all must face death. Each person must assume responsibility for his or her own actions, and be responsible for moral choices and actions. An emphasis is placed on the anticipation of death and the effects of that anticipation on everyday life, thus causing the person to come to an understanding of how death and life are linked. From an existentialist view, it is conceivable that the confrontation with death during a suicidal crisis may cause suicidal individuals to experience aloneness and personal responsibility for their experience. Thus, the manner of death chosen may be fully akin to the manner of life chosen—both are the result of reflection. Death through suicide or any other means is not the enemy that it is in other perspectives (Charmaz, 1980:242).

Existentialism is linked with the phenomenological method of inquiry. This approach starts with an examination of the point of view of the experiencing person. Experience is studied from the inside—from what it appears to be to the involved person. What is dying to those who are experiencing it? This method tries to study the phenomenon directly and to discover how it is constituted. In studying attempted suicide, one would conduct interviews with failed suicides to determine what they were thinking during their crisis. By comparing patterns one can determine parallels among the various suicidal experiences (Charmaz, 1980:51–56).

Alienation

Alienation may occur when an individual feels that he or she is not in control of a situation. Karl Marx, for example, noted that laborers are separated, or alienated from, nature itself, and that capitalism separates workers from each other and from their work. The realization of human potential and creativity is thereby prevented, according to Marx. Thus, alienation results in a loss of self or a lack of self-realization.

A sense of powerlessness may result, leading to hopelessness over time, then a feeling of helplessness (Charmaz, 1980:260). Individuals may not be wholly aware of their alienation and may feel frustrated, worthless, dependent, and powerless without connecting their feelings to the social structure.

This woman contemplates suicide as a solution to her feelings of alienation and social isolation. Her suicide gesture elicits a response from another to indicate the meaningfulness of her life.

These feelings are likely to be intensified by the individuals' acceptance that they reflect who they are and what they may become. Such assessments may lead to feelings of hopelessness. Alienation may, therefore, lead to suicide.

As shown by the above theoretical perspectives on suicide, the "whys" of suicide are not always easy to explain. One thing is clear: For the survivors of a completed suicide, guilt is often associated with the event. Individuals may feel that they contributed to the suicide. "If only" they had acted differently, the suicide might not have happened.

SOCIAL FACTORS, SIGNS, AND METHODS

Social Factors

The relation between suicide and the variables associated with it is not simple and easily understood. Nonetheless, some of these variables include age, sex, marital status, and socioeconomic level (Kastenbaum & Aisenberg,

1976:252–271). As noted later in this chapter, suicide is rare in childhood, rises sharply during adolescence and early adulthood, and peaks with persons aged 75 to 84.

With relation to marital status, the suicide rate is lower for the married than for those never married, and highest for the widowed, divorced, and separated. These data on marital status fit Durkheim's theory that suicide is a function of social integration. Individuals with children commit suicide less than the childless (Ezell, Anspaugh, & Oaks, 1987:164).

Suicide rates tend to be highest at both extremes of the socioeconomic ladder. Certain professions such as physicians, dentists, and lawyers tend to be particularly suicide-prone, while the suicide rates of teachers and clergy are rather low.

More suicides occur in heterogeneous urban areas than in more homogeneous rural areas. Nostalgic times like the Christmas season and "renewal of life" times like spring are the most frequent times of year for suicides, with fewest suicides committed in the summer. Suicides occur most often on Saturday and Monday, the end and beginning of the routine workweek. Protestant faiths have higher rates than Catholics, and the Jewish faith has the highest rate (Ezell, Anspaugh, & Oaks, 1987:164).

Signs

The person who commits suicide will tend to talk about the attempt prior to the act. Repeated talk of killing oneself should be taken seriously. Other than the outright statement "I am going to kill myself," more subtle verbal clues might include "I'm not the person I used to be," "You would be better off without me," "I can't stand it anymore," "Life has lost its meaning for me," and "Nobody needs me anymore."

Behavioral clues might include giving away valued personal possessions, getting one's house in order as if ready for departure, unexplained frequent crying, changes in daily behavior such as beginning to take long walks at night, poor sleeping habits, loss of appetite, inability to concentrate, a sudden change in appearance, a sudden shift in the quality of school work, and the sudden withdrawal from various organizations. The following factors tend to describe an individual at high risk of committing suicide: lethal weapon readily available, history of prior suicide attempts, detailed suicide plan, feelings of hopelessness and helplessness, severe personal loss such as health problems or bereavement, and alcohol or drug abuse (Ezell, Anspaugh, & Oaks, 1987:163).

Methods

Listed in decreasing order of frequency, the ways of committing suicide in the United States are firearms (especially handguns), drug overdose, cutting and stabbing, jumping from high places, toxic gas inhalation, hanging, and drowning (Ezell, Anspaugh, & Oaks, 1987:165). While women *attempt* suicide more often, men more often *complete* suicide. Since men are more likely to use firearms in suicide attempts and women more likely to use drugs, the higher male success rate is clearly at least partially attributable to method chosen.

BOX 8.2 **HOW YOU CAN HELP IN A SUICIDAL CRISIS**

1. *Recognize the clues to suicide.* Look for signs of hopelessness and helplessness. Listen for suicide threats and words of warning. Notice if the person becomes withdrawn and isolated.

2. *Trust your own judgment.* If you believe someone is in danger of suicide, act on your beliefs. Don't ignore the signs of suicide.

3. *Tell others.* Share knowledge with parents, friends, teachers, employers, or other people who might help. If you have to betray a secret to save a life, do it. Don't worry about breaking a confidence if someone's suicidal plans are revealed to you.

4. *Stay with a suicidal person.* Don't leave a suicidal person alone if you think there is immediate danger. Stay until help arrives or the crisis has passed.

5. *Listen.* Encourage a suicidal person to talk. Don't give false reassurances that "everything will be okay." Listen and sympathize with what the person says.

6. *Urge professional help.* Offer to make an appointment for and go with the person for professional help, if that is what it takes. Call your community Hotline or crisis number for suggestions.

7. *Be supportive.* Show the person that you care. Help to make the person feel worthwhile and wanted.

From *Too Young to Die: Youth and Suicide* by Francine Klagsbrun, p. 96. Copyright © 1976 by Francine Klagsbrun. Reprinted by permission of Houghton Mifflin Company.

ADOLESCENT SUICIDAL BEHAVIOR

Suicidal deaths are virtually nonexistent before age 5 and are rare in the age group of 5 to 9 years. The policy of the U.S. Division of Vital Statistics is to not even report the deaths of children under 8 as suicides, regardless of what

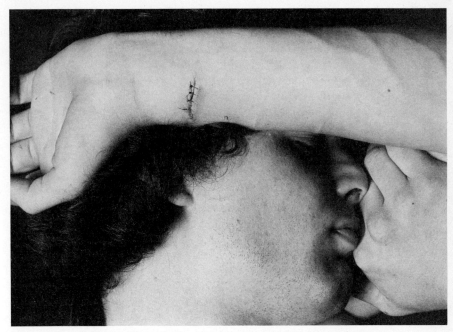

This young man has cut his wrist in a suicide gesture. His problems are now compounded by the fact that he must live with the stigma of a failed suicide attempt.

data may have been entered on a given death certificate—"other," "unknown," and "unspecified causes" are the classifications used for these deaths. Similarly, suicide is uncommon in the cohort of children between the ages of 10 and 14 (Smith, 1985:103). A noticeable shift, however, marks the age group beginning with age 15.

Every 90 minutes one teenager in the United States will take his or her own life, while every nine minutes a teenager will make an attempt to kill himself or herself (Coleman, 1987:1). Adolescent and young-adult suicide is not unique to contemporary times, but the significance of the problem has recently emerged in the United States, especially since 1960. In recent years, the media has called attention to the cluster suicide phenomenon (several suicides occurring in the same community—often teenagers from the same high school) so that parents and educational personnel have become even more aware of the problem.

The suicide rate for the 15-to-24-year-old age group in 1960 was 5.2 per 100,000. By 1980, however, the rate was 12.3 per 100,000. What accounts for this increase? The numbers could reflect a greater willingness today to report a death as a suicide. Also, the taboo nature of identifying suicide is not as significant today as in 1960. Suicide is now the third leading cause of death in this age group (following accidents and homicides), and is the second leading cause of death among persons aged 15 to 19 years (U.S. Vital Statistics, 1981). Since 1980, however, the number of deaths by suicide among teenagers has begun to level off, possibly due to the decline in the use of mind-altering drugs and to the increased attention given to children at risk of taking their own lives (Brody, 1987:16).

Accidents and homicides are viewed by many researchers as disguised suicides (Coleman, 1987:1). Many drug overdoses, fatal automobile accidents, and related self-destructive eating and alcoholic disorders are uncounted teen suicides. Thus, the total number of adolescent suicides may be greater than reported.

Geographically, Nevada is first in youth suicides, and New Mexico is second. In taking their own lives, boys tend to use violent means such as guns and hanging, though girls seem to be turning to violent means also (Brozan, 1986). Perhaps by using violent means, these adolescents are suggesting that they indeed are serious about their attempts. These are more than a "cry for help."

Suicides of individuals within the early stages of life are especially difficult to understand, since adolescents and young adults are just "growing up" and beginning to launch out into the world. On the other hand, complex forces are at work: adolescent frustrations related to growing up and making the transitions to adulthood; others' expectations to "act like an adult," yet at times not being "old enough" for certain behaviors. It is no wonder that the suicide rate in this age group is as high as it is. Suicide becomes an available solution to one's problems. When stress is experienced, a constricted view of future possibilities and a momentary fix on present escapes may hold sway. A tendency to impulsive action and limited alternative problem-solving ability may turn suicidal fantasies into suicidal behaviors. As noted at the beginning of this chapter, suicide is an answer (though permanent) to a set of temporary problems. The problem is gone, but so is life.

The letter below (Berman, 1986:151), written by a 17-year-old who took his life, apparently indicates that death was the solution to this adolescent's dilemmas. He lived with various problems but tended to keep his pain mostly to himself.

Dear Mom, Dad, and everyone else,

I'm sorry for what I've done, but I love you all and I always will, for eternity. Please, please, please don't blame it on yourselves. It was all my fault and not yours or anyone else's. If I didn't do this now, I would have done it later anyway. We all die some day, I just died sooner.

Love,
John

After John's body was found, people began to piece together his life and to fill their own with the inevitable "if only's." This reconstruction of an interpretation after the event of suicide follows the dramaturgical approach. Box 8.3 shows how some colleges are handling suicide threats.

BOX 8.3   **WHAT COLLEGES HAVE LEARNED ABOUT SUICIDE**

DANIEL GOLEMAN

All new students at the University of California, Los Angeles, receive in their registration packet a six-page pamphlet on suicide. Among other things, they are urged to watch for fellow students who exhibit certain warning signs: people who are chronically depressed and hint that they won't be around long, for example, or who give away prized possessions. The booklet lists eight phone numbers for students to call, from the campus counseling center to the university police.

U.C.L.A.'s effort is typical of the reaction at many colleges and universities to the rise in suicides among American youths in the last 30 years. From 1981 to 1983, the rate was about 8.7 per 100,000 youths, compared with 6.9 in 1973. Sometimes, they occur in clusters. This month, three students from the same Omaha high school committed suicide.

A school's role in preventing the deaths of despondent students is complicated by the question of liability. "Say a student who is seeing a college counselor threatens suicide and has a plan, but the therapist does not take the threat seriously," said Gary Pavela, a professor at the University of Maryland Law School. "If the student commits suicide, then both the college and the counselor could be held liable." Leighton Whitaker, a Swarthmore College psychologist who advises college officials on suicides, explained it another way: "A college is under a legal obligation to assess and refer for proper treatment any suicidal student who comes to their attention."

A turning point in colleges' attention to the problem came in 1967, when Congress made it illegal to discriminate against the handicapped, including the emotionally handicapped, in admitting students. This has meant that applicants cannot be asked about psychiatric problems and that a larger number of troubled students may find their way to campuses, Dr. Whitaker said.

In any case, psychologists say, the college community is well-suited to helping troubled young people and preventing suicides. The close

(continued on next page)

contact among students and faculty members heightens the probability of spotting those at risk. Many campuses hold special classes for resident assistants, the students who supervise dormitories. At U.C.L.A., for example, they are instructed to watch for certain danger signs, such as weeping for no apparent reason, drawing back from friends or suffering social or academic crises.

"The resident assistants are told to err on the side of safety," said Morris Holland, an assistant vice chancellor for student development.

"The numbers of suicides here vary greatly from year to year," he continued. "Over the last five years, it has been between one and five each year, on a campus of 35,000 students. It happens rarely, but we're prepared when it does."

"There are about 50 threats for every successful suicide among students," Dr. Whitaker said. And while threats are far more common among college women than among men, men are three to four times more likely to succeed in killing themselves—an imbalance that is also true for the population at large. "Women are more able to cry out for help with their emotional needs than are men," Dr. Whitaker said. "Twice as many women students as men seek help from college counselors. The higher risk is the silent and isolated college man who does not turn to anyone for help."

At Indiana University in Bloomington, resident assistants are warned not to challenge a student who threatens suicide, analyze motives or try to handle the situation themselves. "It's sometimes useful to find a small piece of the problem that can be dealt with positively, such as getting an 'incomplete' on a course the student is worrying about," said Nancy Stockton, a campus psychologist. Students who seem to be at serious risk are often asked to take health leaves and get psychological help, in which case their grades for the last term—which are frequently low—are removed from their transcript. A condition for the student's return may be a letter from a psychotherapist.

"A suicide arouses immense anxiety among everyone who knew the student, as well as a great deal of guilt," said Ben Lieber, dean of students at Amherst College and formerly a dean at Columbia University. "Everyone thinks that if only they had done something else it wouldn't have happened. It helps to be as open as possible with them about the circumstances of the suicide, to let them know how common attempts are and generally to treat it as something that is not shameful, but is genuinely tragic."

The Adolescent in the Family and with Peers

Since adolescents are caught between childhood and adulthood, the often intense and conflictual task of separating from the world of family can be more difficult when family dynamics interfere with the child's move toward self-sufficiency. Parents of suicidal adolescents have been found to display more overt conflict, including threats of separation and divorce. The loss of a parent occurring prior to the child's twelfth year is also positively correlated with suicide. Suicidal adolescents report receiving little affection, hold negative views of their parents, describe time spent in their family as unenjoyable, have been found to have deficient problem-solving skills, tend to have a higher-than-average use of drugs and alcohol, and see themselves as different from their parents (Berman, 1986:157–8).

Active peer involvement may be the support needed to discourage suicide behavior, for such activity is negatively correlated with a depressive mood in adolescence. Suicidal adolescents tend to show greater withdrawal from, and less involvement with, the school milieu. On the other hand, suicidal adolescents tend to have more frequent and serious problems with peers, to be more interpersonally sensitive, and to be less likely to have a close confidant (Berman, 1986:159). Since adolescents are highly suggestible by nature, suicidal adolescents are especially vulnerable to influence since they often lack reinforcing role models. Such adolescents may also be low in self-esteem and ego strength. Thus, suicidal behavior by one may lead to an epidemic of followers.

Teenage Suicide Clusters

Clusters of teenage suicides have been noted in the media, where imitation is generally cited as the cause. Madelyn Gould and David Shaffer (1986) studied the variation in the numbers of suicides and attempted suicides by teenagers in the greater New York area two weeks before and two weeks after four fictional films were broadcast on television in the fall and winter of 1984 and 1985. The number of attempts in the period after the broadcasts was significantly greater than the number before the broadcasts, leading the researchers to conclude that some teenage suicides are imitative.

Another study by David Phillips and Lundie Carstensen (1986) examined the relation between 38 nationally televised news or feature stories about suicide from 1973 to 1979 and the fluctuation of the rate of suicide among American teenagers before and after these stories. The observed number of teenage suicides within seven days after these broadcasts was significantly greater than the number expected. The more networks carrying a story on suicide, the greater was the increase in suicides thereafter. Teenage suicides increased more than adult suicides after stories about suicide. The researchers concluded that the best available explanation is that television stories on suicide trigger additional suicides, perhaps because of imitation (Phillips & Carstensen, 1986).

Age by itself does not *cause* suicidality. The person most vulnerable to suicide in the United States, however, is a white male between the ages of 75 and 84. The traditional, assertive, achievement-oriented role of a typical, middle-aged male may not be as adaptable to the retirement situation as the traditionally more passive, nurturant role assumed by a typical, middle-aged woman. Thus, the greater change in behavior and self-esteem necessitated in the older man may create more stress and depression if he is unable to find satisfaction in this new situation. A greater potential for suicidal behavior results (Aiken, 1982:114).

Danger Signals and Methods

The *threat* of suicide is uncommon in the aged—they simply kill themselves, and their attempts rarely fail. Danger signals for suicide among the elderly include depression, withdrawal, bereavement (especially within the last year), isolation, expectation of death from some cause, retirement, loss of independence, physical illness, desire and rational decision to protect survivors from financial disaster, philosophical decision (e.g., no more pleasure or purpose in life), decreased self-esteem, and organic mental deterioration (Eddy & Alles, 1983:169–171).

Frequent methods used by the elderly to kill themselves are guns, drugs, hanging, and jumping. More subtle means, such as not eating, not taking medication, drinking too much, delaying medical treatment, or taking physical risks, are also used (Ezell, Anspaugh, & Oaks, 1987:171). Sometimes the elderly will "give up" psychologically, and this triggers biological changes that increase potential for disease.

Robert Kastenbaum (1986:196) notes other findings about suicide in later life: (1) Most elderly people do *not* have suicidal thoughts. (2) When suicidal intentions exist, the probability of a completed act of self-destruction is higher than at other ages. (3) Suicidality is less frequent among married older people who stay in touch with their children and relatives, and who have not had a suicide or an attempt in their family. (4) The suicidal older person is more depressed and sees self-destruction as an acceptable action.

Rational Suicide

There have been times in history when misery was so common and the outlook so bleak that suicide probably seemed a reasonable option. As Mark Twain was quoted at the beginning of the chapter, there are times in life when we would like to die temporarily. The Judeo-Christian tradition, however, has generally advocated life and strongly urged that life not be disposed of, no matter what the situation. For the elderly, to decide to take one's life tends to be a more rational or philosophical decision. As we saw in Chapter 7 in the discussion on euthanasia, elderly individuals and others today seem to be asking if life is to be valued under all conditions because it has intrinsic value, or if the value of life is relative to the circumstances. Box 8.4 describes one couple's final days, and suggests that the value of life for them *was* relative to the circumstances.

BOX 8.4

AFTER 60 YEARS OF MARRIAGE, COUPLE DECIDES TO LEAVE WORLD TOGETHER

Julia Saunders, 81, had her hair done. Her husband, Cecil, 85, collected the mail one final time and paused to chat with a neighbor. Inside their mobile home, they carefully laid out a navy blazer and a powder-blue dress.

After lunch, the Saunders drove to a rural corner of Lee County and parked. As cows grazed in the summer heat, the couple talked. Then Cecil Saunders shot his wife of 60 years in the heart and turned the gun on himself.

Near the clothes they had chosen to be buried in, the couple had left a note:

"Dear children, this we know will be a terrible shock and embarrassment. But as we see it, it is one solution to the problem of growing old. We greatly appreciate your willingness to try to take care of us.

After being married for 60 years, it only makes sense for us to leave this world together because we loved each other so much."

On the floorboard of the car, Cecil and Julia Saunders had placed typewritten funeral instructions and the telephone numbers of their son and daughter.

Then they consummated their suicide pact, becoming two of the more than 4,000 elderly Americans authorities say will commit suicide this year.

"What struck all of us was how considerate, how thoughtful they were to all concerned about killing themselves," said Sheriff's Sergeant Richard Chard, who investigated the August 19 murder–suicide. "They didn't want to impose or be a bother to anyone. Not even in dying."

Julia's dimming eyesight, heart congestion and a stroke had driven Cecil to place his wife in a nursing home earlier this year. But she became hysterical over what she said was poor care there, and Cecil brought her home, said neighbors at the mobile home park where the couple had lived since 1974.

(continued on next page)

Box 8.4, continued

"You never saw him without her," said Vera Whittimore, 67. "If there ever was true love, they had it. I think they were just tired of living and couldn't wait for God to take them."

The Saunders had hot dogs and beans for lunch, then drove their Caprice to pastureland 5½ miles from their mobile home, parking on the grassy shoulder.

As thunderstorms rumbled in the distance, they talked.

"I can picture in my mind them sitting there," Chard said. "Maybe they spoke about how things were when they were young. Then he leaned over and gave her a farewell kiss."

The bodies were found by workers from nearby Owl Creek Boat Works, who called police.

In Philadelphia, a police officer stood by as the Saunders' son, Robert, 57, was told of his parents' death. His parents wanted no tears shed over their decision to die. The note they left for Robert and his sister, Evelyn, 51, ended with a wish:

"Don't grieve because we had a very good life and saw our two children turn out to be such fine persons. Love, Mother and Father."

Associated Press. *Minneapolis Star and Tribune,* October 4, 1983, p. 12A.

While suicide is usually treated as the product of mental illness or a desperate cry for help used by someone who does not really want to die, it can be considered a rational act. **Rational suicide** is presumably suicide in which the individual is not insane, in which the decision is reached in unimpaired, undeceived fashion, and in which the choice made is not a bad thing for that individual to do (Battin, 1982). Certainly, one could argue that the Saunders' behavior, described in Box 8.4, was rational homicide/suicide. Seeming to fit the case of the Saunders is Jacques Choron's description (1972:96–97) of rational suicide as implying "not only that there is no psychiatric disorder but also that the reasoning of the suicidal person is in no way impaired and that his motives would seem justifiable, or at least 'understandable,' by the majority of his contemporaries in the same culture or social group."

Richard Brandt (1986:339) notes that the person contemplating suicide is clearly making a choice between future world courses—one future world course that includes his or her imminent demise versus several possible ones that contain death at a later point. While one cannot have precise knowledge about many features of the latter category of world courses, it is certain that all scenarios end with death sooner or later. To determine the best (or rational) choice, the person must answer one question: Which option would I choose if I had the best information, when all my personal desires are taken into account? It is not just a question of what is preferred now.

Certainly one's desires, aversions, and preferences may change after a short while. When one is in a state of despair, nothing but the thing he or she cannot have—the love of a particular person or a job, for example—may seem desirable. The passage of time is likely to reverse all this. If one acts, then, on the preferences of today alone, when the emotion of despair seems more than one can stand, death might seem preferable to life. If one allows for the preferences of the weeks and years ahead, however, when many goals might be enjoyable and attractive, life might be found to be preferable to death. Thus, Brandt (1986) is suggesting that a future world course might well be different from that of the hour.

Brandt (1986) further suggests that one must take into account the infirmities of one's "sensing" machinery. Knowing that the machinery is out of order will not tell one what results it would give if it were working. Thus, the best recourse might be to refrain from making any decision in a stressful frame of mind. If decisions have to be made, one must recall past reactions made in a normal frame of mind to events such as those of the moment. To the Saunders after 80 years of life, the future world course clearly does not look to be "enjoyable and attractive."

CONCLUSION

Just what constitutes a suicide is not clear today. Many persons display suicidal behavior with constant risk taking and gambling with their lives. If death results from such behavior, however, it is often classified as accidental or natural. Sociologists argue that suicidal persons construct their meanings of suicide and motivations for committing it out of collective values upon which the social structure rests. Meanings of suicide arise out of what people think, feel, and do.

Suicidal persons are more likely to be adolescents or very elderly, male, and alone. Though age by itself does not cause suicidality, the person most vulnerable to suicide is a white male between the ages of 75 and 84. Suicidal persons tend to talk about the attempt prior to the act and often display observable signs of suicide. Males are perhaps more successful at completing suicide than females because they tend to use a more lethal weapon—firearms. For suicidal persons, this act becomes an easy solution to their problems—a permanent answer to a temporary set of problems. Suicide can be a rational act, and one does not have to be insane to take one's own life.

BOX 8.5 **A FEW WORDS ON SUICIDE: DON'T TRY IT!**

A few months ago, I tried to commit suicide. The reason I did this was that I could no longer find happiness within me. I know that sorrow and pain are parts of life, but so are joy and laughter. I wasn't getting enough of the happiness that should be in everyone's life. I felt that, no matter how hard I tried to be a good, kind, thoughtful person, I failed. My best just wasn't good enough for people. This was making me miserable, and a miserable person is a burden to others. I didn't want to live the rest of my life feeling the way I was feeling, so I decided to end it all and find out what my Lord thought of me. It was wrong. I know that society thinks it's wrong. That's why, when I made the decision to commit suicide, I really wanted to die. Having to survive and face the music, so to speak, seemed worse than death itself.

I'm hoping now, though, that you won't make me feel as though I should be ashamed of myself. You see, I'm really glad to be alive, and I even believe I have a bright future. Someday I might even have children, and I don't want them to think badly of me. I know they won't if you don't.

I've learned to be stronger: I've done this by becoming a little more selfish. But that is necessary, or else you'll lose yourself to others and become their puppet. I've learned to make demands of others. The big one I'm making now is that you just keep giving me affection.

Sincerely,
Don't Try Suicide

Taken from the *Boston Globe*, Boston, MA, July 7, 1981, p. B13.

In the event that one does not take the advice in Box 8.5 and suicide is completed, we provide some suggestions for dealing with the aftermath of suicide.

1. Be available to the survivors by taking the initiative to help. Do not hesitate to visit them, even if you do not know what to say. Just being present shows that you care.

2. Discourage guilt feelings for suicide tends to result from long-term feelings. Thus, grievers should not blame themselves with the "if only" feelings.

3. Be truthful and honest at all times.

4. Discourage self-pity and encourage the individual to become involved in activities.

5. Encourage the griever to express his or her real feelings. Help guide the individual toward thinking ahead to the future.

SUMMARY

1. Suicide has been around for as long as recorded history.

2. Suicide has historically been viewed in different ways in different places.

3. The meaning of suicide is problematic.

4. In the late 1800s French sociologist Emile Durkheim noted that suicide is related to one's degree of social integration.

5. The dramaturgical approach to suicide uses action or the metaphor of the drama to explain behavior.

6. The existentialist perspective on suicide may view the choice of death as being like the choice of life—both the result of reflection; death is not seen as "the enemy."

7. If one feels alienated and powerless, suicide may appear to be a solution.

8. The person most vulnerable to suicide in the United States is a white male between the ages of 75 and 84.

9. The person who commits suicide will tend to talk about it prior to the act.

10. The most frequent method of completed suicide is firearms.

11. The rational suicide approach suggests that a person does not have to be mentally ill to take his or her own life.

12. Some researchers have concluded that the media contribute to cluster suicides by teenagers.

DISCUSSION QUESTIONS

1. Discuss why the meaning of suicide continues to be problematic today.

2. Give examples of Durkheim's four types of suicide.

3. How does the dramaturgical approach view suicide?

4. How does an existentialist philosophy perspective explain suicide?

5. Describe signs of suicide. What should you do if you observe some of these signs in a friend?

6. Discuss why the suicide rate tends to be high among adolescents and the elderly.

7. The term *rational suicide* implies that one does not have to be mentally ill to take one's own life. Discuss whether you feel that one can be sane and take one's own life.

8. Discuss your reaction to Julia and Cecil Saunders' deaths.

GLOSSARY

Alienation   A cause of suicide in which one does not feel in control and does not feel a part of a situation, often resulting in a lack of self-realization and a feeling of powerlessness and hopelessness.

Altruistic suicide   A form of suicide in which the individual is overly integrated into society and willing to die for the group.

Anomic suicide   A form of suicide that results from a lack of regulation of the individual when the norms governing existence no longer control that individual.

Dramaturgical perspective   An approach to suicide that uses the metaphor of the drama to explain behavior.

Egoistic suicide   A form of suicide in which the person is inadequately integrated into the society.

Existentialist philosophy   An approach to suicide which states that the manner of death chosen may be like the manner of life chosen; death is not the enemy as viewed by some perspectives, but is, rather, the result of reflection.

Fatalistic suicide   A form of suicide in which the individual experiences too much control by society, possibly leading to feelings of oppression under extremely strict rules.

Rational suicide   A form of suicide in which the individual is not insane and is aware of what he or she is doing.

REFERENCES

Aiken, Lewis R. 1982. *Later Life,* Second Ed. New York: Holt, Rinehart and Winston.
Alvarez, A. 1971. *The Savage God: A Study of Suicide.* London: Weidenfeld and Nicolson.

Battin, Margaret P. 1982. *Ethical Issues in Suicide.* Englewood Cliffs, NJ: Prentice-Hall.

Berman, Alan L. 1986. "Helping Suicidal Adolescents: Needs and Responses." In Charles A. Corr & Joan N. McNeil (Eds.), *Adolescence and Death.* New York: Springer Verlag, pp. 151–166.

Boston Globe. 1981. "A Few Words on Suicide: Don't Try It." July 7, p. 13B.

Brandt, Richard B. 1986. "The Morality and Rationality of Suicide." In Robert F. Weir (Ed.), *Ethical Issues in Death and Dying,* Second Ed. New York: Columbia University Press, pp. 330–344.

Brody, Jane E. 1987. "Child Suicides: Common Causes." *The New York Times.* March 3, p. 16.

Brozan, Nadine. 1986. "Adolescent Suicides: The Grim Statistics." *The New York Times.* January 13, p. 16.

Charmaz, Kathy. 1980. *The Social Reality of Death.* Reading, MA: Addison Wesley.

Choron, Jacques. 1972. *Suicide.* New York: Scribner's.

Coleman, Loren. 1987. *Suicide Clusters.* Boston: Faber & Faber.

Curran, David K. 1987. *Adolescent Suicidal Behavior.* Washington, DC: Hemisphere.

Donne, John. 1930. *Biathanatos,* reprint of the first edition, 1644. New York: Facsimile Text Society.

Douglas, Jack D. 1967. *The Social Meanings of Suicide.* Princeton, NJ: Princeton University Press.

Durkheim, Emile. 1951. *Suicide: A Study in Sociology.* New York: Free Press. (Originally published in 1897.)

Eddy, James M., & Wesley F. Alles. 1983. *Death Education.* St. Louis: Mosby.

Ezell, Gene, David J. Anspaugh, & Judy Oaks. 1987. *Death and Dying: From a Health and Sociological Perspective.* Scottsdale, AZ: Gorsuch Scarisbrick.

Farberow, Norman L. 1975. *Suicide in Different Cultures.* Baltimore, MD: University Park Press.

Goleman, Daniel. 1986. "What Colleges Have Learned about Suicide." *The New York Times.* February 23.

Gould, Madelyn S., & David Shaffer. 1986. "The Impact of Suicide in Television Movies." *The New England Journal of Medicine, 315* (September 11), pp. 690–694.

Guillon, Claude, & Yves LeBonniec. 1982. *Suicide, Its Use, History, Technique and Current Interest.* Paris: Editions Alain Moreais.

Kastenbaum, Robert J. 1986. *Death, Society and Human Experience,* Third Ed. Columbus, OH: Merrill.

Kastenbaum, Robert, & Ruth Aisenberg. 1976. *The Psychology of Death.* New York: Springer Verlag.

Klagsbrun, Francine. 1976. *Youth and Suicide.* New York: Pocket Books.

Mayo Clinic. 1985. "Suicide in America." *Mayo Clinic Health Letters* (September).

Minneapolis Star and Tribune. 1983. "After 60 Years of Marriage, Couple Decides to Leave World Together." October 4, p. 12A.

News and Courier. 1989. "Human Cost Figured for Homicide, Suicide." Charleston, SC, August 21.

Parsons, Talcott. 1949. *The Structure of Social Action.* New York: The Free Press.

Phillips, David P., & Lundie L. Carstensen. 1986. "Clustering of Teenage Suicides after Television News Stories about Suicide." *The New England Journal of Medicine, 315* (September 11), pp. 685–689.

Smith, Walter J. 1985. *Dying in the Human Life Cycle.* New York: Holt, Rinehart and Winston.

Theodorson, George A., & Achilles G. Theodorson. 1969. *Modern Dictionary of Sociology.* New York: Thomas Y. Crowell.

U.S. Vital Statistics. 1981.

SUGGESTED READINGS

Corr, Charles A., & Joan N. McNeil. 1986. *Adolescence and Death.* New York: Springer Verlag.

An anthology covering numerous issues on adolescence and death, this book devotes one section to helping suicidal adolescents and the survivors of suicide.

Curran, David K. 1987. *Adolescent Suicidal Behavior.* Washington, DC: Hemisphere.

Based on the premise that suicidal adolescents are significantly disturbed and historically troubled individuals, much of this book on adolescent suicidal behavior in America is devoted to discussion of suicide attempts rather than completed suicides.

deCatanzaro, Denys. 1981. *Suicide and Self-Damaging Behavior: A Sociobiological Perspective.* New York: Academic.

Covers a broad spectrum of the many aspects of suicide.

Johnson, S. W., & L. J. Maile. 1987. *Suicide and the Schools: A Handbook for Prevention, Intervention, and Rehabilitation.* Springfield, IL: Thomas.

A good reference for school personnel working with students.

Weir, Robert F. 1986. *Ethical Issues in Death and Dying,* Second Ed. New York: Columbia University Press.

While this anthology is broader in scope than suicide, nonetheless a large segment of the book is devoted to ethical issues surrounding it.

CHAPTER 9

Children and Death

—

The way I see it, we die in the same order we were born. It's the only fair way of working it!

CHARLES SCHULZ AND KENNETH F. HALL, *Two-by-Fours*

9 Despite a new openness to death in the United States, as discussed in Chapter 1, children are generally not encouraged to express themselves on the topic of dying and death. As Jane Sahler (1978:XV) in writing about children and death notes, "One of the fascinating things about children is the naive, simplistic way in which they approach the unknown. Yet it is this very naiveté that makes their questions the most difficult to answer." Children usually have no prior experience on which to base their reactions, thus their earliest death experiences are unique to each of them.

Research on very young children's conceptions of death still does not have an adequate understanding of their responses. Yet there is a need to look more carefully at the dynamics of the young and their families relating to the concept of death. This chapter will address children's understanding of death from a developmental perspective—breaking the children into age groups. As with any life cycle approach, the division lines between ages often overlap rather than serve as clear-cut absolute divisions. However, this is a way to understand children's conceptions of death at various ages of their lives.

The chapter will also discuss dying children and their parents and siblings and how to explain death to children. In trying to understand children's concepts of death and of their dying, we must also include significant others involved in this relationship.

CHILDREN'S UNDERSTANDING OF DEATH

A child growing up in the United States today seldom experiences many aspects of the life cycle. Replacing life on the farm near grandparents and other extended family, as was the case earlier in the century, urbanization and mobility have contributed to a separation from this older generation and other extended family. Thus, the child today is often removed from dying grandparents due to distance or their removal to a hospital or nursing home.

Largely gone are the days when the child lives in the household with a dying grandparent. Death has been moved from the home to more institutionalized settings, a fact summed up by the statement of the little boy who said, "I don't want to go to the hospital because that is where you go to die." That is where Grandfather had been taken the last time the little boy saw him alive. After going to the hospital, Grandfather had become a corpse. The process of the grandfather's dying was not part of the daily routine in the family's home.

Gone are the days when the majority of children were reared on farms experiencing the life cycle daily—animals were born and animals died. Birth and death were commonplace to their socialization. Gone are the days when siblings and relatives were born at home and died at home.

The media expose children to dying and death, but often on television death is viewed as reversible—an individual "dies" on a program this week and reappears in another show the next week. Thus, a child today can acquire the idea that death is only temporary, having received his or her only death education from the media. A shortcoming of television as a death educator for children is its inability to respond to questions children may have. One cannot call into the set and expect to receive an answer. One little boy, raised in the television era, expressed his confusion with this question, "Dad, are we alive or on tape?" Another boy, upon being told that his grandfather had died, asked, "Who shot him?" He was so accustomed to seeing people die from gunshots on television that this was his concept of death.

The process and the event are, therefore, removed and foreign to children. This fact exaggerates their natural tendency to deny the facts of death. Just how do children conceptualize death? While the following discussion looks at children in various age groups, one must remember that ages and stages are in no way absolute. Each child must be interpreted with an understanding of his or her experience and the family's cultural heritage.

Birth to Age 3

By six months an infant perceives differences in caregivers and the degree to which physical and emotional needs are being met. One cannot have a concept of death until the beginning of thought, as evidenced by the emergence of symbolic function between 18 and 24 months. It has been suggested that the origin of death anxiety is in the traumatic separation from mother at the time of birth (Hostler, 1978:7). The delight of peek-a-boo lies in the relief of the intermittent terror of separation. Under age five, death is perceived as separation, but separation from one's caregiver is a terrifying thought.

Erik Erikson (1963) observed that an infant "decides" early in life whether the universe is a warm and loving place to be. On this primitive, yet momentous, early subconscious conclusion is based, to a large degree, the ability to deal with threats and difficulties in later life. We must not assume that the small child has no concept or grasp at all of death, and we must be concerned about the effects of a given death upon his or her life.

A toddler recognizes that a pet is alive and a table is not. The toddler's vocabulary normally includes "to die" by age two and a half and "to live" by age three (Hostler, 1978:7). While the two-year-old child dying in a hospital has no real concept of his or her death, he or she does have a real appreciation of the altered patterns of care and the separation from usual caregivers.

Psychologist Jean Piaget concluded that children progress in stages of cognitive development, with each qualitatively better than the preceding one (Ginsburg & Opper, 1979). Small children can grieve over the loss of something only at the point that they have realized that things (and people) are not permanent. This quality, which he called *object constancy*, would have to precede any sense of loss. Piaget observed that this happens somewhere around one year to 18 months of age.

Ages 3 through 5

From stepping on an ant to seeing a dead animal lying beside the road to losing a beloved pet, the first experience of most children with death often involves an animal.

The permanency of death is not clear in early childhood, as evidenced by this story told to the author about a three-and-a-half-year-old whose father had been killed six months earlier in an auto accident. One day the little boy's mother came in and said, "I have a surprise for you." The little boy replied, "Is Daddy coming home?" On another occasion, this same little

Regardless of how much adults may wish to protect their children from death, it will always be a part of a child's experience.

boy was building a miniature house. He placed a person inside it, and was asked to identify the individual. "Oh, that's Daddy. He's asleep for 100 years." Daddy is not dead; he is simply away on a trip or in a deep sleep. Death is not permanent to young children.

When our daughter was five years old, she attended the funeral of an elderly friend of ours. After the service and the final viewing, the casket was closed and sealed. At this point Cindy tugged on my coat, and I bent down on my knees to have horizontal eye contact with her (life is a world of knees to small children). "But, Daddy, how is Mrs. Kirby going to breathe in there?" she asked. Again, for a five-year-old it is difficult to grasp a concept of death. Death is still not permanent, since one still needs to breathe.

The practicality of young children comes out in another story of a five-year-old whose mother had died. While waiting in the airport to fly from Kentucky to Texas to bury the child's mother, she looked up at her father and said, "Daddy, can you cook?" In this traditional family, where the father brought home the bacon, and the mother cooked it, the child's concern was whether or not the father could fill the lost role.

Maria Nagy (1948) interviewed 378 Hungarian children from three to 10 years of age, ranging across a broad spectrum intellectually and religiously. She asked the younger children to draw pictures concerning death, and those over seven to write down everything they could think of about death. Children aged three to five found death to be reversible and not final; separation and abandonment are, therefore, seen as equivalent to death.

Since Nagy's research was conducted in the 1930s in Hungary, one could surmise that many children had heard much about death from relatives and neighbors who had gone through World War I in Europe. Children's deaths were much more common than in the current era.

Ages 6 to 10

At the age of six the better coordinated child has such motor mastery that he or she can ride a bicycle without holding the handles and can sing a song at the same time. The child begins to view the world from an external point of view, and language skills are becoming communicative and less egocentric. The first major separation from home occurs, and the child enters the world of school where teachers and adults other than parents become the models for identification. While magical thinking persists, the child gains in the ability to test reality (Hostler, 1978:11).

A sense of moral judgment continues to develop during ages six to 10. The child attains an understanding that rules are of human origin, and that he or she can participate in their origin and modification. The child is mastering school and social skills, and interprets that experience based on an external point of view—schoolmates, teachers, other adults, readings, and the media.

Calvin and Hobbes by Bill Watterson

Reprinted by special permission of Universal Press Syndicate.

Between the ages of six and 10, the evolution of the concept of death as a permanent cessation of life begins. However, the cognitive obstacles to abstract thought—the child's persistence in egocentrism, animism, and magical thinking—prevent its completion. Psychosocial experiences at home and in one's community influence the development of the death concept (Hostler, 1978:16). Death is linked to forces in the outside world and becomes

> scary, frightening, disturbing, dangerous, unfeeling, unhearing, or silent. Death can be invisible as a ghost, or ugly like a monster, or it can be a skeleton. Death can be a person, a companion of the devil, a giver of illness, or even an angel (Lonetto, 1980).

Death is viewed as a *taker,* something violent that comes and gets you like a burglar or a ghost. It is personified, an external agent that catches you—a scary skeleton or a bogeyman to be run away from or handled by magic. Though death is beginning to be viewed as final, one can outmaneuver it. Children in this age group do not accept the fact that death must happen to everyone, especially them. There is a fear, however, that it is contagious, something that can be caught like a cold (Schaefer & Lyons, 1986:20–21).

BOX 9.1   **MOTHER GOOSE: TEACHER OF DEATH**

> Childhood, a famous poet once wrote, is "the kingdom where nobody dies."
>
> A University of Minnesota psychologist would take issue with that. To illustrate his thesis, Dr. John Brantner tells this story:
>
> > A young couple was determined to shield their children from the facts of death. They took extraordinary precautions never to mention the word, or allude to the eventual fate of all men. One day they were at a rented beach house, about ready to romp down to the ocean for a day in the sun, when the father glanced out the window and saw a dead dog in the road they

would have to cross. Quickly he drew the blinds and, while his wife distracted the children, called the proper authorities and told them to come and get the carcass.

Within the hour the victim of a speeding motorist had been removed and the father, peeking through the blinds, told his wife it was all right to go to the beach. The family got outside and was about to cross the road separating the beach house from the shore when the little girl looked up at her father and asked, "Daddy, what happened to the dead dog?"

Brantner believes that, by the time children are able to speak, they have some awareness of the reality of death. How do they learn about it?

One way is TV. Brantner cites a recent study which found that, on the average, a child who watches the tube for ten years will see no fewer than 13,500 violent deaths. "And the odds are great that he doesn't see a single natural death," the psychologist adds.

Another, surprising teacher of death is that nice little old lady, Mother Goose. Brantner pulls out the comprehensive *Oxford Dictionary of Nursery Rhymes* as evidence. Consider *The Death and Burial of Poor Cock Robin.*

Who killed Cock Robin?
"I," said the sparrow,
"With my little bow and arrow,
I killed Cock Robin."

Who saw him die?
"I," said the fly,
"With my little eye,
I saw him die."

And on it goes, through the funeral, grave digging, burial, and final tolling of the bell.

Consider this little ditty:

There was an old woman who had three sons,
    Jerry and James and John,
Jerry was hanged, James was drowned,
    John was lost and never was found;
And there was an end of her three sons,
    Jerry and James and John!

Rhymes were a common conveyance of such grim news, Brantner believes, because, back when the classic children's verse came to be,

(continued on next page)

death was much more of an immediate reality for those who recited them. "Until 1900," the professor said, "67 percent of everyone who died was under the age of 15. It was a common part of growing up that you had younger brothers and sisters who died."

Verses not only described peaceful passings. They also were not hesitant to speak of murder, drownings, hangings, and other violent ends, all in light couplet. And death became the ultimate punishment.

Barnaby Bright was a sharp cur,
He always would bark if a mouse did but stir,
But now he's grown old, and can no longer bark,
He's condemned by the parson to be hanged by the clerk.

Or this one . . . :

Little Dicky Dilver
Had a wife of silver;
He took a stick and broke her back
And sold her to the miller;
The miller wouldn't have her
So he threw her in the river.

Death was to be mourned, the rhymes told their reciters:

Granfa' Grig had a pig
    In a field of clover;
Piggie died, Granfa' cried
    And all the fun was over.

Fatalism? That can be found, too, as in:

Now I lay me down to sleep,
I pray the Lord my soul to keep;
And if I die before I wake,
I pray the Lord my soul to take.

Nature's destruction of the body comes across grotesquely in this bit of verse:

On looking up, on looking down
She saw a dead man on the ground;
And from his nose unto his chin,
The worms crawled out, the worms crawled in.

Then she unto the parson said,
Shall I be so when I am dead?
O yes, O yes, the parson said,
You will be so when you are dead.

Even pitiful but benign Old Mother Hubbard recounts death, with a magical twist. The second stanza goes like this:

She went to the baker's
　To buy him some bread;
But when she came back
　The poor dog was dead.

She went to the undertaker's
　To buy him a coffin;
But when she came back
　The poor dog was laughing.

What's a child to make of that?

There's little doubt about life's brevity, however, in this well-known rhyme:

Solomon Grundy,
Born on a Monday,
Christened on Tuesday,
Married on Wednesday,
Took ill on Thursday,
Worse on Friday,
Died on Saturday,
Buried on Sunday,
This is the end
Of Solomon Grundy.

Your kids don't hear nursery verse? What about fairy tales? Again, the classics are rife with violence and death.

Remember what the giant in *Jack and the Beanstalk* repeated with lust?

Fee-fi-fo-fum,
I smell the blood of an Englishman.
Be he alive, or be he dead,
I'll grind his bones to make my bread.

Hansel and Gretel roast the witch in her own oven. Dorothy is trapped in Oz until the wicked witch of the west could be liquidated.

And Henny-Penny, the paranoid little chick who thought the sky was falling down, leads four friends, Turkey-Lurkey, Goosey-Poosey, Duckey-Daddles and Cocky-Locky, to decapitation by the fox.

Bluebeard, a misogynist turned mass murderer, began as a children's story.

(continued on next page)

Some tales have been changed. In the first version of *The Three Little Bears* there is no Goldilocks, but a little old woman who plays the intruder. Upon being discovered by the Bears she jumps out the window to an uncertain fate. The narrator speculates that she possibly broke her neck.

Before Walt Disney got hold of them, the Three Little Pigs were a morbid bunch. The wolf consumed the first two for lunch, but the third, who declined his invitations to dinner, boiled the beast and ate him for supper. And lived happily ever after.

Richard Gibson, *The Minneapolis Star,* Minneapolis, MN, April 11, 1973, p. 1C. Reprinted with permission of the Star Tribune.

EXPLAINING DEATH TO CHILDREN

Robert Kavanaugh (1972:126), a psychologist and former priest, refers to children as "little people." He sees them as "compact cars instead of Cadillacs," traveling the same roads of life and going the same places as big cars. While they are more vulnerable and fragile, they have all the parts and purposes of big people. They are ready and capable to talk about anything within the framework of their own experience. Little people can handle any situation adults can handle comfortably and should do anything big people should do, as long as they are physically able, notes Kavanaugh (1972:137).

Too often we big people fail to give the little people credit, and we try to shield them from information. Rather than their not being able to take it, could it not be that it is we who feel uncomfortable talking about death, and thus avoid the topic altogether? Avoidance is not the best solution, as noted in this example of needless worry and frustration (Dickinson, 1986:83):

> A four-year-old girl was not told about her puppy's traumatic death by a mowing machine for two or three weeks afterwards. She was allowed to search for him "frantically" every day. She even put out food and would worry at night that he was cold or hungry.

John Bowlby (1980) argues that young children can mourn in a similar way to healthy adults. For this to happen, the child should participate fully in what is taking place during and after the death. Rather than withhold information, parents should encourage questions and give answers. Kavanaugh (1972:132) suggests that we allow children to talk freely and ask their own questions, without any adult speeches or philosophic nonanswers, let them ramble, talk crudely if they wish, change the subject, or present unanswerable questions without being squelched. The child should always be supported in a "comforting way" with an assurance of a continued relationship.

Be Honest and Open

Being honest and straightforward with children in talking about dying and death is a good rule of thumb. To give concrete answers, rather than abstract ones, is a realistic way to handle the topic. Answer the child's questions as they are asked. If your answer is unsatisfactory, the child will probably ask a follow-up question in a few seconds or a few hours. If the child asks something you cannot answer, be honest and say you do not know. If you cannot explain something, find someone who can.

Answer directly, but do not be too detailed with your responses. When a small child asks where they came from, you do not go into minute detail about the sperm and the ovum forming a zygote. You state that you came from your mother. If the child is not satisfied, the next question may then be, "How did I get in my Mommy?" At this point, I refer the question to Mother.

The same is true if the child asks, "Daddy, what makes the car run?" I tell him that the car has an engine. If he or she then asks a follow-up question as to what makes the engine run, I refer the child to our local mechanic, since my technical skills are severely limited. The point is that the child's questions should be answered *as they occur*, not postponed in the hope that they will be forgotten.

If parents are open to discussing death, opportunities will present themselves such as dead flies, mosquitoes, birds, and animals beside the road. When the explanation is postponed until the death of someone or something deeply loved by the child, either the emotional turmoil will complicate the acceptance of the reality of death or the concept of death may preclude for that occasion the appropriate emotional response.

To bury a deceased pet is a positive learning exercise in relating to death. The animal is cold, still, and not alive—it is dead. That is reality. For parents *and* children, conducting the burial together can be a very meaningful experience.

BOX 9.2   **OPEN COMMUNICATION IS IMPORTANT**

> As we listen to our children, remember that it's important to make sure that we hear what they're saying, not what we *think* they should be saying. We might expect our child to feel lonely or sad, but what comes out of him is that he's relieved or feeling guilty that the person died.
>
> *(continued on next page)*

His feelings may be very different from what we ourselves are feeling. The temptation is to try and change him.

Telling a child he shouldn't feel a certain way, judging his feelings, is an automatic turn-off. Don't judge him, just listen. He has a right to his feelings. They're part of him and he needs to work them out. What he needs to know is that he is not alone; that you're there to help him; that you accept the way he is, bad feelings and all; and that you're trying to empathize. Maybe you've felt that way, too—if so, you can understand what's happening inside him right now. Reassure him that it's okay, it's normal to have these emotions, and that eventually the pain will pass.

Dan Schaefer & Christine Lyons. 1986. *How Do We Tell the Children? A Parent's Guide to Helping Children Understand and Cope When Someone Dies.* New York: Newmarket Press, p. 85.

Avoid Euphemisms

Try to avoid **euphemisms,** softer but less accurate terms, when talking to a child about death. Use words such as *dead, stopped working,* and *wore-out*—simple words to establish the fact that the body is biologically dead (Schaefer & Lyons, 1986:31). One child was told that Grandfather's heart was bad and stopped working. This seemed to satisfy the child. Couched in a different way, however, another child was told, "Grandfather can breathe easier now," implying that Grandfather is still breathing. This child wanted to join his grandfather because he had asthma and would welcome the chance to "breathe easier." He was told, however, that he was too young to join Grandfather (Dickinson, 1986:83).

"Dead" is a difficult word to say, but to use a euphemism like "went to sleep" may make it difficult for the child to go to sleep at night. If Grandad "went to sleep," and is then buried in a box underground or destroyed through cremation, that is probably not what the small child wants. Thus, the objective is to stay awake and *not go to sleep.* Parents wonder why the child is still awake at 10 P.M., after having been put to bed at 8.

To use euphemisms such as "went away," "departed this life," or "passed away" may cause the child to expect the deceased to return, as if from a trip. Even to suggest that "he's gone to heaven and will live forever" is confusing to a child when this is said through heavy tears and upset emotional feelings.

The death of a four-year-old's younger sister was explained to her as "being too sick to live with us so she went to visit Grandmother in heaven

THE FAMILY CIRCUS
by Bil Keane

Copyright 1985
The Register and Tribune
Syndicate, Inc.

"Well, yes — we'll see Granddad someday when we go to heaven."

"Could I just wait in the car?"

Reprinted with special permission of King Features Syndicate, Inc.

and would never come home again." She was frightened for months afterward because "whenever anyone did not feel well, I thought they would go away forever too" (Dickinson, 1986:83).

In recalling childhood memories of death, children who were told that the deceased had "gone to heaven" had been comforted (Dickinson, 1986). They had been told that "heaven was a happy place," thus all was well in the world of fantasy of these children.

Rabbi Harold Kushner (1981) cautions, however, that to try to make a child feel better by stating how beautiful heaven is, and how happy the deceased is to be with God, may deprive the child of a chance to grieve. By doing such, we ask a child to deny and mistrust his or her own feelings, to be happy when sadness is desired. Kushner notes that the child's right to feel upset and angry should be recognized. One should also be cautious that the child not feel that the deceased *chose* to leave and "go to heaven." It should be made clear that the person did not wish to leave or "desert," as the child may feel.

Anthropologist Colin Turnbull (1983) describes death as being like it was before birth—a state of nothingness. Ask someone to describe what it was like prior to birth, and you will probably not receive much of an answer.

To suggest that after death there is "no place" to describe—a nothing—would deny children a defined place to imagine. But then with the vast imagination of children, perhaps this might be more creative for them than a vague description of a "big house in the sky."

After you have made an effort to avoid euphemisms and gotten across the fact that the person is dead, the next step is to explain what is going to happen next. Tell the child about the body being moved from the hospital to the funeral home. Alert the child that funeral arrangements will be made (if this is the case), and that a funeral will follow. Outline the format of a funeral itself, then talk about going to the cemetery (if this is the case) and burying the body in the ground.

Show Emotion

It is important that the child know it is okay to show emotion when someone dies. Since it is a very sad time, the child should be told that everyone is upset and that many may be crying. If the child feels like crying, he or she should be assured that crying is okay, normal. It should also be explained that just because some people do not show emotion does not mean that they did not love the dead person (Schaefer & Lyons, 1986:33).

You probably cannot "overhug" a child during these times. It is important to always reassure the child that you care for him or her. Hugs and tears are very compatible expressions. Do not apologize for crying. Your crying in front of the child gives assurance that crying is okay.

Rabbi Earl Grollman (1967) defines crying as the sound of anguish at losing a part of oneself in the death of one who is loved. Since children often cry when they have hurt themselves, would it not follow that it would be natural to cry when "losing a part of oneself?" Grollman observes that tears and sorrowful words help the child feel relieved. Given the display of emotions, the dead person or pet seems more worthy—tears are a natural tribute paid to the deceased. The child misses the one who is gone and wishes the person were still around.

In recalling their first childhood experiences with death, some individuals indicated that crying was not acceptable and even had negative consequences (Dickinson, 1986:83–84). A 15-year-old was spanked with a hairbrush for crying over the death of her puppy. A 10-year-old was "smacked" by her uncle to "make her stop crying at the funeral." Some were told that it was not "grown-up" to cry. For many, their first childhood memories of death included recalling that it was the first time they had seen their fathers cry. No one commented that it was the first time they remembered seeing their mothers cry.

Several college students in recalling their first childhood experiences with death (Dickinson, 1986:85) noted that they watched others' reactions, then responded accordingly. Since children are watching adults, a parental

Adults model appropriate bereavement behavior for their children. The best thing adults can do for children is to be well-adjusted, secure, and loving people.

role model of expressing oneself in front of children might be very beneficial to the socialization of children. Children then would not feel a need to hide in the closet to cry, or to cry in their pillow at night, as some reported. One child noted the positive experience of his parents and sibling sitting down together to have a good cry at the death of his pet—this pointed out to him the warmth of the family in sharing this common event. It was not a burden he carried alone—his family grieved with him. It is comforting to know that others care.

According to former professional football player Rosey Grier, it is okay to cry. He sings a song in which he notes it is all right for women, men, girls, *and* boys to cry. For little boys to cry is not "sissy." If Rosey Grier says it is all right, it must be okay. Anthropologist Ashley Montagu (1968) agrees with

Rosey Grier when he states that women enjoy a superior use of their emotions because they can express themselves through crying.

Some men feel that "real men" do not cry because it is not macho to cry. They will wear dark glasses on the cloudiest of days, if they fear they may cry at a funeral. Several years ago, our teenage daughter attended the funeral of a friend with me. After leaving the cemetery on a very cloudy day, she said to me, "Dad, you were right." I said, "About what?" She said, "Nearly all the men at the graveside services were wearing dark sunglasses to hide the fact that they might cry." Males hold back the tears and develop psychosomatic disorders like peptic ulcers. "Is this a superior use of emotions?" Montagu would ask.

What favors are we doing our children by teaching them that it is not okay to cry? It is okay to laugh, why should it not also be okay to express feelings through crying?

THE DYING CHILD

As we have discussed, Kavanaugh (1972:139) says that little people enjoy the same human rights as their bigger counterparts. They have a right, therefore, to know if they have a fatal condition. When kept in ignorance, children, like adults, will rarely grow beyond the initial stage of denial and isolation. Not telling denies children of the peace and dignity that can be theirs in the final stage of acceptance and resignation.

Knowledge Is Kindness

The diagnosis of death should be made known to children as soon as the decision is clear and final (Kavanaugh, 1972:139–140). Especially in the case of the child who is dying, physicians, nurses, and family obviously need delay-time to bring their own emotions under control. We now know how to treat the dying child kindly. Knowledge is kindness, ignorance is cruel. The child is the patient whose life is being lost and whose concerns are pre-eminent. Kavanaugh (1972:143) notes that when children have known the truth about their condition, and were allowed to talk about it openly, they have been as brave as any adult.

Reasons for the advice given above by Kavanaugh (1972:140–143) are based on several observations. First, the dying child is no ordinary child. The ordinary process of maturing quickens through lengthy illness with confinement, suffering, and deprivation. Children ill for a long time usually exhibit a maturity beyond their calendar years.

Second, children's consciences are more tender and concerned than most adults are in a position to know. Deathbed children uninformed of their fate will often own guilt for the sadness and poorly veiled tears they witness around their bed. They can sense the phoniness around them, and they may tend to believe they are being punished for something evil they have done. Their isolation is heightened in their heavy concerns. Nothing is sadder than for a dying child to learn of his or her fate from playmates.

Finally, moderately aware and normally alert children know what is predicted for them in the signs they see—they recognize their plight from seeing dying scenes on television. They may ponder why the physician comes so often, why everyone is so nice to them, and why all the gifts. Either a child shares what he or she knows about his or her dying, or the final weeks and months become a lonely vigil, a sentence to fear and guilt, confinement, and confusion.

How do we tell a child about his or her dying condition? Kavanaugh (1972:142–143) notes that to adults brave enough to listen, this is not a valid question. The child will do the telling, if we create an atmosphere in which the child can make all appropriate deductions. The child's talk will flit in and out of the awful revelation.

The Child Needs Support

Who should do the telling or serve as a catalyst for it? Kavanaugh (1972:143) says that anyone strong enough to take the consequences by being a regular visitor, a trusted confidant, and a patient listener can be the catalyst. Many adults cannot qualify.

From her research with hospitalized, terminally ill children between the ages of six and 10, Eugenia Waechter (1985) agrees with Kavanaugh's conclusions. Her findings indicate that, despite efforts to shield a child from knowledge of the seriousness of his or her illness, the anxiety of those close to the child is likely to alter the emotional climate in the family. This may occur to such a degree that the child will develop suspicions and fears about his or her condition. Often they will feel that awareness of their condition is knowledge they are not supposed to have, so the silence of those nearby isolates children from needed support.

The question of whether a child should be told is meaningless, notes Waechter (1985). No curtain of silence should exist around the child's most intense fears. Support must especially be made available for them during and following actual encounters with death on pediatric wards. Support is needed to allow introspective examination of attitudes and fears related to death in general and to the death of children in particular.

In working with children with cancer, Yehuda Nir (1987:64) concludes that children's ability to cope with the stress of cancer is important in the way they deal with the illness itself and with the treatment. Feelings of helplessness and vulnerability dominate, often leading to regressive behavior. Withdrawal and refusal to participate in the treatment are seen almost immediately at the onset of the disease in young children. Because these types of behavior interfere with the medical management of the illness, resistance to treatment is circumvented by such methods as the use of general anesthesia and hypnotic relaxation techniques. While these interventions are medically justified, they intensify the child's feelings of passivity and helplessness.

Nir (1987) further notes that regression can take the form of acute separation anxiety. When the parents are unable to stay overnight in the hospital, they often speak with the child by phone. After talking with their parents, young children sometimes fall asleep with the telephone receiver in their laps, as if to maintain contact with what has become elusive.

BOX 9.3 **WOMAN SENDS "LOVE LETTERS" TO 465 SERIOUSLY ILL CHILDREN**

A woman whose 7-year-old son died of cancer four years ago now offers cheer to hundreds of ailing children in a monthly newsletter packed with jokes, puzzles, and stories.

"I can't cure them, but I know how to make them smile while they're here," said Linda Bremner, 40.

Her 10-page newsletters, called Love Letters, go to 465 children with terminal or long-term illnesses in 35 states and four other countries. Ms. Bremner said she began writing to seriously ill children in 1984, after the death of her only child, Andy.

"After my son died, I was cleaning out his drawers and I found his address book with the addresses of about 20 children who, like himself, had cancer.

"Remembering how important mail was to Andy, I wrote to them," she said. "What I didn't expect was that they wrote me back and that lit a fire under me," she said.

Stephen Lopez said the newsletter made his three-week hospital stay "much funner." "I like the dot-to-dots and the mazes most," said the 12-year-old, who suffers from a behavior disorder.

"It's the passion of my life. Nothing has ever made me feel this good," said Ms. Bremner.

"When I lose one of my kids I grieve," she said. "But it gives me a fervor, and I sit down and write some more letters." The newsletters carry games, puzzles, jokes, and "witty and whimsical" stories, said Ms. Bremner, who has made it a rule never to mention diseases or symptoms.

But sometimes her correspondents address serious topics when they write back, and she draws on her experiences with Andy. One 13-year-old girl wrote that she was being teased by classmates because her hair was falling out. "Andy had lost his hair five times and it grew back, so I wrote her and told her it would grow back, too," Ms. Bremner said. When the girl's hair finally grew back, she sent a little lock of blond hair with a note that read, "You were right—it grew back," Ms. Bremner recalled.

In the beginning, she was sending handwritten letters, she said. Now her pen pals get the newsletter, which is drafted on a computer. About a dozen volunteers help design and mail them.

Adapted from an Associated Press article in the *News and Courier*, Charleston, SC, July 30, 1988, p. 3A.

Families that seem best equipped to cope are those who develop a therapeutic alliance with the pediatric oncologist (Nir, 1987:65). This alliance buffers and protects the child from much of the pain and stress of the daily treatment routines. Another group of parents who seem successful in reducing stress are those with strong religious beliefs, notes Nir.

Through observing and talking to leukemic children ages three to nine in a hospital, anthropologist Myra Bluebond-Langner (1978) concluded that most of them knew not only that they were dying, but that this was a final and irreversible process. Children may wish and need to be open about their condition, but adults are often traumatized by a child's openness and honesty. Bluebond-Langner notes that the age of the children is not as important in their self-awareness of their dying as their experience with the disease and its treatment.

The founder and executive director of Children's Hospice International, Ann A. Dailey, says,

> Kids intuitively know when they are dying and they tend not to have the fears that adults have. But they want to know what it is going to feel like. Will someone be with them to hold their hand? Will a grandmother who died last year be there to greet him? Families need to cry together, to tell how much they are going to miss each other (Gamarekian, 1987:19).

Though one may not know what to say to a dying child or feel skilled in this area, it is imperative that we show support to them and let them know that we care. Support of others is important throughout life, whether relating to a terminally ill person or otherwise. This point is illustrated in the following story told by Rabbi Kushner (1985).

> A little boy had gone to the store, but was late in returning home. His mother asked, "Where were you?" He said, "I found a little boy whose bicycle was broken, and I stopped to help him." "But what do you know about fixing bicycles?"

his mother asked. "Nothing," the little boy replied, "I sat down and cried with him."

Many times, we may not know how to fix the situation, but like the little boy in the story, we can give support to the individual in other ways.

PARENTS OF THE DYING CHILD

Although there are many problematic aspects of parenting, none is as devastating to the parent as the loss of a child through death. This was observed by Ronald Knapp (1986:13), based on his interviews with 155 families suffering the loss of a child ranging in age from one to 28. The death of a child represents in a symbolic way the death of the parent, who will die along with the child, only to survive in a damaged state with little or no desire to live today or plan for tomorrow.

The truth is, we often take our children for granted. While one can *imagine* the loss of a child, how often does one have such thoughts? Even so, such thoughts bear little resemblance to reality. For parents who have lost a child through death, however, the reality of the situation lingers forever. A friend whose son had recently died told me that the stark reality hit him in the face every morning when he woke up and realized that this was not just a bad dream—his son was really dead.

Four years after the death of his son, Eric Wolterstorff said (Buursma, 1987:6):

> We took him too much for granted. Perhaps we all take each other too much for granted. The routines of life distract us; our own pursuits make us oblivious; our anxieties and sorrows, unmindful. The beauties of the familiar go unremarked. We do not treasure each other enough. He was a gift to us. . . . When the gift was finally snatched away, I realized how great it was. Then I could not tell him. . . . The pain of the no more outweighs the gratitude of the once was. Will it always be so?

Though the parent can never be really prepared for the end, as the dying child continues to lose ground, one reaches a point where resignation begins to replace hope for survival, and the inevitable end slowly comes into focus (Knapp, 1986:62). The character of hope changes from hoping for survival to hoping for a full range of living in the time available and for a comfortable, pain-free death. When parents consciously accept the fact that death is imminent, they become totally absorbed in the life of that child and try to make each day a memorable occasion.

Knapp (1986:67) notes that parents "live" the child's death over and over in their imaginations, as the end is near. This imaginery scenario takes them from the moment of death through the funeral of the child. Parents may wish to keep the child at home so that he or she will not die in strange surroundings. When one is able to make the decision to terminate all further treatment and let the disease take its course, a sense of tranquility results, and parents are ready to release their hold. Sometimes parents must take on the painfully hard task of telling the child that it is all right to let go, it is all right to stop fighting, it is all right to die. Giving permission to die is difficult. Sometimes it only takes gentle encouragement from parents, gentle persuasion that all has been done, and that nothing more remains.

BOX 9.4   # THE ART OF CONSOLING

JOE WARD

As anyone knows who has ever tried, it is difficult to talk to a parent who has lost a child. Julie McGee, coordinator of the Louisville chapter of The Compassionate Friends—an organization of bereaved parents—says no one who has not lost a child can really understand how it feels.

She says bereaved parents themselves recognize how misguided were their past efforts to console a friend or relative in the same situation. So the organization has compiled the following list of do's and don't's:

Do

Be available to listen, to run errands and to help with housework and other children.

Say you are sorry about what happened to their child and about their pain.

Allow them to express grief without holding back. Listen if they want to talk about the child, as much and as often as they want to.

Encourage them to be patient with themselves, not to expect too much of themselves and not to impose any "shoulds" on themselves.

Talk to them about the special endearing qualities of the child who has died.

Give special attention to the child's brothers and sisters at the funeral and later.

Reassure parents about the care their child received, but be careful not to say anything that is obviously not true.

Don't

Avoid them because you are uncomfortable.

Say you know how they feel unless you have lost a child yourself.

(continued on next page)

Tell them they've grieved long enough and "ought to be feeling better by now." Your guess at an appropriate timetable probably is short. Avoid telling them, in general, what they "should" feel and do.

Change the subject when they mention their dead child.

Worry about mentioning their child's name. You won't make them think of him or her; they probably are doing that anyway.

Try to point out some bright side. They don't want to hear, "At least you have your other children," or "At least you can have another child," or, "At least you had the child for a while."

Try to commiserate with them by saying the child's case was bungled by the doctors or the hospital or someone else involved. They will be plagued by guilt and feelings of inadequacy without any help from you.

SIBLINGS OF THE DYING CHILD

When a newborn comes into the family, siblings of the baby often feel neglected. Most of the attention seems to go to the baby, therefore the young siblings often have a pity party for themselves. Presents are given to the baby, and adults carry on about the new arrival. All this time the siblings may be jealous because they do not seem "special."

A similar situation may occur in the family when a sibling is dying. The energies of parents, grandparents, and significant others seem to be directed toward the dying child, who seems to be receiving all of the attention.

In a study of siblings of children with cancer (Sourkes, 1981), it is noted that parents, in fact, do provide them with less attention, causing them to feel lonely and neglected. Siblings are also distressed by the visibility of the illness and their tendency to identify with it. They are distressed by the treatment process and may feel guilty about being healthy.

Even during remission, siblings are neglected by parents who must catch up on the instrumental tasks of daily living (Spinetta, 1981). Sibling anger begins to surface most clearly during remission when their loss of parental attention becomes even more prominent than at diagnosis.

In a study of 65 children between the ages of four and 16 who were the siblings of deceased children, McCown and Pratt (1985) confirmed previous studies indicating that 30 to 50 percent of surviving children demonstrate increased behavior problems following the death of a sibling. Their studies showed that children in the middle age group, six to 11 years, developed more behavior problems than other age groups. Reasons cited for more problems in this age group are that the loss of a sibling at this phase may lead to a sense of vulnerability and inferiority, and for the child in this age group who is making the transition to concrete thought, the event and cause of sibling death may evoke confusion. The increased behavior problems may be a reflection of that confusion and concern.

David Adams and Eleanor Deveau (1987:284) note that, after a child's death, many siblings fear minor physical symptoms and worry about death occurring at the same age. Siblings resent parents for their preoccupation with the dead child and blame them for their inability to protect them during illness. Parents are often so consumed by their own grief that they have little energy left to help surviving children. Problems also develop when parents expect surviving siblings to surpass or equal the achievements of a deceased child or to replace the deceased brother or sister.

Peer support and special attention for the siblings of dying children are especially needed, but it is a time of limited resources and energies in the home. Teachers in particular need to be alert to the special concerns and needs of these children. The personal worth of surviving siblings needs to be reinforced. They too wish to be noticed and given some love and care.

BOX 9.5 **DID I REALLY LOVE MY BROTHER?**

ELIZABETH RICHTER

"Everybody told me to be strong for my parents and to be quiet because I might make them more upset. Everyone told me to put my feelings aside, like my feelings weren't as important as my parents'. I never cried until about a year later, when it hit me that my sister Sandy wasn't around." That's how 18-year-old Lisa describes her own grieving for an older sister who was murdered.

"When I was told my brother had died, I just left the room. I couldn't even cry. My father cried, although he had never cried in his life. Because I couldn't cry, I began to wonder if there was something wrong with me. Did I really love my brother?" That is the way 18-year-old Sharon reacted to her little brother's dying of a brain tumor.

Children are not supposed to die—or so we like to think. But, of course, they do. When a child dies, it means not only the loss of a young life but also the death of parents' hopes and dreams.

(continued on next page)

Many professionals believe that schools need to do more to comfort surviving children. Too often, when survivors return to school, there is no acknowledgement of the death of a brother or sister.

Sandra Fox, director of the Good Grief Program at Judge Baker Guidance Center in Boston, says, "Teachers want to avoid the subject of death. It's not malicious. It's just they are afraid to say the wrong things. They tend to err on the side of being supercautious."

Psychologist Gerald Koocher believes that death education classes could be useful in giving young people a chance to think about the issues of dying and death before being confronted with personal loss. We obviously cannot just pat siblings on the head and tell them everything will be okay.

Adapted from *U.S. News and World Report,* August 4, 1986.

SUDDEN INFANT DEATH SYNDROME

Sudden, unexpected infant death is a major type of death in infants between the ages of one week and one year in the United States—an estimated 10,000 deaths per year. According to a study by the Foundation for the Study of Infant Deaths, these babies do not cry out as if in pain, but simply die quietly in their sleep, after becoming unconscious. **Sudden infant death syndrome (SIDS)** is usually defined as the sudden, unexplained death of an infant where no cause is found through a postmortem examination (DeFrain, Taylor, & Ernst, 1982:11–12).

Historically, unexpected, unexplainable deaths of infants were routinely attributed to the mother's lying on the baby, since mothers often slept with infants. If they woke and found the baby dead, they assumed that they had lain on the child, smothering and crushing it. Perhaps the earliest recorded such death is in the Bible in 1 Kings 3:19: "And this woman's child died in the night, because she overlaid it." It is believed that SIDS was occurring long before it was recognized and accepted as a diagnostic label (Beckwith, 1978).

Etiology

The **etiology** of SIDS deaths show that they occur more often in winter and spring when respiratory illnesses are frequent, and autopsies show inflammation in windpipes in a high number of SIDS deaths. There is a higher incidence among blacks, poor families, and babies born to teenage mothers. Deaths are more frequent in infants with low alertness scores at birth and in infants born to mothers using drugs or who smoke and have premature babies (Cope, 1980).

Data reported by Cope (1980) are supported in a more recent study by Southall and colleagues (Southall, Alexander, Stebbens, Taylor, & Jancaynski, 1987), who monitored breathing movements of 301 infants who had had a sibling die of SIDS. The infants were then compared to a control group of 170 infants, matched by postnatal age. Researchers found that the mothers of the SIDS siblings smoked and consumed alcohol more often during pregnancy than the mothers of control babies. The siblings had lower Apgar (alertness) scores and were more often breast-fed than were controls.

Most deaths occur when the baby is sleeping and usually occur between midnight and 9 A.M. The peak age for death is between two and four months of age. Death occurs rapidly, and the child turns blue and limp, apparently from lack of oxygen. Clues to SIDS are present in the brain, which should alert the infant to breathe harder, but research is inconclusive on the linkage to brain dysfunction (Cope, 1980).

J. B. Beckwith (1978) by the late 1970s had catalogued 73 different theories for the cause of SIDS, and noted that new ideas were being published almost on a weekly basis. Viral infections have been viewed as a link to SIDS (Valdes-Dapena, 1980), and are evident in autopsies of some babies, but not all. Evidence from postmortem studies shows elevated levels of a thyroid hormone triiodothyronine (T-3) in 44 out of 50 victims (Rowley, 1981). This may be an important step in determining the cause, and we hope, the cure for SIDS. It is not clear, however, when the elevation of T-3 occurred—prior to birth or after the death.

If T-3 has an influence on breathing and heart beat, an infant with an elevated level of T-3 should perhaps be put on a monitor (DeFrain, Taylor, & Ernst, 1982:14). Apparently, all infants experience numerous short periods of not breathing, a condition called *apnea*. A home **apnea monitor** is frequently used in the management of infants at increased risk for SIDS, and helps alert parents to breathing irregularities by sounding an alarm when breathing stops. Home apnea monitoring remains unproven, however, since some infants have died despite evaluation by infant apnea programs (Ward, Keens, Chan, Chipps, Carson, & Deming, 1986).

BOX 9.6 **RESEARCHER LINKS HEART DEFECT WITH NEARLY HALF OF CRIB DEATHS**

A newly discovered defect in the hearts of some babies may be responsible for half of all cases of sudden infant death syndrome. The new evidence suggests that these babies' hearts frequently have a defect in their electrical stimulation. The malfunction could make their hearts stall when they begin to speed up for any reason.

While the discovery does not provide immediate new ways to prevent crib deaths, the researchers say it may someday help identify babies who are at high risk so they could be treated with drugs. Dr. Daniel C. Shannon, co-author of the study at Massachusetts General Hospital, speculated the defect could result from immaturity or from damage triggered by an infection or toxin encountered as a fetus.

Adapted from an Associated Press article in the *News and Courier*, Charleston, SC, December 10, 1987, p. 1-A.

Recent death-scene investigations (Bass, Kravath, & Glass, 1986) of 26 cases of infants brought into an emergency room with presumptive diagnoses of SIDS, revealed strong circumstantial evidence of accidental death in six cases and found various *possible* causes of death, other than SIDS, in 18 other cases. These researchers suggest that many sudden deaths of infants may have a definable "cause" other than SIDS, but question the extremely high rate reported in the population of low-socioeconomic status served by their hospital (Bass, Kravath, & Glass, 1986).

Parents of SIDS Children

When an infant dies suddenly and unexpectedly, the sense of loss and grief may be overwhelming. When that sudden death is due to a known cause, the concrete character of the event can be incorporated into the normal rationalization of mourning. When death is due to an unknown mechanism, however, as in SIDS, feelings of inadequacy in caring for the child are reinforced for both medical staff and parents (Mandell, McClain, & Reece, 1987).

Since there are still many questions remaining unanswered about SIDS, parents have a tremendous guilt feeling and shoulder the responsibility for the infant's death. Marital conflict, difficulties with surviving children, and anxiety about the health of future children are often experienced. With the cause of death being questionable, the parents are likely to undergo a police interrogation, in addition to the stress of having lost their infant. In an era of child abuse, the parents may be suspected of smothering the child.

Young parents whose baby dies of SIDS have probably not experienced the death of a close relative, thus they are not familiar with the social and emotional aspects of grief and mourning. The death of one's baby is traumatic under any conditions, but the sense of not knowing how to mourn adds to the difficulties of socially adjusting to the loss. The parents and siblings experience "anomic grief," a grief without the traditional supports of family, church, and community.

A survey of newly trained local SIDS counselors in North Carolina (Kotch & Cohen, 1985) reported that sharing the autopsy report with bereaved parents was a valuable part of the counseling process and removed some of the mystery surrounding the diagnosis. The autopsy report, by documenting that the child died a natural death, may relieve some families of the feeling that they were somehow responsible for the death.

My own discussions with parents who have lost a child through SIDS suggest that friends may turn on them as if they are criminals. In addition, parents tend to blame each other for the death—"if only you had. . . ." Parents become victims because SIDS is both personally traumatic and complicated with problems of social interaction. The uncertainty of the cause of death is frustrating to the parents and medical staff, and clouds the whole issue from a societal perspective. A SIDS death is probably one of the more traumatic experiences a parent can experience.

CONCLUSION

Rather than trying to protect the young from death talk, we need more open communication channels on this topic. Children from an early age have a concept of death, and terminally ill children seem to know that they are dying. We need to stop pretending that children cannot handle this topic. It is okay for children (and adults) to show emotions like crying when they feel so inclined. It is okay to feel the way one feels—moral judgments should not be attached to feelings. One feels the way one feels, and we should not try to be judgmental.

We adults must be alert to the questions of children on dying and death. In speaking to a group of sixth-graders a few years ago on the topic of dying and death, my frustration was trying to decide who to call on when a dozen or more hands at a time were up from these 40 children. Each had his or her own concerns, and they were sincere, legitimate interests. I remember one little boy asking if it were true that one would die from getting embalming fluid on the skin. I tried to assure him that this would not likely be a cause of death, but this was a genuine *concern* of his. When our son was six, he asked, "Daddy, do we eat dead people?" Since we eat *dead* cows and pigs, why not people? We certainly do not eat *live* cows and pigs. The questions are there from these "little people," and we "big people" must respond by answering in a way that respects the question.

Dying children and significant others surrounding these children need a strong support system. It is important to let the child and family know that others care. Though one may not know what to say in such situations, this should not keep one away from the death environs. Go and visit to show that you care. Parents who have lost a child through SIDS not only have lost their child, but face a suspicious public that questions the real cause of death—double punishment.

SUMMARY

1. Due in part to an urbanized and industrialized society, and in part to the artificial messages of the media, children are removed from death.

2. The permanency of death is unclear to young children, who tend to see death as reversible.

3. Children can take just about anything adults can dish out, including discussing the topics of dying and death.

4. Honesty and openness in relating to children about death is very important.

5. Avoid euphemisms when talking to children about death.

6. It is okay to express emotions through crying. Adults can sanction this behavior by not hiding their own tears when they are sorrowful. By seeing big people cry, children can know that crying is normal behavior.

7. Dying children should be told their diagnosis and kept informed of their prognosis. They seem to know when they are dying anyway, so why make them bear this burden all alone? Knowledge is kindness.

8. Dying children and parents and siblings of dying children need the support of others.

9. Research on Sudden Infant Death Syndrome (SIDS) is inconclusive as to the causes of SIDS deaths, though recent research suggests that a defect in the electrical stimulation of the heart may be correlated with SIDS.

DISCUSSION QUESTIONS

1. Discuss your first childhood memory of death. How old were you? Who or what died? What do you remember about this event?

2. When you were growing up, how was death talked about in your family?

3. Discuss the various perceptions of death as one goes from birth to age 10. What shortcomings do you find with a life-cycle approach?

4. Analyze the Mother Goose stories in this chapter. What are some of the themes in these "kiddie" rhymes?

5. Put yourself in the place of a parent with a terminally ill child. How do you think you would relate to this child?

6. List as many euphemisms as you can to identify dying and death. Why do you think euphemisms are used with death?

7. Why is knowledge kindness in relating to a dying child?

8. What is SIDS? Is this a new or an old phenomenon?

9. Discuss why adults tend to avoid talking about death with children.

GLOSSARY

Apnea monitor   A device to detect the temporary stopping of breathing in infants.
Etiology   The science of causes or origins.
Euphemisms   Words or phrases that, while less expressive or direct, are considered less distasteful or less offensive than other words or phrases.
Sudden infant death syndrome (SIDS)   The sudden, unexplained death of an infant where no cause is found through a postmortem examination.

REFERENCES

Adams, David W., & Eleanor J. Deveau. 1987. "When a Brother or Sister Is Dying of Cancer: The Vulnerability of the Adolescent Sibling." *Death Studies, 11*:279–295.
Bass, M., R. E. Kravath, & L. Glass. 1986. "Death-scene Investigation in Sudden Infant Death." *New England Journal of Medicine, 315* (July 10):100–105.
Beckwith, J. B. 1978. *The Sudden Infant Death Syndrome.* DHEW Publication No. HSA 75-5137. Washington, DC: U.S. Government Printing Office.
Bowlby, John. 1980. *Attachment and Loss,* Vol. III. New York: Basic Books.
Bluebond-Langner, Myra. 1978. *The Private Worlds of Dying Children.* Princeton, NJ: Princeton University Press.
Buursma, Bruce. 1987. "Scholar Wrestles with Son's Death." *News and Courier,* Charleston, SC. August 2, p. 6D.
Cope, L. 1980. "Research Finding Clues to Crib Deaths." *Minneapolis Tribune,* Minneapolis, MN. June 4.
DeFrain, John, Jacque Taylor, & Linda Ernst. 1982. *Coping with Sudden Infant Death.* Lexington, MA: Lexington Books.
Dickinson, George E. 1986. "Childhood Memories of Death." In Gary H. Paterson (Ed.), *Children and Death.* London, Ontario: King's College Press, pp. 81–90.
Erikson, Erik. 1963. *Childhood and Society.* New York: Norton.
Gamarekian, Barbara. 1987. "A Support Network for Dying Children." *The New York Times.* June 25, pp. 19–20.

Gibson, Richard. 1973. "Mother Goose: Teacher of Death." *The Minneapolis Star*, April 11.

Ginsberg, Herbert, & Sylvia Opper. 1979. *Piaget's Theory of Intellectual Development*, Second Ed. Englewood Cliffs, NJ: Prentice-Hall.

Grollman, Earl. 1967. *Explaining Death to Children*. Boston: Beacon Press.

Hostler, Sharon L. 1978. "The Development of the Child's Concept of Death." In Olle Jane Z. Sahler, *The Child and Death*. St. Louis: Mosby, pp. 1–25.

Kavanaugh, Robert E. 1972. *Facing Death*. Baltimore, MD: Penguin Books.

Knapp, Ronald J. 1986. *Beyond Endurance: When a Child Dies*. New York: Schocken Books.

Kotch, Jonathan B., & Susan R. Cohen. 1985. "SIDS Counselors' Reports of Own and Parents' Reactions to Reviewing the Autopsy Report." *Omega*, 16:129–139.

Kushner, Harold S. 1981. *When Bad Things Happen to Good People*. New York: Schocken Books.

Kushner, Harold S. 1985. Lecture given in Charleston, SC, on October 20.

Lonetto, Richard. 1980. *Children's Conceptions of Death*. New York: Springer Verlag.

Mandell, F., M. McClain, & R. M. Reece. 1987. "Sudden and Unexpected Death." *American Journal of Diseases of Children*, 141 (July):748–750.

McCown, Darlene E., & Clara Pratt. 1985. "Impact of Sibling Death on Children's Behavior." *Death Studies*, 9:323–335.

Montagu, Ashley. 1968. *The Natural Superiority of Women*, Rev. Ed. New York: Collier Books.

Nagy, Maria. 1948. "The Child's Theories concerning Death." *Journal of Genetic Psychology*, 73:3–27.

News and Courier. 1988. "Woman Sends 'Love Letters' to 465 Seriously Ill Children." Charleston, SC, July 30.

Nir, Yehuda. 1987. "Post-Traumatic Stress Disorder in Children with Cancer." In John E. Schowalter, Penelope Buschman, Paul Patterson, Austin Rutsches, Margot Tallmar & Robert Stevenson (Eds.), *Children and Death: Perspectives from Birth through Adolescence*. New York: Praeger, pp. 63–72.

Richter, Elizabeth. 1986. "Did I Really Love My Brother?" *U.S. News and World Report*, August 4.

Rowley, J. 1981. "Crib Death Discovery May Lead to Simple Test for the Disease." *Minneapolis Tribune*, Minneapolis, MN, November 6.

Sahler, Olle Jane Z. 1978. *The Child and Death*. St. Louis: C. V. Mosby.

Schaefer, Dan, & Christine Lyons. 1986. *How Do We Tell the Children? A Parents' Guide to Helping Children Understand and Cope When Someone Dies*. New York: Newmarket Press.

Schulz, Charles, & Kenneth F. Hall. 1965. *Two-by-Fours: A Sort of Serious Book about Children*. Anderson, IN: Warner.

Sourkes, B. 1981. In J. Kellerman (Ed.), *Psychological Aspects of Childhood Cancer*. Springfield, IL: Thomas.

Southall, D. P., J. R. Alexander, V. A. Stebbens, V. G. Taylor, & R. E. Jancaynski. 1987. "Cardiorespiratory Patterns in Siblings of Babies with Sudden Infant Death Syndrome." *Archives of Disease in Childhood*, 62 (July):721–726.

Spinetta, J. J. 1981. "The Siblings of the Child with Cancer." In J. J. Spinetta & P. Deasy-Spinetta (Eds.), *Living With Childhood Cancer*. St. Louis: Mosby, pp. 137–140.

Turnbull, Colin M. 1983. *The Human Cycle.* New York: Simon and Schuster.

Valdes-Dapena, Maria A. 1980. "Sudden Infant Death Syndrome: A Review of the Medical Literature, 1974–1979." *Pediatrics, 66:*597–613.

Waechter, Eugenia H. 1985. "Children's Awareness of Fatal Illness." In Sandra G. Wilcox & Marilyn Sutton (Eds.), *Understanding Death and Dying,* Third Ed. Palo Alto, CA: Mayfield, pp. 299–306.

Ward, Joe. 1980. "The Art of Consoling." *The Louisville-Courier Journal,* Louisville, KY. July 27.

Ward, S. L., T. G. Keens, L. S. Chan, B. E. Chipps, S. H. Carson, & D. D. Deming. 1986. "Sudden Infant Death Syndrome in Infants Evaluated by Apnea Programs in California." *Pediatrics, 77* (April):451–458.

SUGGESTED READINGS

Linda Edelstein. 1984. *Maternal Bereavement: Coping With the Unexpected Death of a Child.* New York: Praeger.

A book dealing with women and the loss of a child, with special emphasis on mourning and bereavement, the mother–child relationship, putting one's life back in order, and emotional and social supports.

Sherry E. Johnson. 1987. *After a Child Dies: Counseling Bereaved Families.* New York: Springer Verlag.

Though written for practitioners counseling survivors of families who have experienced the death of a child, this book could be read by anyone experiencing bereavement following the death of a child.

Ronald J. Knapp. 1986. *Beyond Endurance: When a Child Dies.* New York: Schocken Books.

An excellent book based on in-depth interviews with 155 families who have lost a child through death.

Gary H. Paterson (Ed.). 1986. *Children and Death.* London, Ontario: King's College Press.

An anthology from a conference on children and death covering the topics of the child's point of view on death, the adult experience of a child's death, the role of education, and support systems for terminally ill children.

Pyltes, Marian S. 1988. *Death and Dying in Children's Literature: A Survey and Bibliography.* Jefferson, NC: McFarland.

A survey of children's literature critiquing books on folklore, one's own death, and the deaths of pets, friends, and relatives.

Dan Schaefer & Christine Lyons. 1986. *How Do We Tell the Children? A Parent's Guide to Helping Children Understand and Cope When Someone Dies.* New York: Newmarket Press.

Covers the topics of children's thinking on death, explaining death to children, grief and healing, and children and funerals.

John E. Schowalter, Penelope Buschman, Paul R. Patterson, Austin H. Kutscher, Margot Tallmer, & Robert G. Stevenson. 1987. *Children and Death.* New York: Praeger.

An anthology on children's concepts of death, the emotional impact of disease, and coping with childhood death.

FOUR

Understanding the Bereavement Process

—

CHAPTER 10

Cross-Cultural Understanding of Dying, Death, and Bereavement

—

Some children love to watch the cremations. The skull is usually the last thing to be burned. Sometimes it collapses with a loud pop, like a balloon bursting. When that happens, the children clap their hands.

ALEXANDER CAMPBELL, *THE HEART OF INDIA*

295

10 Death is an event occurring in all societies, yet it evokes an incredible variety of responses. At the moment of death, survivors in some societies remain rather calm, some cry, while others mutilate their own bodies. Some societies officially mourn for months, yet others complete the ritual within hours. Family involvement in preparation of the corpse for the funeral ritual exists in many societies, while others call professional funeral directors to handle the job.

The variety of responses to death is further noted by Richard Huntington and Peter Metcalf in *Celebrations of Death: The Anthropology of Mortuary Ritual* (1979:1). They state that corpses are burned or buried, with or without animal or human sacrifice; they are preserved by smoking, embalming, or pickling; they are eaten—raw, cooked, or rotten; they are ritually exposed as dead or decaying flesh or simply abandoned; they are first dismembered and treated in a variety of ways. Funerals are times for avoiding people or holding parties, for weeping or laughing, for combat or sexual orgies.

Societal Management of Death-Related Emotions

Though they vary significantly, all societies seem to have some social mechanism for managing death-related emotions and reconstructing family interaction patterns modified by death. These customs are passed down from generation to generation and are an integral part of a society's way of coping with a major event like death.

The study of death rituals is a positive endeavor. Regardless of whether societal customs call for festive or restrained behavior, the issue of death throws into relief the most important cultural values by which people live their lives and evaluate their experiences (Huntington & Metcalf, 1979). Life becomes transparent against the background of death, and fundamental social and cultural issues are revealed.

Anthropologists do not claim to have a special understanding of the mystery of death, but they can recount the collective wisdom of many cultures. The entire web of human social interrelations is founded on many invisible and indirect meanings that are bestowed on various individuals (Cuzzort & King, 1980:55). While we cannot actually see a mourner or a mortician, we can observe those who occupy such statuses. Until we are informed that they occupy such statuses (and are expected to behave accordingly), however, we cannot respond in an appropriate way.

The anthropologist is concerned as a scientist with the meanings that different events have for different societies. A true understanding of various rituals and activities results from an immersion in the culture. While the anthropologist cannot determine what is in the mind of the person acting, similar events observed over time can result in some understanding of the behavior within that context. Marvin Harris (1974:4) notes that human life is not merely random or capricious. Since one does not expect dreamers to explain their dreams, lifestylers should not be expected to explain their lifestyles. Through careful observation over time, one can come to a better understanding of why people do what they do.

Why Study Cross-Cultural Death Rituals?

Why should a student of death and dying become familiar with the death customs of other cultures? Our culture is characterized all too often by **ethnocentrism**—we tend to think that our way is the superior way. Just because another society's customs differ from our own does not mean they are wrong. When we compare different death-related customs, the similarities between cultures are often greater than the differences. As you read this chapter, note the many parallels that exist between our death customs and those of others.

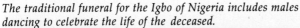
The traditional funeral for the Igbo of Nigeria includes males dancing to celebrate the life of the deceased.

Being familiar with cross-cultural death customs should help us to better understand the American concept of death. To blame a supernatural force or a physician or someone else for one's death is functional in both literate and nonliterate societies—an explanation for the death and a scapegoat to relieve one's guilt feelings. While some nonliterate groups might attribute a death to the ghost of a deceased ancestor, a literate group might blame medical personnel.

Almost all societies seem to have a concept of soul and immortality. For some, a belief in a soul concept explains what happens in sleep and after death. For others, the belief in souls explains how the supernatural world becomes populated (Tylor, 1873). Much of the ritual performed at death is related to the soul and an appeasement of the beings in the spiritual world. This spiritual dimension of death plays a significant role in the social structure of societies that hold such beliefs.

For many groups, the souls of the dead become ghosts. These ghosts may take up residence, and, after a short period of wandering, may cease to exist. Some cultures have conversations with ghosts and make offerings to them—sometimes referred to as the *cult of the dead* (Taylor, 1980). These ghosts are not worshipped but simply maintain a relationship with a spirit that acts as a guide and protector and confers power. To have a guardian spirit is a positive experience in some societies. Ghosts are not unique to nonliterate cultures but seem to also exist in literate societies (e.g., the United States).

This chapter will present various death rituals and discuss the functions of such activities. In no way are these various cultures representative of all. Some examples may appear bizarre to the reader, but keep in mind that our own death rituals may appear strange to persons from other cultures.

DEATH AS A RITE OF PASSAGE

Death is a transition, but only the last in a long chain of transitions, according to Huntington and Metcalf (1979:93). The moment of death is related not only to the process of afterlife, but to the process of living, aging, and producing progeny. Death relates to life—to the recent life of the deceased and to the life he or she has procreated and now leaves behind. There is an eternity of sorts on either side of the line that divides the quick from the dead. Life continues generation after generation, and in many societies it is this continuity that is focused on and enhanced during the rituals surrounding a death.

One of the best-known accounts of death as one of a series of such **rites of passage** through the life cycle comes from Van Gennep (1909/1960) in his treatment of funerals. He had expected that the element of separation would be more marked in funerals than other rites of passage, but his evidence demonstrated that it is the transitional or the liminal that dominates mortuary ritual and symbolism. Van Gennep (1909/1960:164) noted social status aspects of ritual and mourning:

> The length of the period [of mourning] increases with the closeness of the social tie to the deceased and with higher social standing of the dead person. If the dead man was a chief, the suspension affects the entire society.

However, persons for whom no rites are performed,

> are the most dangerous dead. They would like to be reincorporated into the world of the living and since they cannot be, they behave like hostile strangers toward it. They lack the means to subsistence which the other dead find in their own world and consequently must obtain them at the expense of the living (Van Gennep, 1909/1960:160).

Individuals are often considered to be composed of several components, each of which may have a different fate after death (Palgi & Abramovitch, 1984:117). The purpose of the destruction of the corpse, whether through cremation, burial, or decomposition, is to separate the components—the various bodies and souls.

For the Lugbara of Uganda (Middleton, 1965) when people die, they cease to be "people of the world outside" and become "people who have died" or "people in the earth." Death marks the beginning of an elaborate rite of passage as a dead man has relations with both living and dead kin.

THE RITUAL OF MOURNING AT DEATH

Ritual can be defined as "the symbolic affirmation of values by means of culturally standardized utterances and actions" (Taylor, 1980:198). A **ceremony** is a given complex of rituals associated with a specific occasion. People in all societies are inclined to symbolize culturally defined feelings in conventional ways. Ritual behavior, therefore, is an effective means of expressing or reinforcing these important sentiments.

Rituals differ from other behavior in that they are formal—stylized, repetitive, and stereotyped (Rappaport, 1974). Rituals are performed in special places and occur at set times and include liturgical orders—words and actions set forth previously by someone.

Functions of rituals include validation and reinforcement of values, reassurance in the face of psychological disturbances, reinforcement of group ties, facilitation of status change by acquainting persons with their new roles, relief of psychological tensions, and restabilization of patterns of interaction disturbed by a crisis (Taylor, 1980). Ritual, however, can also have negative functions by causing tensions.

This Japanese funeral emphasizes the social status of the man who has died. The living honor the dead and thereby create a symbolic community consisting of their ancestors and living members of their families.

Whereas death rituals in the United States are generally subdued, gloomy affairs, some societies engage in spirited activities. The Bara people in Madagascar, for example, engage in "drunken revelry" at a funeral—rum is consumed, sexual activities occur, dancing takes place, and contests involving cattle occur (Huntington & Metcalf, 1979). Among the Cubeo of South America, simulated and actual ritual coitus is part of the mourning ritual (Goldman, 1979). The dances, ritual, dramatic performances, and the sexual license are intended to transform grief and anger into joy.

The Display of Emotions

An examination of ethnographic data from 78 societies (Rosenblatt, Walsh, & Jackson, 1976) that sought to identify the essence of universal grief behavior shows that it is a near universal that death is associated with emotions, and that the most usual expression among the bereaved is crying. The study further concluded that, if there are gender differences in emotions during bereavement, the women tend to cry and self-mutilate more than men. Men tend to direct anger and aggression away from the self. One of the traditional theories suggested to explain such gender differences in emotional expression was that it may be easier to socialize women than men to be overtly nonaggressive; thus crying may represent a female expression of aggression.

Another explanation was the belief that women will be more affected by the loss from a death because of their stronger attachments through their role as mothers. On the other hand, women may not experience death more strongly, but they may simply be used by the society as the ones to symbolize publicly, in burdensome or self-injuring ways, the loss that all experienced. The researchers concluded on the basis of data from these 78 societies that the kind of data needed to "explain" the emotional difference by gender is lacking.

Paul Rosenblatt and colleagues (1976) note that most societies have developed mechanisms to control the anger of the bereaved and channel it along nondestructive paths. Ritual specialists help to minimize anger leading to disruptive social behavior. In a country so deritualized as the United States, funeral directors may provide a positive role in developing sets of norms for mourning behavior.

The expression of emotions ranges from complete abstinence to amplified wailing, notes Effie Bendann's *Death Customs: An Analytical Study of Burial Rites* (1930). She states that after a death the aborigines of Australia and Melanesia indulge in the most exaggerated forms of weeping and wailing. They display other manifestations of emotional excitement seemingly because of grief for the departed. At the end of a certain designated time period, however, they cease with metronomic precision and the would-be mourners indulge in laughter and other forms of amusement.

An outgoing display of emotions is found among the Kapauku Papuans of West New Guinea (Pospisil, 1963). Their ritual at death requires the relatives of the deceased to give a formal expression of their grief as soon as the soul leaves the body. They weep, eat ashes, cut off their fingers, tear their garments and net carrying bags, and smear their faces and bodies with mud, ashes, or yellow clay. A loud sing-song lamentation follows.

As noted above, mourning often falls most heavily on the women. For example, women among the Cheyenne Indians cut off their long hair and gash their foreheads so that the blood flows (Hoebel, 1960). If the deceased was killed by enemies, they slash their legs until caked with dried blood. Mourning gives the women their own masochistic outlet. Cheyenne men, on the other hand, simply let down their hair in mourning and do not bother to lacerate themselves.

The Dinka women of the Sudan (Deng, 1972) cut their leather skirts and cover their bodies with dirt and ashes for as long as a year. Widows among the Swazi in Africa (Kuper, 1963) shave their heads and remain "in darkness" for three years before given the duty of continuing the lineage for the deceased through the **levirate,** or required marriage with her husband's brother. Mourning imposed on the Swazi husband is less conspicuous and of shorter duration.

In the United States some funeral directors have noted that occasionally individuals "carry on to the point of fainting" but catch themselves before completely passing out. If such behavior is expected within a subculture, some will comply. However, a more stoic approach appears to be normative in the United States. For example, when President John F. Kennedy was assassinated in Dallas in 1963, Jacqueline Kennedy was praised by the media for "holding up well." Her reaction was probably one of shock more than bravery.

Types of Weeping

One could argue that people display the outward emotion of crying at the time of death because they are sad. Perhaps it is not as simple as that. Anthropologist A. R. Radcliffe-Brown (1964) notes two types of weeping. Reciprocal ritual weeping, where two parties cry over each other, affirms the existence of a social bond between two or more persons, and is an occasion for affirming social ties. Although participants may not actually feel these sentiments that bind them, participation in various rites will strengthen whatever positive feelings they do have. The second type of ceremonial weeping is one-sided, where one person weeps over a passive person or object. In the second type, one cries over the remains of a significant other, and expresses the continued sentiment of attachment despite the severing of this social bond.

Richard Huntington and Peter Metcalf (1979) observe that Radcliffe-Brown was strongly influenced by the French sociologist Emile Durkheim. Durkheim (1965) had argued in 1912 that the emotions developed are feelings of sorrow and anger, which are made stronger by participation in the burial rite, while Radcliffe-Brown claimed that those participating in ceremonial weeping come to feel emotion that is not sorrow but togetherness. What Durkheim finds significant is the way other members of society feel moral pressure to put their behavior in harmony with the feelings of the truly bereaved. Even if one feels no direct sorrow, weeping and suffering may result. Thus, to say that one weeps because of sadness may be too simplistic.

In conclusion, cross-cultural studies of the ritual of mourning at death reveal that a double standard prevails among some cultures—different "scripts" for different genders. Women in many societies, including the United States, are expected to display more of their emotions than men. Mourning rituals also tend to last for a set period of time in many societies.

ATTITUDES TOWARD DEATH

In some societies death is viewed as a continuation of life, simply in a different form. Death may be accepted by some as a natural part of life—the "final

The feast of the dead in Peru demonstrates the belief in the continuity of relationships between the living and the dead.

stage of growth," as Elisabeth Kübler-Ross notes. Yet for others, death is the end of everything. For example, the Navaho Indians (Habenstein & Lamers, 1963) have no belief in a glorious immortality for the soul, and believe that death is the end of everything good. Likewise, the Semai of Malaya (Dentan, 1968) talk about life after death, but most admit they do not believe in it. Thus, attitudes toward death are partly reflected in beliefs about what happens after death.

In our own culture, a popular belief is that the dead and the living are separated from each other. Yet, like many cultures, we periodically pay respect to the dead through All Saints Day and Memorial Day (Decoration Day). For example, people in New Orleans still throng cemeteries on All Saints Day (Marcus, 1988). Burial places bloom with white and yellow chrysanthemums, and family tombs are scrubbed and whitewashed as in the past. A century ago in New Orleans on All Saints Day crowds poured into cemeteries from dawn to dusk. Families gathered for picnics, entertained friends, and told stories about the dead. Even today, All Saints Day remains a holiday for New Orleans municipal employees.

The continuity between the living and the dead is elaborated in ideas of reincarnation and in other ways found in non-Western as well as Western societies. For example, many Japanese today think that a person's spirit belongs to the same family and the same local community before and after death (Nagamine, 1988:67). A person's spirit gradually fades away from its family as time goes on. The Japanese do not clearly distinguish the dead from the living and seem to recognize the continuity between life and death.

BOX 10.1 **HOPI ATTITUDES TOWARD DEATH**

The Hopi Indians viewed life and death as a phase of a recurrent cycle. Death was an important change in individual status because it represented an altered state for the person involved. The Hopi believed that a duality of being existed in each person—a soul and a body expressed as a "breath-body." A person dying on earth literally was reborn in the afterworld. Corpses were washed and given new names before burial. The breath-body's pattern of existence would supposedly be the same in the domain of the dead as it had been on earth—when it died in the afterworld, it would be reborn on earth.

During their elaborate ceremonies, the Hopi performed specific rites for making the desires of the living known to the dead. Thus, the living solicited the active aid of the dead. The dead returned symbolically to earth at given times through katchina performers [masked and costumed individuals who impersonated spirits of the dead].

W. H. Oswalt, 1986. *Life Cycles and Lifeways.* Palo Alto, CA: Mayfield, p. 174.

The Igbo in Nigeria (Uchendu, 1965) believe that death is important to join the ancestors. Without death, there would be no population increase in the ancestral households and thus no change in social status for the living Igbo. The **lineage** system is continued among the dead. Thus the world of the dead is a world full of activities.

The Ulithi of Micronesia are not morbid or defeated by death, according to William A. Lessa (1966). Their rituals afford them some victories, and their mythology provides a hope for a happy life in another realm. Though their gods are somewhat distant, they assure that the world has an enduring structure, and their ancestral ghosts stand by to give more immediate aid when merited. Thus, after expressing their bereavement, rather than retreating, they spring back into their normal work and enjoyment of life.

For the Dunsun of North Borneo, few events focus more on the beliefs and acts concerned with the non-natural world than the death of a family member (Williams, 1965:39). While death is considered a difficult topic about which everyone is fearful of talking, it must, nonetheless, be prepared for since it causes great changes.

The Abkhasians on the coast of the Black Sea (Benet, 1974) view death as irrational and unjust. The one occasion when outbursts of feeling are permitted is at a funeral—wailing and scratching at one's flesh are permitted. Box 10.2 provides more detail on this culture.

BOX 10.2 **ABKHASIANS—THE LONG-LIVING PEOPLE**

Over 125,000 native Abkhasians live mostly in rural areas on the coast of the Black Sea in Abkhasia, a country about half the size of New Jersey. These people do not have a phrase for "old people." Those over one hundred years of age are called "long-living people." Most of the aged work regularly, performing light household tasks, working in the orchards and gardens, and caring for the animals.

These long-living people seem to enjoy fairly good health in their "old age." Close to 40 percent of the aged men (over age 90) and 30 percent of aged women have good vision—they do not need glasses for any sort of work. Nearly half have "reasonably good hearing." Most have their own teeth, and their posture is unusually erect.

Why do these people live so long? First, they have no retirement status but simply decrease their expected work load as they grow older. Second, they do not set deadlines for themselves, thus, no sense of urgency is accepted in emergencies.

Third, overeating is considered dangerous, and fat people are regarded as sick. When eating, they take small bites and chew slowly, thus insuring proper digestion. Leftovers are not eaten. Milk and vegetables make up 74 percent of their diet. The aged average 1900 calories per day—500 less than the U.S. National Academy of Science recommends for those over 55. They do not use refined sugars, and drink water and honey before retiring in the evening. A fermented drink (like buttermilk) with a high food value and useful for intestinal disorders is drunk. They eat a lot of fruit. Meat is eaten only once or twice per week. They usually cook without salt or spices. A dry red wine not fortified with sugar and with a low alcohol content is drunk. Few of them smoke, and they do not drink coffee or tea. Their main meal is at lunch (between 2 and 3 p.m.), and their supper is light. Between meals they eat fruit or drink a glass of fermented milk. They have a relaxed mood at mealtimes and eat slowly.

Fourth, stress is avoided by reducing competition. Fifth, they exercise daily. Sixth, their behavior is fairly uniform and predictable. Seventh, moderation is practiced in everything they do.

(continued on next page)

Though some social scientists question the longevity of the Abkhasians, they do seem to have their act together regarding health habits. Much of the above is advice we have often heard but failed to put into practice. Perhaps we should adhere to some of the Abkhasians' practices. Who knows, we might even live longer—if that is a goal to be sought.

Based on Sula Benet, 1974, *Abkhasians: The Long-Living People of the Caucasus.* New York: Holt, Rinehart and Winston.

CUSTOMS AT DEATH

As will be discussed in Chapter 12, a professional is called upon in the United States to prepare the body for final disposition, since we are a very specialized society with a high division of labor. The funeral director takes the body away and returns it later for viewing. The kin and friends in the United States normally play no significant role in handling the corpse. Compared with most societies, our culture is unique in the level of professional specialization relative to the preparation of the corpse and the actual disposal of the body. Most of the cultures discussed in this section encourage families and friends to become very involved in preparing the corpse for its final disposition.

Norms Prior to Death

Some societies have specific norms just prior to the death. It is important in many societies, including the United States, that one be with the dying person at the time of death. So often it is said, "If only I had gotten there a few minutes earlier . . ." A visit prior to death allows one to say goodbye. Among the Dunsun of North Borneo (Williams, 1965), relatives come to witness the death. The dying person is propped up and held from behind. When the body grows cold, the social fact of death is recognized by announcing "he exists no more" or "someone has gone far away."

The Salish Indians of the Northwest United States (Habenstein & Lamers, 1963) leave the dying person alone with an aged man who neither receives pay nor is expected to have any special qualifications for the task. One near death must confess his or her misdeeds to this person. The confession is to prevent the ghost from roaming the places once frequented in life.

The Ik of Uganda (Turnbull, 1972) place the dying person in the fetal position since death for them represents a "celestial rebirth." (Box 10.3 provides additional description of the Ik culture; also see Turnbull, 1972.) The

Magars of Nepal (Hitchcock, 1966) purify a dying person by giving him or her water that has been touched with gold.

Having a cultural framework prescribing proper behavior at the time of death provides an established order and perhaps gives comfort to the bereaved. These behavioral norms give survivors something to do during the dying process and immediately thereafter, thus facilitating the coping abilities of the bereaved.

BOX 10.3 **THE IK OF UGANDA**

The Ik of Uganda were relocated by the government prior to World War II in order to use their territory for a national park. As a result, these 2000 nomads had to abandon their hunting and gathering way of life and turn to horticulture—a sedentary way of life for which they had no preparation. This resulted in a mere subsistence level of living, with starvation the norm.

The Ik quickly evolved from a very loving, caring family system where mutuality, reciprocity, cooperation, and sharing were normal, to a survival-of-the-fittest system where children were put out of the house on their own at age three. Self-interest soon became the motivating theme in their daily existence—stealing, treachery, and deceit followed. With social disintegration complete, no individual had any concern or consideration for anyone else.

These "loveless people" changed from the epitome of a solid family structure to that of a fractured family. With love being lethal—one could not afford to care for another as food supply and water were so limited—marriage and procreation were rare. Why bother to marry and have children if one literally cannot afford such a relationship? Family sentiment and love were luxuries the Ik could not afford. At the verge of starvation, such luxuries could mean death. Is it not a singularly foolish luxury to die for someone already dead, or weak, or old?

Based on Colin M. Turnbull, 1972, *The Mountain People,* New York: Simon and Schuster.

Handling the Corpse

Cleaning the Body   Family members' preparation of the body for final disposition, especially cleaning the body, is very evident in some societies. For the Bornu in Nigeria (Cohen, 1967), family members are required to wash the body, wrap it in a white cloth, place it on a **bier,** a structure for viewing and/or carrying, and take it to the burial ground. Similarly, the Semai in Malaya (Dentan, 1968) have the housemates bathe the corpse and sprinkle it with perfume or sweet-smelling herbs to mask the odor of decay. They then wrap the body in swaddling.

The Mapuche Indians of Chile (Faron, 1968) sometimes smoke the body, then wash and dress it in the person's best clothes, lay it out on a bier in the house, and place the body in a pine coffin. Among some groups in South Thailand (Fraser, 1966), the body is held and bathed with water specifically purified with herbs and clay. The corpse is then rinsed and dried and all orifices plugged with cotton.

In the French West Indies (Horowitz, 1967) the neighbors wash the body with rum and force a liter or more of strong rum down the throat as a temporary preservative before dressing and placing the body on a bed. Rather than use a strong drink like rum, the Zinacantecos of Mexico (Vogt, 1970) pour water into the mouth of the deceased about every half hour to "relieve thirst" while the grave is being dug.

BOX 10.4 **FUNERAL HOME PROPOSED FOR SPECIAL RITUALS OF INDIANS**

The strange odyssey of Steve Perion, the man who wants to open a funeral home in Minneapolis for American Indians, has already taken him to the State Capitol posing for pictures with Gov. Rudy Perpich and to City Hall looking for money.

He has impressed politicians with his business acumen and collected a stack of letters praising his sensitivity from people he hardly knows. "His particular expertise in and commitment to serving the funeral needs of the American (Indian) community here would fill a desperate need," says Minneapolis DFLer Rep. Karen Clark, who acknowledges she barely knows him.

Perion has huddled with financial analysts and come away with a polished business plan for success based on death—60 indigent Indian deaths a year will mean $15,600 in gross profits.

So goes the balancing act for Perion, a Chippewa Indian who admits he has no money of his own. Entering an arena where many Indian families can't afford even the simplest of funerals, he is trying not to be viewed as an opportunist. But Perion, who claims his will be the first funeral home for Indians in urban America, is quickly enlisting support by promising the city's large Indian community a perspective other funeral homes can't match and promising financiers a steady cash flow from county welfare payments for indigent deaths.

"The issue is sensitivity," said the Rev. James Notebaart, director of the Catholic Indian Ministries in south Minneapolis. "It's really a clash of cultures—the urban economic life and culture and the (Indian) tradition of living off the land and living without dollars. . . . The business of burying the dead costs money and there's often a clash there."

As Perion moves to bridge the two worlds using a yellow Ford station wagon as a hearse, the task also can be tiring. That point was driven home only last week as Perion coordinated a wake for a 38-year-old Sioux woman who died in Duluth. Between Tuesday and Friday, Perion had gone to Duluth to get the body, used a Richfield funeral home to prepare it for burial and then had overseen a 24-hour wake at the American Indian Center on Franklin Avenue in Minneapolis.

Then there was a 10-hour drive with the coffin to Belcourt, N.D., for another wake and burial. In between, there was the haggling by phone with a North Dakota funeral home that wanted a consulting fee of nearly $400. And finally, there were arrangements with the family to place a hatchet in the coffin—an Indian custom to ward off evil spirits—and to put tobacco between the body's fingers to feed the spirits.

Perion's fee, excluding the price of the poplar wood coffin: $927. "It's really amazing. When I get through with a funeral, I'm exhausted," he said.

It is that commitment that has won Perion friends. "I see a pretty big need," said Philip Gleason, co-owner of Gleason Mortuary in Richfield where Perion uses space for embalming. "The white man does not understand the Indian and his traditions. . . . (Perion's) all set to go, you might say, if he can come up with a building."

Perion's financial plan, written with the help of economic development experts, lists start-up costs of $100,245—more than half of which would go to buy a four-wheel-drive funeral coach and two new Buicks. Regarding the size of the building he'll need, Perion said: "The square footage is based on how many Indians will die in the first year—how many will die in Minneapolis and St. Paul, and how many calls I'll get out of that."

But he also stresses the sensitivity he will bring to the role. He advertises his familiarity with the water drum ceremony, during which an Indian elder wraps an animal hide around a canister of water that symbolizes the purification of the spiritual world. Perion talks also of the star quilt burial rite, in which a large quilt with a star in the middle hangs behind the casket during the wake and is often then used to wrap the body before burial.

And he talks of the pain of burying his own people.

His most heart-wrenching Indian funeral? That, says Perion, might be the time the family of an Indian infant who had died wanted to wrap the body in a blanket just before the casket was closed. But when the family began wailing and wouldn't let the body go, Perion finally found himself having to pry the body from them. "I'll never do that again," he said.

Others agree the uniqueness of Indian burials can make them challenging. "They have evening wakes that last the entire (night)," said Les Rosecke, a funeral director at Albin Funeral Chapel in south Minneapolis. The funeral home, which Rosecke said handles an estimated 35 Indian burials a year, is considered to have the largest number of Indian funerals locally. Of a funeral home for Indians, he said: "We certainly would cooperate with them."

As Perion searches for money and a funeral home, the supports continue to roll in. "I tell ya', I think it would be a marvelous idea if it works," said Mary Williams, a funeral director in Duluth who once worked with Perion. "It's a culture that's very unique to itself—different rituals, different time considerations. (Steve's) very much involved in tribal activities.

Mike Kaszuba, *Minneapolis Star Tribune*, October 9, 1989. Reprinted with permission of the Star Tribune, Minneapolis-St. Paul.

Other Customs Regarding the Corpse   In addition to cleaning the corpse, many groups spend time decorating the body. For example, the Tiwi of Australia (Hart & Pilling, 1960) wrap the body in bark. The Qemant of Ethiopia (Gamst, 1969) wrap the body in a piece of white cloth and cover it with a mat of woven grass. Tewa Indians in Arizona (Dozier, 1966) bury a woman in her wedding outfit and wrap a man in a blanket for burial. After cleaning the body, the Ulithi in Micronesia (Lessa, 1966) cover it with a tuberous plant and decorate the head and hands with flower garlands.

The Konyak Nagar in India (Furer-Haimendorf, 1969) place the **cadaver** on a bier. Six days after the funeral, the head is wrenched from the body, and the skull is placed in an urn hollowed from a block of sandstone. For

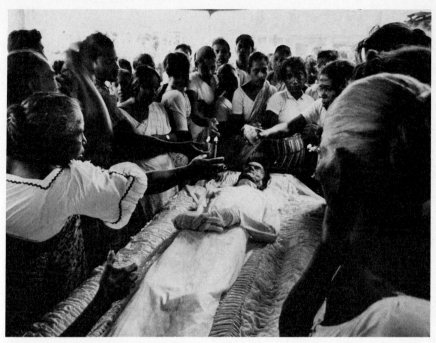

This Buddhist funeral in Ceylon demonstrates the communal nature of the special care taken in preparing the body for final disposition.

three years the skull is given portions of food and beer whenever the kinsmen celebrate a feast.

Bronislaw Malinowski (1929) reports that the Trobriand Islanders continually handle the remains throughout the death ritual. The body is **exhumed** (removed from its grave or tomb) twice and cut up. Some of the bones are peeled out of the carcass, handled, and given to different individuals. The sons of the deceased are expected to suck some of the decaying matter when they are cleaning the bones.

Among the Yạnomamö Indians of Venezuela and Brazil (Chagnon, 1983), the body of one dying in an epidemic is placed on a tree platform and allowed to decay. After several months, an elderly man is appointed to strip the remaining decayed flesh from the bones, which are then cremated. Under normal circumstances, the body of a deceased Yạnomamö is burned, the ashes are mixed with boiled plantain soup and then eaten at a feast. This **endocannibalism** is supposed to put the warriors in an appropriate frame of rage prior to going out to kill the enemy. Such behavior is considered a supreme form of displaying friendship and solidarity for the Yạnomamö.

BOX 10.5 **THE YĄNOMAMÖ**

Approximately 12,000 Yąnomamö Indians live in Venezuela and Brazil in villages ranging in size from 40 to 250 inhabitants. Being horticulturalists, the Yąnomamö grow 85 percent of their food. They occasionally enjoy the delicacies of caterpillars, roasted spiders, and armadillos.

The Yąnomamö are a very aggressive and fierce people living in a state of chronic warfare and believing it is the "nature of men to fight." Because they define themselves as fierce, they act accordingly. The "fierceness" of the Yąnomamö is exemplified by their gruesome methods of infanticide and abortion, their raiding parties where men are killed and women raped and captured as wives, their games of chest pounding, side slapping, club pounding and ax fights played at village feasts, their chopping on their wives with machetes to "show their love," and 24 percent of adult males dying in warfare.

Women's status among the Yąnomamö is not high. They perform the bulk of the garden work, while men do the initial heavier groundbreaking duties with their digging sticks. Almost daily, the men lie in their hammocks getting high on hallucinogenic drugs. The drugs are taken from the bark of the ebene tree and shot into their nostrils in a powdery form. Though side effects of the drug are vomiting, runny nose, and watery eyes, the men have contact with the deceased ancestors while under the drug's influence. Husbands beat their wives, and brothers will trade their sisters to other groups of brothers for wives for themselves.

Competition and aggressiveness are certainly prevalent in the United States, especially among the middle class. We too are a somewhat fierce people. We have a reputation of high crime and violence and of cutthroat economics. While not like the Yąnomamö, the United States would likely fall closer to the Yąnomamö on a continuum with aggressive behavior at one end and passive behavior at the other.

Based on Napoleon A. Chagnon, *Yąnomamö: The Fierce People,* Third Ed. New York: Holt, Rinehart and Winston, 1983.

From the customs cited above, it seems significant in most societies that the body be cleaned and steps taken to assure a tolerable odor prior to final disposition. A reverence for the body also seems prevalent. As in the United States, it is important in many other societies that the deceased "look good" to the mourners.

The body is not exhumed to take various parts home in the United States, but some individuals have been known to keep the **cremains** (remains from cremation) in a vase in the home or to carry them around in their purse. Others take photographs of the deceased or collect important reminders to be placed in scrapbooks or albums. According to Judy Tatelbaum (1980), keepsakes like photographs, clippings, and stories about the deceased can provide a satisfying memorial later on. Fearing that we will be unable to remember the deceased distinctly enough, we desire a "piece" of the person we loved.

BURIAL RITES

As noted in Chapter 4, Bronislaw Malinowski (1948) stressed the roles of religion and magic as a means of reducing death anxiety and fears. A. R. Radcliffe-Brown (1965) argued for a different interpretation, suggesting that rites may contribute to death anxiety and insecurity. These are simply different explanations for the same rites. Conrad Kottak (1982) notes that for one raised within the cultural tradition of a particular society, performance of the rite does relieve anxiety—it is the socially approved means to do so. On the other hand, anxiety may result *because* the rite exists. A common stress may be produced by participation in the rite, thus enhancing the social solidarity of the participants.

Functions

The term *function* refers to the extent to which some part or process of a social system contributes to the maintenance of that system. Function means the extent to which a given activity promotes or interferes with the maintenance of a system (Cuzzort & King, 1980:172). Robert Merton (1957) distinguished between two forms of social function. **Manifest functions** are objective consequences for the person, subgroup, or social system that contribute to its adjustment and are so intended. **Latent functions** are consequences that contribute to adjustment but are not so intended. While manifest functions are the official explanations of a given action (e.g., going to a funeral to pay respects to the deceased and to let the survivors know that you care), latent functions are the sociological explanations (e.g., a funeral really becomes a family reunion).

Rather than leave all corpses to environmental elements, an event like a burial rite obviously has some positive consequences for the survivors of the deceased. Burial rite functions can be enumerated as follows. First, burial rites are the reaffirmation of group structure and social cohesiveness of the individuals suffering loss. Second, they give meaning and sanction to the separation of the dead person from the living. Third, burial rites help effect the transition of the soul to another, otherworldly realm. Fourth, they assist in the incorporation of the spirit to its new existence. Fifth, according to Melvin Williams (1981), for middle-class Americans in Pittsburgh, Pennsylvania, for example, a funeral may establish, validate, and reinforce social status, whereas for the lower class, funerals tend to be rites of intensification and solidarity putting aside feuds and squabbles for the moment.

To assure that the spirit will be born again, some societies go to great lengths. For example, the Dunsun of North Borneo (Williams, 1965) kill animals to accompany the deceased on the trip to the land of the dead. The Ulithi in Micronesia (Lessa, 1966) place a loincloth and a gingerlike plant in the right arm of the deceased so that gifts can be presented to the custodian at the entrance of the world. For the Zinacantecos of Mexico (Vogt, 1970), a chicken head is put in a bowl of broth beside the head of the corpse. The chicken allegedly leads the inner soul of the deceased. A black dog then carries the soul across the river.

In Southwestern Nigeria the Yoruba (Bascom, 1969) have a man with a live chicken precede the carrier of the corpse, plucking out feathers and leaving them along the trail for the soul of the deceased to follow back to town. Upon reaching the town gate, the chicken is killed by striking its head against the ground. The blood and feathers are then placed in the grave so that others will not die. A second chicken is killed and its blood put in the grave so the soul of the deceased will not bother the surviving relatives.

Soul houses are built in some parts of Appalachia (Gaines, 1981) to provide protection for the deceased from evil spirits, wild animals, grave robbers, and other unwelcome visitors. These little houses are placed directly over the grave. Some are box-shaped concrete slabs, while others have rooftop structures. The more elaborate of the soul houses are miniature homes with actual tin roofs, gutters, drainpipes, carpets, furniture, and various objects dear to the deceased.

Thus, burial rites serve the functions of maintaining relations with ancestral spirits, reaffirming social solidarity, and restoring group structures dismembered by death. Burial rites not only reaffirm group structure, but enhance social cohesiveness.

Variations

As expressions of mourning vary with cultures, different burial rites tend to be widespread among societies. The depth of the burial area, the place of disposal, and the importance of the status of the deceased are examined here.

In the old days of the wild West in the United States, a man was buried "six feet under with his boots on." It is true that graves were six feet deep in earlier periods of United States history, but today graves are less than six feet deep—typically around four and a half feet in depth with 18 inches of dirt above the top of the casket/vault. With sealed, heavier caskets today—often placed within a steel or concrete vault—it is not necessary to place the body so deep in the ground, as was the case with an unsealed pine box of an earlier period.

The Kalingas of the Philippines (Dozier, 1967) bury adults in six-feet-deep and three-feet-wide graves. The Mardudjara aborigines of Australia (Tonkinson, 1978) dig a rectangular hole about three-feet deep, line the bottom with leafy bushes and small logs, then perform the **interment.** Similarly, the Semai of Malaya (Dentan, 1968) dig the grave two- to three-feet deep. Among the Abkhasians near the Black Sea (Benet, 1974), women are buried 10 centimeters deeper than men.

Some societies keep the corpses in or near the home of the deceased. The Yoruba of Nigeria (Bascom, 1969), for example, dig the grave in the room of the deceased. An adult man among the Lugbara of Uganda (Middleton, 1965) is buried inside his first wife's hut in the center of the floor. The Swazi of Africa (Kuper, 1963) bury a woman on the outskirts of her husband's home. Such a practice is not limited to African countries, however, as is noted in Box 12.9.

One's rank or status in the community or village may determine the final disposition of the remains. The Barabaig of Tanzania (Klima, 1970) place women and children out in the surrounding bush where they are consumed by the hyena. Only certain male and female elders will receive a burial. Box 10.6, about the Kapauku Papuans, further details the importance of one's position in the community determining how and where burial or final disposition will occur.

BOX 10.6 **BURIAL RITES AMONG THE KAPAUKU PAPUANS**

Among the Kapauku Papuans of West New Guinea, burial rites are determined by the deceased's status and cause of the death. The simplest burial is given to a drowned man whose body is laid flat on the bank of a river and protected by a fence erected around it. The body is then abandoned to the elements. Very young children and individuals not particularly liked and considered unimportant are completely interred. Children, women, and the elderly who were unimportant but loved are tied with vines into a squatting position and semi-interred with the head above ground. A dome-shaped structure of branches and soil is then constructed to protect the head.

(continued on next page)

A respected and loved adult male among the Kapauku Papuans receives a tree burial. Tied in a squatting position, the corpse is placed in a tree house with a small window in front. Corpses of important individuals, who are feared by their relatives, and of women who died in childbirth require a special type of burial. Their bodies are placed in the squatting position on a special raised scaffold constructed in the house where death occurred. The house is then sealed and abandoned.

The most elaborate burial among the Kapauku Papuans is given to a rich headman. A special hut is built on high stilts. The body is tied in a squatting position, and a pointed pole is driven through the rectum, abdomen, chest cavity and neck with its pointed end supporting the base of the skull. The body is then placed in the dead house with the face appearing in the front window of the structure. The body is pierced several times with arrows to allow the body fluids to drain away. Years later, the skull of the respected man may be cleaned and awarded a second honor of being placed on a pole driven into the ground near the house of the surviving relatives.

Excerpt from *The Kapauku Papuans of West New Guinea* by Leopold Pospisil, copyright © 1963 by Holt, Rinehart and Winston, Inc., reprinted by permission of the publisher.

In death, as in life, one's social status determines how one is treated. Whether one is buried or left to the elements is often determined by gender, age, standing in the community, and cause of death. If buried in the ground, even the depth of burial may vary by one's social position: additional evidence of the social nature of the meaning of death, as discussed in Chapter 2.

CONCLUSION

As discussed in Chapter 2, dying is more than a biological process. One does not die in a vacuum but in a social milieu. An act of dying has an influence on others because it is a shared experience. The sharing mechanism is death-related meanings composed of symbols.

Since death meanings are socially constructed, patterns of correct or incorrect behavior related to dying and death will largely be determined within the social setting in which it occurs. Death-related behavior of the dying person and of those relating to him or her is in response to meaning, relative to the audience and the situation. As noted, death-related behavior is shared, symboled, and situated.

Because death generally disrupts established interaction networks, shared "scripts" aid in providing socially acceptable behavior for the bereaved. Such scripts are essential because they prevent societal break-downs while providing social continuity. Burial rituals are important in assuring social cohesion at the time of family dismemberment through death. Since death is a family crisis (see Dickinson & Fritz, 1981), appropriate networks for coping must be culturally well grounded.

Death-related meanings are socially created and transmitted. Through participant observation, small children learn from others how to respond to death. If children are sheltered from such situations, their socialization will be thwarted. As noted in this chapter, family involvement plays an important role in most societies as individuals prepare for death, as they prepare the corpse for final disposition, and in burial rituals that follow. Therefore, whether death rituals involve killing a chicken, scraping the meat from the bones of the corpse, crying quietly, wailing loudly, mutilating one's own body, or burning or burying the corpse, all bereavement behavior has three interconnected characteristics—it is shared, symboled, and situated.

SUMMARY

1. Customs for caring for the dying prior to death assist both the dying individual and the survivors in coping with the impending death.

2. Death for some is viewed as the end, while for others it is viewed as a continuation of life in a different form.

3. While mourning rituals tend to be commonplace in different cultures, the prescribed behavior is effected by the social status and gender of the individuals involved.

4. Some social groups mourn for a few hours after death, while others mourn for months or years.

5. The depth of burial often varies by the gender and socioeconomic status of the deceased.

6. Burial rituals serve the functions of appeasing the ancestral spirits and the soul of the deceased, bringing the kin together, reinforcing social status, and restoring the social structure.

7. In most societies the body of the deceased is cleaned and prepared for burial. Some groups even keep parts of the body for ornamental or special purposes.

DISCUSSION QUESTIONS

1. Why is it important to learn about bereavement patterns in other cultures?

2. Cite as many death-custom similarities between other cultures and the United States as you can. Cite death-custom differences between other cultures and the United States.

3. What is your own concept of *soul?* How is your concept of soul similar to and different from some other cultures' soul concept? How does such a concept relate to death?

4. Drawing on your own knowledge, discuss any United States behavior patterns for the dying just prior to death. How do these customs compare to those cited in this chapter?

5. Describe mourning rituals commonly found in the United States. Mourning rituals may differ by region of the country or ethnicity. Discuss these differences.

6. It is suggested that an explanation of crying at the time of death may be rather complex. Discuss the types of crying over a death.

7. A professional generally prepares the corpse for final disposition in the United States, but this is not universally true. Discuss the importance of the family being involved in preparing the body for final disposition.

8. In death as in life gender discrimination occurs. Discuss with a local funeral director the differences in funerals for males and females. Do you notice discrepancies in grave markings (e.g., size of the stone and length of epitaphs) between males and females?

9. Unlike many societies where squatting occurs, in the United States we basically give birth and are buried in a horizontal position. Why do you suppose the United States has a "laid-back" approach from the womb to the tomb? Can you cite advantages and disadvantages to horizontal burials?

10. What are some of the functions of burial rites in this chapter?

GLOSSARY

Bier   A framework upon which the corpse and/or casket is placed for viewing and/or carrying.

Cadaver   A dead human or animal body usually intended for dissection.

Ceremony   A given complex of rituals associated with a specific occasion.

Cremains Cremated remains—what is left after cremation.

Endocannibalism The Yąnomamö Indian practice of eating the ashes of the deceased in order to charge a warrior up prior to going into battle and to display friendship and solidarity.

Ethnocentrism Literally means "culture-centeredness." The belief that one's own culture is superior to others.

Exhume To remove a corpse from its place of burial.

Interment The act of depositing a corpse in a grave or tomb.

Latent function Behavioral consequences that are not intended (e.g., a funeral brings the family together usually in an amiable way).

Levirate A marriage rule whereby a widow marries her deceased husband's brother.

Lineage A group of relatives who trace their descent unilineally from a common ancestor.

Manifest function Behavioral consequences that are intended and overt (e.g., going to a funeral to pay respects to the deceased).

Rites of passage Ceremonies centering around transitions in life from one status to another (e.g., baptism, marriage ceremony, the funeral).

Ritual The symbolic affirmation of values by means of culturally standardized utterances and actions.

REFERENCES

Bascom, William. 1969. *The Yoruba of Southwestern Nigeria.* New York: Holt, Rinehart and Winston.

Bendann, Effie. 1930. *Death Customs: An Analytical Study of Burial Rites.* New York: Knopf.

Benet, Sula. 1974. *Abkhasians: The Long-Living People of the Caucasus.* New York: Holt, Rinehart and Winston.

Campbell, Alexander. 1958. *The Heart of India.* New York: Knopf.

Chagnon, Napoleon A. 1983. *Yąnomamö: The Fierce People,* Third Ed. New York: Holt, Rinehart and Winston.

Cohen, Ronald. 1967. *The Kanuri of Bornu.* New York: Holt, Rinehart and Winston.

Cuzzort, Ray P., & Edith W. King. 1980. *Twentieth Century Social Thought,* Third Ed. New York: Holt, Rinehart and Winston.

Deng, Francis M. 1972. *The Dinka of the Sudan.* New York: Holt, Rinehart and Winston.

Dentan, Robert K. 1968. *The Semai: A Non-Violent People of Malaya.* New York: Holt, Rinehart and Winston.

Dickinson, George E., and Judy L. Fritz. 1981. "Death in the Family." *Journal of Family Issues.* September 2: 379–384.

Dozier, Edward P. 1966. *Hano: A Tewa Indian Community in Arizona.* New York: Holt, Rinehart and Winston.

Dozier, Edward P. 1967. *The Kalinga of Northern Luzon, Philippines.* New York: Holt, Rinehart and Winston.

Durkheim, Emile. 1965. *The Elementary Forms of the Religious Life.* New York: The Free Press.

Faron, Louis C. 1968. *The Mapuche Indians of Chile.* New York: Holt, Rinehart and Winston.

Fraser, Thomas M., Jr. 1966. *Fishermen of South Thailand: The Malay Villagers.* New York: Holt, Rinehart and Winston.

Furer-Haimendorf, Christoph Von. 1969. *The Konyak Nagar: An Indian Frontier Tribe.* New York: Holt, Rinehart and Winston.

Gaines, Judith. 1981. "Appalachia Comes Alive in Studying Tombstones." *Louisville Courier-Journal,* Louisville, KY, November 1, p. 5.

Gamst, Frederick C. 1969. *The Qemant: A Pagan–Hebraic Peasantry of Ethiopia.* New York: Holt, Rinehart and Winston.

Goldman, I. 1979. *The Cubeo: Indians of the Northwest Amazon.* Urbana, IL: University of Illinois Press.

Habenstein, Robert W., & William M. Lamers. 1963. *Funeral Customs the World Over.* Milwaukee: Bulfin.

Harris, Marvin. 1974. *Cows, Pigs, Wars and Witches.* New York: Vintage Books.

Hart, C. W. M., & Arnold R. Pilling. 1960. *The Tiwi of North Australia.* New York: Holt, Rinehart and Winston.

Hitchcock, John T. 1966. *The Magars of Manyan Hill.* New York: Holt, Rinehart and Winston.

Hoebel, E. Adamson. 1960. *The Cheyennes: Indians of the Great Plains.* New York: Holt, Rinehart and Winston.

Horowitz, Michael M. 1967. *Morne-Paysan: Peasant Village in Martinique.* New York: Holt, Rinehart and Winston.

Huntington, Richard, & Peter Metcalf. 1979. *Celebrations of Death: The Anthropology of Mortuary Ritual.* Cambridge: Cambridge University Press.

Klima, George J. 1970. *The Barabaig: East African Cattle-Herders.* New York: Holt, Rinehart and Winston.

Kottak, Conrad P. 1982. *Cultural Anthropology,* Third Ed. New York: Random House.

Kuper, Hilda. 1963. *The Swazi: A South African Kingdom.* New York: Holt, Rinehart and Winston.

Lessa, William A. 1966. *Ulithi: A Micronesian Design for Living.* New York: Holt, Rinehart and Winston.

Malinowski, Bronislaw. 1929. *The Sexual Life of Savages.* New York: Harcourt, Brace and World.

Malinowski, Bronislaw. 1948. *Magic, Science and Religion, and Other Essays.* Boston: Beacon Press.

Marcus, Frances Frank. 1988. "An Invitation to Become the Life of the Cemetery." *The New York Times.* New York, NY, November 1, p. 8.

Merton, Robert K. 1957. *Social Theory and Social Structure,* Rev. Ed. New York: The Free Press.

Middleton, John. 1965. *The Lugbara of Uganda.* New York: Holt, Rinehart and Winston.

Nagamine, Takahjko. 1988. "Attitudes toward Death in Rural Areas of Japan." *Death Studies,* 12:61–68.

Oswalt, W. H. 1986. *Life Cycles and Lifeways*. Palo Alto, CA: Mayfield.

Palgi, Phyllis, & Henry Abramovitch. 1984. "Death: A Cross-Cultural Perspective." *Annual Review of Anthropology*, 13:385–417.

Pospisil, Leopold. 1963. *The Kapauku Papuans of West New Guinea*. New York: Holt, Rinehart and Winston.

Radcliffe-Brown, A. R. 1964. *The Andaman Islanders*. New York: The Free Press.

Radcliffe-Brown, A. R. 1965. *Structure and Function in Primitive Society*. New York: The Free Press.

Rappaport, Roy A. 1974. "Obvious Aspects of Ritual." *Cambridge Anthropology*, 2:2–60.

Rosenblatt, P. C., R. Walsh, and A. Jackson. 1976. *Grief and Mourning in Cross Cultural Perspective*. New Haven: Human Relations Area Files Press.

Tatelbaum, Judy. 1980. *The Courage to Grieve*. New York: Lippincott and Crowell.

Taylor, Robert B. 1980. *Cultural Ways*, Third Ed. Boston: Allyn and Bacon.

Tonkinson, Robert. 1978. *The Mardudjara Aborigines*. New York: Holt, Rinehart and Winston.

Turnbull, Colin M. 1972. *The Mountain People*. New York: Simon and Schuster.

Tylor, E. B. 1873. *Primitive Culture*. London: John Murray.

Uchendu, Victor C. 1965. *The Igbo of Southeast Nigeria*. New York: Holt, Rinehart and Winston.

Van Gennep, A. 1909. *Les Rites de Passage*. Paris: Nourry. M. B. Vizedom & G. L. Caffee (Transl.) 1960. *The Rites of Passage*. Chicago: University of Chicago Press.

Vogt, Evon Z. 1970. *The Zinacantecos of Mexico: A Modern Maya Way of Life*. New York: Holt, Rinehart and Winston.

Williams, Melvin D. 1981. *On the Street Where I Lived*. New York: Holt, Rinehart and Winston.

Williams, Thomas R. 1965. *The Dunsun: A North Borneo Society*. New York: Holt, Rinehart and Winston.

SUGGESTED READINGS

Badone, Ellen. 1989. *The Appointed Hour*. Berkeley: University of California Press.

An examination of death in Brittany that is concerned primarily with the complex, mutually reinforcing, and interdependent relationships between responses to death and transformations in Breton social organizations.

Bendann, Effie. 1930. *Death Customs: An Analytical Study of Burial Rites*. New York: Knopf.

A thorough anthropological analysis of death customs, including an analysis of burial rites, causes of death, attitudes toward the corpse, mourning, and beliefs in the afterlife.

Blackburn, Stuart H. 1988. *Singing of Birth and Death*. Philadelphia: University of Pennsylvania Press.

Based on data gathered in India, the author takes the reader through translated performances sung in different bow song festivals from birth to death.

Counts, Dorothy Ayers, & David R. Counts. 1985. *Aging and Its Transformations: Moving toward Death in Pacific Societies.* Washington, DC: University Press of America.

A discussion of aging and dying in the South Pacific.

Habenstein, Robert W. & William M. Lamers. 1963. *Funeral Customs the World Over.* Milwaukee: Bulfin.

A review of the cultures of the world especially helpful in cross-cultural study of the various practices of funeralization in all cultures.

Huntington, Richard, & Peter Metcalf. 1979. *Celebrations of Death: The Anthropology of Mortuary Ritual.* Cambridge: Cambridge University Press.

An anthropological analysis of dying and death, including universals and culture, death as transition, and the royal corpse and the body politic.

Metcalf, Peter. 1982. *A Borneo Journey into Death.* Philadelphia: University of Pennsylvania Press.

This ethnographical approach to dying and death includes the topics of the soul, celebrating the ancestors, and the cosmology of the ancestral spirits.

Stannard, David E. 1977. *The Puritan Way of Death.* New York: Oxford University Press.

A portrayal of death in the Western tradition, including discussions of death, childhood, and burial.

Watson, James L. and Evelyn S. Rawski (Eds.). 1988. *Death Ritual in Late Imperial and Modern China.* Berkeley, CA: University of California Press.

Essays on both Chinese ritual practice and belief structures as they relate to death rites—the performance of required acts, variations in form, and attitudes behind practices.

CHAPTER 11

The History of Bereavement and Burial Practices in American Culture

—

As long as the cemetery is being filled with a fresh stream of the recently dead, it stays symbolically a live and vital emblem, telling the living of the meaning of life and death.

W. LLOYD WARNER, *THE LIVING AND THE DEAD*

11 This chapter traces the development of bereavement practices in America from the Puritans to the present. As death bereaves family members, friends, and more distant relatives, the survivors generally follow established rituals to care for the corpse, to reaffirm the solidarity of important groups, to create a new status for the dead person, and to comfort each other in such a way that they can eventually resume their roles in society. These rituals were established in time, and come to us from the past. Therefore, we need an historical explanation to fully understand them.

We deal with historical explanations every day, but we seldom consider what constitutes an historical explanation. Historians mainly determine chronology and context in order to demonstrate causation and coincidence in human affairs. We begin with chronology in order to determine the order in which events or processes occurred. This in itself has a certain explanatory value; for example, it is useful to know that discovery of the germ theory of disease preceded the widespread use of embalming in America. Too often, however, history begins and ends with chronology, and students are stuck with memorizing names and dates. History also explores the context of events to help explain them. For example, it is easier to understand the development of the funeral parlor if we see it in the context of developments in the domestic parlor.

Sometimes, historians can use chronology and context to determine causation. Knowing, for example that rural cemeteries preceded the public parks movement in America, we might conclude that cemetery reforms caused the parks movement. More frequently, however, chronology and context allow us only to identify coincidences (events or processes that occurred during the same period of time). Especially in social and cultural history, this chronicle of coincidences is crucial because people think analogically as much as they think logically. They do not isolate problems or ideas when they are faced with them; instead their whole range of prior experience affects their decision. In evaluating embalming, for example, few people treated the preservation of the corpse as a discrete issue. Instead, it coincided with other issues such as the importance of appearances in a consumer culture, the sanitary movement, the germ theory of disease, the privacy of the home, a stress on the "natural," a respect for surgery and surgeons, and the need to delay many funerals for distant relatives to return home.

Likewise, history shows that bereavement is but one part of a social construction of reality that changes through time. Bereavement practices are virtually inseparable from prescriptions for dying and descriptions of death, just as the whole American way of death is inseparable from the American way of life. Therefore, this chapter explains how changes in the American way of life brought changes in the American way of death and bereavement. It traces the historical roots of our bereavement practices so that we can begin to trace the routes of future change.

LIVING DEATH, 1600–1830: THE REFORMED TRADITION

Between 1600 and 1830, death was a living part of the American experience. Most people in this primarily agricultural period were well acquainted with death. In New England towns, for example, if people escaped death in their own homes, they still heard the toll of the funeral bell, encountered the funeral procession winding through the streets, or saw the stark *memento mori* of the graveyard. Even more, death was highlighted by the intellectual and emotional framework of the Reformed Tradition.

The Reformed Tradition was the one part of the Protestant Reformation that most influenced colonial Americans. Although most colonists followed the beliefs of the Reformers, the New England Puritans made the most convincing synthesis of their ideas and attitudes. In their view, a sovereign God ruled over an earth inhabited by depraved people. God displayed his sovereignty in "special providences" in which He intervened in the natural or social world. One such providence was death.

Because of original sin and their own sinfulness, Puritans knew they deserved death and damnation. They also celebrated, however, the fact that God freely elected a select few for salvation. Therefore, they approached death with an amazing ambivalence. They believed that "the last Enemy was Death; and God had made that a friend too" (Sewall, 1973:1, 599). Death

When death was viewed as a part of life, the body of the deceased was laid out in the home and friends of the bereaved visited to offer their condolences.

was an enemy for several reasons: It was painful, a punishment for sin, a possible prelude to everlasting hellfire, and meant separation from loved ones. Death was a friend, however, because it ended the pain and the earthly pilgrimage of the deceased, served as a "sanctified affliction" (Geddes, 1981:31)—either confirming a saint's faith or converting a sinner—and could open the gates to Heaven. Indeed, it was both a friendly enemy and a fearful friend.

Unlike modern thanatologists, the Puritans encouraged each other to fear death. They increasingly used that strong human emotion to rouse people from their psychological and spiritual security. Puritans knew that they would die, but not *when* they would die, or if they were among the elect. Therefore, they admonished themselves and each other to be constantly prepared for death. "It will do you no hurt. You will Dy not One Minute the sooner for it," argued Cotton Mather, "and being fit to Dy, you will be the more Fit to Live" (Geddes, 1981:64–65). Over and over again, they prayed, "Lord, help me to redeem the time!" Like modern thanatologists, they felt an awareness of death could improve the quality of their lives, and that they had a role to play in the work of God's redemption. Indeed, for them, dying, death, and bereavement were opportunities to glorify God by demonstrating human dependence on divine providence.

The deathbed was the final place of preparation. Dying Puritans received visitors who wanted to help provide "a lift toward heaven." Unlike Catholics, who relied on the sacramental rite of Extreme Unction, the Puritans focused on the state of the dying person's soul and mind. They prayed together, read the Bible, and urged active acceptance of the will of God.

In the same way, "the funeral was another opportunity for the bereaved to turn affliction into spiritual growth through resignation to, and joyful acceptance of, the will of God" (Geddes, 1981:104). Most Puritan deaths occurred at home. The family sent out for midwife-nurses to care for the corpse, ordered a coffin, and notified friends and relatives not already present. Puritans considered the corpse a mere shell of the soul. They simply washed it, wrapped it in a shroud, and placed it in the coffin. They embalmed bodies only to transport them to other towns for burial, or to prevent an offensive stench in hot weather.

Friends and relatives visited the home to console and congratulate the bereaved. They brought gifts of food to allow the survivors to mourn and to prepare the funeral. In this way, as in their own participation in the funeral, they reaffirmed the solidarity of the covenanted community. The funeral itself usually took place within a few days of death, and it followed the simple guidelines of the 1644 Westminster Confession: "When any person departeth this life, let the dead body, upon the day of Buriall, be decently attended from the house to the place appointed for publique Buriall, and there immediately interred, without any ceremony" (Geddes, 1981: 110–124).

Pallbearers, ministers, and civil officials were commonly invited to a funeral with a gift of gloves. Wealthier families might also bestow scarves and/or memorial rings, and give gloves to anyone who marched in the procession. These items were the common symbols of mourning in a colonial society, but more elaborate mourning apparel was also available. The tolling of the town bell announced the onset of a funeral, and participants gathered at the home for prayer and the procession.

Puritans prayed not for the soul of the deceased but for the comfort and instruction of the living. They believed that judgment occurred at death and that the dead were beyond human aid, so they prayed to reaffirm their faith and to glorify their God. For example, upon the death of his two-year-old daughter, Samuel Sewall had his surviving children read passages from the Bible. John read Ecclesiastes 3 on the acceptance of the seasons of life, Elizabeth read Revelation 22 on the theme of hope, Hannah read Psalm 38 on the mercy of God, and young Samuel asked for God's comfort in Psalm 102 (Sewall, 1973:1, 364). In addition to prayers, Puritans might also read an **elegy,** which generally depicted the dead person as a saint freed from the world and entering eternal bliss. Such elegies confirmed the new, separate status of the deceased, helping to bring grief under control, and provided a good example for structuring life after bereavement. Sometimes a copy of the elegy was pinned to the coffin or hearse for the funeral procession (Geddes, 1981:130–131).

The mourners walked from the home to the graveyard, where the men of the family, or the **sexton,** had opened a grave. They carried the coffin on a bier, covered with a black cloth "pall"—both of which were the property of the town instead of the church, as was the custom in England. During the procession, mourners were supposed to "apply themselves to meditations and conferences suitable to the occasion." At the gravesite, the pallbearers lowered the coffin into the earth, and the grave was refilled (Geddes, 1981:111, 133–135).

After the burial, the mourners returned home where they shared food, drink, prayers, and comforting words. The family thanked the pallbearers and participants, and sometimes gave additional presents. They might also request the minister to deliver a funeral sermon, which would occur not on the day of burial, but at the next regular meeting of the congregation. Sometimes families had such sermons and/or the elegies published and distributed to friends as *memento mori*. At a later date, the family might also erect a marker over the grave to proclaim the imminence of death or God's promise of salvation. Such markers near the much-frequented meetinghouse were another way of maintaining the vitality of death in early American culture (Geddes, 1981:139–140; Ludwig, 1966).

The Puritan funeral was the primary social institution for channeling the grief of survivors. It provided for the disposition of the body and the acknowledgment of the absence of the deceased. It drew the community together for mutual comfort, and it allowed mourners to honor the dead, to express their sorrow at separation, and to demonstrate their acceptance of God's will. After the funeral, Puritans expected mourners to return to their calling and to resume their life's work. They did not approve elaborate or extended mourning of the sort that became customary in the 19th century because it undermined the cheerful resignation to God's will that was essential to the Puritan experience.

Reforming the Reformed Tradition

In 1802, Nathaniel Emmons delivered a magnificent funeral sermon called "Death without Order." In it, he reviewed the Puritan orthodoxy about death, observing that "in relation to God, death is perfectly regular; but this regularity he has seen proper to conceal from the view of men." Emmons saw the uncertainty of death as a demonstration of God's sovereignty and human dependence, and as a way of teaching people "the importance and propriety of being constantly prepared for it." He, however, also saw that, despite the fact of death's disorder, multitudes of Americans had resolved "to observe order in preparing to meet it" (Emmons, 1842:3, 29–38). Between the 1730s and the 1830s, such orderly Americans were influenced by the Enlightenment, the American Revolution, Unitarianism, and Evangelicalism—and all of these were influenced by an underlying market revolution. These movements slowly but surely reformed the Reformed Tradition, and gave Americans an eclectic tradition from which to fashion new beliefs and behavior about dying, death, and bereavement.

The Enlightenment replaced the Puritans' providential God with a First Cause who designed the universe to operate by orderly and observable natural laws, and it replaced depraved dependent Puritans with Enlightened, rational people. Enlightened people, therefore, viewed death not as a time of judgment, but as a natural occurrence. They looked for a serene and stoic death, and a simple, emotionally controlled funeral. Because Enlightened ideas were exchanged almost entirely among the educated classes of the Eastern seaboard, they had little immediate impact on American bereavement practices. In conjunction with the social forces of the American Revolution, however, the Enlightenment eventually affected American society.

In most areas of America, a basically Puritan way of death persisted until the 19th century, especially in rural areas where religion remained the focus of life. The increasing specialization and commercialization of life, however, eventually shaped death customs, too. During the 18th century, economic, geographic, and population growth began to produce cities, social stratification and diversity, political dissent, and cultural controversy. Anxiety over the ideology of opportunistic individualism that produced many of these internal conflicts combined with extended imperial control to produce a Revolution that reinforced Enlightenment ideas of rationality and activity. The

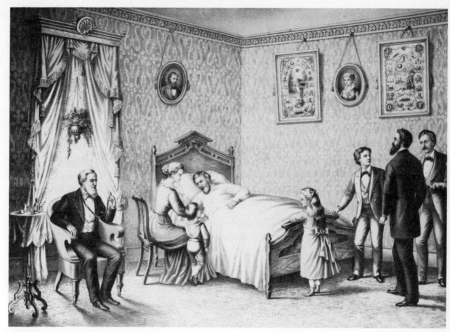

During the early part of the 19th century, Americans socialized their children to view dying as a natural process to be accepted by all members of the family.

Revolution "acted as an inspirational model of human beings' power to alter their own lives, to think new thoughts, to act on the best ideas of humanity, to liberate themselves from the dead weight of the past" (Gross, 1976:191). As a newly independent people pursued life, liberty and happiness, they no longer depended on God's will; instead they made their own plans—plans which did not include death as a fact of life.

In religious developments, both Unitarianism and Evangelicalism accepted the enhanced view of human nature and human agency. The Unitarian gospel of "capitalism, theism, liberalism, and optimism" appealed especially to the commercial and professional classes of Boston—America's cultural capital in the 19th century (Howe, 1970:21). The Unitarians, however, were influential far beyond their numbers. Many people in other denominations accepted their progressive optimism—which derived from conceptions of a beneficent God. Unitarians were viewed by others as being basically good people whose lives were the best evidence of their religiosity, and they were admired for their rational approach to religion. Almost all Americans accepted the mid-19th century rural cemetery reform that began in Brahmin Boston.

Outside of Boston, more Americans were affected by revivalistic Evangelicalism than by Unitarianism. The Second Great Awakening of American

Evangelicalism began in the 1790s as a response to the Enlightenment, and grew throughout the 19th century. Evangelicals stressed the Bible, a conversion experience, and a Christian life (and death). They preached God's persuasiveness more than His arbitrary power, His moral government rather than the ideas of predestination and election, and willful sinfulness more than innate depravity. Therefore, although Evangelicals generally approached death from a Puritan position, they believed that God offered salvation, and people could take it if they willed. Consequently, evangelicalism offered assurance to the saved, even as it heightened the anxiety of the unregenerate. With the idealization of home and family, this could account for the abundant literature on the death of children as parents agonized over an ailing child "hoping all the while that death would terminate its sufferings, and fearing that something worse would be the result." After 1850, however, the romanticization of childhood overcame ideas of infant damnation, provided more assurance to worried parents, and tipped the delicate balance of evangelical belief from anxiety to assurance. By that time, however, Evangelicalism had begun to be affected by sentimentalism, scientific naturalism, and liberal theology, as well as the social and institutional developments of the dying of death.

THE DYING OF DEATH, 1830–1945

Separate Spheres: The Rise of the Middle Class

Between 1830 and 1945, the ideas and institutions with which Americans approached death changed in a process that an English author of 1899 called "The Dying of Death." This process brought "the practical disappearance of the thought of death as an influence bearing upon practical life" ("The Dying of Death," 1899:364–365), and the tactical appearance of funeral institutions designed to keep death out of sight and out of mind.

Both ideas and institutions were the product of a new American middle-class, a group of people trying to distinguish themselves from the European aristocracy and from the American common people. Alexis de Tocqueville saw the middle-class as "an innumerable multitude of men almost alike, who, without being exactly rich or poor, possess sufficient property to desire the maintenance of order" (Tocqueville, 1945:2, 145); contemporary historians see them as substantial property owners, professionals, businessmen and merchants, shopkeepers and skilled artisans, commercial farmers, and their families. They possessed property, but their property (and the hope of increasing it) also possessed them, intensifying their fear of death. For the acquisitive member of the middle-class, "the recollection of death is a constant spur. . . . Besides the good things that he possesses, he every instant fancies a thousand others that death will prevent him from trying if he does not try them soon." Therefore, the middle-class wanted death with order.

One strategy for achieving death with order was the ideology of separate spheres. In the course of the 19th century, middle-class people separated management from labor, men's work from the home, and women's work from men's. They also tried to separate death from life, both intellectually and institutionally. Increasingly, specialists (either medical or clerical or academic) revised ideas of death, while other specialists segregated the funeral from the home, and the cemetery from the city.

Both separation and specialization were strategies of control, an increasingly important idea in Victorian society. Nineteenth century Americans worked for self-control, social control, and control over nature. They saw self-control as the key to character, and sexual control as the key to marriage. In separating their homes from their shops, they tried to control both spheres of their lives. The home would be a controlled environment for reproduction and **socialization,** while the workplace would be a controlled environment for increased production and time-discipline. Schools served as a transition from one controlled environment to another, while asylums provided controlled environments for societal deviants. Science and technology attempted to make the whole continent a controlled environment. Therefore, it should not surprise us that the same class that practiced birth control should also devise forms of death control (Hale, 1971:25; Howe, 1970:304; Rosenberg, 1973:137).

Intellectual Influences

In the process of the dying of death, the three most important intellectual influences were Romanticism and sentimentalism, scientific naturalism, and liberal religion. Romanticism was an intellectual response to the rationality and uniformity of the Enlightenment. Romantics discarded the Enlightenment idea of God as First Cause of a mechanistic universe operating according to predictable natural cycles. Instead, they emphasized the emotional and intuitive communion with the Oversoul (or Cosmos) in a mysteriously organic nature. Asher B. Durand depicted the essential correspondence of God, nature, and humanity in his painting *Kindred Spirits* (1849). It shows painter Thomas Cole and poet William Cullen Bryant in a beautiful natural setting, kindred to each other, to nature, and to the spirit that informed them all.

Such Romantic naturalism converted death from an untimely, unnatural event into a natural, conclusive communion with nature. In Romantic poetry, such as Bryant's "Thanatopsis" or "A Forest Hymn," death was swallowed up in the teeming life of the landscape. Such soothing conceptions of natural death encouraged people to accept their demise. At the same time, such Romantic ideas influenced the inception of rural cemeteries, which institutionalized Romantic naturalism, even as they provided the consolations of Mother Nature to mourners.

During the latter part of the 19th century, mourners were expected to dress for the part. In this picture, the pallbearers wore mourning clothes, black sashes and badges, and dark hats.

The Romantic emphasis on emotions led to simple sentimentalism, which was "part of the self-evasion of a society committed to laissez-faire industrial expansion and disturbed by its consequences" (Douglas, 1977). As Americans began to experience the hard-headed rationalism of the Industrial Revolution, they began to create counterpoints to the "railroad principle" of American life. These counterpoints included the conventions of romantic love, the cult of true womanhood, the idealization of childhood, the home as "haven in a heartless world," residential suburbs, and an "emotional revolution" that bound family members with ties of intimacy. Domestic intimacy heightened the sense of loss upon the death of a "loved one," and required public outlets for the expression of private grief (Douglas, 1977:12–13, 200–226).

For most of the 19th century, the main outlet for the grief of sentimentalism was the **ritual** of mourning, including the funeral, but also extending beyond it. This ritual differed markedly from the simple Puritan rite as mourners immersed themselves in grief to become, through their expressive (and often excessive) emotions, the central feature of the ritual. It allowed many members of the middle-class (especially the women, who were supposed to be creatures of the "heart") to indulge in grief as "therapeutic self-indulgence." Like other forms of sentimentality, the sentimental mourning ritual counterpointed "the real world" because it forced all mourners to consider the power of personal connections in their lives. It turned people from life to death, from the practical to the ceremonial, from the ordinary to the extraordinary, and from the banal to the beautiful (Taylor, 1980:39–48).

Belief in the beauty of death and the funeral was new to the 19th century as the middle-class used its aesthetic awareness to beautify corpses, door badges, caskets, casket backdrops, hearses, horses, funeral music, cemeteries, monuments, mourning costume, and death itself. In the process, they made death so artistic that it almost became artificial, and, therefore, less fearful. At the same time, concerned with an etiquette of proper social relations, people used the beauty of the funeral to preserve appearances among their middle-class peers. Finally, the middle-class called for "taste" and "refinement" in funerals as mourning rituals served to distinguish them from the common folk (Farrell, 1980:110–111).

Especially around the mid-1800s, the tastefully refined middle-class funeral was a dark and formal affair. After death, which still generally occurred in the home, the family either cleaned and dressed the deceased, or, if possible, hired an undertaker to care for the corpse. If they had secured an undertaker, he would place a black badge over the doorbell or door knocker to indicate the presence of mourning and to isolate the intimate family from the unwanted intrusions of everyday life. The family would also close window shades and drapes. Sometimes they draped black crepe over pictures, mirrors, and other places throughout the house (Habenstein & Lamers, 1962:389–444).

By the time of the funeral, family members had swathed themselves in black mourning garb that symbolized the intimacy of relationship to the deceased and the depth of grief. After the funeral, custom encouraged the continued expression of grief, as widows were expected to spend a year in "deep" mourning, and a year in "second" mourning. For the first year, a bereaved woman wore dull black clothes, matched by appropriately somber accessories. In the second year, she gradually lightened her appearance by using a variety of materials in somewhat varying colors. Widowers and children were supposed to follow a similar regimen, but in practice, women bore the burden of 19th century mourning. Social contact and correspondence followed similar rules, with widened social participation or narrowed black borders on stationery as indicators of different stages of mourning.

The funeral ceremony itself reflected and affected the somber atmosphere in which it occurred. In the mid-1800s, people were invited to funerals with hand-delivered printed cards. By the end of the century, the **obituary** began to serve as a funeral notice, and the telephone allowed people to deliver their own invitations without leaving the house of mourning. Once invited, people generally came to the house, offered condolences to the bereaved family, viewed the corpse, and sat in chairs arranged in the parlor by the undertaker. Sometimes, however, the funeral took place in church, in which case people would process from the home to the church. In either place, services were generally extended affairs in which ministers counterbalanced fears of death, decay, and damnation with hopes of regeneration and resurrection. Funerals might include music and hymns, but the central feature of the ceremony was the sermon, which combined an elegy with exhortations for repentance and renewal. This gloomy funeral was not, however, the only type of sentimental funeral. As the 19th century proceeded, a more hopeful sentimentality entered funeral services as middle-class religious liberalism began to domesticate death (Habenstein & Lamers, 1962:389–444; Hillerman, 1980:101; Stannard, 1980:26).

In Box 11.1's modern-day obituary of H. P. Murphy, the highlights of his life are noted. Unlike many obituaries today, a personal touch is found here. The importance and pride of family are stressed—a sort of continuation of life through his children. It is more than the facts of Mr. Murphy's life; what made him "special" to others is noted. As was true in the mid-1800s, the obituary today is a way of informing the public of this vital statistic—death—and of the forthcoming event of final disposition.

BOX 11.1   **HENRY P. MURPHY, WAS AN INSTITUTION IN DORCHESTER, AT 86**

Dorchester lost one of its institutions Friday. Henry P. (Harry) Murphy died in Carney Hospital, Dorchester, after a short illness. He was 86.

Although he was born in Charlestown before the turn of the century and took his early education in that closely knit section of the city before serving in the U.S. Navy during World War II, it was as a citizen of St. Mark's Parish in Dorchester that Harry Murphy made his mark.

His job as an attendance supervisor for the Boston School Department brought him into contact with people of all ages and backgrounds. His face was a familiar one to many families as he went about his business in the days when playing hookey from school was considered a serious sin.

He retired 16 years ago, but his interest—and pride—in the world around him, specifically his family, his Somoset street neighborhoods (spell that Ward 16), and St. Mark's Parish, never waned.

His devotion to his late wife, Mary (Livingston), who died in 1975 after a long illness at home, and his constant attention to the affairs of his active family were the stuff of Harry Murphy's life.

His oldest son, Paul, served for many years as a state representative from Ward 16 before being named presiding justice at West Roxbury

District Court. To have a son reach such peaks of accomplishment was the ultimate reward for a father like Harry Murphy.

Add to that the fact that his only daughter, Mary, proved her mettle in the groves of academe and beyond before moving to Connecticut with her husband, Len Manchuck, and raising a family; that his son, Albert, made his way to a responsible position in the probation section of Roxbury District Court; that his son, Joseph, worked and studied enough to gain appointment as vice-principal of Boston Technical High School; and that his youngest, James, has become a successful educator in Stoughton, and you know that Harry Murphy, husband, father, and citizen, was a successful man.

A funeral Mass for Mr. Murphy will be said Wednesday at 10 A.M. in St. Mark's Church, Dorchester.

Mr. Murphy was a charter member of the Bunker Hill American Legion Post and a member of the Bunker Hill Council of the Knights of Columbus. He was a 50-year member of St. Mark's Holy Name Society.

He leaves his daughter, Mary V. Manchuck of Stamford, Conn.; four sons, Joseph A. of Scituate, James J. of Brockton, Albert J. and Judge Paul Murphy, presiding justice of West Roxbury District Court, both of Dorchester; a sister Gertrude FitzGerald of Quincy; 14 grandchildren and two great-grandchildren.

Burial will be in Mount Benedict Cemetery, West Roxbury.

Boston *Sunday Globe,* June 21, 1981, p. 39. Reprinted courtesy of The Boston Globe.

After the funeral, the procession continued to the cemetery, which was, as we shall see, beautified in order to belie the presence of death. There, the body was interred, and people returned home, not like the Puritans to resume their life's work, but like Victorians to extend their expressions of emotional grief. Mourning garb was one symbol of such sorrow, but mourning portraits and consolation literature were other ways to prolong the period of lamentation.

In the early 19th century, embroidered or painted mourning pictures flourished as a form of memorialization. These pictures often showed stylized graveyard scenes including such standard features as the weeping willow, the gravestone and **epitaph** (tombstone inscription) of the deceased, the mourners, and a *memento mori.* These remained popular until the 1830s, when printed memorials with spaces for names and dates came into vogue. During the middle third of the century, posthumous mourning portraiture also flourished, depicting the deceased with conventional symbols of mortality like the broken shaft or roses held with blooms downward. These paintings were drawn from the corpse, and they expressed "the desire for the restoration of the dead through art." All of these forms of mourning art provided icons for the bereaved to contemplate as a part of the extended mourning ritual (Lloyd, 1980:71–89).

Consolation literature allowed people to share their grief without sharing it with people they knew. It showed mourners that they were not alone in the house of sorrow, and it showed them the emotional and moral benefits of their heartache. Consolation literature included obituary poems and memoirs, mourner's manuals, prayer guidebooks, hymns, and books about heaven. Such writings inflated the importance of dying and the dead by every possible means; they sponsored elaborate methods of burial and commemoration, communication with the next world, and microscopic viewings of a sentimentalized afterlife. Books like *Agnes and the Key of Her Little Coffin* (1857) or *Stepping Heavenward* (1869) or *The Empty Crib: The Memorial of Little Georgie* (1873) all featured and championed the ideal of "the sensitized mourner" (Douglas, 1977:240–249).

To the modern mind, these sentimental expressions of grief may seem forced, overdone, or even false. Such attitudes, however, tell more about us than about our Victorian ancestors. "Nineteenth century Americans mourned well" because they gave themselves symbols, rituals, and time in which to work out their feelings. We do not understand this because of important intervening historical forces, one of which was scientific naturalism.

If sentimentality was one way of controlling the hard fact of death, scientific naturalism was another. Although it systemized the hard-headed rationalism that sentimentalism tried to smother, it contributed to the dying of death, as the middle-class used the "laws" of science like they used the "customs" of etiquette to legitimize their cultural values.

"What strikes the historian," writes Burton J. Bledstein (1976:55), "is the totality of the mid-Victorian impulse to contain the life experiences of the individual from life to death by isolating them as science." Another instance of the ideology of separate spheres, the rise of science in the last half of the 19th century allowed Americans to invoke authority for "those scientific plausibilities which fitted most conveniently into their social needs and presuppositions" (Bledstein, 1976:55). An integral part of the social construction of reality, science isolated the mystery of death as "a matter of fact," and interpreted that fact in order to reduce the impact of death on practical life.

Scientific naturalists insisted first that death was "natural, a product of natural causes, the same as any other natural phenomenon, and that these causes are bound to the fixed, and as we believe beneficent, laws of the universe" (Johnson, 1896:77). Their insistence on the "natural" quality of death complemented the natural death of Romanticism, but the scientific fact of death eliminated providential intervention and the possibility of death as punishment.

Consequently, scientific naturalists insisted that death was painless, and that all people could eventually attain an "easy," natural death at an advanced age. Pain, which (like fear) was an important part of the Puritan world, lost its cultural relevance in the 19th century. With the discovery of ether in the 1840s and the coining of the word *painkiller* in the 1850s, Americans applied physical and mental anaesthetics to kill the pain of death ("Pain, Life, and Death"). Magazine articles constantly stressed "the modern belief that the process [of dying] is easy," as easy and "as painless as falling asleep" ("The Fear of Death," 1912:21). In so doing, they eliminated a major reason for people to think seriously about death.

Other scientific and medical innovations persuaded many Americans that death might be postponed or prevented. Even before the demographic transition, they began to treat death as an occurrence of old age, an idea that encouraged people to postpone or pre-empt preparation for death. In addition, some prominent medical researchers asserted that even old age was a curable congenital disease, and asked "Why Not Live Forever?" Indeed, when Elie Metchnikoff, the head of the Pasteur Institute in Paris, claimed that cultured milk products could combat the "autointoxication" of old age, Americans immediately began to buy yogurt and buttermilk. Especially between 1900 and 1920, the prestige of science convinced many Americans that individual physical immortality might be imminent (Farrell, 1980:60–61).

Other scientific naturalists admitted individual mortality, but promoted a species immortality whereby "we are immortal if we but form a sturdy link in the great chain of life." Influenced by Darwin's idea of natural selection, these scientists viewed death as "an inevitable corollary to the advancement of the species" (Hutchinson, 1893:637). Therefore, they advised Americans not to take death personally, but to accept it as part of human progress. This species perspective did not prevent individuals from dying, but it did turn their attention from death and the deceased to survivors and posterity. As we shall see, this species perspective of death and immortality was institutionalized in "life" insurance.

By itself, scientific naturalism had almost no impact on American bereavement practices. In conjunction with religious liberalism and the culture of professionalism, however, scientific naturalism did affect changes in funeral service.

Religious liberals tried to reconcile new scientific knowledge with traditional religious interpretations of death. Between 1850 and 1930, liberals like Henry Ward Beecher and Phillips Brooks enunciated "the attitudes and values of a new urban middle-class" (Clark, 1978:3). They combined scientific naturalism, higher Biblical criticism, Romantic idealism, and sentimentality in order to show the place of evolution in God's plan, the place of death in evolution, and the progress of life through death to an exalted immortality. In addition, changing ideas of death and immortality brought them into the arena of funeral reform.

Henry Ward Beecher was the most popular and influential of liberal clergymen. His pulpit at the Plymouth Congregational Church of Brooklyn Heights gave him opportunities for public speaking and publication, and he became a "symbol for a middle-class America" (Clark, 1978). He rejected the Evangelicalism of his youth, and preached instead a gospel of divine immanence, natural law, and human hope. He accepted scientific naturalism, and wrote an article for the first issue of the *Popular Science Monthly*. He believed that God acted primarily in the world through natural laws, and that people responded naturally to God by electing their own salvation. Eventually, he even rejected the doctrine of everlasting punishment in hell.

Beecher viewed death as the first step up toward heaven, as God's call to "Come home!" "I would not, for the world, bring up a child to have that horror of death which hung over my own childhood," claimed Beecher, because "the thought of death was to me awful beyond description" (Beecher, 1859:194–195). Instead, he wanted people to see that "a funeral is the nearest place to heaven," and that sorrow was inappropriate. He suggested:

> When friends have gone out from us joyously, we should go with them to the grave, not singing mournful psalms, but scattering flowers. Christians are wrong to walk in black, and sprinkle the ground with tears, at the very time when they should walk in white, and illumine the way by smiles and radiant hope. The disciples found angels at the grave of Him they loved; and we should always find them too, but that our eyes are too full of tears for seeing (Beecher, 1858:189).

At his own funeral in 1887, Beecher's family reversed the somber formality of the Victorian funeral by making sure that "no emblem of parting or sorrow was there, but the symbols of love, and faith, and hope, the glad tokens of eternal reward, such as befitted his life, his death, and his fame" (Handford, 1887:47–49). On a practical, pastoral level, other ministers counseled people to follow Beecher's example. They celebrated death as a passage to eternal life, not as a moment of judgment. They tried to soothe survivors instead of promoting self-examination or preparation for death. They worked with funeral directors to effect funeral reforms. In 1913, Lyman Abbott recalled the achievements of liberal funeral reform:

> We have done much to Christianize our farewells to those who have gone before us into the next stages of life. We no longer darken the rooms that now more than ever need the light and warmth of the sun; we no longer close the windows as if to shut out Nature at the moment when we are about to give back to Mother Earth all that was mortal in the earthly career now finished; we no longer shroud the house in black, we make it sweet with flowers; for the hymns of grief we are fast substituting the hymns of victory; for words charged with a sense of loss we

listen to words that hold wide the door of hope and faith; and on the memorials which we place where they lie who have vanished from our sight we no longer carve the skull and crossbones, the hourglass and the scythe—we recall some trait or quality of achievement that survives the body and commemorates the spirit ("There Are No Dead," 1913:979).

Such changes, thought Abbott, helped people "to think of life as one and indivisible, of immortality as our possession, here and now, of death as normal change in an eternal process of growth" (There Are No Dead," 1913:979–980).

By defining death as part of evolutionary progress propelled by an immanent and merciful God, liberals allowed bereaved Americans to approach death optimistically. This new definition of death derived from ideas of Romanticism, scientific naturalism, and religious liberalism. Together with the institutional innovations of cemetery superintendents, life insurance agents, and funeral directors, these ideas caused the dying of death in America.

Institutional Influences

Like religious liberalism, cemetery reform derived from Romantic naturalism, middle-class family sentimentality, and scientific concerns. In 1895, a writer in *American Gardening* wrote that "the modern garden cemetery like the modern religious impulse seeks to assuage the cheerlessness and the sternness of life and to substitute the free and gracious charity of One who came to rob death of its hideousness" ("Extracts," 1895:108). By the 1830s, many physicians had begun to worry about the possible health hazards of city graveyards. By the same time, commercial development had raised the price of land on which graveyards were located, and Romantic ideas of landscape architecture had begun to affect the aesthetically oriented members of the middle class. Also, space limitations of city graveyards prevented the possibility of family plots, and many of the burial places had become overcrowded, unkempt, and unsightly.

The solution to these problems was the rural cemetery, a landscaped garden in a suburban setting. In 1831, Mount Auburn Cemetery was founded four miles west of Boston, and its success stimulated the spread of such cemeteries all over the country. In rural cemeteries, family plots averaging 300 square feet were nestled among trees and shrubs upon the slopes of soft hills, or on the shores of little lakes. Paths curled throughout the grounds, passing lots enclosed by stone coping or wrought iron fences and surmounted by a monument of some sort. Such cemeteries were invented to bury bodies and to ease the grief of survivors; to bring people into communion with God, with Nature, and with deceased family and friends, and to teach them important lessons of life; to surround bereavement with beauty and to divert the attention of survivors from death to the setting of burial; and to display "taste" and "refinement" and to reinforce the class stratification of the status quo (Bender, 1973:196–211; French, 1975:69–91; Rotundo, 1973:231–242).

The founders of Mount Auburn were liberal Unitarian reformers, progressive professionals and businesspeople who considered the cemetery in the context of social developments of their day. They equated the family with the garden, and imagined both as a counterpoint to a society of accumulation. In the same way that upper-middle-class families moved to suburbs where curved roads and greenery contrasted with the grid-block plan of the cities and offered space to raise a family, they moved from the "cities of the dead" to rural cemeteries that offered space to "plant" a family.

During this period of "the discovery of the asylum," social deviants were located in restorative rural settings that would rehabilitate people away from the contaminating influence of urban life. Like insane asylums, orphanages, and penitentiaries, many of these reformers saw the cemetery as an "asylum" from urban ills. In the cemetery, "the weary and worn citizen" was also rehabilitated. Cleaveland (1847:13–14, 26) noted:

> Ever since he entered these greenwood shades, he has sensibly been getting farther and farther from strife, from business, and care. . . . A short half-hour ago, he was in the midst of a discordant Babel; he was one of the hurrying, jostling crowd; he was encompassed by the whirl and fever of artificial life. Now he stands alone in Nature's inner court—in her silent, solemn sanctuary. Her holiest influences are all around him.

The rehabilitation of the rural cemetery paralleled the philosophy of education found in the common school. Like the new compulsory schools, rural cemeteries responded to middle-class fears of mobilization of the masses in the Age of Jackson. Educational reformers like Horace Mann both reflected and affected cemetery proponents in their belief that "sentiment is the great conservative principle of society," and that "instincts of patriotism, local attachment, family affection, human sympathy, reverence for truth, age, valor, and wisdom . . . constitute the latent force of civil society" (Tuckerman, 1856:338–342).

Like these other reforms of antebellum society, rural cemeteries "took the public mind by storm." Cities and towns throughout the United States established rural cemeteries, and people flocked to visit them. In New York, Baltimore, and Philadelphia, Andrew Jackson Downing estimated that over 30,000 people a year toured the rural cemeteries. Consequently, he wondered whether they might not also visit landscaped gardens without graves. In articles like "Public Cemeteries and Public Gardens" and "The New York Park," Downing (1921:28–40, 374) advanced the idea that would eventuate in New York's Central Park and in a new direction for cemetery development.

The new direction was the lawn-park cemetery emphasizing a new aesthetic—efficiency—and the absence of death. By the end of the century, members of the Association of American Cemetery Superintendents routinely wrote in journals like *Park and Cemetery* that "a cemetery should be a beautiful park. While there are still some who say 'a cemetery should be a cemetery,' . . . the great majority have come to believe in the idea of beauty" (Simonds, 1919:59). This new aesthetic emphasized the open meadows of the beautiful style over the irregular hill-and-dale outcroppings of the picturesque style and the irregular outcroppings of obelisks and monuments in the unregulated rural cemetery. This aesthetic coincided with considerations of efficiency as the uncluttered landscape required less upkeep than the enclosures and elaborate monuments of the rural cemetery. Finally, this aesthetic buried death beneath the beauty of the design. Andrew Jackson Downing (1921:59) had said that "the development of the beautiful is the end and aim of all other fine arts. . . . And we attain it by the removal or concealment of everything uncouth or discordant." The cemetery superintendents practiced what Downing preached. "Today cemetery making is an art," said one superintendent in 1910, "and gradually all things that suggest death, sorrow, or pain are being eliminated" (Hare, 1910:41).

Cemetery superintendents eliminated suggestions of death by banning lot enclosures and grave mounds, and by encouraging fewer gravestones and fewer inscriptions. They banned lot enclosures (fencing or stone coping) because they broke up the unified landscape, blocked the path of the lawn mower, and signified a "selfish and exclusive," possessive individualism. While grave mounds obstructed the view and the lawn mower, they also reminded people of death. Without them, a cemetery lot would evoke "none of the gruesomeness which is invariably associated with cemetery lots. . . . *No grave mounds are used,* so save the headstones, *there is nothing to suggest the presence of Death*" (Smith, 1910:539).

BOX 11.2 **FOREST LAWN**

SONG BY TOM PAXTON

Oh, lay me down in Forest Lawn in a silver casket,
Put golden flowers over my head in a silver basket.
Let the drum and bugle corps blow taps while cannons roar,
Let sixteen liveried employees pass out souvenirs from the funeral store.
I want to go simply when I go, and they'll give me a simple fun'ral there,
I know.

(continued on next page)

With a casket lined in fleece,
And fireworks spelling out "rest in peace."
Oh, take me when I'm gone to Forest Lawn.

Oh, lay me down in Forest Lawn—they understand there.
They have a heavenly choir and a military band there.
Just put me in their care, and I'll find my comfort there, with sixteen planes
  in last salute, dropping a cross in a parachute.
I want to go simply when I go, they'll give me a simple fun'ral there, I
  know.
With a hundred strolling strings.
And topless dancers in golden wings,
Oh, take me when I'm gone to Forest Lawn.

Oh come, come, come, come,
Come to the church in the wildwood,
Kindly leave a contribution in the pail.
Be as simple and as trusting as a child would
And we'll sell you a church in the dale.

To find a simple resting place is my desire,
To lay me down with a smiling face comes a little bit higher.
My likeness done in brass will stand in plastic grass,
And weights and hidden springs will tip its hat to the mourners filing past.
I want to go simply when I go.
And they'll give me a simple fun'ral there, I know.
I'll sleep beneath the sand, with piped in tapes of Billy Graham.
Oh, take me when I'm gone to Forest Lawn.
Rock of Ages, cleft for me, for a slightly higher fee.
Oh, take me when I'm gone to Forest Lawn.

Some superintendents did not want to save the headstones either, proposing instead "a cemetery where there is no monument, only landscape" (*Association,* 1889:59). Most superintendents favored sunken stones at the site of the grave. Howard Evarts Weed (1912:94), author of the influential *Modern Park Cemeteries,* argued that "with the headstones showing above the surface we have the old graveyard scene, but buried in the ground they do not appear in the landscape picture and we then have a park-like effect." Some superintendents zoned the cemetery to permit monuments only on large "monument lots." This allowed the superintendent, like a realtor, to charge premium prices for such lots and for prime locations for corner lots or hillside or lakeside property. This **social stratification** of the cemetery allowed for the social mobility of the dead, as ambitious dead people moved to better "neighborhoods" as their survivors saw fit. Where they could not ban or limit the number of monuments, superintendents tried to make them as unobtrusive as possible, preferring horizontal monuments to the earlier upright markers, and preferring sorted inexpressive inscriptions to the poetic epitaphs of earlier times. They wanted to replace the *memento mori* of earlier stones with "forgetfulness" as they buried death with the dead (Farrell, 1980:122–127).

BOX 11.3 **GRAVE REMARKS**

I'll Write My Own Epitaph Before I Leave, Thank You

Epitaphs are footnotes chiseled on tombstones.

They are parting shots taken at or by the deceased. They can be patriotic, poetic, profound or pathetic. They can be wise, witty or just weird. They can glorify, be grievous or gruesome.

Few of them have summed up a person's attitude toward life as well as one found in a Georgia cemetery:

I told you I was sick!

Perhaps the most famous epitaph is one credited to W. C. Fields, written for himself:

On the whole I'd rather be in Philadelphia.

But Fields' epitaph was not used and his tombstone in Forest Lawn (Glendale, California) contains only his vital statistics.
Here are some others.

Epitaph from Kilmurry Churchyard, Ireland:

This stone was raised to Sarah Ford.
Not Sarah's virtues to record,
For they're well known to all the town,
No Lord, it was raised to keep her down.

From Streatham Churchyard, England:

Here lies Elizabeth, my wife for 47 years, and this is the first damn thing she ever did to oblige me.

(continued on next page)

Epitaph on one of three tombstones in a family burial plot in Niagara Falls, Ontario:

Here I lie between two of the best women in the world; my wives. But I have requested my relatives to tip me a little toward Tillie.

In a Falkirk, England, cemetery:

At rest beneath this slab of stone
Lies stingy Jimmy Wyatt;
He died one morning just at ten,
And saved a dinner by it.

Here's one from Boot Hill, Dodge City, Kansas, that reflects a popular epitaph theme:

Here lies the body of Mannie,
They put him here to stay;
He lived the life of Riley
While Riley was away.

From Burlington Churchyard, Mass.,

Sacred to the memory of Anthony Drake
Who died for peace and quietness sake,
His wife was constantly scolding and scoffin',
So he sought repose in a twelve-dollar coffin.

Railroad conductor Charles B. Gunn's tombstone in Colorado Springs, Colo., contains these words:

Papa—Did you wind your watch?

And in a Moultrie, Ga., cemetery:

Here lies the father of twenty-nine
He would have had more but he didn't have time.

From Burlington, Mass., again:

Here lies the body of Susan Lowder
Who burst while drinking Seidlitz powder;
Called from the world to her heavenly rest
She should have waited till it effervesced.

On a hanged sheep-stealer from Bletchley, Bucks, England:

Here lies the body of Thomas Kemp
Who lived by wool and died by hemp.

Abraham Newland, a lonely London Banker, who wrote his own epitaph:

Beneath this stone old Abraham lies;
Nobody laughs, and nobody cries.
Where he has gone, and how he fares,
Nobody knows and nobody cares.

In a Thurmont, Md., cemetery:

Here lies an atheist—All dressed up and no place to go.

And in a Stowe, Vt., cemetery:

I was somebody. Who is no business of yours.

An infant's epitaph in a Plymouth, Mass., cemetery:

Since I have been so quickly done for
I wonder what I was begun for.

In a Uniontown, Pa., cemetery:

Here lies the body of Jonathan Blake;
Stepped on the gas instead of the brake.

Written by a widow on her adulterous husband's tombstone in an Atlanta, Ga., cemetery:

Gone. But not forgiven.

Similarly, a Middlesex, England, widow put this on the gravestone of her wandering husband:

At last I know where he is at night!

An "old maid's" epitaph in Scranton, Pa.:

No hits, no runs, no heirs.

At Cripple Creek, Colo., an epitaph to a man who died by accident:

Within this grave there lies poor Andy;
Bit by a snake no whiskey handy.

Another one from Cripple Creek:

Here lies the bones of a man named Zeke,
Second-fastest draw in Cripple Creek.

(continued on next page)

Near Atlanta, Ga., a cemetery hosts this unique epitaph:

Due to lack of ground in this cemetery,
two bodies are buried in this one plot.
One of them was a politician, the other
was an honest man.

An English epitaph over the grave of Sir John Strange, a lawyer:

Here lies an honest lawyer, and that is Strange.

Epitaph to Joseph Crump, a musician:

Once ruddy, and plump
But now a pale lump
Beneath this same hump
Lies honest Joe Crump
What, tho' by Death's thump
He's laid on his rump
Yet up he shall jump
When he hears the last triumph.

An 1890 epitaph of Arthur C. Hormans of Cleveland, Ohio, puts this in startlingly clear perspective:

Once again I wasn't. Then I was. Now I ain't again.

Superintendents tried to structure cemetery services "to mitigate the harshness and cruelty of death and its attendant details and ceremonies" (Seavoy, 1906:488) and to provide a sort of grief therapy for bereaved individuals. They encouraged private, family funerals, and they tried to remove or conceal the uncouth and discordant aspects of interment. They carted the dirt away from the grave, or they hid it beneath cloth, flowers, or evergreens. They lined the grave with cloth to make it look like a little room. They suggested changes in religious services, and they escorted mourners away from the grave before filling it in order to avoid the finality of death. In all of these services, "everything that tends to remove the gloomy thoughts is done. . . . The friends cannot but leave the sacred spot with better, nobler thoughts, freed from the gloom and terror that otherwise would possess them" (Hay, 1900:46).

A second institutional innovation, life insurance, tried to exorcise the anxiety and financial insecurity that would otherwise possess people contemplating death. Established about the same time as rural cemeteries, life insurance flourished after 1850. In 1850, 48 companies held policies valued at $97 million; by 1920, 335 companies recorded 65 million policies worth $40 billion. Life insurance contributed to "the practical disappearance of the thought of death as an influence bearing upon practical life," and thus it contributed to the dying of death (U.S. Bureau of the Census, 1975:1050–1059).

Life insurance emerged from the same historical context as rural cemeteries and funeral reform; it assumed the uniformity and continuity of death as a natural occurrence. Life insurance depended on the science of statistics and on a species perspective of death and immortality that focused attention, not on the life of the individual policyholder, but on the lives of beneficiaries. Like the rural cemetery, it was praised for its educational benefits as it taught lessons of self-reliance, forethought, thrift, discipline, and (very) delayed gratification. For these reasons, clergymen like Henry Ward Beecher endorsed the system of life insurance, responding to critics that in effect, God helps those who help themselves. Also, life insurance accentuated the importance of the family, as did Romantic sentimentalism and the family plot of the rural cemetery. Finally, life insurance provided families with money to pay for elaborate funerals, a fact that affected both the development of funeral service and of the history of bereavement.

Like burial service, funeral service also changed between 1850 and 1920. Because "the growing wealth and prosperity of our country has caused people to demand something more in accordance with their surroundings" (Benjamin, 1882:3), and because funeral directors cultivated a "steadily advancing appreciation of the aesthetics of society" (Funeral Directors, 1883:3), the new funeral would be, like the 19th-century cemetery, a work of art. As cemetery superintendents used their art to hide the uncouth and discordant aspects of death, so did funeral directors use "the varied improvements in (their) art . . . to conceal much that is forbidding in (their) calling" (National Funeral Directors Association, 1882:5). As cemetery superintendents institutionalized "the modern religious impulse" to "assuage the cheerlessness and sternness of life," the funeral director worked to "adopt some philosophy or some new customs and ideals that will make death less of a tragedy" ("The Ideas of a Plain Country Woman," 1913:42).

The demand for a new funeral service came from the American middle class, but it was created and supplied by casket manufacturers and funeral directors. The National Funeral Directors Association was founded in 1882 in Rochester, New York, the home of the Stein Casket Manufacturing Company. The association's official journal was *The Casket*, founded and funded for several years by the Stein Company. As this suggests, the first widespread innovation in funeral service was the casket, a stylish container for the corpse. Before 1850, most Americans were laid to rest in a coffin, a six-sided box that was constructed to order by the local cabinetmaker. By 1927 "the old wedge-shaped coffin [was] obsolete. A great variety of styles and grades of caskets [were] available in the trade, ranging from a cheap, cloth-covered pine box to the expensive cast-bronze sarcophagus" (Gebhart, 1927:8). The rectangular shape of the new caskets complemented the artwork in concealing the uncouth corpse. In applying for a casket patent in 1849, A. C. Barstow explained:

> The burial cases formerly used were adapted in shape nearly to the form of the human body, that is they tapered from the shoulders to the head, and from the shoulders to the feet. Presently, in order to obviate in some degree the disagreeable sensations produced by a coffin on many minds, the casket, or square form has been adopted (Habenstein & Lamers, 1962:270, 251–310).

The adoption of the word *casket* also accelerated the dying of death, as the word had previously denoted a container for something precious, like jewels.

Accepting the associated idea of the preciousness of the body, Americans decided that a dead-looking corpse looked out of place in an elaborate silk-lined casket. Rather than remove the casket, they decided to stylize the body. Originally a way of preserving bodies for shipment home from Civil War battlefields or western cities, embalming soon became a way of preserving appearances. Responding to the germ theory of disease and the public health movement, funeral directors attempted to gain professional status by emphasizing the disinfectant qualities of embalming. Most funeral directors, however, wanted simply "to retain and improve the complexion" so that the corpse would look "as natural as though [it] were alive" (Hohenschuh, 1921:82, 88). To do this, they began to cosmetize the corpse, and to clothe and position the body naturally. They replaced the traditional shroud with street clothes, and they tried "to lay out the body so that there will be as little suggestion of death as possible." By 1920, they succeeded so well that a Boston undertaker supposedly advertised (Dowd, 1921:53):

For composing the features,	$1
For giving the features a look of quiet resignation,	$2
For giving the features the appearance of Christian hope and contentment,	$5

Bereavement practices were affected by the change from coffin to casket and by the "restorative art" of the embalmer; they were also changed by the movement of the funeral from the domestic parlor to the funeral parlor. As they began banishing death from their homes to hospitals, they started moving the funeral from the family parlor to a specialized funeral parlor. After the Civil War, middle-class Americans began to exclude the formal parlor from their homes and to replace it with a "living room." At the same time, funeral directors wanted full control of the corpse and the funeral. The ease and efficiency of directing funerals in a funeral home made them more profitable. In spite of all these benefits, however, the transition to the funeral parlor was a slow process, extending well into the twentieth century (Farrell, 1980:172–177).

Both in the domestic parlor and in the funeral parlor, the procedure of the turn-of-the-century funeral changed. In conjunction with the reform forces of religious liberalism, funeral directors began to redirect funerals to be shorter, more secular, and more soothing. They shortened the service by trying to revise the long sermon with its exhortations of repentance and renewal. Although some clerics resisted, funeral directors wanted the sermon redirected from theology to psychology, from preaching to grief therapy, and from the state of survivors' souls to the state of their emotions. The funeral director took care of all the details of the funeral and performed as much as a stage manager as a mortician. "Really it is much the same," wrote one director, "I work for effect—for consoling and soothing effect" ("The Man Nobody Envies," 1914:68–71).

After 1880, funeral directors used their arts and the culture of professionalism to effect a massive change in the American way of bereavement. Professionalism was part of the middle-class strategy of specialization. It required education in an area of expertise and an ethic or service, and it provided autonomy and income for its practitioners. The American undertaker sought professional status because it would help him to become "enough of an *authority* to convince his clients, without offense, that there are better methods than are prescribed by custom" (Hohenschuh, 1921:9). Etiquette books reinforced this culture of professionalism by advising readers that "the arrangements for the funeral are usually left to the undertaker, who best knows how to proceed" (Wells, 1887:303). To the middle-class people who feared death anyway, this established a situation in which the public passively accepted changes in funeral service suggested by funeral directors (Hohenschuh, 1921:9; Wells, 1887:303).

Indeed, restraint and passivity became the watchwords of 20th-century bereavement. If the funeral director was a stage manager, then the family was the audience, responding to the drama in prescribed ways in the hopes of achieving a catharsis of death. Instead of the expressive grief of the sentimental funeral, the family was expected to contain and control their emotions and to meet death stoically. At the turn of the century, some religious liberals saw grief as lack of faith in the imminence of immortality. Others reacted to the central place of the mourners in the mournful Victorian funeral, and charged that "over-much grief would seem mere selfishness" (Mayo, 1916:6). Over and over again, writers proclaimed that "the deepest grief is the quiet kind" (Sargent, 1888:51). An 1890s etiquette book suggested that "we can better show our affection to the dead by fulfilling our duties to the living, than by giving ourselves up to uncontrolled grief" (Pike & Armstrong, 1980:125). Portraying grief as a selfish ploy to stop the ongoing business of life, these reformers called for controlled and private grief. In the long run, they predicted the modern practice of grief therapy in which grief is seen as a disorder by people who still want death with order (Mayo, 1916:6; Pike & Armstrong, 1980:125; Sargent, 1888:51).

With this new ideal of grief, Americans reduced their symbolic expressions of sorrow—mourning wear, for example, which declined after World War I—because extended grief offended others who preferred to live for life. In concealing mourning, Americans reversed the 19th-century tradition that *required* good mourning. Like cemetery superintendents and funeral directors, Americans in general began to conceal the uncouth and discordant emotion of grief. Thus, modern grief isolates the mourners and forces them to discover their own private mourning ritual. It dictates the appearance of control and the dying of death (Hillerman, 1980:104–105; Oxley, 1887:608–614).

BOX 11.4 **THE DISPLAY OF THE DEAD**

Truly, we need to do away with some of the false ideas of Death which are shown in so many gruesome ways at funerals, and strive to give the young a different and truer idea of what the passing away of a soul means. The awfulness of some funerals is nothing short of criminal, especially as it affects the minds of the young. If there is work cut out for the minister of today, it is the enlightenment of his people on the subject of death and the funeral. But the minister must, first of all, imbibe a wholesome lesson of self-restraint for himself, and abolish the fulsome and tiresome eulogy which is the bane of so many funerals. He must learn for himself, and teach to his people, the beauty and solemnity of the brief service as prescribed by his church and attempt nothing more, and he must also relentlessly oppose the tendency which exists to turn the modern funeral, especially in the country, into a picnic. The present outpouring of a heterogeneous mass of folk from every point of the countryside is a farce that cannot be too soon abolished. A funeral is essentially a time for the meeting of the family and relatives and the closest friends, and the fewer the number of outsiders present the better. Nor is there anything quite so barbarous as the present custom at so many funerals of "viewing the remains" by a motley collection of folk, many of whom never even knew the dead in life, or, if they did, never thought enough of him to come and see him. The vulgar curiosity that prompts "a last look" at the loved one cannot be too severely denounced. Only second to it is the pretentious line of vehicles that "escorts the remains to the grave" and the mental calibre of a community that bases the popularity of a man on the number of carriages that follow him to the grave!

If there is a crying need of the gospel of simplicity it is in connection with funerals. It seems inconceivable that Death should be made the occasion for display, and yet this is true of scores of funerals. The flowers, including those fearful conceptions of the ignorant florist, such as "Gates Ajar"; the quality of casket and even of the raiment of the dead, the "crowd" at the "obsequies," the number of carriages in the "cortege"—oh, oh, "what fools these mortals be," to say naught of the wicked and wanton waste of much-needed money. It is difficult to conceive that a national love of display should have become so deep-rooted as to lead to the very edge of the grave!

Ladies' Home Journal, September 1903. Courtesy *Ladies' Home Journal* magazine.

The modern bereavement practices described in Box 11.4 proceeded from a simple desire to make death as painless for survivors as for the deceased. It came from a widespread cultural attempt "not to mention trouble or grief or sickness or sin, but to treat them as if they do not exist, and speak only of the sweet and pleasant things of life" ("Ideas," 1913:42). This dying of death came from the desire of the middle-class for control—of self, society, and the environment. It ended exactly where de Tocqueville (1945:2, 4) predicted:

> As they perceive that they succeed in resolving without resistance all the little difficulties their practical life presents, [the Americans] readily conclude that everything in the world can be explained, and that nothing in it transcends the limits of the understanding. Thus they fall to denying what they cannot comprehend.

Denying and disguising death, middle-class Americans achieved, on the surface at least, the dying of death.

THE RESURRECTION OF DEATH, 1945 TO THE PRESENT

Although Americans sought a death sentence for death, the Judge granted only life imprisonment. Consequently, although death had disappeared from the streets, Americans worried that this hardened killer might escape. After World War II, some Americans suggested instead that death had been rehabilitated, and like 19th-century "resurrectionists," they began to resurrect death. Presently Americans are deciding between the dying of death and "living with dying."

The Atomic Age

On August 6, 1945, the United States dropped a single atomic bomb on the Japanese city of Hiroshima. It exploded in the air, with a heat flash that inflamed clothing within a half-mile radius and trees up to a mile and a half. The shock wave followed soon after, rupturing internal organs. Finally, the blast blew bodies at 500 to 1000 miles per hour through the flaming, rubble-filled air. The bomb destroyed everything within 8000 feet, killed at least 70,000 people, and destroyed or damaged 98 percent of Hiroshima's buildings. The effects of atomic radiation have disfigured or killed thousands more, and the whole world bears the psychological scars of the blast.

President Truman announced the explosion:

> It is an atomic bomb. It is a harnessing of the basic power of the universe. . . . What has been done is the greatest achievement of organized science in history.

One of the scientists, Albert Einstein, responded "Ach! The world is not ready for it." Within a year, Einstein argued that "the unleashed power of the atom has changed everything save our modes of thinking, and we thus drift toward unparalleled catastrophe."

The atomic bomb and the arms race did, however, begin to change our mode of thinking about death. In a prescient 1947 article on the social effects of the Bomb, Lewis Mumford predicted that, in the Atomic Age,

> Life is now reduced to purely existentialist terms: existence towards death. The classic other worldly religions undergo a revival; but even more quack religions and astrology, with pretensions to scientific certainty, flourish; [so do] new cults. The young who grow up in this world are completely demoralized: they characterize themselves as the generation that drew a blank. The belief in continuity, the sense of a future that holds promises, disappears; the certainty of sudden obliteration cuts across every long-term plan, and every activity is more or less reduced to the life-span of a single day, on the assumption that it may be the last day. . . . Suicide becomes more frequent . . . and the taking of drugs to produce either exhilaration or sleep becomes practically universal. . . .
>
> These conditions—as unfamiliar to the experience of the race as the atom bomb itself—must lead to grave psychological disruptions. We can posit the familiar forms of these regressive actions: escape in fantasy would be one; purposeless sexual promiscuity would be another; narcotic indulgence would be a third.
>
> Not a single life [will yet have] been lost in atomic warfare; nevertheless death has spread everywhere in the cold violence of anticipation (Mumford, 1947:9–20, 29–30).

"The Far Side" cartoon reprinted by permission of Chronicle Features, San Francisco, CA.

"Wouldn't you know it! Now the Hendersons have the bomb."

"For the first time in six centuries," says Edwin Shneidman (1973:189), "a generation has been born and raised in a thanatological context, concerned with the imminent possibility of the death of the person, the death of humanity, the death of the universe, and, by necessary extension, the death of God." "The bomb," said philosopher William Barrett (1958:65), "reveals the dreadful and total contingency of human existence. Existentialism is the philosophy of the atomic age." Indeed, the Bomb did lead many postwar people to the philosophy of existentialism, which began with the reality of death, worked through anxiety and alienation, and culminated with individuals condemned to the freedom to undertake responsible action in the world. Like the "God Is Dead" theology of the 1960s, atomic existentialism returned Americans to the basic fact of death.

The threat of "megadeath" has also taken the traditional future away from young people. Twenty-eight percent of high school seniors in 1975 to 1978 believed that "nuclear or biological annihilation will probably be the fate of all mankind in my lifetime." Even younger children are aware of the Bomb, and many are pessimistic about the possibilities of preventing a nuclear war. "Others report deep despair, a sense of living totally for today, anger at adults for appearing impotent to do anything, and varying degrees of ability to commit to a future or to invest in their own personal capacity to do anything about one." This affects not only the way that children live their lives, but the way they deal with death. "What happens to the child's concept of death and capacity to cope with death in a rational way," asks one researcher, "when death ceases becoming an end state of the growth process, or an incidental accidental happening, but rather becomes a catastrophic threat for all humans by our own doing?" (Greenwald & Zeitlin, 1987:21, 30–31).

The apocalyptic possibility of nuclear megadeath reminded many people of the fragility of life and the uncertainty of existence—ideas that the Puritans could surely appreciate. Because the historical context was different, however—now people could plan their own extinction—the effects were different. Instead of experiencing death in life as an incentive for righteousness, people experience the "death in life" that comes from psychic numbing. In psychic numbing, we block our capacity to feel as strongly about other aspects of everyday life. In extreme cases, we become emotionally dead; in most cases, we are merely schizophrenic, ignoring the threat of the Bomb, and consequently ignorant of the ways we might try to reduce the threat (Lifton & Falk, 1982:103–106).

BOX 11.5 **LATE NIGHT THOUGHTS ON LISTENING TO MAHLER'S NINTH SYMPHONY**

BY LEWIS THOMAS

I cannot listen to Mahler's Ninth Symphony with anything like the old melancholy mixed with the high pleasure I used to take from this music. There was a time, not long ago, when what I heard, especially in the final movement, was an open acknowledgement of death and at the same time a quiet celebration of the tranquility connected to the process. I took this music as a metaphor for reassurance, confirming my own strong hunch that the dying of every living creature, the most natural of all experiences, has to be a peaceful experience. I rely on nature. The long passages on all the strings at the end, as close as music can come to expressing silence itself, I used to hear as Mahler's idea of leave-taking at its best. But always, I have heard this music as a solitary, private listener, thinking about death.

Now I hear it differently. I cannot listen to the last movement of the Mahler Ninth without the door-smashing intrusion of a huge new

thought: death everywhere, the dying of everything, the end of humanity. The easy sadness expressed with such gentleness and delicacy by
that repeated phrase on faded strings, over and over again, no longer
comes to me as old, familiar news of the cycle of living and dying. All
through the last notes my mind swarms with images of a world in
which the thermonuclear bombs have begun to explode, in New York
and San Francisco, in Moscow and Leningrad, in Paris, in Paris, in
Paris. In Oxford and Cambridge, in Edinburgh. I cannot push away the
thought of a cloud of radioactivity drifting along the Engadin, from the
Moloja Pass to Ftan, killing off the part of the Earth I love more than
any other part.

I am old enough by this time to be used to the notion of dying, saddened by the glimpse when it has occurred but only transiently
knocked down, able to regain my feet quickly at the thought of continuity, any day. I have acquired and held in affection until very recently
another sideline of an idea which serves me well at dark times: the life
of the Earth is the same as the life of an organism: the great round being
possesses a mind: the mind contains an infinite number of thoughts and
memories: when I reach my time I may find myself still hanging around
in some sort of midair, one of those small thoughts, drawn back into
the memory of the Earth: in that peculiar sense I will be alive.

Now all that has changed. I cannot think that way anymore. Not
while those things are still in place, aimed everywhere, ready for
launching.

This is a bad enough thing for the people in my generation. We can
put up with it, I suppose, since we must. We are moving along anyway,
like it or not. I can even set aside my private fancy about hanging
around, in midair.

What I cannot imagine, what I cannot put up with, the thought that
keeps grinding its way into my mind, making the Mahler into a hideous
noise close to killing me, is what it would be like to be young. How do
the young stand it? How can they keep their sanity? If I were very
young, sixteen or seventeen years old, I think I would begin, perhaps
very slowly and imperceptibly, to go crazy.

There is a short passage near the very end of the Mahler in which
the almost vanishing violins, all engaged in a sustained backward
glance, are edged aside for a few bars by the cellos. Those lower notes
pick up fragments from the first movement, as though prepared to
begin everything all over again, and then the cellos subside and dis-

(continued on next page)

appear, like an exhalation. I used to hear this as a wonderful few seconds of encouragement: we'll be back, we're still here, keep going, keep going.

Now, with a pamphlet in front of me on a corner of my desk, published by the Congressional Office of Technology Assessment, entitled "MX Basing," an analysis of all the alternative strategies for placement and protection of hundreds of these missiles, each capable of creating artificial suns to vaporize a hundred Hiroshimas, collectively capable of destroying the life of any continent, I cannot hear the same Mahler. Now, those cellos sound in my mind like the opening of all the hatches and the instant before ignition.

If I were sixteen or seventeen years old, I would not feel the cracking of my own brain, but I would know for sure that the whole world was coming unhinged. I can remember with some clarity what it was like to be sixteen. I had discovered the Brahms symphonies. I knew that there was something going on in the late Beethoven quartets that I would have to figure out, and I knew that there was plenty of time ahead for all the figuring I would ever have to do. I had never heard of Mahler. I was in no hurry. I was a college sophomore and had decided that Wallace Stevens and I possessed a comprehensive understanding of everything needed for a life. The years stretched away forever ahead, forever. My great-great grandfather had come from Wales, leaving his signature in the family Bible on the same page that carried, a century later, my father's signature. It never crossed my mind to wonder about the 21st century; it was just there, given, somewhere in the sure distance.

The man on television, Sunday midday, middle-aged and solid, nice-looking chap, all the facts at his fingertips, more dependable looking than most high-school principals, is talking about civilian defense, his responsibility in Washington. It can make an enormous difference, he is saying. Instead of the outright death of eighty million American citizens in twenty minutes, he says, we can, by careful planning and practice, get that number down to only forty million, maybe even twenty. The thing to do, he says, is to evacuate the cities quickly and have everyone get under shelter in the countryside. That way we can recover, and meanwhile we will have retaliated, incinerating all of Soviet society, he says. What about radioactive fallout, he is asked. Well, he says. Anyway, he says, if the Russians know they can only destroy forty million, this will deter them. Of course, he adds, they have the capacity to kill all two-hundred-and-twenty million of us if they were to try real hard, but they know we can do the same to them. If the figure is only forty million, this will deter them, not worth the trouble, not worth the risk. Eighty million would be another matter, we should guard ourselves against losing that many all at once, he says.

If I were sixteen or seventeen years old and had to listen to that, or read things like that, I would want to give up listening and reading. I would begin thinking up new kinds of sounds, different from any music heard before, and I would be twisting and turning to rid myself of human language.

The threat of the end of the world had taken away some of the traditional consolations of the dying and bereaved, including three cultural conceptions of immortality: biosocial (immortality through reproduction); natural (immortality through the continuity of Nature); and creative (immortality through creative endeavors). It has forced people to reconsider their faith in the future, or to place their faith fully in spiritual immortality, a choice that is difficult in a secular society (Fulton & Gottesman, 1981).

Thanatology

The thanatological context of the postwar world has led some people to examine our reservation as a culture to discuss the death that faces us. In 1955, Geoffrey Gorer published "The Pornography of Death" in which he showed that death was the taboo topic of modern civilization. In 1959, Herman Feifel edited *The Meaning of Death,* an interdisciplinary attempt to restore death to cultural consciousness. In 1963 Jessica Mitford blasted "the American way of death" in her book of the same title. Elisabeth Kübler-Ross's *On Death and Dying* in 1969 advised Americans that they can play a significant role in the lives of the dying. Daniel Maguire (1982:502–513) even argues that Americans have experienced a "revolution in death consciousness." Most of these people have promoted the Puritan position, "Life is not comprehended truly or lived fully unless the idea of death is grappled with honestly" (Feifel, 1959).

Kübler-Ross has been particularly influential in the institutionalization of these ideas, as Americans have re-examined their practices of death and bereavement in the hospice movement, in changing medical treatment of the terminally ill, in the legal changes like living wills, in alternative funeral practices, and in better support groups for the bereaved. As they created a new fluidity in American practices of dying and bereavement, many of these thanatologists have realized the creative possibilities of the past. They have learned that the American way of death and bereavement has deep intellectual, institutional, and emotional roots in American culture, and they know that our way of death will be hard to change. In a country that conspires to cover up unpleasantness, it will be difficult (if not impossible) to make Americans confront the mysterious reality of death. At the same time, by showing the social *construction* of reality, history teaches us that rituals of dying and bereavement *do change* when people act. It offers hope that Americans can free themselves from the restrictions of the past by recognizing their history and by adapting rituals from the past to meet their human needs. Indeed, in more ways than one, it helps us "to redeem the time."

Box 11.6 presents one man's contemporary reflection on bereavement customs of the past. The author illustrates many of the major perspectives presented in this chapter—especially the "dying of death" in contemporary American mourning rituals.

BOX 11.6 **AT A COUNTRY FUNERAL**

WENDELL BERRY

> Now the old ways that have brought us
> farther than we remember sink out of sight
> as under the treading of many strangers
> ignorant of landmarks. Only once in a while
> they are cast clear again upon the mind
> as at a country funeral where, amid the soft
> lights and hothouse flowers, the expensive
> solemnity of experts, notes of a polite musician,
> persist the usages of old neighborhood.
> Friends and kinsmen come and stand and speak,
> knowing the extremity they have come to,
> one of their own bearing to the earth the last
> of his light, his darkness the sun's definitive mark.
> They stand and think as they stood and thought
> when even the gods were different.
> And the organ music, though decorous
> as for somebody else's grief, has its source

in the outcry of pain and hope in log churches,
and on naked hillsides by the open grave,
eastward in mountain passes, in tidelands,
and across the sea. How long a time?
Rock of Ages, cleft for me, let me hide my
self in Thee. They came, once in time,
in simple loyalty to their dead, and returned
to the world. The fields and the work
remained to be returned to. Now the entrance
of one of the old ones into the Rock
too often means a lifework perished from the land
without inheritor, and the field goes wild
and the house sits and stares. Or it passes
at cash value into the hands of strangers.
Now the old dead wait in the open coffin
for the blood kin to gather, come home
for one last time, to hear old men
whose tongues bear an essential topography
speak memories doomed to die.
But our memory of ourselves, hard earned,
is one of the land's seeds, as a seed
is the memory of the life of its kind in its place,
to pass on into life the knowledge
of what has died. What we owe the future is not a
new start, for we can only begin
with what has happened. We owe the future
the past, the long knowledge
that is the potency of time to come.
That makes of a man's grave a rich furrow.
The community of knowing in common is the seed
of our life in this place. There is not only
no better possibility, there is no
other, except for chaos and darkness,
the terrible ground of the only possible
new start. And so as the old die and the young
depart, where shall a man go who keeps
the memories of the dead, except home
again, as one would go back after a burial,
faithful to the fields, lest the dead die
a second and more final death.

CONCLUSION

This historical approach to death has gone full circle from living death, to the dying of death, to the resurrection of death. This change of attitude has taken place over a 400-year period. One of the real assets of history is its ability to demonstrate causation and coincidence in human affairs by determining chronology and context.

In this chapter we have discussed bereavement and burial practices in the United States from the early beginnings of European settlement. While European influences were obviously present in this development, a "breaking away" from the European aristocracy is evidenced by middle-class Americans in the 1830s. Certainly various "isms" played significant roles in the shaping of American bereavement and burial practices. An historical perspective blends the various influences on the development of American death customs as we know them today.

With the developing of cemeteries, building of funeral homes, and the establishing of life insurance companies, certain needs of Americans have been fulfilled. Security comes from the sheer orderliness and structure of these "institutions." One should know what to "expect" from these services, and payment turns the responsibility over to the professionals. We Americans differ significantly from nonliterate societies where such functions are completed within the kin network. However, paying someone else to perform a service fits middle-class Americans' specialization and division of labor.

It is important that the consumer stay well informed about burial practices and insurance in our society through staying abreast of various funeral home regulations and different life insurance offerings. It is also significant with the threat of nuclear war that the public be well-informed and actively involved in seeking peace and avoiding such a war. Perhaps this recent "resurrection of death" in an atomic age will be history behind us that will not continue into the future.

SUMMARY

1. Historians mainly determine chronology and context in order to demonstrate causation and coincidence in human affairs.

2. Rural Americans between 1600 and 1930 were well acquainted with death; it was commonplace.

3. The Reformed Tradition of the Protestant Reformation stressed that death and damnation were deserved, but God had elected a select few for salvation. Thus, death was approached with ambivalence.

4. Death was feared by the Puritans, who prayed not for the soul of the deceased but for the comfort and instruction of the living. The funeral was the main social institution for channeling the grief of Puritan survivors.

5. The Enlightenment replaced depraved dependent Puritans with rational people who viewed death as a natural occurrence rather than a time of judgment. Unitarianism and Evangelicalism accepted this view of human nature.

6. Between 1830 and 1945, as a middle-class America emerged, "the dying of death" occurred as funeral institutions designed to keep death out of sight and mind appeared.

7. Important intellectual influences on "the dying of death" were romanticism, sentimentalism, scientific naturalism, and liberal religion.

8. At the middle of the 19th century, the rural cemetery evolved—a landscaped garden in a suburban setting. Life insurance was established at this time to remove anxiety and financial insecurity.

9. Death was resurrected after 1945 with the ushering in of the atomic age.

DISCUSSION QUESTIONS

1. Describe and discuss the Puritan view of death. Describe the procedures and atmosphere surrounding the typical Puritan funeral.

2. How did the Enlightenment affect the Reformed Tradition of funerals and view of death?

3. Discuss influences of the following on the "Dying of Death": romanticism and sentimentalism, scientific naturalism, and liberal theology.

4. What are the influences of the following occupations upon the "Dying of Death": life insurance agents, cemetery superintendents, and funeral directors.

5. Describe and explain the reforms that have taken place over the years in the construction and maintenance of the cemetery.

6. What effect has the dropping of the atom bomb had on American death conceptions?

7. Describe the changes that have taken place with regard to the role of the family in funeralization.

GLOSSARY

Elegy A song or poem expressing sorrow, especially for one who is dead.

Epitaph An inscription, often on a tombstone, in memory of a deceased person.

Obituary Notice of a death, usually with a brief biography.

Ritual A behavioral form prescribed by custom or law, often associated with religion.

Sexton A church custodian charged with the upkeep of the church and parish buildings and grounds.

Socialization The learning process through which an individual is taught to be accepted in his or her society.

Social stratification A ranking of social status (position) in groups; upper, middle, and lower classes are basically distinguished in the United States' social class system, for example, while India's stratification is a caste system.

REFERENCES

Abbott, Lyman. 1913. "There Are No Dead." *Outlook, 104* (August 30): 979–980.

Association of American Cemetery Superintendents. 1889. *3,* p. 59. Beecher, Henry Ward. 1858. *Life Thoughts.* Boston: Phillips, Sampson.

Barrett, William. 1958. *Irrational Man: A Study in Existential Philosophy.* New York: Doubleday.

Barry, Wendell. 1973. "At a Country Funeral" in *The Country of Marriage.* San Diego: Harcourt, Brace, Jovanovich.

Beecher, Henry Ward. 1859. *Notes from Plymouth Pulpit.* New York: Derby and Jackson.

Beecher, Henry Ward. 1866. *Royal Truths.* Boston: Tichnor and Fields.

Bender, Thomas. 1973. "The 'Rural Cemetery' Movement." *New England Quarterly,* 47 (June):196–211.

Benjamin, Charles L. 1882. "Essay." *The Casket, 7,* (February):2.

Bledstein, Burton J. 1976. *The Culture of Professionalism: The Middle Class and the Development of Higher Education in America.* New York: Norton.

Clark, Jr., Clifford E. 1978. *Henry Ward Beecher: Spokesman for a Middle-Class America.* Urbana, IL: University of Illinois Press.

Cleaveland, Nehemiah. 1847. *Green-Wood Illustrated.* New York: R. Martin.

Douglas, Ann. 1977. *The Feminization of American Culture.* New York: Knopf.

Dowd, Quincy L. 1921. *Funeral Management and Costs: A World-Survey of Burial and Cremation.* Chicago: University of Chicago Press.

Downing, Andrew Jackson. 1921. *Landscape Gardening,* 10th ed. New York: Wiley.

"The Dying of Death." 1899. *Review of Reviews, 20* (September):364–365.

Emmons, Nathaniel. 1842. "Death without Order." In Jacob Ide, (Ed.), *The Works of Nathaniel Emmons, 3.* Boston: Crocker & Brewster, pp. 29–38.

"Extracts." 1895. *Park and Cemetery, 5* (August):108.

Farrell, James J. 1980. *Inventing the American Way of Death,* 1830–1920. Philadelphia: Temple University Press.

"The Fear of Death." 1912. *Harper's Weekly, 56* (October 5):21.

Feifel, Herman (Ed.). 1959. *The Meaning of Death.* New York: McGraw-Hill.

French, Stanley. 1975. "The Establishment of Mount Auburn and the 'Rural Cemetery' Movement." In *Death in America*: pp. 69–91. Philadelphia: University of Pennsylvania Press.

Fulton, Robert, & David J. Gottesman. 1981. "Loss, Social Change and the Prospect of Mourning," Unpublished paper.

"Funeral Directors." 1883. *The Casket, 8* (June).

Gebhart, John C. 1927. *The Reasons for Present-Day Funeral Costs,* Unpublished.

Geddes, Gordon. 1981. *Welcome Joy: Death in Puritan New England.* Ann Arbor, MI: U.M.I. Research Press.

Greenwald, David S. and Steven J. Zeitlin, 1987. *No Reason to Talk About It: Families Confront the Nuclear Taboo.* New York: W. W. Norton.

Gross, Robert A. 1976. *The Minutemen and Their World.* New York: Hill and Wang.

Habenstein, Robert W., & William M. Lamers. 1962. "The Pattern of Late 19th Century Funerals." *The History of American Funeral Directing.* Milwaukee: Bulfin, pp. 389–444.

Hale, Nathan G. 1971. *The Origin and Foundations of the Psychoanalytic Movement in the United States, 1876–1918.* New York: Oxford University Press.

Handford, Thomas W. (Ed.) 1887. *Beecher: Christian Philosopher, Pulpit Orator, Patriot and Philanthropist.* Chicago: Donahue, Henneberry, pp. 47–49.

Hare, Sidney J. 1910. "The Cemetery Beautiful." *Association of American Cemetery Superintendents, 24*:41.

Hay, Mrs. E. E. 1900. "Influence of Our Surroundings." *Association of American Cemetery Superintendents, 14*:46.

Hillerman, Barbara. 1980. "Chrysallis of Gloom: Nineteenth Century Mourning Costume." In Martha V. Pike and Janice Gray Armstrong (Eds.), *A Time to Mourn: Expressions of Grief in Nineteenth Century America.* Stony Brook, NY: The Museums at Stony Brook, p. 101.

Hohenschuh, W. P. 1921. *The Modern Funeral: Its Management.* Chicago: Trade Periodical Company.

Howe, Daniel Walker. 1970. *The Unitarian Conscience: Harvard University Press, 1805–1861.* Cambridge: Harvard University Press.

Hutchinson, Woods. 1893. "Death As a Factor in Progress." *North American Review, 156* (May):637.

"The Ideas of a Plain Country Woman." 1913. *Ladies Home Journal, 30* (April):42.

Johnson, J. B. 1896. "A More Rational View of Death." *Proceedings of the Association of American Cemetery Superintendents. Association of American Cemetery Superintendents, 10*:77.

Kübler-Ross, Elisabeth. 1969. *On Death and Dying.* New York:Macmillan.

Lifton, Robert Jay and Richard Falk. 1982. *Indefensible Weapons: The Political And Psychological Case Against Nuclearism.* New York: Harper and Row.

Lloyd, Phoebe. 1980. "Posthumous Mourning Portraiture." In Martha V. Pike and Janice Gray Armstrong (Eds.), *A Time to Mourn: Expressions of Grief in Nineteenth Century America.* Stony Brook, NY: The Museums at Stony Brook.

Ludwig, Allen. 1966. *Graven Images: New England Stonecarving and its Symbols.* Middletown, CT:Wesleyan University Press.

"The Man Nobody Envies: An Account of the Experiences of an Undertaker." 1914. *American Magazine,* 77 (June):68–71.

Mayo, Wyndham R. 1916. "Address." *Association of American Cemetery Superintendents,* 2: 51.

Mitford, Jessica. 1963. *The American Way of Death.* New York: Simon & Schuster.

McGuire, Daniel. 1982. "The Revolution in Death Consciousness," *Thought,* 57:227 (December).

Mumford, Lewis. 1947. "Atom Bomb: Social Effects," *Air Affairs, 1* (March):370–382; reprinted as "Assumptions and Predictions," Lewis Mumford. 1954. *In the Name of Sanity,* New York: Norton, pp. 10–33.

Oxley, J. MacDonald. 1887. "The Reproach of Mourning." *Forum, 2* (February):608–614.

Pike, Martha V., & Janice Gray Armstrong (Eds.). 1980. *A Time to Mourn: Expressions of Grief in Nineteenth Century America.* Stony Brook, NY: The Museums at Stony Brook.

Rosenberg, Charles E. 1973. "Sexuality, Class, and Role in Nineteenth Century America." *American Quarterly, 25*(May):137.

Rotundo, Barbara. 1973. "The Rural Cemetery Movement." *Essex Institute Historical Collections, 109* (July): 231–242.

Sargent, A. H. 1888. "Country Cemeteries." *Association of American Cemetery Superintendents.* 2:51.

Seavoy, Mr. 1906. "Twentieth Century Methods." *Park and Cemetery, 15* (February):488.

Sewall, Samuel. 1973. *The Diary of Samuel Sewall.* M. Halsey Thomas (Ed.). 2 vol. New York: Farrar, Straus and Giroux.

Shneidman, Edwin. 1973. "Megadeath: Children of the Nuclear Family." *Deaths of Man.* Baltimore: Penguin Books.

Simonds, O. C. 1919. "Review of Progress in Cemetery Design and Development with Suggestions for the Future." *Association of American Cemetery Superintendents,* 24:41.

Smith, Bayley. 1910. "An Outdoor Room on a Cemetery Lot." *Country Life in America,* 17 (March):539.

Stannard, David E. 1980. "Where All Our Steps Are Tending: Death in the American Context." In Martha V. Pike and Janice Gray Armstrong (Eds.), *A Time to Mourn: Expressions of Grief in Nineteenth Century America.* Stony Brook, NY: The Museums at Stony Brook, p. 26.

Taylor, Lawrence. 1980. "Symbolic Death: An Anthropological View of Mourning Ritual in the Nineteenth Century." In Martha V. Pike & Janice Gray Armstrong (Eds.), *A Time to Mourn: Expressions of Grief in Nineteenth Century America.* Stony Brook, NY: The Museums at Stony Brook, pp. 39–48.

Tocqueville, Alexis de. 1945. *Democracy in America.* New York: Vintage Books (Originally published 1835).

Tuckerman, Henry. 1856. "The Law of Burial and the Sentiment of Death." *Christian Examiner, 61* (November):338–342.

U.S. Bureau of the Census. 1975. *Historical Statistics of the United States, Colonial*

Times to 1970, pp. 1050–1059. Washington, DC: Department of Commerce, Bureau of the Census.

Warner, W. Lloyd. 1959. *The Living and the Dead.* New Haven: Yale University Press.

Weed, Howard Evarts. 1912. *Modern Park Cemeteries.* Chicago: R. J. Haight.

Wells, Richard A. 1887. *Decorum: A Practical Treatise on Etiquette and Dress of the Best American Society.* Springfield, MA.: King, Richardson.

SUGGESTED READINGS

Farrell, James. 1980. *Inventing the American Way of Death, 1830–1920.* Philadelphia: Temple University Press.

Examines the transformation from the Puritan Way of Death to the American Way of Death. Includes intellectual and institutional changes, and concludes with a case study of how such changes affected a single county.

Geddes, Gordon. 1981. *Welcome Joy: Death in Puritan New England.* Ann Arbor, MI: U.M.I. Research Press.

Good descriptive study, rich in detail. Particularly good on the Puritan funeral and bereavement.

Habenstein, Robert, & William Lamers. 1962. *The History of American Funeral Directing.* Milwaukee: Bulfin.

Prepared for the National Funeral Directors Association, this detailed study is a good history of the development of the profession.

Jackson, Charles O. (Ed.) 1977. *Passing: the Vision of Death in America.* Westport, CT: Greenwood Press.

A collection of classic essays on death in America, a few of which have been superseded by more recent work in the area.

Pike, Martha, & Janice Gray Armstrong (Eds.). 1980. *A Time to Mourn: Expressions of Grief in Nineteenth Century America.* Stony Brook, NY: The Museums at Stony Brook.

A beautifully illustrated collection of excellent essays, a must for anyone who wants to see and feel the grief of 19th century America.

Stannard, David (Ed.). 1975. *Death in America.* Philadelphia: University of Pennsylvania Press.

The December 1974 special issue of *American Quarterly,* with an added essay on the cemetery as a cultural institution, by Stanley French.

CHAPTER 12

The Funeral: Expression of Contemporary American Bereavement

You must express your grief at the loss of a loved one and then you must go on. The eyes of the dead must be gently closed and the eyes of the living must be gently opened.

JAN BRUGLER, INDIAN LAKE (OHIO) HIGH SCHOOL STUDENT

12 Most anthropologists agree that there has been no civilization discovered and studied that has not in some form given evidence of a funeralization process. This process varies greatly from culture to culture, but the basic elements of the recognition of the death—a rite or ritual and the final disposition of the body—have their counterparts in every culture. As we concluded in Chapter 10, funeral rituals allow individuals of every culture to maintain relations with ancestors, while uniting family members, reinforcing social status, fostering group cohesiveness, and restoring the social structure of the society.

SOCIAL AND CULTURAL ROOTS OF AMERICAN FUNERALIZATION

In contemporary American culture the process of final disposition of the body should be studied within its cultural and historical context. As we discovered in Chapter 10, it is wrong to believe that funeralization is either unique to western culture, or has been invented or created by it. To bury the dead is a common social practice. The methods to accomplish burial, and the meanings associated with it, are culturally determined.

This process requires the involvement of a functionary, who may be a professional, tradesperson, religious leader, servant, or even a member of the family. The functionary in each society is closely associated with the folkways and mores of the culture and its philosophical approach to life and death.

The Hebrew scripture reveals in the 50th Chapter of Genesis (Verse 2) that physicians embalmed the body of Jacob, the father of Joseph. This is followed by a detailed description of the funeral and burial. The historian Herodotus records embalming preparation as early as circa 484 BC. These two documents and archeological discoveries of earlier cultures give evidence of the disposition of the dead.

It is often stated that Egypt had a secret process for the preservation of the dead. The Egyptian embalming process, however, is fully described in several sources. There is perhaps no ancient culture that provides more evidence of its burial procedures than the great number of Egyptian mummies available for observation and study.

The Egyptians believed that the soul made a journey following death. According to their beliefs, this journey took approximately 3000 years followed by the soul's returning to the body it had left. This belief required the preservation of the body so that the soul, upon its return, would have a final destination. In addition to the embalming procedures, the Egyptians attempted to exclude air and moisture from the body by the liberal use of wrappings, oils, and gums. They also practiced elaborate encasement and burial of the remains. Such attempts at body preservation were obviously effective as evidenced by the many specimens still in existence today.

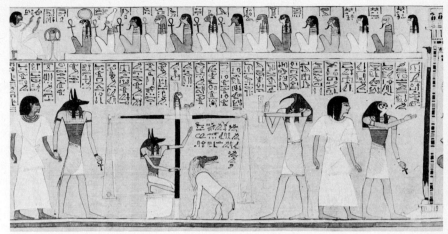

The most elaborate and famous burial customs are the Egyptian customs.

BOX 12.1 **DEATH IN ANCIENT EGYPT**

The earliest burials known in Egypt date to a period well before 3000 B.C. and display evidence, through funerary gifts in the graves, of a belief of continued existence after death. The earliest graves were very simple affairs consisting of shallow circular or oval pits in the ground where the body was placed in a fetal position. The introduction of methods to protect the body from the filling of the pit was motivated by a desire to improve the conditions for the dead.

During the middle and late Predynastic Period (before 3100 B.C.) the practice of wrapping the body in animal skins gradually gave way to other forms of protection, particularly the use of basket trays upon which the body was laid out. Wooden coffins, made of rough planks joined by dowels, became common by the end of the Predynastic Period (circa 3200 B.C.). By the beginning of the Fourth Dynasty (2613 B.C.), a significant number of burials occurred in which the body was placed in a coffin in a fully extended position.

The main advance in Predynastic tomb design (before 3100 B.C.) was the gradual introduction of wood-roofed graves, thus creating an underground chamber within which the coffin could be placed and separated from the sand. The pits were often lined with mud-plaster or wood therefore providing an additional barrier between the body and the ground. An important consequence of the added separation

(continued on next page)

between the body and the filling of the grave, however, was the loss of the natural preservative effects of direct contact with the dry sand which served to preserve some of the soft tissues through rapid drying.

Wrapped bodies of the first three dynasties were not truly mummified, since no treatment other than the use of linen bandages and resin was employed. By the Fourth Dynasty, however, evidence was found of deliberate attempts to inhibit decomposition by removal of the soft internal organs from the body—accomplished by means of an incision in the side of the abdomen. Removal of the liver, intestines, and stomach improved the chances of securing good preservation because the emptied body-cavity could be dried more rapidly. The removed organs were deposited in a safe place in the tomb in order for the body of the deceased to be complete once more in the netherworld.

Bandages soaked in resin were carefully molded to the shape of the body in order to reproduce the features, particularly in the face and the genital organs. As the resin dried, it consolidated the linen wrapping in position, preserving the appearance of the body for as long as it remained undisturbed. The corpse itself decomposed very rapidly within this linen shell, leaving the innermost wrappings in close contact with the skeleton.

An important factor in the development of the Egyptian tomb was the necessity to provide storage space for the items of funerary equipment considered essential for continued use by the deceased in the hereafter. A significant part of the material provided for the dead took the form of actual offerings of food and drink—required for the "very survival" of the deceased before enjoying all the other possessions in the tomb. Because of the need to provide offerings of food at the tomb, the tomb had to combine the function of a burial-place with that of a mortuary chapel in which the priests could officiate.

The Egyptians believed there were two main spiritual forms of the deceased. The *Ka* was supposed to dwell in the tomb in the mummified body. The *Ba* was usually represented as a human-headed bird, which left the body at the time of death, and was free to travel in the tomb during the daytime but returned to dwell in the mummy at night. The Predynastic cultures may have believed that continued existence after death resembled earthly life, also a popular belief in later times.

A. J. Spencer. 1982. *Death in Ancient Egypt.* New York: Penguin Books.

In many cultures the religious beliefs of the people influence their funeral and burial practices. Such was the case on the European continent during the medieval period of the feudal estates. Each landholder or lord was responsible for the people who worked for him and were members of the lord's extended family. These lords had a chaplain or religious person as a part of their staff, and they became responsible for the care and burial of the dead.

In the structure of the Christian church, priests were assigned to certain duties during specified hours. It is suggested that our use of the word *sexton* today comes from the practice of assigning the priest in charge of the sixth hour (in Latin, *sex*) with the burial of the dead and the supervision of the churchyard or cemetery.

As western civilization developed and progressed, there is evidence that many of the functionaries were anatomists, doctors, or artists. Each profession wanted to preserve the human body to further its own interests and offered to do so in return for the availability of bodies for study and research. Still in existence today are anatomical plates that daVinci drew from his observations of human specimens.

With the advent of the discovery of the circulatory system of the body, circa 1600, and the possibility of diffusion of preserving chemicals through that system, more sophisticated methods of embalming the body were developed. Dr. Hunter of England and Dr. Gannal of France, independently of each other, furthered the process in the early 1600s. In France, this work coincided with the advent of the bubonic plague. During this period of time, extensive attempts were made to preserve the bodies of the dead to protect the health of those who survived the plague.

BOX 12.2

> Historically, through a considerable period of time, the pattern of mortuary behavior in any society is subject to change, although basic death beliefs remain fundamentally unchanged. The roots of American funeral behavior extend back in a direct line several thousand years to early Judeo-Christian beliefs as to the nature of God, man, and the hereafter, and, in turn, these beliefs and practices were influenced to some extent by even earlier beliefs and practices.
>
> Habenstein, Robert W., & William M. Lamers. 1962. *The History of American Funeral Directing.* Milwaukee: Bulfin.

EARLY AMERICAN FUNERAL PRACTICES

During the colonization of America, early evidence exists of the care and burial of the dead. There is, however, no evidence of any attempt at body preservation, even though the body was bathed and dressed prior to burial. This was usually done by nurses, midwives, or members of the family. It was not until the time of the Civil War that embalming was promoted to temporarily preserve the body for return to the soldier's home. Some reports credit this practice to a military doctor by the name of Thomas Holmes. It was not until the late 1800s and early 1900s that states began to promote the practice of embalming to protect the public's health. With the advent of the practice of embalming, laws were soon passed to regulate both the practice and the practitioner.

The current practitioner of the funeral profession evolved from the artisan or cabinetmaker (invariably a man who built the casket as part of his trade) and the livery owner (who provided the special vehicles needed at the time of the funeral—particularly the hearse and special buggies for the family). As the public came to expect the services associated with the casket and transportation, persons began to specialize in providing these services, and the funeral functionary of today evolved as a provider of these services.

With the development of contemporary funeral practices over the past 90 years, it is interesting to observe the kind of facilities evolving to provide these services. It was not customary to hold funerals in the church in colonial America. The Puritans gave little importance to the funeral and seemed only to demand proper and reverent disposition of the dead by burial. Almost without exception, death occurred in the home. It was, therefore, expected that the dead would be bathed, dressed, put in a casket, and laid out (viewed) in the home. The funeral rite was either in the home or at the gravesite. When the first practitioners began to specialize in the burial of the dead, they continued to use the home for this purpose. They often would acquire a large house in the community and convert it to use as a "funeral home." It should be noted that the word *home* was associated with this facility, and today is still the most commonly used term to describe funeral facilities.

BOX 12.3 **NEW FUNERAL OPTION FOR THOSE IN A RUSH**

The convenience and high technology of drive-through banks and hamburger places have come to the funeral world. A Chicago funeral home has set up a drive-through service with cameras and a sound system that let on-the-go visitors pay their respects, sign the funeral reg-

Box 12.3, continued

ister and view the remains of the loved one round the clock without ever leaving the car.

Carloads of working people pressed for time, as well as bus loads of senior citizens confined to wheelchairs, have paraded through the drive-in at Gatling's Funeral Home on the city's South Side to see the images of embalmed friends and relatives on a television screen covered by a white canopy that is lit up at night.

The owner, Lafayette Gatling, a former construction worker who says he used to feel uncomfortable himself paying his respects in soiled work clothes, added the drive-through service two years ago. "The working person doesn't have time to come in," Mr. Gatling said. "They want to see the body but they don't want to have to wait. I always thought there should be some way they could see the body any time they want."

The procedure goes something like this: Visitors, cautioned to drive through slowly, ride to a speakerphone and push a button for service. An attendant in a control room asks whom they wish to see. "I would like to view the remains of John Doe," the visitor says into the speakerphone. "You may proceed," the attendant says, using controls to turn on the lights and cameras over the body of the deceased lying in one of the rooms.

The motorist then signs the register, conveniently tucked underneath the speakerphone, and drives a couple of feet to the viewing area where a head shot of the loved one in a coffin instantly appears on a 25-inch screen. The picture lasts three seconds, but visitors can push a button to request to see the loved one over and over again, and some stare at the screen for half an hour. When the car moves on, the next in line takes its place.

The feature has been a hit with visitors, who are used to ordering hamburgers and fries from a drive-through, a comparison that Mr. Gatling finds insulting. "We're dealing with remains here—I wouldn't compare that with food," Mr. Gatling said. "The only thing similar is the speaker system."

Drive-up windows displaying a single coffin came on the scene briefly several years ago at a few funeral homes in Florida and California, but there have been none using the complex system of relays, switches and timers needed to accommodate requests to see as many as a dozen bodies as the Gatling Funeral Home allows.

(continued on next page)

Mr. Gatling is now seeking a patent for the system. And he is planning bigger and better things for his funeral home, which already sells flowers and sympathy cards for mourners who forgot theirs and holds weddings in the main chapel on off-days. In addition to adding more chapels and parlors, he plans to make videotapes of the remains and the funeral services, which he hopes to sell to the bereaved.

Others worry about what all this convenience could do to the funeral business. "You could have the curious going through and checking out who happens to be laid out today," said W. Timothy Simms, president-elect of the Illinois Funeral Directors Association. "It lends a circus atmosphere to the services. It seems we're in a changing world."

Bernard Beck, an associate professor of sociology at Northwestern University, agreed, saying: "There seems to be no end to the need to save time. There has been a loosening of our communal ties. Still this is a way of putting in an appearance."

It was only natural that with specialization, special facilities would be developed for the funeral ceremony. The influence of the family and the church is readily seen in that most facilities try to provide both a homelike atmosphere for the gathering of the community and a chapel-like atmosphere for the funeral service. If the family chooses not to use a church for the funeral service, the funeral home provides a similar setting. Approximately 50 percent of the funerals today are held in churches, and the remaining 50 percent are held in funeral homes or cemetery chapels. The Department of Commerce of the United States Government estimates that approximately 22,000 funeral homes serve the families of the approximately 2.1 million annual deaths.

BOX 12.4 **THE DECLINE OF MOURNING**

A decade ago, anthropologist Geoffrey Gorer wrote a much reprinted article on "the pornography of death." Gorer's point, also made by German theologian Helmuth Thielicke, is that death is coming to have the same position in modern life and literature that sex had in Victorian times. Some support for the theory is provided by the popular movie *The Loved One*, which turns death into a slapstick dirty joke.

Is grief going underground? People want briefer funeral services, says Dr. Quentin Hand, an ordained Methodist minister who teaches at the theological school of Georgia's Emory University. "No one wants a eulogy any more—they often ask me not to even mention Mother or Father." Even those much scolded death-deniers, the undertakers, seem to sense that something is missing. Dean Robert Lehr of the Gupton Jones College of Mortuary Science in Dallas says that whereas students used to study only embalming, they now go in heavily for "grief psychology and grief counseling." Explains Lehr: "There are only 16 quarter hours in embalming now and 76 in other areas. We're in a transition period."

The outward signs of mourning—veils and widow's weeds, black hat and armbands, crepe-hung doorways—are going the way of the hearse pulled by plumed horses. There is almost no social censure against remarrying a few months after bereavement in what one psychiatrist calls "the Elizabeth Taylorish way" (referring to her statement six months after husband Mike Todd was killed in a plane crash: "Mike is dead now, and I am alive"). Many psychologists who have no quarrel with the life-must-continue attitude are dubious about the decline in expression of grief. Psychology Professor Harry W. Martin of Texas Southwestern Medical School deplores the "slick, smooth operation of easing the corpse out, but saying no to weeping and wailing and expressing grief and loneliness. What effect does this have on us psychologically? It may mean that we have to mourn covertly, by subterfuge—perhaps in various degrees of depression, perhaps in mad flights of activity, perhaps in booze." In his book, *Death, Grief and Mourning*, anthropologist Gorer warns that abandonment of the traditional forms of mourning results in "callousness, irrational preoccupation with and fear of death, and vandalism."

Whether or not such conclusions are justified, the take-it-in-stride attitude can make things difficult. Gorer cites his brother's widow, a New Englander, whose emotional reticence, combined with that of her British friends, led her to eschew any outward signs of mourning. As a result, "she let herself be, almost literally, eaten up with grief, sinking into a deep and long-lasting depression." Many a widow invited to a party "to take her mind off things" has embarrassed herself and her hostess by a flood of tears at the height of the festivities. On occasion,

(continued on next page)

Gorer himself "refused invitations to cocktail parties, explaining that I was mourning; people responded to this statement with shocked embarrassment, as if I had voiced some appalling obscenity."

Funerals seem ever harder to get to in a high-pressure, computerized way of life. But the social repression of grief goes against the experience of the human race. Mourning is one of the traditional "rites of passage" through which families and tribes can rid themselves of their dead and return to normal living. Black funeral parades, Greek klama (ritual weeping), Irish wakes—each in their own way fulfills this function. Orthodox Jewish families are supposed to "sit *shiv'ah*"; for seven days after the burial they stay home, wearing some symbol of a "shredded garment," such as a piece of torn cloth, and keeping an unkempt appearance. Friends bring food as a symbol of the inability of the bereaved to concern themselves with practical affairs. For eleven months sons are enjoined to say the prayers for the dead in the synagogue twice a day.

By no means all observers agree that the decline of such demanding customs is a bad thing. The old rituals, while a comfort and release for some, could be a burden to others. And grief expressed in private can be more meaningful than the external forms. London psychiatrist Dr. David Stafford-Clark thinks that the new attitude toward death should be considered in the context of "the way the whole structure of life has changed since World War II, particularly the very different attitude toward the future which has arisen. It is a much more expectant attitude—an uncertain one, but not necessarily a more negative one."

THE CONTEMPORARY AMERICAN FUNERAL

Most people use the words *death, grief,* and *bereavement* confusedly, which can lead to difficulty in communication. The words are closely interrelated, but each has a specific content or meaning. As discussed in Chapter 1, death is that point in time when life ceases to exist. *Death* is an event. It can be attached to a certain day, hour, and minute. *Grief* is an emotion, a very powerful emotion. It is triggered or stimulated by death. Although one can have anticipatory grief prior to the death of a significant other, grief is an emotional response to death. *Bereavement* is the state of having lost a significant other to death. Alternative processes—such as denial, avoidance, and defiance—have been shown by psychologists and psychiatrists to be only aber-

rations of the grief process and, as such, are not viable means of grief resolution.

The ultimate method of final disposition of the body should be determined by the persons in bereavement. Those charged with these decisions will be guided by their personal values and by the norms of the culture in which they live.

With approximately 70 percent of American deaths occurring in hospitals or institutions for the care of the sick and infirm, the contemporary process of body disposition begins at the time of death when the body is removed from the institutional setting. Most frequently the body is taken to a funeral home. There, the body is bathed, embalmed, and dressed. It is then placed in a casket selected by the family. Typically, arrangements are made for the ceremony, assuming a ceremony is to follow. The funeral director, in consultation with the family, will determine the type, time, place, and day of the ceremony. In most instances, the public rite or ceremony will have a religious content (Pine, 1971). The procedure described above is followed in approximately 75 percent of funerals. Alternatives to this procedure will be examined later in this chapter.

Following this ceremony, final disposition of the body is made by either earth burial (80 percent), cremation (15 percent), or entombment (5 percent). (These percentages are approximate national averages and will vary by geographical region.) The bereavement process will then be followed by a period of postfuneral adjustment for the family.

HOW THE FUNERAL MEETS THE NEEDS OF THE BEREAVED

Paul Irion (1956) has described the following needs of the bereaved: reality, expression of grief, social support, and meaningful context to the death. For Irion, the funeral is an experience of significant personal value insofar as it meets the religious, social, and psychological needs of the mourners. Each of these dimensions is necessary to return bereaved individuals to everyday living and, in the process, resolve their grief.

The *psychological* focus of the funeral is based on the fact that grief is an emotion. Edgar Jackson (1963) has indicated that grief is the other side of the coin of love. He contends that if a person has never loved the deceased—had an emotional investment of some type and degree—he or she will not grieve upon death. Evidence of this can easily be demonstrated by the number of deaths that we hear, see, or read about daily that do not have an impact on us unless we have some kind of emotional involvement with those deceased persons. We can read of 78 deaths in a plane crash and not grieve over any of them unless we personally knew one or more of the individuals killed. Exceptions to the above might include the death of a celebrity or public figure, when people experience a sense of grief even though there has never been any personal contact.

In his original work on the symptomatology of grief, Erich Lindemann (1944) stressed this concept of grief and its importance as a step in the resolution of grief. He defines how the emotion of grief must support the reality and finality of death. As long as the finality of death is avoided, Lindemann (1944) believes grief resolution is impeded. For this reason, he strongly recommends that the bereaved persons view the dead. When the living confront the dead, all of the intellectualization and avoidance techniques break down. When we can say, "He or she is dead, I am alone, and from this day forward my life will be forever different," we have broken through the devices of denial and avoidance, and have accepted the reality of death. It is only at this point that we can begin to withdraw the emotional capital that we have invested in the deceased and seek to create new relationships with the living.

On the other hand, viewing the corpse can be very traumatic for some. Most people are not accustomed to seeing a cold body and a significant other stretched out with eyes closed. Indeed, for some this scene may remain in their memories for a lifetime. Thus, they remember the cold corpse, not the warm, responsive person. Whether or not to view the body is not a cut-and-dried issue. Many factors should be taken into account when this decision is made.

Grief resolution is especially important for family members, but others are affected also—the neighbors, the business community in some instances, the religious community in most instances, the health-care community, and the circle of friends and associates (many of whom may be unknown to the family). All of these groups will grieve to some extent the death of their relationship with the deceased. Thus, many people are affected by the death. These affected persons will seek not only a means of expressing their grief over the death but also a network of support to help cope with their grief.

Sociologically, the funeral is a social event that brings the chief mourners and the members of society into a confrontation with death. The funeral becomes a vehicle to bring persons of all walks of life and degrees of relationship to the deceased together in one place for expression and support. It is for this reason that in our contemporary culture the funeral becomes an occasion to which no one is invited but all may come. This was not always the case, and some cultures make the funeral ceremony an "invitation only" experience. It is perhaps for this reason that private funerals (restricted only to the family or a special list of persons) have all but disappeared in our culture. (The possible exception to this statement is the funeral for a celebrity—where participation for the general public is limited to media coverage.)

At a time when emotions are strong, it is important that human interaction and social support become a high priority. A funeral can provide this atmosphere. To grieve alone can be devastating because it becomes necessary for that lone person to absorb all of the feelings into him- or herself. It has often been said that "joy shared is joy increased"; surely grief shared will be grief diminished. People need each other at times when they have intense emotional experiences.

A funeral is in essence a one-time kind of "support group" to undergird and support those grieving persons. A funeral provides a conducive social environment for mourning. We may either go to the funeral home to visit with the bereaved or for the purpose of working through our own feelings of grief. Most of us have had the experience of finding it difficult for the first time to discuss the death with a member of the family. We seek the proper atmosphere, time, or place. It is during the funeral, the wake, the shiva, or the visitation with the bereaved where we are provided the opportunity to express our condolences and sympathy comfortably.

Anger and guilt are often deeply felt at the time of death and will surface in words and actions. They are permitted within the funeral atmosphere as honest and candid expressions of grief, when at other times, they might bring criticism and reprimand. The funeral atmosphere says in essence "You are okay, I am okay; we have some strong feelings, and now is the time to express and share them for the benefit of all." Silence, talking, touching, feeling, and all means of sharing can be expressed without the fear of it being inappropriate.

The third function of the funeral is to provide a *theological* or *philosophical* perspective to facilitate grieving and provide a context of meaning in which to place one of life's most significant experiences. For the majority of Americans, the funeral is a religious rite or ceremony (Pine, 1971). For those who do not possess a religious creed or orientation, death will find definition or expression in the context of the values that the deceased and the grievers find important. Theologically or philosophically, the funeral functions as an attempt to bring meaning to the death and life of the deceased individual. For the religiously oriented person, it will perhaps contain a belief or understanding of an afterlife. For others, it may be seen only as an end of biological life and the beginning of symbolic immortality caused by the effects of one's life on the lives of others. The funeral should be planned in order to give meaning to whichever value context is significant for the bereaved.

"Why?" is one of the most often asked questions at the moment of death or upon being told that someone we know has died. Though it cannot provide the final answer to this question, the funeral can place death within a context of meaning that is significant to those who mourn. If it is religious in context, the theology, creed, and articles of faith confessed by the mourners will give them comfort and assurance as to the meaning of death. Others who have developed a personally meaningful philosophy of life and death will seek to place the death in that philosophical context.

Cultural expectations require that we typically dispose of the dead with ceremony and dignity. The funeral can also ascribe importance to the remains of the dead.

The Needs of Children and Their Attendance at Funerals

For children, as well as their adult counterparts, the funeral ceremony can be an experience of value and significance. At a very early age, children are interested in any type of family reunion, party, or celebration. To be excluded from the funeral may create questions and doubts in the mind of children as to why they are not permitted to be a part of an important family activity.

Another consideration in denying the child an opportunity to participate in post-death activities is what goes through the child's mind when such participation is denied. Children deal with other difficult situations in life, and when denied this opportunity, many will fantasize. Research suggests that these fantasies may be negative, destructive, and at times more traumatic than the situation from which the child is excluded.

Children also should not be excluded from activities prior to the funeral service. They should be permitted to attend the visitation, wake, or shiv'ah. (In some situations it would be wise to permit children to confront the deceased prior to the public visitation.) It is obvious that children should not be forced into this type of confrontation, but, by the same token, children who are curious and desire to be involved, should not be denied the opportunity.

Children will react at their own emotional levels, and the questions they ask will usually be asked at their level of comprehension. Two important rules follow: Never lie to the child, and do not overanswer the child's question.

At the time of the funeral, parents have two concerns about their children's behavior at funerals. The first is that they are worried that the child will have difficulty observing the grief of others—particularly if the child has never seen an adult loved one cry. The second is that parents themselves become confused when the child's emotional reactions may be different from their own. If the child is told of a death and responds by saying "Oh, can I go out and play?" the parent may interpret this as denial or a suppressed negative reaction to the death. Such a reaction can increase emotional concern on the part of the parent. However, if the child's response is viewed as only a first reaction, and the child is provided with loving, caring, and supportive attention, the child will ordinarily progress into an emotional resolution of the death.

The final reasons for involving children in post-death activities are related to the strength and support that they give other grievers. They often provide positive evidence of the fact that life goes on. In other instances, having been an important part of the life of the deceased, their presence is symbolic testimony to the immortality of the deceased. Furthermore, it is not at all unusual for a child to change the atmosphere surrounding bereavement from one of depression and sadness to one of laughter, verbalization, and celebration. Many times the child does this through his or her normal behavior, without any understanding of the kind of contribution being made.

BOX 12.5 **CHILDREN AND FUNERALS**

Before the visit to the funeral home children should be told that they will have a chance to see grandma, if they desire. They should be told that she is no longer breathing, that she is not just "asleep"; that she is no longer alive. They might be told that she does not look exactly the way she used to, but that this is all right; that it is easier to say "goodbye" if it is possible to see the person and be certain that they appear calm and at peace. They should be told that they may have questions, some of which will be hard to answer.

Children, depending on their age, will react differently to viewing the deceased. Children between five and ten years of age seem to ask many questions; they tend to be more open than adolescents. Older children usually experience and express stronger emotions than younger children. They need assurance that this, too, is all right. Children need assurance that they may have questions even after this last "goodbye" visit and that every attempt will be made to help find the answers.

The same sort of approach is indicated when preparing a child for attendance at a funeral or for a visit to the cemetery. In general, it is easier to include children in the entire course of the funeral than to exclude them from part or all of the activities and then try to deal with their subsequent inability to understand what happened at the funeral.

In order to be most supportive of their children when a friend or family member has died, parents should be told that it is natural for chil-

(continued on next page)

dren to want to be included in funeral activities. They should be advised that advance preparation, some explanation and time for questions will provide children with the support and understanding needed for respectful involvement. Parents should be told that children are welcome to come to the funeral home, that staff will be pleased to assist the parents in this work, and that children should be invited to attend and even participate in funeral service activities.

Parents should be told to invite and encourage children to be part of the funeral service—but not to force them or coerce them into participating. If the parents are having a difficult time because of the death, the children can be brought to services in the care of a close friend or relative with whom they are comfortable. If there is some concern that the children might have a difficult time at the funeral, it is best to encourage attendance and, at the same time, see that supportive people are available to them.

William Lamers. 1986. "Helping the Child to Grieve." In Gary H. Paterson (Ed.), *Children and Death*. London, Ont.: King's College Press, pp. 105–120.

THE AMERICAN PRACTICE OF FUNERAL SERVICE

Education and Licensure

Earlier in this chapter we indicated that with the evolution of the funeral there likewise has been an evolution of a funeral functionary. Our contemporary American culture refers to that functionary as a funeral director. One hundred years ago this functionary was a "layer out of the dead," often a member of the family who physically and emotionally could perform the necessary tasks of bathing the body, closing the eyes and mouth, and dressing the body. It was not unusual for a midwife or other person who provided nursinglike services in the community to be called on to assist the family. Early advertisements indicate that nurses did offer such services.

The advent of the cabinetmaker and livery person has been discussed, and out of this transition evolved the funeral director. As early as the 1890s, the various states began to enact legislation to protect the public's health by licensing embalmers. The early licenses directed their attention to the embalming process, and it was not until the decades of the 1920s and 1930s that licensing agencies began to regulate the other aspects of the funeral and the operation of funeral homes.

BOX 12.6

Clarence Darrow, discussing an ancestor reported to have been an undertaker, said: "One could imagine a more pleasant means of livelihood, but, almost any trade is bearable if the customers are sure."

The rationale for this licensure was based upon the felt need to protect the public, primarily in the financial area. However, regulations also addressed themselves to the conduct of the funeral where the cause of death was due to a contagious disease. Another issue of public health protection was the transportation of the dead from the place of death to the location of final disposition. Public health authorities claim that the regulation of the treatment of the dead has significantly contributed to the advanced standard of health of our country.

Based on these concepts, the licensing agencies most often charged with responsibility to regulate the funeral industry have been the various state boards of health. In some states, special boards were established for the regulation and enforcement procedures.

Licensure has been reserved to the individual states and includes three basic licenses. A license as an *embalmer* permits a person to legally remove the dead from the place of death and prepare the body through the process of embalming for viewing and **funeralization.** All states require persons who function in this regard to be licensed. A second license to practice as a *funeral director* permits the holder to arrange the legal details of the funeral, including the preparation of the death certificate and counseling with the family to arrange, plan, and implement the kind of funeral desired for the deceased. A third license is one that permits the licensee to practice mortuary science— an all-inclusive specialty that covers the practices of both embalming and funeral directing.

A few states have a license for a funeral director, a license that may be held by only one person in each firm (usually the owner or manager) and that serves to give the licensing agency control over all of the practitioners within that firm. A greater number of states have created a funeral home license or permit that is required to be issued to each funeral home and permits the state to close the funeral home by the withdrawal of the license without taking action against the licensees employed by that firm. In addition to every state requiring embalmers to be licensed, 49 states and the District of Columbia require practitioners to be licensed as funeral directors. The exact number of states requiring funeral home licenses or permits is hard to determine inasmuch as some are required by law, some by regulation, and some by local ordinance. Approximately one-half of the states have some requirement that governs the operation of a funeral home.

The qualifications for licensure deal basically with age, citizenship, and specific education. As of 1990 (with exception of Colorado, which has no current basic educational requirements for embalmer's and funeral director's licenses), all states require a high school education and professional preparation in mortuary college. In addition, eight states require one academic year of college in addition to the professional preparation, and 21 states require two academic years of college in addition to the professional preparation. Following the academic training, and in some instances before academic training is begun, all states require an internship or apprenticeship period. This varies from one to three years. The variance is directly related to the amount of college and professional training required. Upon the completion of academic and internship or apprenticeship requirements, applicants for licensure are required by all states to successfully pass a qualifying examination prior to the issuance of the license to practice.

Approximately five percent of the licensees in the United States are women. However, in the last decade, the number of women entering colleges of funeral service education and becoming licensed has greatly increased.

As of 1990, 14 states mandate continuing education to renew the license to practice. There is also an Academy of Professional Funeral Service Practice that provides a voluntary program of continuing education.

BOX 12.7 **SHOULD FUNERAL DIRECTORS PROFESSIONALIZE?**

RAYMOND DeVRIES, ASSOCIATE PROFESSOR, SAINT OLAF COLLEGE

Like many other occupations, funeral directors would like to be thought of as professionals. Should we as consumers support the attempts of funeral directors to become more professional?

Our first response to this question is, "Yes, of course." But let's not be so hasty. We must first consider what it is that makes an ordinary job a "profession." How do we distinguish a profession from a regular job? One way is to list the features or traits of occupations commonly accepted as professions. If asked which occupations are professions, most of us would answer: Physician, lawyer, minister. What sets these occupations apart? They are characterized by:

1. a specialized body of knowledge

2. a long period of training

3. an orientation toward service rather than profit

4. a commonly accepted code of ethics

5. legal recognition (most often through licensure)

6. a professional association

Implicit in this definition is the assumption that professionals have the best interest of the public in mind. After all, they submit to a long period of training, look forward to serving others, abide by a code of ethics, and police themselves through their professional associations. All occupations should become professions!

But this is not the only way to define a profession. Others look more cynically on the role of professions in society. George Bernard Shaw said, "Professions are a conspiracy against the laity." What did he mean? Shaw's comment hints at an alternative definition of the professions, a definition that suggests that there is just *one* distinguishing characteristic of the professions: *power*. Professions are those occupations that have accumulated enough power to control the definition and substance of their work. For example, this view contends that physicians are professionals by virtue of their complete control of matters of health. Through their associations they control the number and training of doctors, they limit the practices of competitors (e.g., chiropractors, nurse-practitioners), they set rates of reimbursement for health care. Adherents to this view point out that professionals in fact incapacitate us: they limit our choices, make us feel unable to help ourselves, encourage dependency.

Should funeral directors become more professional? Not all would agree. Funeral directors subscribe to the first definition and assert that professionals can better attend to the needs of the public. Followers of the second definition conclude that the move toward professionalization would limit competition, drive prices up, and, by promoting dependency, make us less able to deal with death.

The Role Of The Funeral Director

Rabbi Earl Grollman (1972) describes the role of the funeral director as that of a *caretaker, caregiver,* and *gatekeeper*. He indicates that the etymology of the word *undertaker* is based upon the activities of the early undertaker who "undertook" to do for people at the time of death those things that were crucial in meeting their bereavement needs. The funeral director, from the perspective of the community, was viewed as a secular gatekeeper between the living and the dead.

John Brantner (1973), elaborating upon the caregiver role, emphasizes that the funeral director is a crisis intervenor. Support for this idea can be documented in the vast amount of literature on the counseling role of crisis intervenors, who are not clinical practitioners by training but to whom the public turns in the crisis of death.

The funeral director will serve families by determining their needs and responding to them (Raether & Slater, 1974). This service will include, but not be limited to, the funeral (or its alternative) that they will plan and implement together. As a licensee of the state, the funeral director will handle the details requiring the death to be properly recorded and will file permits for transportation and final disposition of the body. The funeral director will serve as a liaison with other professionals working with the family—medical personnel, clergy, lawyers, cemetery personnel, and, when necessary, law enforcement officials.

Body Preparation

While the Egyptian process of embalming required 70 days to perform, body preparation today is completed within a few hours and is more effective and acceptable. Body preparation may be as simple as bathing the body, closing the eyes and mouth, and dressing the body for final **disposition** (placement or disposal). This procedure, infrequently selected, is utilized by families who wish direct disposition. Later in this chapter we will discuss direct disposition where this procedure may be an acceptable and a logical choice.

Nationally, it is estimated that four out of five bodies are embalmed before final disposition. **Embalming**, by definition, is the replacement of normal body fluids with preserving chemicals. This process is accomplished by using the vascular system of the body to both remove the body fluids and suffuse the body with preserving chemicals. The arterial system is used to introduce the chemicals into the body, and the venous system is used to remove the body fluids. This intravascular exchange is accomplished by using an embalming machine. The machine can best be described as an artificial heart outside of the body that produces the pressure necessary to accomplish the exchange of fluids. This, together with procedures to remove the contents of the hollow viscera from the body organs, constitutes the embalming procedure.

In addition to the embalming procedure and the thorough bathing of the body, cosmetic procedures are used to restore a more normal color to the face and hands. When death occurs, the pigments of the skin, which give the body its normal tone and color, no longer function. It is for this reason that creams, liquids, and/or sprays are used to restore color.

The question "Why embalm or cosmetize the dead body?" is based on the assumption that one of the needs of the family is the reality of death, thus the body should be left in its most deathlike appearance. Those who have seen a person die (especially if the dying process was painful, prolonged, and emaciating) know that the condition of the body at the time of death can be very repulsive. Many people cannot accept this condition. It is for this reason that contemporary funeral directors embalm and cosmetize the body.

Another reason for embalming is the mobility of the American population. Viewing, which is practiced in over 75 percent of the funerals today, often requires more than a bathing and dressing of the body. Due to the time involved, embalming is necessary to accomplish a temporary preservation of the body to permit the gathering of the family, which may take as long as two or three days. If the body were to remain unembalmed for this length of time, the distasteful effects of decomposition would create a significant problem for grievers.

Though arguments have been presented favoring embalming, it may not always be necessary or desired. Embalming is not required in all states. In Minnesota, for example, if the body is disposed of within 72 hours, is not transported on a common carrier or across state lines, and/or the person did not die of a contagious disease, embalming is *not* required. If a body is to be cremated and no public viewing is held, embalming would not be necessary. Many consumers just assume that embalming should or must occur.

A frequently asked question is, "If a body is embalmed, how long will it last?" There is no simple answer to this question. It is for that reason that funeral directors talk in terms of "temporary preservation." Most families are interested in a preservation that will permit them to view the body, have a visitation, and allow the body to be present for the funeral. Beyond that, they are not concerned with the lasting effects of embalming.

Final Disposition

Earlier in this chapter we indicated three forms of final disposition and their approximated utilization. Earth burial is by far the most widely used. Almost without exception, earth burial is accomplished within established cemeteries. In some instances, earth burial can be made outside of a cemetery if the landowner where the interment is to be made and the health officer of jurisdiction grant their permission. By law, cemeteries have the right to establish reasonable rules and regulations to be observed by those arranging for burial in them. A person does not purchase property within a cemetery, but rather purchases the "right to interment" in a specific location within that cemetery. Most cemeteries require that the casket be placed in some kind of outer receptacle or burial vault. The cemetery will also control how the grave can be marked with monuments or grave markers.

Cremation is the next most common method of final disposition. Until recently, the **crematory** was generally located within the cemetery. With the increase of cremation as an option for final disposition, however, some funeral homes have now installed crematories. Cremation is accomplished by the use of either extreme heat or direct flame. In either instance, the actual process of reducing the casket (or alternative container) and the body to "ashes" takes approximately two hours. After the cremation, the residue of cremated remains is collected, put in an urn, and disposed of according to the wishes of the family. The cremains may be buried in the earth, scattered in an appropriate or significant place, placed in a **niche** in a **columbarium** (a special room in a cemetery), or placed in some churches where cremains may be memorialized.

BOX 12.8   **A TRUE DIE-HARD FAN:
HE'LL ATTEND GAME IN URN**

Les Boatwright's death won't keep him from going to the Super Bowl today. He'll be there in a small brass urn. Boatwright, 75, died of a heart attack Monday, clutching two Super Bowl tickets as he prepared to place a bet with his bookie, said Boatwright's widow, Midge.

His two sons will take the urn carrying the ashes of the San Jose, California, resident to the Big Game between the San Francisco 49ers and the Cincinnati Bengals, Mrs. Boatwright said. "I told the boys, 'Do it for your daddy,' " she said. Boatwright's 33-year-old son Todd, flew to south Florida with his father's ashes early yesterday. His brother Marc, 37, arrived earlier.

Associated Press. From *The Arizona Daily Star*, Tucson. January 22, 1989, page E3.

Entombment is the least practiced of final disposition options. It consists of placing the body (contained within a casket) in a special building designed for this purpose. Cemeteries offer large buildings **(mausoleums)** as an alternative to earth burial or cremation. In some instances, families may purchase the right to interment in a cemetery, and on the designated space build a private or family mausoleum that will hold as few as one or two bodies or as many as 12 to 16. Both types of mausoleums must be specifically constructed and designed in such a way as to provide lasting disposition for the body. Most states and/or cemeteries regulate the specifications and construction of the mausoleum.

The mausoleum provides families with an additional option for body disposition. Approximately 5 percent of the 2.1 million annual deaths involve entombment as the method of final disposition.

FATHER KEEPS SON'S MEMORY ALIVE WITH CORPSE IN HOME

LOUISVILLE, KY. (AP)–William Sneed's son died November 8 of injuries suffered in an auto accident. He won't be buried. Instead, Sneed said, the body will remain in a casket with a clear plastic top in a room off the family kitchen.

(continued on next page)

"There are three especially painful moments one goes through at the death of a loved one," Sneed said. "The first is at the news of the death, the second when you see the body in the casket at the funeral home, and the third and most difficult is when you have to turn away from the grave site and know you'll never see that person again. We simply decided not to go through that last step."

Sneed obtained a burial permit naming himself custodian of the body of his son, William B. Sneed III, 29. The permit names the place of entombment as the Sneed Family Mausoleum--the room off the kitchen.

There is no law in Louisville that requires burial below ground. Sneed said the decision to keep the body of his son at home really began eight years ago.

"At first, it was like a joke, just between the three of us (himself, his daughter and his son)," he said. "But after talking about it for a while, it got serious. We decided then—I don't remember how long ago it was—that whichever one of us was the first to go, the other two would take care of everything like this."

Sneed said he plans to remodel the interior of his home to accommodate a small chapel at the rear, and the body will be placed there.

Adapted from an Associated Press article in the *Minneapolis Tribune,* Minneapolis, MN, November 20, 1975.

ALTERNATIVES TO THE FUNERAL

People often ask if there are alternatives to the traditional funeral. Three alternatives exist: immediate disposition of the body of the deceased, the bequest of the deceased to a medical institution for anatomical study and research, and the memorial service. Each of these alternatives is defined and discussed below.

Immediate disposition occurs when the deceased is removed from the place of death to the place of cremation or earth burial without any ceremony; proper certificates are filed and permits received in the interim. In these instances, the family is not present, usually does not view the deceased after death, and is not concerned with any further type of memorialization. It is immediate in that it is accomplished as quickly after death as is possible. In this situation the body will not likely be embalmed, and the only preparation will consist of bathing and washing the body. The 1985 National

Funeral Directors Association (NFDA) survey of members found that approximately 5 percent of all deaths involved immediate disposition. The frequency of this procedure differs by region of the country—it is performed most in the South Central part of the United States (approximately 7 percent of cases) and least in New England and the Mountain States (less than 1 percent of cases).

Body-bequest programs have become more well known in the last four decades and permit the deceased (prior to death) or the family (after the death) to donate the body to a medical institution. A compendium of body donation information (NFDA, 1981) indicates that, when the family desires, 75 percent of the donee institutions permit a funeral to be held prior to the delivery of the body to the institution for study or research. Some medical schools will pay the cost of transporting the body to the medical school, while others will not. With regard to expenses, this is the least expensive way of disposition of the body, especially if a memorial service is conducted without the body present. The compendium also indicates that in almost every instance the family may request that either the residue of the body or the cremated remains be returned when it is of no further benefit to the donee. In those instances where the family does not desire to have the body or the cremated remains returned, the donee institution will arrange for cremation and/or earth burial—oftentimes with an appropriate ceremony. People who are considering donating their bodies should be aware of the fact that at the time of death the donee institution may not have the need of a body. If this does happen the family will have to find another institution or make other arrangements for the disposition of the body. The 1985 NFDA survey found that anatomical gifts account for less than one percent of all deaths.

To some, body donation may not appear to be an alternative to the funeral (especially when a ceremony is held prior to the delivery of the bequested body), but inasmuch as the procedure is different from the most common methods of disposition, it may be considered as an alternative. According to the National Funeral Directors Association approximately 7000 such donations are made each year out of 2,099,000 deaths.

BOX 12.10 **WAITING FOR NEW LIFE AT 320 BELOW**

> Dora Kent's head lies in mute repose in a canister of liquid nitrogen, preserved in hope that scientists one day will find a way to thaw it out without damaging the tissues. Perhaps by then, they will also have mastered the problem of cloning a new Dora Kent from its cells. . . .
>
> *(continued on next page)*

The field of cryonics, as the practice of freezing humans is known, has been an obscure one. Cryonics is being studied as a way to sustain life or at least preserve the deceased's healthy organs until they can be donated to an ailing recipient. While scientists work to refine the technique, which is more hypothetical than practical right now, some critics pooh-pooh the whole idea. . . .

There are five cryonics firms in North America—in Florida, Michigan, and California, as well as one in Ontario. Worldwide there are believed to be 16 persons in deep freeze, though there could be others secretly held, according to Jackson Zinn, a lawyer and president of the American Cryonics Society. Five of them are in storage at Trans Time Inc., a cryonics firm in Oakland, California. According to Zinn, since the first body was placed there in 1974, the practice of cryonic suspension has been upheld in the supreme courts. In one case, the court upheld a man's request to undergo the procedure despite his family's objections.

Some clients of Trans Time wear bracelets directing immediate application of the cryonics process upon death. At the concrete, one-story Trans Time warehouse, the client's blood is replaced with a blood substitute and glycerol; the body is then wrapped in foil, placed in a polyethylene bag and suspended upside down in a stainless-steel cylinder filled with liquid nitrogen at 320 degrees below zero. The bodies are placed upside down so that the brain would be last to thaw should there be an accident and some of the nitrogen drain off.

Cryonics is expensive, which would appear to make it an option only for the rich and quirky. The cost of freezing an entire body, says Zinn, is about $125,000. The account is usually set up as a trust in the form of life insurance. A portion of the trust pays for the initial processing and the balance earns interest to pay for maintenance over the years. . . .

In 1986 physiologist and cryonicist Paul Segall anesthetized a laboratory beagle named Miles and placed him in a bin of crushed ice, chilling the dog to about 68 degrees Fahrenheit. Then his blood was removed and replaced with a solution of blood salts, starches, minerals, sugars, buffers, and anticoagulants. As Segall recounts the experiment, Miles was chilled further to about 38 degrees Fahrenheit and then the pumps were shut off. For 15 minutes the chilled beagle was without oxygen or pulse. Then the pumps were turned on, Miles was warmed up to 44 degrees and Segall began restoring the blood. When the normal concentration of blood was reached, Miles was sewn up and shipped off to intensive care.

Within hours the dog was active, and after six days he left the clinic. Since then he has lived at the Segall household. "He stands on his hind legs begging for food; he is very well coordinated; there has been little or no brain damage," says Segall. Trans Time intends similar experiments soon with monkeys.

The cryonicists say there are a number of potential immediate benefits from their research. Suppose a healthy person dies in Oregon in an auto accident. Usually only one or two organs, if any, can be salvaged. But cryonicists contend that if the body could be chilled quickly, the victim's heart could be shipped out for a recipient in California, the lungs to Florida, the corneas to New England and so on—all at a great time advantage. Or, given more time, all the potential organ recipients could be assembled at one transplant site.

Miles Cunningham. 1988. *Insight,* April 11, pp. 22–23.

The *memorial service* is defined as a service without the body present. It is true that every funeral is a memorial service—inasmuch as it is in memory of someone—but a memorial service, by our definition, is an alternative to the typical funeral. It may be conducted on the day of the death, within two or three days of the death, or sometimes as much as weeks or months following the death. The content of the service places little or no emphasis on the death. Instead, it often is a service of acclamation of philosophical concepts. Religious or nonreligious in content, these services can meet the needs of the bereaved.

Organizations exist for consumers called **memorial societies.** Such an example is in Ithaca, New York. The by-laws of this particular nonprofit and nonsectarian organization establish the following as purposes of their society:

1. To promote the dignity, simplicity, and spiritual values of funeral rites and memorial services.

2. To facilitate simple disposal of deceased persons at reasonable costs, but with adequate allowances to funeral directors for high-quality services.

3. To increase the opportunity for each person to determine the type of funeral or memorial service he or she desires.

4. To aid its members and promote their interests in achieving the foregoing.

Thus, such a memorial society would help educate consumers regarding death prior to the actual death of a significant other and present options for final disposition of the body. Likewise, many funeral directors today serve as valuable resource persons by sharing information regarding death with various community groups.

FUNERAL, FINAL DISPOSITION, AND RELATED EXPENSES

Charges made by a funeral home ordinarily involve the services of the professional staff, the use of the funeral home facilities and equipment, transportation, and the casket or other alternate container. In addition, most funeral homes provide burial vaults or other types of outer enclosures for the casket and ancillary items that may be purchased from the funeral director—clothing, register books, acknowledgment cards, and Stars of David, crucifixes, or crosses.

The other major cost of the funeral is the cemetery charges—either for the purchase of cemetery property for the right to interment therein, for mausoleum space, or for an urn for the cremated remains (in some instances, charges will include a space in a columbarium for the urn). Most families will also select, in one form or another, a monument or marker to identify the grave or other place of final disposition.

A final category of expenses incurred by the family is money sometimes advanced by the funeral home at the request of, and as an accommodation to, the family. Such cash advances might include, but are not limited to, the following: charges for opening and closing the grave, crematory costs, honoraria for clergy and musicians, obituary notices, flowers, and transportation costs in addition to the transportation ordinarily furnished by the funeral home.

In a recent survey (NFDA, 1986:7, 42) of members of the National Funeral Directors Association dealing with financial operations in 1985, it was determined that the average cost for an adult funeral in the United States was $3310. This figure is the sum of the charges for the following items (numbers in parentheses are average dollar costs); it does *not* include cemetery charges and cash advances to ministers, musicians, and florists:

Nondeclinable professional service charges ($536)
Transfer to funeral home ($71)
Embalming ($178)
Other preparation ($76)
Use of viewing facilities ($155)
Use of facilities for ceremony ($149)
Hearse ($97)
Limousine ($68)

In addition to providing a service to families in bereavement, funeral directors sell burial merchandise to their customers. Typically the cost of such merchandise comprises approximately 25 percent of the amount collected by funeral directors.

18 gauge steel casket ($1520)
Asphalt burial vault ($500)

The NFDA survey (NFDA, 1986:5) determined that nationally, for every dollar taken in by affiliated funeral homes, money was distributed in the following manner:

32 cents for salaries and benefits
25 cents for merchandise (caskets, vaults, etc.)
21 cents for other operating expenses
13 cents for facilities
 9 cents for before-tax profits

The 1986 NFDA financial survey provides us with a number of other important findings. First, the data suggest that funeral service is a competitive industry. When the cost of an average funeral is compared, the differences between the highest and the lowest prices charged varies less than $600 regardless of demographic category (region of the country, number of families served, number of facilities operated, or metro/rural location) (NFDA, 1986:1).

Second, approximately 70 percent of firms operate only one funeral home facility and another 20 percent operate two facilities (NFDA, 1986:40). Third, on average, 56 percent of all funeral home assets are owned by the funeral home. Funeral directors appear to be more willing to leave their assets within the company than other service professionals (NFDA, 1986:4).

Finally, the average funeral service firm's actual return on net worth is approximately 8 percent—which is comparable to a risk-free certificate of deposit invested in a bank or savings-and-loan. This relatively low return on equity makes funeral service (like other capital-intensive industries) a very difficult one to enter as a new entrepreneur. For the new entrant, the price of land and buildings would result in higher operating expenses to perform the same service as a more established funeral home (NFDA, 1986:1).

Until 1984 there were basically three ways that a funeral home charged for its services and merchandise selected by the family. The first was the *unit method* of pricing. In this procedure, all of the costs involved with the funeral home providing the services (including the staff, the facilities, the automotive equipment, and the casket) were included in a single charge. In making a selection under this procedure, the family looked at a "bottom line" figure to which only other charges paid by the funeral home (e.g., a vault, additional burial merchandise, cash advances) might be added.

The second method was referred to as the *bi-unit* or *tri-unit pricing system*. The bi-unit procedure was to make separate charges for professional services and the casket, and the tri-unit procedure was to separate charges made for professional services, the use of facilities, and the casket selected. This system enabled families to understand the charges for the three basic components making up funeral costs.

A third method of presenting costs was referred to as either *functional, multi-unit,* or *itemization.* (There is an interchange of the use of these terms. However, they usually refer to the same basic procedure.) In this method of pricing, each and every item of service, facility, and transportation was shown as a separate item together with its related cost. With this method there was usually a minimum of eight to ten items listed, and the family decided in each instance whether or not that item would become a part of the funeral service. In 1984 the Federal Trade Commission (FTC) mandated that all American funeral homes itemize their fees and that consumers have access to pricing information over the phone. However, at the present time this procedure is under review.

A major advantage of itemization is the opportunity to provide family members greater flexibility in arranging a funeral and the ability to control costs. The family should have the freedom to decline those items that they do not want, and a proper allowance should be made for such items that are not used. For example, one may ask to see "the pine box"–usually a cloth-covered wood casket or a pressed wood container. These caskets are relatively inexpensive and may or may not be in the display room. If the body is to be transported a great distance to the gravesite or crematorium, perhaps the funeral director's van or station wagon could be used rather than the expensive hearse. Similarly, the consumer should have the right to choose among types of **vault liners.** The greatest advantage of the process of itemization is that one can look carefully at the itemized services and obtain the most adequate services at the best price.

Drawing by D. Reilly, © 1988 The New Yorker Magazine, Inc.

"He'd rest a lot better with thirty per cent off."

There are two major disadvantages of the FTC policy requiring funeral homes to give prices over the phone and to itemize funeral expenses. The first is that when consumers receive prices over the phone it is difficult to make accurate price comparisons. One firm can say that they sell an oak casket for $900, and another will price a *different* oak casket at $2200. It is entirely possible that the price–quality ratio is better for the more expensive casket. A helpful analogy might be to imagine calling two import automobile dealerships—Yugo and Mercedes—to ask each "How much do cars cost in your dealership?" The only way one can make accurate price comparisons is to personally inspect both products carefully. The same is true for the funeral industry. Families are better served when they can make careful comparisons between the costs of services provided by funeral firms prior to the death of a significant other. Most people do not wait until the car breaks down before they shop for a new one. Furthermore, if they did find themselves in this situation, they would not purchase a car over the telephone.

The second disadvantage of the FTC ruling regarding the itemization of funeral expenses is that itemization did not uniformly result in decreasing expenses to families. Prior to the 1984 ruling, many funeral firms included some merchandise and services as part of the standard funeral. With itemization, funeral directors could provide justification to raise the cost for funeral services. The analogy of restaurant pricing may be appropriate at this point—it is often less expensive to order a complete meal than to order food a la carte.

BOX 12.11

President Roosevelt left detailed instructions for his funeral and burial, should he die while President. He directed that the funeral service be simple, that the casket be plain and of wood, that there be no embalming of the body or sealing of the casket and that his grave have no lining.

These instructions were found in a private safe days after his burial, too late to be considered. Consequently, Franklin D. Roosevelt's remains were embalmed, sealed in a copper coffin and placed in a cement vault.

Consumer Survival Kit: The Last Rights: Funerals. 1977. Owings Mills, MD: Maryland Center for Public Broadcasting.

PRENEED FUNERALS: A "NEW" TREND IN PLANNING FUNERALS

One of the more controversial issues today in funeral service is the trend toward **preneed funerals. Prearranging** is the process of arranging funerals in advance of need. This process can include the selection of merchandise, planning the service, determining method of review and final disposition, and the selection of persons to be involved in the funeral. In addition to prearranging, **prefunding,** or the legal commitment of money to pay for the funeral service, is also common. This is usually accomplished through *insurance* or a *trust.* Preneed is a generic term that refers to both processes of prearranging and prefunding (Hocker, 1987:1–2).

According to a 1983 national survey conducted by the National Research and Information Center (cited by Will, 1988:366), 9.2 percent of the American public have made prearrangements for their funerals, and another 62 percent feel that they should make funeral prearrangements with a funeral director. According to James Will (1988:367) and William Hocker (1987:4–11), the reasons why consumers prearrange and/or prefund funerals are the following:

1. To provide a forum for death-related discussions that is not profoundly affected by the grief that naturally accompanies the event of death.

2. To make one's funeral preferences known to one's survivors may assure that survivors will not select a type of funeral that differs from the one desired.

3. To provide an opportunity to personalize the funeral.

4. To plan one's funeral can be one of the last pieces of unfinished business one can accomplish for one's survivors. This action can provide the dying with peace of mind.

5. To give individuals an opportunity to get the most for their money through comparison shopping at a time when they are not faced with urgent need or overwhelmed by grief.

6. To unburden loved ones of the obligation of having to plan and pay for a funeral.

7. To protect an estate from funeral expenses in the future.

8. To assure that funds are available in the future for the type of funeral that is desired.

The problem with preneed funerals from the perspective of consumers and funeral service professionals is that a potential exists for consumer fraud. There have been some consumers who have bought and paid for funerals from unethical funeral salespersons (some licensed and others not) and later found at the time of death that either the firm was no longer in business, the money had not been put in a trust account, and/or the deceased had moved to a location not served by the firm. For these reasons Thomas D. Bischoff (cited by Kelly, 1987:32), Senior Vice-President of the Prearranged Funeral Division of Service Corporation International (the largest chain of funeral homes in the United States and the world), has made the following recommendation:

> We, as funeral service professionals, must encourage that everything be done to minimize these eventualities. We would again suggest that an insurance-funded prearranged funeral program is the best safeguard that the funeral director and the consumer have. Insurance companies are very tightly and closely regulated and are required to maintain sufficient funds on hand to meet requirements. An insurance-funded prearranged funeral program has very little potential for mis-management or fraud and as such should become the standard for the industry.

Ultimately, consumers must protect themselves against fraudulent entrepreneurs and dishonest "get-rich-quick" salespersons. Insurance-funded prearranged funeral programs are important potential safeguards, but the words of Robert W. Ninker (cited by Kelly, 1987:32), Executive Director of the Illinois Funeral Directors Association, should also be heeded.

The best protection a buyer can have is to purchase from a funeral director with a long history of success, after asking and understanding that this person is licensed and, in fact, trusts his funeral funds. . . The buyer should also check references with acquaintances. That is about as much certainty as there is in life. Of course, if the buyer responds to door-to-door sellers or boiler room operations, he is his own victim! No one can protect someone from his own fool-like actions.

CONCLUSION

━━━ Grief is the emotional working through of a significant loss. The funeral is a part of the grief process in contemporary America.

In our discussion, we have described funerals and their alternatives within a cultural and historical perspective. In the United States an evolutionary, not a revolutionary, process has occurred. Americans did not invent the funeral or the funeral functionary. However, contemporary Americans have found an expression for their bereavement.

SUMMARY

━━━ 1. To understand the contemporary funeralization process in the United States, one must understand its cultural and historical context.

2. Embalming, a process as old as 484 BC, was introduced in France and England in the 1600s, and to the United States during the Civil War. Presently four out of five American bodies are embalmed.

3. The contemporary role of funeral director has evolved from the occupations of cabinetmaker and livery owner.

4. Presently there are approximately 22,000 funeral homes in the United States serving the families of the approximately 2.1 million annual deaths.

5. Within the contemporary funeralization process, final disposition of the body is made by either burial (80 percent), cremation (15 percent), or entombment (5 percent). These percentages are approximate national averages.

6. The funeral is designed to meet the psychological, sociological, and theological or philosophical needs of bereaved persons.

7. A person does not purchase property within a cemetery, but purchases the right to interment in a specific location within that cemetery.

8. Alternatives to funerals exist, including immediate disposition, body donation, and memorial services.

9. Funeral bills have been presented to customers utilizing the following pricing systems: unit pricing, bi- or tri-unit pricing, and itemization. The latter is mandated in all states by the Federal Trade Commission. In 1985 the cost of the average adult funeral was $3310.

10. Children should not be excluded from participating in funerals. To do so might have adverse effects on the child's emotional well-being and impede his or her bereavement.

DISCUSSION QUESTIONS

1. Describe how the funeralization process can assist in coping with grief and facilitate the bereavement process.

2. Distinguish between grief, bereavement, and funeralization.

3. Describe and compare each of the following processes: burial, cremation, and entombment.

4. Based on Irion's concept of psychological needs of the bereaved, explain how funeralization can be related to the meeting of each of these needs.

5. Discuss the factors affecting post-death costs and the expenses related to funerals and final disposition.

6. Discuss the psychological, sociological, and theological–philosophical aspects of the funeralization process. How do each of these aspects facilitate the resolution of grief?

7. What would you include in your own obituary if you were to write it?

8. What would be your choice of final disposition of your body? Why would you choose this method, and what effects might this choice have upon your survivors (if any)?

9. What is the difference among preneed, prefunding, and prearranging funerals? What are the advantages and disadvantages of preneed funeral arrangements?

GLOSSARY

Cremation The reduction of human remains by means of heat or direct flame. The cremated remains are called *cremains* or *ashes* and weigh between six and eight pounds. "Ashes" is a very poor description of the cremated remains because they look more like crushed rock or pumice.

Crematory An establishment in which cremation takes place.

Crypt A concrete chamber in a mausoleum into which a casket is placed.

Columbarium A building or wall for above-ground accommodation of cremated remains.

Disposition Final placement or disposal of a dead person.

Embalming A process that temporarily preserves the deceased by means of displacing body fluids with preserving chemicals.

Entombment Opening and closing of a crypt, including the placement and sealing of a casket within.

Funeralization A process involving activities, rites, and rituals associated with the final disposition of the deceased's body.

Itemization A method of pricing a funeral in which every item of service, facility, and transportation is listed with its related cost. A service presently mandated by the Federal Trade Commission.

Mausoleum A building or wall for above-ground accommodation of a casket.

Memorial society A group of people joined together to obtain dignity, simplicity, and economy in funeral arrangements through advanced planning.

Niche A chamber in a columbarium into which an urn is placed.

Prearranging The process of arranging funerals in advance of need. This process can include the selection of merchandise, planning the service, determining method of review and final disposition, and the selection of persons to be involved in the funeral.

Prefunding Legally committing money to pay for the funeral service.

Preneed Funerals A generic term that refers to both processes of prearranging and prefunding funerals.

Urn A container for cremated remains.

Vault or grave liner A concrete container into which a casket or urn is placed for ground burial. Its function is to prevent the ground from settling.

REFERENCES

Associated Press. "A True Die-Hard Fan: He'll Attend Game in Urn." 1989. *Arizona Daily Star*, January 22, p. E3.

Brantner, John P. 1973. "Crisis Intervenor." Paper presented at the Ninth Annual Funeral Service Management Seminar, National Funeral Directors Association, Scottsdale, Ariz. (January).

Cunningham, Miles. 1988. "Waiting for New Life at 320 below." *Insight*, April 11:22–23.

"On Death as a Constant Companion." 1965. *Time*, November 12.

Grollman, Earl A. 1972. Commencement Address, Department of Mortuary Science, University of Minnesota, Minneapolis, MN. (May).

Habenstein, Robert W., & William M. Lamers. 1962. *The History of American Funeral Directing.* Milwaukee: Bulfin.

Hocker, William V. 1987. "Financial and Psychosocial Aspects of Planning and Funding Funeral Services in Advance As Related to Estate Planning and Life-Threatening Illness." An unpublished article distributed by the National Funeral Directors Association.

Irion, Paul E. 1956. *The Funeral: An Experience of Value.* Milwaukee: National Funeral Directors Association.

Irion, Paul E. 1968. *Cremation.* Philadelphia: Fortress Press.

Jackson, Edgar N. 1963. *For the Living.* Des Moines, IA: Channel Press.

Kelly, Thomas E. 1987. "Predict Preneed Vital to Financial Future." *The American Funeral Director.* (February):31–69.

Lamers, William. 1986 "Helping the Child to Grieve." In Gary H. Paterson (Ed.), *Children and Death.* London, Ont.: King's College Press, pp. 105–120.

Lindemann, Erich. 1944. "Symptomatology and Management of Acute Grief." *American Journal of Psychiatry, 101,* (September):141–148.

Maryland Center for Public Broadcasting. 1977. *The Last Rights: Funerals.* Owings Mills, MD: Maryland Center for Public Broadcasting.

National Funeral Directors Association. 1981. "Body Donation: A Compendium of Facts Compiled As an Interprofessional Source Book." Produced by the College of Health Sciences (University of Minnesota) and the National Funeral Directors Association.

National Funeral Directors Association. 1986. *Financial Operations Survey: For Fiscal 1985.* Milwaukee, WI: NFDA.

Pine, Vanderlyn R. 1971. *Findings of the Professional Census.* Milwaukee: National Funeral Directors Association (June).

Raether, Howard C. & Robert C. Slater. 1974. *Facing Death as an Experience of Life.* Milwaukee: National Funeral Directors Association.

Spencer, A. J. 1982. *Death in Ancient Egypt.* New York: Penguin Books.

Wilkerson, Isabel. 1989. "New Funeral Option for Those in a Rush." *The New York Times,* February 23, p. 10.

Will, James. 1988. "Preneed: The Trend toward Prearranged Funerals." In Howard Raether (Ed.), *The Funeral Director's Practice Management Handbook.* Englewood Cliffs, NJ: Prentice-Hall.

SUGGESTED READINGS

Consumers Union. 1977. *Funerals: Consumers' Last Rights.* Mount Vernon, NY: Consumers Union.

A report by Consumers Union on conventional funerals, burials, and alternatives including cremation, direct burial, and body donation.

Habenstein, Robert W., & William M. Lamers 1962. *The History of American Funeral Directing.* Milwaukee: Bulfin.

An excellent source for the study, review, and analysis of the history of funeral directing in the American culture from its introduction in colonial times to present.

Irion, Paul E. 1966. *The Funeral—Vestige or Value?* Nashville: Abingdon Press.

Irion, Paul E. 1968. *Cremation.* Philadelphia: Fortress Press.

Irion, Paul E. 1971. *Humanistic Funeral Service.* Baltimore: Waverly Press.

This series of books gives the serious student an excellent background in the whole area of grief and bereavement as well as their relation to the funeral.

Maryland Center for Public Broadcasting. 1977. *The Last Rights: Funerals.* Owings Mills: Maryland Center for Public Broadcasting.

A detailed report describing funerals, burials, and alternatives including memorial societies, cremations, and organ donations. Issues of cost and specific steps to be considered in burying the dead are discussed. Outstanding resource for lay persons.

Pine, Vanderlyn R. 1975. *Caretaker of the Dead.* New York: Irvington Publishers.

An excellent source to discover the ways in which a society views death and cares for its dead. It is written from both a funeral director's and a sociologist's analytical perspective. Pine is not only a licensed funeral service practitioner but also a professor of sociology at New Paltz University in New York.

Raether, Howard C. 1988. *The Funeral Director's Practice Management Handbook.* Englewood Cliffs, NJ: Prentice-Hall.

A valuable resource on the internal workings of funeral service in America.

CHAPTER 13

The Bereavement Process

—

Only people who avoid love can avoid grief. The point is to learn from it and remain vulnerable to love.

JOHN BRANTNER (IN J. WILLIAM WORDEN, *GRIEF COUNSELING AND GRIEF THERAPY*)

13

If at the conclusion of the funeral service grief work were finished, the process of reintegration of the bereaved into society would be completed. The funeral service and the final disposition of the dead only mark the end of public mourning; however—private mourning continues for some time.

THE BEREAVEMENT ROLE

In earlier chapters we discussed bereavement behavior within historical and cross-cultural perspectives. We have given a general description of the norms and cultural patterns that prescribe proper conduct for the bereaved within American society. When we apply these bereavement norms to particular persons occupying statuses within a group or social situation, we are talking about the **bereavement role.**

In discussing the adaptation to the crisis of becoming ill, Talcott Parsons (1951:426–437) describes the *sick role* as being composed of two rights and two obligations. The first right is for the sick person to be exempted from "normal" social responsibilities. The extent to which one is exempted is contingent upon the nature and severity of the illness. The second right is to be taken care of and to become dependent on others as one attempts to return to normal social functioning. In exchange for these rights, the sick person must express a desire to "want to get better" and must seek technically competent help.

J. D. Robson (1977) suggests that behavior related to the death of a significant other (spouse, parent, etc.) is similar to illness behavior patterns. At the onset of death, the bereaved are exempted from their normal social responsibilities. Depending on the nature and the degree of relationship with the diseased, the bereaved are awarded time away from employment in much the same way as they are given sick leaves—spouses and children may be given a week, while close friends and relatives may only be given time to attend the funeral.

The bereaved are also allowed to become dependent on others for social and emotional support and for assistance with tasks related to the requirements of normal, daily living. In offering this type of support, neighbors and friends call on survivors with gifts of food, flowers, and other expressions of sympathy. This custom led Robert Kavanaugh's brother to ask if "dead people ate meatloaf and chocolate cake" (Kavanaugh, 1972:32).

In exchange for these privileges created by the death of a loved one, those adopting the bereavement role are not only required to seek technically competent help from funeral directors and clergy members, but are expected to return as soon as possible to normal social responsibilities. The bereavement role is considered a temporary one, and it is imperative that all role occupants do whatever necessary to relinquish it within a reasonable period of time. Time extensions are usually granted to spouse and children, but there is a general American value judgment that normal grieving should be completed by the first anniversary of the death.

American folk wisdom would contend that "time heals"—with the intensity of the grief experienced diminishing over time. According to Paul Rosenblatt (1983), however, a more accurate picture of mourning would point out that the time intervals between intense experiences of grief increase with the passing of time. Furthermore, in analyzing 19th-century diaries, Rosenblatt discovered that it was quite common to experience periods of mourning for losses that occurred many years earlier. What is abnormal behavior, from the perspective of the American bereavement role, is the preoccupation with the death of the loved one and refusing to make attempts to return to normal social functioning. Examples of deviant behavior of this type would include the following:

1. Malingering in the bereavement role and memorializing the deceased by refusing to dispose of articles of clothing, personal effects, and living as if one expected the dead to reappear.

2. Rejecting attempts from others who offer social and emotional support, refusing to seek professional counseling, and taking up permanent residence in "Pity City."

3. Rejecting public funeral rituals and requesting that the funeral functionaries merely pick up the body and dispose of it through cremation without any public acknowledgment of the death that has occurred.

4. Engaging in aberrant behavior such as heavy drug or alcohol usage.

5. Rushing into major life changes such as a hasty remarriage or moving to a new home.

Behaviors such as these may be sanctioned by others through social avoidance, ostracism, and criticism. As a consequence, most people are not only encouraged but forced to move through the grieving process.

BOX 13.1 **A WEDNESDAY AFTERNOON**

JANE SOLI

> The hot, humid air of August enveloped us in the crowded car. Sig drove. The Air Force had flown him home from Tahiti. Behind him sat Karen, her arm around Johanna. Peter sat on the other side looking
>
> (continued on next page)

vacantly out the window. Tina sat between Sig and me. The handle of my black purse felt as moist as my sweaty palms. My dress stuck to the skin of my back. How lucky it was that Harmar's Fashion Shop had a black linen dress, size 12. The yellow dotted Swiss I sewed for summer best would not be appropriate today.

The procession crept down Division Street. The neon sign at the Rock County Bank flashed 94 degrees and 3:06. Behind the plate glass of The River Inn, businessmen shook dice for their afternoon coffee. Lois Palmer came out of Hanson's Variety Store carrying a lamp shade.

We turned the corner at the lumberyard, crossed the wagon bridge, then, over the tracks and up the hill. Once in the country the long line of cars moved a little faster. After the turn at Benson's farm the gravel road narrowed. I could see the cemetery.

Why did you die, Dan? Did you have to die when the children were so young? You were lean and fit, physically active, no apparent health problems. You were fine when you went to bed, but I heard your death rattle; a small cough, I thought. You were dead when I came to bed five minutes later.

Is there any money? Will Karen be able to finish her last year of college? How about Peter—he's only seventeen? And then Johanna and Tina, thirteen and eleven. At least Sig is out of school. Such problems. Such a loss. How will I ever manage?

Two things came back to me during those early days of worry, fear, and grief. I recalled twenty years of bridge games with Judy and Elmer and the late-night discussions of death and funerals as we ate brownies and drank coffee. We spoke of our own deaths and our personal wishes. Dan, always the most vocal, stated again and again, "Don't spend any money on me when I am dead," and "Give me a military funeral." There was not a man in the USA more proud to be a Marine than Dan Soli. To hear him tell it, the Marines fought World War II single-handedly. Though he was 33 and the others in boot camp were 18, he was a member of the United States Marine Corps and never mind if the recruits called him "Grandpa."

With Dan's wishes uppermost in my mind, the children and I had the gruesome task of selecting a casket at the Anderson Brothers Mortuary. A basement room displayed a dozen or more for my choice. Mr. Anderson, ever solicitous, hovered over me giving the cost in a hushed voice—$2500, $3000, or, if we wanted the best, it would be $5000. Together we returned to the main floor for my decision. I asked, "What is your cheapest casket?"

"We have a pine box for county paupers at $50." he answered.

"What is your next price?"

"There is a casket we use for servicemen. It is made of wood and covered with grey velour. The flag would go over it. That sells for $100."

"I'll take it," I said quickly. In my mind I was doing rapid arithmetic. Twenty-five hundred dollars would pay for Karen's last year of college.

The entire tenor of our meeting changed. The solicitousness ended. The Anderson brothers conferred in the hallway and practically rushed us out of there.

Dan's wish was fulfilled in that regard; we would spend minimum money. A call to the Veterans of Foreign Wars would insure the military funeral.

The hearse turned into the City Cemetery; we followed. Behind our blue Chevy were twenty more vehicles. To the right I saw the Erickson family plot with remnants of Memorial Day decorations: white plastic crosses with letters in gold—"Mother," "Father," "Sister." We passed the graves of my grandparents, my infant brother, my father.

About one hundred yards into the cemetery the procession came to a stop. I saw the fake grass surrounding the open grave over by the fence. Close by stood the caretaker's tool shed with a barrel for refuse in front. Someone had lettered a crude sign above the barrel. It said, "RUBBAGE." The grave diggers stood behind the tool shed waiting to complete their job.

As the casket moved from the hearse to the waiting pallbearers, the honor guard, smart in their black uniforms, aligned themselves on either side of the men carrying the casket and accompanied them to the gravesite.

The children and I left the car to follow. Tina cried, "I'm too young to be without a father," and clung to me. I had vowed to remain dry-eyed. My silly little purse held a lawn hanky—no Kleenex, no billfold, no lipstick. I would not open that purse.

Friends and relatives surrounded the grave as Pastor Jensen gave the committal service. Somehow the next part took me by surprise. Two of the honor guards stepped forward and together removed the American flag from the casket. With ceremony they folded it in the traditional way and presented it to me—the widow.

The two uniformed men rejoined the honor guard and they all stepped back from the mourners. At the command of the captain they fired a twenty-one gun salute.

(continued on next page)

Box 13.1, *continued*

At that point Peter moved away from the family, raised his trumpet and blew taps for his dad. Sweet, melancholy notes rose plaintively over the gathered crowd. From the other side of the hill came the far-away echo. My heart ached with the pain of that moment.

The worst of the day was over. Everyone returned to the basement of the Lutheran Church for sandwiches, cake, and coffee. The Ladies Aid was famous for their "funeral sandwiches," made from ground pork and beef, and each lady brought her special cake. The choices of cake on the plate seemed endless. People sat around the tables, enjoying the food and visiting. Many expressed their condolences to me. My food remained untouched.

As we were leaving, Alice Overbeck came over to me, reached for my hand and said, "Too bad your husband died, but you'll get over it."

She was wrong; I didn't get over it.

I cry when I hear taps.

Jane A. Soli is the retired secretary to the academic dean of Saint Olaf College.

THE GRIEVING PROCESS

The grieving process, like the dying process, is essentially a series of behaviors and attitudes related to coping with the stressful situation of changing the status of a relationship. As discussed in Chapter 5, many have attempted to understand coping with dying as a series of universal, mutually exclusive and linear stages. However, since most will acknowledge that not all people will progress through the stages in the same manner, we will list a number of coping strategies used as people attempt to resolve the pain caused by the loss of a personally significant relationship.

Robert Kavanaugh (1972) identifies the following seven behaviors and feelings as part of the coping process: shock and denial, disorganization, volatile emotions, guilt, loss and loneliness, relief, and reestablishment. It is not difficult to see similarities between these behaviors and Kübler-Ross's five stages (denial, anger, bargaining, depression, and acceptance) of the dying process. According to Kavanaugh (1972:123), "these seven stages do not subscribe to the logic of the head as much as to the irrational tugs of the heart—the logic of need and permission."

Shock and Denial

Even when a significant other is expected to die, at the time of death there is often a sense in which the death is not real. For most of us our first response is "no, this can't be true." With time our experience of shock diminishes but we find new ways to deny the reality of death.

Some believe that denial is dysfunctional behavior for those in bereavement. However, denial is not only a common experience among the newly bereaved, but also serves positive functions in the process of adaptation. The main function of denial is to provide the bereaved with a "temporary safe place" from the ugly realities of a social world that only offers loneliness and pain.

With time the meaning of loss tends to expand, and it may be impossible for one to deal with all of the social meanings of death at once. For example, if my wife dies, not only do I lose my spouse but I also lose my best friend, my sexual partner, the mother of my children, a source of income, the person who writes the Christmas cards, and so on. Denial can protect me from some of the magnitude of this social loss, which may be unbearable at one point in time. With denial, I can work through different aspects of my loss over time.

Disorganization

Disorganization is that stage in the bereavement process in which one may feel totally out of touch with the reality of everyday life. Some go through the three-day time period just prior to the funeral as if on "automatic pilot" or "in a daze." Nothing normal "makes sense," and an individual may feel that life has no inherent meaning. For some, death is perceived as preferable to life, which appears to be devoid of meaning.

This emotional response is also a normal experience for the newly bereaved. Confusion is normal for those whose social world has been disorganized through death. When my father died, my mother not only lost all those things one loses with a death of a spouse, but she also lost her caregiving role—a social role and master status that had defined her identity in the five years my father lived with cancer. It is only natural to experience confusion and social disorganization when one's social identity has been destroyed.

Volatile Reactions

Whenever one's identity and social order face the possibility of destruction, there is a natural tendency to feel angry, frustrated, helpless, and/or hurt. The volatile reactions of terror, hatred, resentment, and jealousy are often experienced as emotional manifestations of these feelings. Grieving humans are sometimes more successful at masking their feelings in socially acceptable behaviors than other animals, whose instincts cause them to go into a fit of rage when their order is threatened by external forces. However apparently dissimilar, the internal emotional experience *is* similar.

In working with bereaved persons over the past 15 years, I have observed that the following become objects of volatile grief reactions: God, medical personnel, funeral directors, other family members, in-laws, friends who have not experienced death in their families, and/or even the person who has died. I have always found it interesting to watch mild-mannered individuals transformed into raging and resentful persons when grieving. Some of these people have experienced physical symptoms such as migraine headaches, ulcers, neuropathy, and colitis as a result of repressing these intense emotions.

Guilt

Guilt is similar to the emotional reactions discussed above. Guilt is anger and resentment turned in on oneself, and often results in self-deprecation and depression. Typically manifested in statements like "If only . . . ," "I should have . . . ," "I could have . . . ," and "Maybe I did the wrong thing," guilt is a normal part of the bereavement process.

From a sociological perspective, guilt can become a social mechanism to resolve the **dissonance** others feel when unable to explain why someone else's loved one has died. Rather than view death as something that can happen at any time to any one, friends can **blame the victim** of bereavement, and believe that the survivor was in some way responsible for the death—"if he had been a better parent, the child might not have been hit by the car," or "if I had been married to him I might also have committed suicide," or "no wonder he died of a heart attack, her cooking would give anyone high cholesterol." Therefore, bereaved persons are sometimes encouraged to feel guilt because they are subtly sanctioned by others' reactions.

Loss and Loneliness

As we discussed earlier, loss and loneliness are the other side of denial. Their full sense never becomes obvious at once; rather each day without the deceased helps us to recognize how much we needed and depended upon that person. Social situations in which we expected them always to be present seem different now that they are gone. Holiday celebrations are also diminished by their absence. In fact for some, most of life takes on a "something's missing" feeling. This feeling was captured in the 1960s love song "End of the World."

> Why does the world go on turning?
> Why must the sea rush to shore?
> Don't they know it's the end of the world
> 'Cause you don't love me anymore?

Loss and loneliness are often transformed into depression and sadness fed by feelings of self-pity. According to Kavanaugh (1972:118), this effect is

Of all the emotions related to the bereavement process, grief, loss, and loneliness are usually the most intensely experienced feelings.

magnified by the fact that the dead loved-one grows out of focus in memory—"an elf becomes a giant, a sinner becomes a saint because the grieving heart needs giants and saints to fill an expanding void." Even a formerly undesirable spouse, such as an alcoholic, is missed in a way that few can understand unless his or her own heart is involved. This is a time in the grieving process when anybody is better than nobody, and being alone only adds to the curse of loss and loneliness (Kavanaugh, 1972:118).

Those who try to escape this experience will either turn to denial in an attempt to reject their feelings of loss or they will try to find surrogates—new friends at a bar, a quick remarriage, or a new pet. This escape can never be permanent, however, because loss and loneliness are a necessary part of the bereavement experience. According to Kavanaugh (1972:119), the "ultimate goal in conquering loneliness" is to build a new independence or to find a new and equally viable relationship.

Relief

The experience of relief in the midst of the bereavement process may seem odd for some and add to their feelings of guilt. My mother found relief in the fact that my father's battle with cancer had ended, even though this end provided her with new problems. I have observed a friend's relief six months after her husband died. This older friend of mine was the wife of a minister, and her whole life before he died was his ministry. With time, as she built a new world of social involvements and relationships of which he was not a part, she discovered a new independent person in herself that she perceived was a better person than she had ever been.

While relief can give rise to feelings of guilt, like denial, it can also be experienced as a "safe place" from the pain, loss, and loneliness that are endured when one is grieving. According to Kavanaugh (1972:121),

> The feeling of relief does not imply any criticism for the love we lost. Instead, it is a reflection of our need for ever deeper love, our quest for someone or something always better, our search for the infinite, that best and perfect love religious people name as God.

Reestablishment

As one moves toward reestablishment of a life without the deceased, it is obvious that the process involves extensive adjustment and time, especially if the relationship was meaningful. It is likely that one may have feelings of loneliness, guilt, and disorganization at the same time, and that just when one may experience a sense of relief, something will happen to trigger a denial of the death. What facilitates bereavement and adjustment is to fully experience each of these feelings as normal and realize that it is hope (holding the person together in fantasy at first) that will provide the survivor with the promise of a new life filled with order, purpose, and meaning.

Reestablishment never arrives all at once. Rather, it is a goal that one realizes has been achieved long after it has occurred. In some ways it is similar to Dorothy's realization at the end of "The Wizard of Oz"—she had always possessed the magic that could return her to Kansas. And, like Dorothy, we have to experience our loss before we really appreciate the joy of investing our lives again in new relationships.

BOX 13.2 **THE LOSS OF A SIGNIFICANT PERSON**

The loss of a significant person can be one of life's most devastating experiences. Yet, every human relationship is destined to end in loss. Loss is the price paid for relationships that insure survival and participation in the human experience.

The death of a loved one is, of course, the ultimate loss. Death is final and complete. But many little deaths are suffered by all of us along the way. Divorce, desertion, separation, abortion, stillbirth, and rejection mean losses of significant people. Jobs, military service, travel, and geographic moves also take us away from important others. So does placing the aged, mentally retarded, emotionally ill, criminal and delinquent, and putting dependent and neglected children up for adoption or foster care. Further, illness, accidents, and aging can change a loved one so drastically that the person we once knew is gone.

From infancy on our lives are bound up with those of others. We are social beings whose very existence depends on attachment to others. The loss of such an attachment can feel like a threat to life itself. That is not to say that all close ties are ties of love. Love and hate are closely interwoven, and every relationship has some of both. Ambivalence is the essence of every relationship. Whether the relationship is weighted toward positive or negative feelings, however, it has to end. No matter how much we love someone we cannot keep that person alive forever or at our side forever. So loved ones die or go away, and those who are more hated than loved do also, and sometimes we get rid of those whom we do not love in other ways. Such losses bring their own kind of pain because we have had a say in them.

Bertha G. Simos, 1979. *A Time to Grieve: Loss As a Universal Human Experience.* New York: Family Service Association of America, pp. 10–11.

THE FOUR TASKS OF MOURNING

In 1982 J. William Worden published *Grief Counseling and Grief Therapy,* which summarized the research conclusions of a National Institutes of Health study called the Omega Project (occasionally referred to as the Harvard Bereavement Study). Two of the more significant findings of this research are that mourning is necessary for all persons who have experienced a loss through death, and that four tasks of mourning must be accomplished before mourning can be completed and reestablishment can take place.

According to Worden (1982:10), uncompleted grief tasks can impair further growth and development of the individual. Furthermore, the necessity of these tasks suggests that those in bereavement *must* attend to "grief work" because successful grief resolution is not automatic, as Kavanaugh's (1972) stages might imply. Each bereaved person must accomplish four necessary tasks: (1) accept the reality of the loss, (2) experience the pain of grief, (3) adjust to an environment in which the deceased is missing, and (4) withdraw emotional energy and reinvest it in another relationship (Worden, 1982).

Visiting the grave of a loved one can provide the bereaved with an opportunity to accept the reality of the loss and experience the pain of grief.

Accept the Reality of the Loss

Especially in situations where death is unexpected and/or the deceased lived far away, it is difficult to conceptualize the reality of the loss. The first task of mourning is to overcome the natural denial response, realize that the person is dead and will not return.

There are many ways in which bereaved persons can facilitate the actualization of death. The traditional methods are to view the body, attend the funeral and committal services, and visit the final place of disposition. The following is a partial list of additional activities that can assist in making death real for grieving persons.

1. View the body at the place of death before preparation by the funeral director.

2. Talk about the deceased and the circumstances surrounding the death.

3. View photographs and personal effects associated with the deceased.

4. Distribute the possessions of the deceased among relatives and friends.

Experience the Pain of Grief

Part of coming to grips with the reality of death is experiencing the emotional and physical pain caused by the loss. Many people in the denial stage of grieving attempt to avoid pain by choosing to reject the emotions and feelings they are experiencing. Some do this by avoiding places and circumstances that remind them of the deceased. I know of one widow who quit playing golf and stopped eating at a particular restaurant because these were activities that she had enjoyed with her husband. Another widow found it extremely painful to be with her dead husband's twin, even though he and her sister-in-law were her most supportive friends.

J. William Worden (1982:13–14) cites the following case study to illustrate the performance of this task of mourning:

> One young woman minimized her loss by believing her brother was out of his dark place and into a better place after his suicide. This might have been true, but it kept her from feeling her intense anger at him for leaving her. In treatment, when she first allowed herself to feel anger, she said, "I'm angry with his behavior and not him!" Finally she was able to acknowledge this anger directly.

The problem with the avoidance strategy is that it is impossible to escape the pain associated with mourning. According to Bowlby (cited by Worden, 1982:14), "Sooner or later, some of those who avoid all conscious grieving, break down—usually with some form of depression." Tears can afford cleansing for wounds created by loss, and fully experiencing the pain ultimately provides wonderful relief to those who suffer, while eliminating long-term chronic grief.

Adjust to an Environment in Which the Deceased Is Missing

The third task, practical in nature, requires the griever to take on some of the social roles performed by the deceased, or find others who will. According to Worden (1982:15), the aborting of this task is to become helpless by refusing to develop the skills necessary in daily living and ultimately withdrawing from life.

I knew a woman who refused to adjust to the social environment in which she found herself after the death of her husband. He was her business partner, as well as her best and only friend. After 30 years of marriage, they had no children, and she had no close relatives. She had never learned to drive a car. Her entire social world had been controlled by her former husband. Three weeks after his funeral she went into the basement and committed suicide.

The alternative to social withdrawal is to assume new social roles by taking on additional responsibilities. Extended families who always gathered at Grandma's house for Thanksgiving will be tempted to have a number of small Thanksgiving dinners after her death. The members of this family may believe that "no one can take Grandma's place." While this may be true, members of the extended family will grieve better if someone else is willing to do Grandma's work enabling the entire family to come together for Thanksgiving. Not to do so will cause double pain—the family will not gather and Grandma will still be missed.

Withdraw Emotional Energy and Reinvest It in Another Relationship

The final task of mourning is a difficult one for many because they feel disloyal or unfaithful in withdrawing emotional energy from their dead loved one. One of my family members once said that she could never love another man after her husband died. My twice-widowed aunt responded, "I once felt like that, but I now consider myself to be fortunate to have been married to two of the best men in the world."

Other people find themselves unable to reinvest in new relationships because they are unwilling to experience again the pain caused by loss. The quotation from John Brantner at the beginning of this chapter provides perspective on this problem: "Only people who avoid love can avoid grief. The point is to learn from it and remain vulnerable to love."

However, those who are able to withdraw emotional energy and reinvest it in other relationships find the possibility of a newly established social life. Kavanaugh (1972:122–123) depicts this situation well with the following description.

> At this point fantasies fade into constructive efforts to reach out and build anew. The phone is answered more quickly, the door as well, and meetings seem important, invitations are treasured and any social gathering becomes an opportunity rather than a curse. Mementos of the past are put away for occasional family gatherings. New clothes and new places promise dreams instead of only fears. Old friends are important for encouragement and permission to rebuild one's life. New friends can offer realistic opportunities for coming out from under the grieving mantle. With newly acquired friends, one is not a widow, widower, or survivor—just a person. Life begins again at the point of new friendships. All the rest is of yesterday, buried, unimportant to the now and tomorrow.

ASSISTING THE BEREAVED

In his book *Bereavement: Studies of Grief in Adult Life,* Colin Parkes (1972:161) notes that the funeral often precedes the "peak of the pangs" of grief that tends to be reached in the second week of bereavement. The face put on for the funeral can no longer be maintained, and a need exists for the bereaved to be freed to grieve. The most valued person at this time is the one making few demands on the bereaved, quietly completing household tasks, and accepting the bereaved person's vented anguish and anger—some of which may be directed against the helper.

It is important to recognize that the bereaved person has painful and difficult tasks to perform that cannot be avoided or rushed. The best assistance one can offer those in grieving is to encourage them to attend to the four tasks of mourning described earlier.

One can help the bereaved come to grips with the reality of the death by talking about the deceased and encouraging them to conceptualize the loss they are experiencing. Parkes (1972:162) observes that it is often reassuring to the bereaved person when others show they are not afraid to express feelings of sadness. Such expressions make the bereaved person feel understood and reduce a sense of isolation. How people grieve will vary; the important thing is for feelings to emerge into consciousness. How they appear on the surface may be of secondary importance.

BOX 13.3 **GRIEVERS KNOW BEST**

We lost the eldest of our three sons nearly two years ago when he fell from the roof of a building. Keith was only 21 years old. Sometimes I wonder if everyone he knew has forgotten him because his name is never mentioned. I suppose they think they're being kind and don't want to upset me by reminding me that Keith is dead. Believe me, there is never a minute of the day that I am not aware that my son is dead. No one needs to be afraid of "reminding" me.

How I would love to talk about the son I lost with someone who knew him.

I lost my beloved husband over a year ago and when his birthday came around, not a soul mentioned it to me. I spent the day alone—weeping because nobody wanted to risk "stirring up my emotions." It hurt me more wondering if everyone who had known him had forgotten that he had ever lived. Or perhaps they didn't know how much he meant to me. A grieving person *wants* to talk about the one he or she lost. So what if it does bring on a flood of tears? The tears are there anyway, waiting to be shed.

Abigail Van Buren (Dear Abby), *Minneapolis Star and Tribune,* January 3, 1989. Copyright Universal Press Syndicate.

It is not uncommon for one approaching a newly bereaved person to be unsure as to how to react. Parkes (1972:163) suggests that while a conventional expression of sympathy can probably not be avoided, pity is the last thing the bereaved person wants. Pity makes one into an object—the bereaved person somehow becomes pitiful. Pity puts the bereaved person at a distance from, and in an inferior position to, the intended comforter. Parkes maintains it is best to get conventional verbal expressions of sympathy over as soon as possible and to speak from the heart or not at all. There is not *a* proper thing to say at this time; a trite formula serves only to widen the gap between the two persons.

The encounter between the bereaved and the visitor may not seem satisfactory, since the helper cannot bring back the deceased and the bereaved person cannot gratify the helper by seeming helped (Parkes, 1972:163). Bereaved people do, however, appreciate the visits and expressions of sympathy paid by others. These tributes to the dead confirm to the mourner the belief that the deceased is worth all the pain. The bereaved are also reassured that they are not alone and feel less insecure.

While many bereaved people are frightened and surprised by the intensity of their emotions, reassurance that they are not going mad and that this is a perfectly natural behavior can be an important contribution of the helper (Parkes, 1972:164–165). On the other hand, absence of grief in a situation where expected, excessive guilt feelings or anger, or lasting physical symptoms should be taken as signs that all is not going well. These persons may require special help, and the caregiver should not hesitate to advise the bereaved to get additional help if the caregiver is uncertain about the course of events.

GRIEVING PARENTS AND THE LOSS OF AN INFANT

Adaptation to the death of a loved one is always difficult. However, the death of a child is typically regarded as the most difficult of all deaths. As we discussed in Chapter 9, the death of a child goes against the natural order—parents are supposed to die before their children. Furthermore, the death of a child symbolically threatens the family's hope for a future.

In order to conceptualize the nature of loss involved in the death of a child, we should remember that the relationship of a parent with a child begins long before birth (Raphael, 1983:230–231). For each parent, from the time of conception, the child becomes a source of fantasy—the imagined child he or she will become. These hoped-for extensions of self are very common among expectant parents. As the pregnancy progresses, the fantasy relationship with this imagined child intensifies with the selection of the name for the baby, the rehearsal for parenting, the fantasies shared with others, and finally the birth of the child. With the death of a newborn or a still-birth, the bubble of one's fantasy world is suddenly burst.

The death of an infant places severe strains on parents and members of the family—a sense of loss that will likely persist over a number of years. Studies show (Nicol, Tompkins, Campbell, & Syme, 1986) that up to one third of mothers experience a marked deterioration in their health and well-being after the loss of an infant.

Mourning the death of a fetus or newborn baby differs from mourning the death of another loved one (Furman, 1978). Mourning is a dual process of detachment from the loved one that is moderated by identification. The bereaved take into themselves aspects of the deceased, but because a fetus or newborn has not lived long enough as a separate person, the parents have little to take into themselves of their baby. Thus, they suffer detachment without identification. Parents must readjust their self-image with the knowledge that the baby will never again be part of them.

Support from Health-Care Professionals

To assist the parents with their adjustment, it is important they receive support from those around them. In a study of 130 parents who had experienced a **perinatal death,** Judith Murray and Victor Callan (1988:242) discovered that a consistent predictor of better adjustment was the parent's level of satisfaction with the comfort and support provided by physicians, nurses, and other hospital staff. Parents who were pleased with the level of support they received from medical personnel were also less depressed and had higher levels of self-esteem and psychological well-being. Furthermore, emotional support from partners, family, and hospital staff was linked to fewer grief reactions and better overall adjustment (Murray & Callan, 1988:237). Therefore, support from others can go a long way to facilitate parental bereavement at the death of a child.

Hospital-based intervention is especially necessary and helpful to parents experiencing the death of a newborn or a stillbirth, and medical personnel are in a unique position to assist parents in their grief (Davis, Stewart, & Harmon, 1988:242). However, while the majority (70 percent) of bereaved parents wish to discuss their concerns with their physician (Clyman, 1979), 50 percent of parents received no physician follow-up, and many others had no contact with their physicians until a regularly scheduled postpartum check (Rowe, et al., 1978). Thus, while parents seem to desire medical personnel to acknowledge their feelings of shock, guilt, and grief, such wishes do not seem to be fulfilled in many instances.

Part of the emotional support needed by parents involves encouraging them to accept the reality of death, express their feelings of loss, and then validating these feelings. Communication and understanding by the medical staff will serve as a great source of support and comfort. By being available,

TABLE 13.1

Behavior of Professionals Identified to Be Helpful by Grieving Parents

HELPFUL BEHAVIORS	PRIMARY RESPONSIBILITY FOR THIS BEHAVIOR
1. Informs the parents immediately of the condition of the baby.	Doctor
2. Expresses feelings over the baby's death with consoling words to parents.	Doctor/Nurse
3. Provides as much factual information surrounding the baby's death as is available.	Doctor/Nurse
4. Describes the appearance of the baby in factual and tender terms before bringing the baby to them.	Doctor/Nurse
5. Encourages parents to see and hold the baby and stays with them while they initially examine the baby.	Doctor/Nurse
6. Touches parents affectionately and appropriately; words are not always necessary.	Doctor/Nurse
7. Encourages parents to grieve openly.	Doctor/Nurse
8. Acknowledges the baby's death at first contact with parents and daily thereafter; does not act like death has not occurred.	Doctor/Nurse
9. Spends extra time with the parents to provide time to review the events surrounding the baby's death.	Doctor/Nurse

*Patricia Estok & Ann Lehman. 1983. "Perinatal Death: Grief Support for Families." *Birth* (March) *10*:1 p. 19. By permission of Blackwell Scientific Publications, Inc.

medical personnel can help to reduce the isolation parents often feel at this difficult time. Since grief is a necessary process, whenever bereavement is facilitated, the parents become subject to a lower risk for psychological and physical disturbances.

Table 13.1 identifies various ways in which professionals can contribute to the adjustment of grieving parents.

Parental Involvement with Professional Helpers: Perinatal Deaths

The death of a fetus or newborn infant is stressful not only for parents and siblings, but also for all people who are involved with the child. Increasingly, parents are being included in the direct care of critically ill children until the time of death and following. Familiarity with the types of procedures and decisions that parents may face at the death of their child is essential. Most bereaved parents will learn about hospital procedures and how to share in decision making only when they are faced with such a situation.

The nursing procedures are fairly clear, and nurses are instructed to respond in ways that can help in the socioemotional adjustments. The nurse notifies a nursing–social worker counselor at the time of admission concerning the fetal death or infant trauma. Even baptism is offered by some hospitals, where it may be done by anyone in the absence of a chaplain. The pastoral care department of a hospital is notified, as is the communications department, so that accurate information is available to others.

In the case of stillbirths, fetal deaths, and infant deaths, the parents may be given the option to see and hold their infant, to learn the baby's gender, and to decide on autopsy and funeral arrangements. The medical staff explains what the parents can expect the baby to look like. Believing that the age of siblings is the major factor in determining their involvement in these settings, Furman (1978:217) notes:

> Adolescents should decide for themselves. Elementary grade children are helped by attending a service but not helped by seeing a malformed dead body. Children under school age are particularly not helped by seeing their dead brother or sister, but they are sometimes helped by being in the company of the parents at the time of the funeral.

The extent of individual involvement depends upon the preference of individual family members.

The nurses' responsibility includes attaching identification bands to wrist and ankle, measuring the weight, length, and head circumference, taking footprints and possibly a handprint, and completing standard forms. These forms might include a fetal death certificate, an authorization for autopsy, and a record of the death for the receptionist. Medical photographs may be taken by the medical photographer of a full front and back view, as well as close-ups of any abnormalities. These are used by physicians to describe the infant's medical condition. The nurse is also encouraged to take nonmedical photographs that include the infant in a blanket, unclothed, a close-up of the face, and the parents holding the child if they so desire. These pictures are given to the counselor and later to the parents.

The dead infant is wrapped in a blanket, labeled, and taken to the morgue. In the case of a fetus, the body is sent to pathology with a surgical pathology lab slip. The physician may request that the placenta be included in the case of spontaneous abortions or fetal deaths. Genetic studies may also be requested; these might include a cord blood sample, a placenta sample, fresh tissue such as gonadal tissue or connective tissue around the kidneys, skin sample, and a complete genetic study that is sent to the state laboratory. The nurse then completes a checklist for assisting parents experiencing perinatal deaths, and she or he may, if procedure calls for it, place an identifier by the name tag at the entrance to the mother's room.

Hospitals with a special program to help the survivors of fetal and infant deaths provide nursing, medical, social work, and/or pastoral counselors who may assist the surviving parents and siblings. Time is taken to explain and help in the following matters: (1) autopsies and hospital procedures after death; (2) funeral or cremation options (arrangements for the disposition of the body are required in most states if the fetus was at least 20 weeks); (3) the nature and expression of grief and mourning; (4) coping with the reactions of friends and relatives; (5) other children in dealing with the death of their brother or sister; and (6) decisions regarding another pregnancy. Monthly meetings of bereaved parents can be established to provide a setting for sharing and learning about grief. These experiences of sharing with other parents allow for reality-based comparisons and for active support of other parents whose loss is also great.

While this list of hospital procedures is by no means complete, it does, however, outline what parents of spontaneous abortion, stillbirth, fetal death, or neonatal death may encounter. The attitudes and responses of physicians, nurses, and others may vary greatly. At times, for example, the helpers are in need of socioemotional support along with parents and siblings. Many hospitals, on the other hand, have not dealt with the special needs of families experiencing perinatal deaths. While these practices are becoming more common around the country, one should not be surprised if a nurse or physician appears stunned at the request of a parent to spend some time with the body of their child. We can only hope that the human values of medical care will prevail over bureaucratic values as the welfare of the whole person is taken into account in the medical arena. This can be accomplished most effectively if parents are provided with accurate information, encouraged to ask questions, given plenty of time to make decisions, and given opportunities to share their experience in parental bereavement with others.

THE DEATH OF PETS: A SPECIAL KIND OF GRIEVING

According to Jack Kamerman (1988:112), the death of pets represents an opportunity to study attitudes and behaviors toward human death. Such a loss often represents a child's first experience with death, and the stance taken by parents influences a child's attitude toward human death encountered later on. For example, in a study of college students recalling their first childhood experience with death (Dickinson, 1986:88), a pet was involved for 15 percent of the students—birds, cats, chickens, cows, dogs, fish, mice, toads, and turtles.

Sociological issues are clarified by examining the death of pets, such as the process by which human traits are attributed to animals. For many individuals, a pet is a significant member of the family. People talk to pets and care for them as if they were their children. Pets often live with a family as many years as children live at home prior to leaving for college or emancipation. Pets can make people feel needed, can relieve loneliness, and can serve as friends and companions. Such a death is a traumatic experience for family members. As would occur for any other member of the family, the resulting dismemberment leaves a big void.

Unlike the person losing a friend or relative who receives outpourings of sympathy and support, one who loses a pet often receives ridicule for overreacting, for being foolishly emotional, and expressing grief over the death of an animal (Brody, 1985). There has not traditionally been a funeral or an acceptable time of mourning or standard words of comfort for friends to speak on the death of a pet. Grief, however, is a natural response to the loss of any significant object, person, or circumstance. Such attachments can be made to any pet—a rat, a guinea pig, a bird, or a fish—providing the animal provides emotional gratification. To a child, for whom a pet offers the most secure and certain acceptance, the loss can be especially painful.

Many individuals go through an agonizing separation when they lose a pet. Their symptoms are very similar to those experienced within the process of bereavement for a significant other. As with the death of a person, when a pet dies suddenly, as in an accident, guilt is a common reaction. Putting an animal to sleep may also leave one with a feeling of guilt.

Pets in the Lives of the Elderly

Companion-animal visits sponsored by community volunteers to nursing homes offer residents opportunities for conversation, sensory stimulation, tactile warmth, and ongoing relationships with others (Savishinsky, 1988:143). The effectiveness of these visits derives in part from the symbolic meanings (fears, hopes, values, and identities) that people attribute to pet animals.

People project onto their pets, and onto their animals' deaths, some of the qualities of human kinship (Savishinsky, 1988:142). Sometimes animals thought to have died of loneliness and grief are believed to mirror the way in which people respond to the loss of their own family members. Discussion of such experiences enables individuals to share their own feelings of grief, fear, and loss.

Having a Pet "Put to Sleep"

Like other professionals dealing with issues related to dying and death, veterinarians are also concerned about discussing euthanasia and giving bad news to pet owners (Edney, 1988). Fears and anxieties experienced by the clinician wanting to succeed in curing the pet's illness make it difficult for the veterinarian breaking the bad news. A prime fear is that the owner will blame the veterinarian for the animal's illness. If veterinarians can understand that blaming the professional is a normal grief reaction, they can learn to depersonalize this reaction.

When contemplating having an animal put to sleep, Herbert Nieburg and Arlene Fischer (1982) suggest asking the owner whether the pet can do the things it once enjoyed, whether there is more pain or pleasure in its life, whether the animal has become bad-tempered and snappish as a result of old age or illness, whether it has lost control of its bodily functions, and whether one can afford the expense and time involved in keeping a sick pet alive. Whatever the final decision, this is not an easy choice for an individual to make.

Disposal of Pets after Death

When a pet dies, many people arrange for disposal through their veterinarians or the local sanitation department. Though many people today may not choose to bury their pets, there are about 500 pet cemeteries in the United States used by 2 percent of pet owners (*News and Courier*, 1987). The choice of pet caskets runs the gamut from simple fiberglass caskets ranging from

$45 to $150, depending on size, to an actual child's casket. Casket, plot, and perpetual care average $300, but a body bag and temporary marker can be purchased for about half that amount (Langley, 1987). Markers for grave sites come in bronze and granite. In addition to the pet's name and dates for birth and death, markers often bear an affectionate word from the owner, an engraving of the dog's face, or a photo of the pet embedded in the bronze or granite. According to Box 13.5, however, the cost of pet burials for the military is bothering certain officials.

BOX 13.5 **BASE PET CEMETERIES TO LOSE ARMY FUNDING**

> The Army, facing shrinking budgets and skeptical Capitol Hill over-seers, has promised to stop spending taxpayer funds to build and maintain pet cemeteries. The rhubarb over Rover's remains ended recently when the House Armed Services Committee, which had questioned a $16,674 pet burial plot at Fort Gordon, Georgia, last year, published an Army statement halting the practice.
>
> "Army policy regarding pet cemeteries has been reviewed, and new guidance is being issued to installations," the Army statement said. "The policy does not permit new pet cemeteries, and the use of (government) funds for maintenance and repair of cemeteries is prohibited." Existing pet cemeteries will be maintained by volunteers—or restored to their natural state—and Army personnel will be encouraged to use "commercial incineration" instead.
>
> Associated Press. Adapted from *The News and Courier,* Charleston, SC, March 17, 1989, p. 6A.

Cremation is another alternative to dispose of one's deceased pet, whether by *communal cremation* or *separate cremation.* The former is less expensive and involves cremation in groups, with ashes distributed according to the law. Separate cremation allows the remains to be placed in an urn. Costs of communal cremation by a pet cremation service in South Carolina, for example, range from $35 to $60 depending on the size of the animal, and separate cremation costs range from $50 to $100.

The final disposition of pets is of such concern that the following was proposed to the American Animal Hospital Association by the Professional Animal Disposal Advisory Council (Cooke, 1988):

> The recognition of the importance of the human/companion-animal bond as it relates to the veterinary profession has mandated changes in methods of disposing of pet animal carcasses. Recent legal decisions make it especially impor-

tant to provide pet owners with a complete description of their options. In view of the fact pet owners view the final disposition of their pets in terms of human reference, it is important the attending veterinarian avoid the responsibility of providing the disposal options whenever possible. Pet disposal services should be turned over to outside contractors whenever possible, in order to avoid implications that veterinarians are purveyors of these services.

Suggestions by the Professional Animal Disposal Advisory Council include:

1. acceptable methods of pet disposition, such as burial or cremation when available, or the use of landfills

2. outline of suggested disposition procedures and a full-disclosure consent form, signed by the client, and used in all hospitals to relieve the veterinarian of future legal ramifications

3. sealing of the body in a sturdy plastic bag sufficient in size and strength to contain the entire pet and its body fluids

The grave of a pet indicates the meaningful relationship that existed between the pet and its owner.

4. proper identification of the body and storage in a freezer

5. identification of pets known to have diseases contagious to human beings and/or other pets

CONCLUSION

In this chapter we have discussed the grieving process, bereavement roles, normal adaptations to experiences of loss, the four tasks of mourning, and special grieving issues related to the loss of children and pets. We have attempted to demonstrate that the bereaved *must* attend to grief work because successful grief resolution is not automatic. This grief work refers to Worden's (1982) four necessary tasks of bereavement—accepting the reality of the loss, experiencing the pain of grief, adjusting to an environment in which the deceased is missing, and withdrawing emotional energy and reinvesting it in other relationships.

"Sometimes a cute card just isn't appropriate, Jane."
Reprinted by permission of Universal Press Syndicate.

Grievers need support and assistance in the bereavement process. One can help the bereaved come to grips with the reality of the death by talking about the deceased and encouraging survivors to conceptualize the loss they are experiencing. It is often reassuring to the bereaved person when others show they are not afraid to express feelings of sadness. Such expressions make the bereaved person feel understood and reduce a sense of isolation.

Many well-meaning friends find it difficult to find proper words to say. Unfortunately their discomfort often causes them to do nothing. Even trite words are better than no words at all. One well-known slogan says, "When you care enough to send the very best, send a Hallmark." When comforting bereaved friends, however, a better personal slogan might be, "When you care enough to send the very best, send yourself." At this time the very best we have to offer is our own caring presence.

SUMMARY

1. The bereavement role is a temporary role that gives one the right to be exempted from normal social responsibilities and to become dependent upon others.

2. Abnormal bereavement behavior is preoccupation with the death of the loved one and refusal to attempt return to normal social functioning.

3. The grieving process is similar to the dying process in that it is a series of behaviors and attitudes related to coping with the stressful situation of changing the status of a relationship.

4. It is important in grieving to let feelings emerge into consciousness and not be afraid to express feelings of sadness.

5. It is not uncommon to be unsure as to how to act around a newly bereaved person.

6. Rather than suggesting that "time heals," an accurate description of the mourning process would point out that the time intervals between intense experiences of grief increase with the passing of time.

7. There are seven behaviors and feelings that are part of the normal bereavement process: shock and denial, disorganization, volatile emotions, guilt, loss and loneliness, relief, and re-establishment.

8. All persons who have experienced a loss through death will need to attend to the four necessary tasks of grief work before mourning can be completed and re-establishment can take place. These tasks involve accepting the reality of the loss, experiencing the pain of grief, adjusting to an environment in which the deceased is missing, and withdrawing emotional energy and reinvesting it in other relationships.

9. Mourning the death of a fetus or newborn baby differs from mourning the death of another loved one because parents must suffer detachment without identification.

10. The death of a pet often represents a child's first experience with death, and the stance taken by parents influences a child's attitude toward human death encountered later on.

11. Many individuals go through an agonizing separation when they lose a pet. Their symptoms are very similar to those experienced within the process of bereavement for a significant other. However, unlike those losing a friend or relative who receive outpourings of sympathy and support, those who lose a pet often receive ridicule for overreacting, for being foolishly emotional, and for expressing grief over the death of an animal.

DISCUSSION QUESTIONS

1. How can one avoid "deviant" or "abnormal" behavior regarding the bereavement role? What are some functions of defining bereavement roles as "deviant" or "abnormal?"

2. What is the relation between time and the feelings of grief experienced within the bereavement process?

3. Discuss how the seven stages of grieving over one's death can also be applied to losses through divorce, moving from one place to another, or the amputation of an arm or leg.

4. Describe the four necessary tasks of mourning. What are some of the practical steps one can take to accomplish each of these tasks?

5. What does Parkes mean by the statement: "The funeral often precedes the 'peak of the pangs'"? How can one assist friends in bereavement?

6. What are the special problems encountered in the death of a child and in a perinatal death?

7. Explain how suggestions related to medical procedures involved in perinatal deaths might better help parents cope with the death of children.

8. What are some of the signs of aberrant bereavement? What could you do to assist people experiencing abnormal grief symptoms?

9. In what ways are deaths of pets and deaths of significant others similar with regard to the bereavement process? What are some special problems related to the death of a pet?

GLOSSARY

Bereavement role Behavioral expectations for the bereaved, structured around specific rights and duties.

Dissonance An inconsistency in beliefs and values relative to a particular social situation that causes personal discomfort or tension for the individuals involved.

Blaming the victim A strategy developed by individuals to relieve the dissonance experienced when innocent people suffer loss.

Perinatal death The death of a child during or around its birth.

REFERENCES

Brody, Jane E. 1985. "Loss of a Pet Often Agonizing for Owners." *The News and Courier,* Charleston, SC (October 27), p. 14E.

Clyman, Ronald I., Charlotte Green, Cynthia Mikkelsen, Jane Rowe, and Linda Ataide. 1979. "Do Parents Utilize Physician Followup after the Death of Their Newborn?" *Pediatrics,* 64:655–667.

Cooke, David C. 1988. "Animal Disposal: Fact and Fiction." In William J. Kay, *et al.* (Eds.), *Euthanasia of the Companion Animal.* Philadelphia: The Charles Press, pp. 224–234.

Davis, Deborah L., Marguerite Stewart, & Robert J. Harmon. 1988. "Perinatal Loss: Providing Emotional Support for Bereaved Parents." *Birth* (December), *14:*242–246.

Dickinson, George E. 1986. "Childhood Memories of Death." In Gary H. Paterson (Ed.), *Children and Death.* London, Ont: King's College Press, pp. 81–89.

Edney, Andrew T. B. 1988. "Breaking the News: The Problems and Some Answers." In William J. Kay, Susan P. Cohen, Herbert A. Nieburg, Carole E. Fudin, Ross E. Grey, Austin H. Kutscher, and Mohamed M. Osman (Eds.), *Euthanasia of the Companion Animal.* Philadelphia: The Charles Press, pp. 181–185.

Estok, Patricia, & Ann Lehman. 1983. "Perinatal Death: Grief Support for Families," *Birth* (Spring), *10:*19.

Furman, E. 1978. "The Death of a Newborn: Care of the Parents." *Birth Family Journal, 5:*214.

Kamerman, Jack B. 1988. *Death in the Midst of Life.* Englewood Cliffs, N.J.: Prentice-Hall.

Kavanaugh, Robert E. 1972. *Facing Death.* Baltimore: Penguin Books.

Langley, Lynne. 1987. "Pet Cemeteries First Stop on Way to Hound Dog Heaven." *News and Courier,* Charleston, SC, September 13, p. 1D.

Murray, Judith, & Victor J. Callan. 1988. "Predicting Adjustment to Perinatal Death." *British Journal of Medical Psychology,* 61:237–244.

News and Courier, 1987. "Pet's Death Can Be as Grievous as Person's." Charleston, SC, March 24, 1987, p. 7A.

Nicol, M. T., J. R. Tompkins, N. A. Campbell, & G. J. Syme, 1986. "Maternal Grieving Response after Perinatal Death." *The Medical Journal of Australia,* 144:287–289.

Nieburg, Herbert A., & Arlene Fischer. 1982. *Pet Loss.* New York: Harper & Row.

Parkes, Colin M. 1972. *Bereavement: Studies of Grief in Adult Life.* New York: International Universities Press.

Parsons, Talcott. 1951. *The Social System.* Glencoe, IL: The Free Press.

Raphael, Beverly. 1983. *The Anatomy of Bereavement.* New York: Basic Books.

Robson, J. D. 1977. "Sick Role and Bereavement Role: Toward a Theoretical Synthesis of Two Ideal Types." In Glenn M. Vernon (Ed.), *A Time to Die.* Washington, DC: University Press of America, pp. 113–120.

Rosenblatt, Paul. 1983. *Bitter, Bitter Tears.* Minneapolis: University of Minnesota Press.

Rowe, Jane, Ronald Clyman, Charlotte Green, Cynthia Mikkelsen, Jeannette Haight, and Linda Ataide. 1978. "Followup of Families Who Experience a Perinatal Death." *Pediatrics, 62*:166–170.

Savishinsky, Joel S. 1988. "The Meanings of Loss: Human and Pet Death in the Lives of the Elderly." In *Euthanasia of the Companion Animal.* William J. Kay, Susan P. Cohen, Herbert A. Nieburg, Carole E. Fudin, Ross E. Grey, Austin H. Kutscher, and Mohamed M. Osman (Eds.), Philadelphia: The Charles Press, pp. 138–147.

Simos, Bertha G. 1979. *A Time to Grieve: Loss as a Universal Human Experience.* New York: Family Service Association of America.

Worden, J. William. 1982. *Grief Counseling and Grief Therapy: A Handbook for the Mental Health Practitioner.* New York: Springer-Verlag.

SUGGESTED READINGS

Grollman, Earl. 1982. *What Helped Me When My Loved One Died.* Boston: Beacon Press.

Collection of personal stories of parents, wives, husbands, children, and friends.

Kay, William J., Susan P. Cohen, Herbert A. Nieburg, Carole E. Fudin, Ross E. Grey, Austin H. Kutscher, and Mohamed M. Osman (Eds.). 1988. *Euthanasia of the Companion Animal: The Impact on Pet Owners, Veterinarians, and Society.* Philadelphia: The Charles Press.

An anthology of recent studies on relating to the death of pets and the effect of dying and death of pets on humans.

Manning, D. 1984. *Don't Take My Grief away from Me.* Herford, TX: In-Sight Books.

Assistance for the bereaved in how to respond to "unhelpful friends."

Raphael, Beverly. 1983. *The Anatomy of Bereavement.* New York: Basic Books.

An encyclopedialike reference book on human grief and bereavement.

Worden, J. William. 1982. *Grief Counseling and Grief Therapy: A Handbook for the Mental Health Practitioner.* New York: Springer-Verlag.

A very practical reference guide for the professional and lay grief counselor.

CHAPTER 14

Epilogue

Practical Issues Relating to Dying and Death

Lament

Listen, children:
Your father is dead.
From his old coats
I'll make you little jackets;
I'll make you little trousers
From his old pants.
There'll be in his pockets
Things he used to put there,
Keys and pennies
Covered with tobacco;
Dan shall have the pennies
To save in his bank;
Anne shall have the keys
To make a pretty noise with.
Life must go on,
And the dead be forgotten;
Life must go on,
Though good men die;
Anne, eat your breakfast;
Dan, take your medicine;
Life must go on;
I forget just why.

Edna St. Vincent Millay

14 The previous chapters in this book have been largely concerned with preparation for dying and death, both our own and that of others. This final chapter, the epilogue, will relate to practical issues of living like wills, organ donations, insurance, and nutrition and exercise. We will also discuss the current status of thanatology in professional schools and of death education in general.

WILLS

Wills to Provide for Dependents and Dispose of Property

"You need a will whether you are single or married, old or young, healthy or ill," according to Eric Schurenberg of *Money* (1987:76). Real property, which includes land and that attached to it such as a house (as opposed to personal property—any other property such as clothes or cars), is transferred in only three ways—through a deed, a will, or inheritance. The latter two deal with property transfer at death. In order to personally determine who receives one's property after death, it is important to have a will. A **will** is a legal document in which one states how property and possessions are to be distributed after death. Each of the 50 states has its own laws regarding wills, thus what is true of one state may not necessarily apply to other states.

If one dies without a will **(intestate)**, that individual has no control over who receives what, and the distribution is made by the state. Classes of heirs are established by the various states to determine how the property passes, if no will was made. Typically, if one is married at the time of death, the spouse receives the inheritance. If they have children, they also take from the inheritance (to be held in trust until they reach a certain age, if minors). If the decedent was single, the parents are usually next in line to inherit. If the parents are dead, the brothers and sisters usually inherit, followed by grandparents, and aunts and uncles. For example, if a college student dies without a will and has no spouse or children, the sports car would go to the

MOMMA MELL LAZARUS

MOMMA! ARE YOU WORKING ON YOUR "LAST WILL AND TESTAMENT" AGAIN ?!

BOY, NOBODY ELSE SPENDS SO MUCH TIME THINKING ABOUT DYING!

EVERYONE ELSE HAS OTHER THINGS TO LOOK FORWARD TO.

Reprinted by permission of Mell Lazarus and Creators Syndicate.

"And my newish Cadillac, with no equity and only
57 more payments, goes to my trusted banker."

Reprinted by permission of Universal Press Syndicate.

parents, not to a brother or sister. If one dies intestate and without heirs, that person's property goes to the state (the legal term for this is **escheat**).

A will is therefore essential, if one does not want the state to determine the distribution of his or her property. Thus, a well-executed will can provide an orderly distribution of property, get the decedent's assets to the people he or she wants to have them, can reduce the expense in probate court, and allows the **testator** (one making the will) to name an individual of his or her choosing to administer the estate and someone to be legally responsible for young children rather than have the court appoint an administrator and place minor children (in the event of a single parent).

In order to make out a will, the following criteria generally apply, though this may vary by states:

1. The person must be at least 18 years of age

2. The person must be of sound mind (know the nature of the document)

3. The will must be in writing

4. The will must be signed by the testator

5. The will must have two witnesses to the signing

6. The will must be dated

A will can be broken in most states by proving in court one of the following: Coercion took place in the signing of the will, fraud occurred, the person had undue influence in making out the will, or the testator was incompetent. A will can be revoked in most states by destroying it through burning or tearing it up, remarrying or divorce, or by writing another will. Wills can be changed by adding an amendment called a **codicil**—made at a later date in accordance with the same formalities required for the validity of the original will. A codicil allows one to amend the will by adding new provisions without having to rewrite it entirely. The will should be kept in a safe place, and family members should be notified as to its whereabouts.

Though not recognized by all states, a **holographic will** is one written wholly in one's own handwriting and does not generally require witnesses. A holographic will also must be signed by the testator.

Though the majority of Americans do not have a will, wills are not simply for the rich. They can be drawn inexpensively—a simple will executed by most attorneys would cost in the area of $150. More complex estate planning is also available through attorneys specializing in estate planning. As Box 2.4 noted, however, fairness may not always seem fair in wills.

Living Wills

A **living will** is a document that states that one does not want medical intervention if the technology or treatment that keeps one alive cannot offer a reasonable quality of life or hope for recovery. Although only 9 percent of Americans have living wills, thirty-eight states, including the District of Columbia, have laws saying that living wills are valid representations of a patient's wishes ("Specific Instructions Needed in Living Wills," 1989, p. 9F).

Despite a growing acceptance of living wills, the issue is still complicated by emotion and questions of when a will should be invoked. Many persons are reluctant to take steps leading to a patient's death, and some are willing to withhold further medical treatment, but do not want to disconnect existing life support ("Making a Living Will," 1985, p. 20).

If considering a living will, one should check to make certain that such a will is legal in the state of residence. After the will is drawn up (see the sample in Box 14.1 for an idea of what is included in such a will), make several copies of the living will and share it with your physician and family members. Your attorney should also have a copy in his or her office. This is not something you should limit to one copy, lock up in your safety deposit box, and keep a big secret. Share the news with family, friends, and especially your physician.

BOX 14.1 **A LIVING WILL**

> To my family, my physician, my lawyer and all others whom it may concern:
>
> Death is as much a reality as birth, growth, maturity, and old age. Death is the one certainty of life. If the time comes when I can no longer take part in decisions for my own future, let this statement stand as an expression of my wishes and directions, while I am still of sound mind.
>
> If at such a time the situation should arise in which there is no reasonable expectation of my recovery from extreme physical or mental disability, I direct that I be allowed to die and not be kept alive by medications, artificial means or "heroic measures." I do, however, ask that medication be mercifully administered to me to alleviate suffering even though this may shorten my remaining life.
>
> This statement is made after careful consideration and is in accordance with my strong convictions and beliefs. I want the wishes and directions here expressed carried out to the extent permitted by law. Insofar as they are not legally enforceable, I hope that those to whom this will is addressed will regard themselves as morally bound by these provisions.
>
> Signed _____
> Date   _____
> Witness _____
> Witness _____
>
> William E. Phipps, 1987. *Death: Confronting the Reality.* Atlanta, GA: John Knox Press, p. 200.

ORGAN DONATIONS

Human organ transplants have long been cloaked in a special aura of mystery and sometimes fear, linked to religious concerns about the sanctity of the body and even to frightening fictional stories like that of Frankenstein (Malcolm, 1986:8). Because of the sensitive nature of the topic, human organ transplants have not been widely discussed by society.

In many urban areas today kidney foundations, eye banks, and transplant centers will supply donor cards and arrange for transplants when death occurs. There are many kinds of tissues or organs used for transplantation including eye, skin, bone, tendon, bone marrow, kidney, liver, pancreas, blood vessel, lung, and heart. While some of these transplant operations are still in the areas of research, techniques are constantly improving.

BOX 14.2   **THE RECYCLED MAN**

Consider this scenario: Dan Smith is injured in a boating accident. Physicians certify that his brain has quit functioning. Although medical equipment can maintain his heartbeat, he is dead. A nurse enters his Social Security number into a computer and the screen flashes "Universal Donor." The display notes that Dan's wife had approved his decision (and signed up herself).

The hospital calls the local organ and tissue center, and late that evening doctors remove Dan's pancreas, liver, kidneys, lungs, and heart. They also take more than 70 kinds of tissue—corneas, skin, bones, ligaments and tendons, veins and middle ears—with procedures so careful that the family can still have an open-casket funeral the next day.

Within 24 hours, elements of Dan's body are used to release two kidney patients from the rigors of dialysis. His heart saves a 40-year-old father of two. His lungs give life to a steelworker and a grandmother. His liver saves a college student and his pancreas is transplanted to a young diabetic.

In the next few days, he gives hearing to one child and eyesight to two others. His skin helps two burned firefighters. Other tissues aid in reconstructive surgery. Some of his bones are freeze-dried for dental and other use; some tissues are assigned to research labs.

Computer networks help allocate the material, allowing physicians to find a proper match (hip and knee bones, for example, are cut to fit specific patients) and all transplant results are fed into a data bank shared by clinicians and researchers.

The collective value of these procedures runs to millions of dollars. The lives saved and suffering relieved are priceless. Yet the cost of Dan's tissues and organs is zero. All were donated.

This is no futuristic daydream. Each of the medical techniques and communication technologies described above exists today.

Joel L. Swerdlow. 1989. *The Washington Post,* June 25, p. 3B. Excerpted from *Matching Needs, Saving Lives* published by The Annenberg Washington Program of Northwestern University.

The first modern human organ transplant was a kidney transplant in 1950 in Chicago (Cooper & Lanza, 1984:1). The first liver transplant was performed in 1963 in Denver (Ezell, Anspaugh, & Oaks, 1987:178). Transplantation received especially wide coverage in the media with the transplantation of the first human heart by Christiaan Barnard in South Africa in 1967. There is an increasing tendency today for individuals to donate their organs and tissues upon death to the living. By 1984, transferring human organs into other bodies was occurring over 100 times a day in the United States (Malcolm, 1986:8). There were 24,000 eyes or corneas transplanted, 6,968 kidneys, 346 hearts, 308 livers, 87 pancreases, and 30 heart–lung combinations.

The National Conference on Uniform Laws developed the Uniform Anatomical Gift Act to help answer questions concerning transplantations, and all 50 states had adopted the act with slight variations by 1971 (Ezell, Anspaugh, & Oaks, 1987:181). The act advocates that a person be over 18 years of age to donate part or all of his or her body upon death. If the body or body part has not been donated prior to death, a family member may do so, with permission based on the priority of the relationship. The priority is as follows: spouse, adult son or daughter, parents, adult sibling, legal guardian, or another party responsible for disposition of the body.

BOX 14.3

UNIFORM DONOR CARD of ____name of donor____. In the hope that I may help others, I hereby make this anatomical gift, if medically acceptable, to take effect upon my death. The words and marks below indicate my desires.

I give: a. _____ any needed organs or parts
          b. _____ only the following organs or parts *specify the organs(s) or parts(s)*

for the purposes of transplantation, therapy, medical research or education:

          c. _____ my body for anatomical study if needed

Signed by the donor and the following two witnesses in the presence of each other:

Signature of donor	Date of birth of donor
Date signed	City and state
Witness	Witness

Various problems affect human transplantations. Whether or not the donor and donee tissues are compatible can be a problem. There is often a chronic shortage of donors, thus sometimes producing a difficult decision in selecting among potential recipients. A lack of a legal definition of death in some states prevents surgeons from removing healthy organs when brain activity has stopped, but the heart and lungs are still functioning. A lack of a nationwide communications network to coordinate information presents a problem for human transplantations.

Another problem is the question of who will pay for expensive transplantation procedures. A few public insurers have recently decided in favor of coverage for heart and liver transplants. Kidney transplants have been covered since 1973 under Medicare's end-stage renal disease program. Though the costs of solid organ transplants are expensive, the benefits are substantial when one considers that they may be life-saving. Average estimated total first-year costs of solid organ transplant procedures are $95,000 for heart transplants, $35,000 for kidney transplants, $130,000 for liver transplants, and $35,000 for pancreas transplants (Ezell, Anspaugh, & Oaks, 1987:185).

As more and more transplants are desired to make living more comfortable or to prolong life, and if insurance does not cover many of the operations, who receives organ and tissue transplantations may be limited to those who can afford such surgery. A sort of survival of the fittest behavior may then result regarding transplantations. Thus, this sensitive topic may become even more touchy.

BOX 14.4 **JAMIE FISKE STORY INSPIRED 7-YEAR-OLD BOY TO DONATE ORGANS**

Mickie Knutson and her 7-year-old son, Chad, had been watching television news reports about Jamie Fiske's liver transplant last November, and they left the boy confused.

"Chad asked me what it was, and I explained," Mickie Knutson recalled Wednesday. "He said, 'Mom, when I go to heaven I'll have a new body.'"

Then, she said, he talked about the child whose liver went to Jamie Fiske, and said: "When I die, I'd like to be able to do that."

"It hits you hard," she said. "You don't expect a 7-year-old to talk about donating his organs. But that was Chad's wish."

"And now it's come true."

Chad, his brother Trent, 4, and a 16-year-old neighbor, Carol Jo Zack, died Sunday night when a train struck the vehicle in which they were riding at a crossing south of Duluth.

On Tuesday, Chad's heart, kidneys and corneas were removed for use in five transplants.

One kidney was placed in a 33-year-old man at the University of Minnesota Hospitals, and the other was flown to New York state for use in a transplant there.

Another team of University Hospitals surgeons transplanted Chad's heart into 11-year-old Krista Larose of Bethel Tuesday morning, but she died later that night.

"It was a perfectly good heart, and the operation went very well," said Dr. R. Morton Bolman. But he said that doctors had been unable to tell before the surgery that the young girl's failing heart had caused such extensive damage to her lungs that no transplant could have worked. And with her fast-failing heart, the transplant was her only hope for survival, he said.

The corneas, which can be preserved for a long time, are expected to be used for later transplants.

Authorities said Chad and the others died instantly when the all-terrain vehicle on which the three were riding collided with an Amtrak

(continued on next page)

passenger train just a quarter-mile from the boys' home in Holyoke, Minnesota.

Chad was rushed by ambulance 20 miles to St. Luke's Hospital in Duluth and placed on a life-support system for nearly two hours before he was pronounced "brain dead," said his father, Roy Knutson.

(Brain death means total and permanent cessation of all brain function. It is the only way that death can be diagnosed when machines are keeping the heart and other organs working.)

The newscasts concerning Jamie Fiske "came to me when we were at the hospital," Mickie Knutson said in a telephone interview.

"His only real injury was to his head. His condition was perfect for it (donating his organs). We remembered what Chad had said."

The Knutsons said they waited in the hospital through the night for a second medical opinion and then waited for Chad's grandfather to arrive for one last look at the child. Chad's body was then flown to Minneapolis.

"We feel with all our hearts that it was God's hands which kept Chad breathing long enough to get to the hospital and fulfill Chad's physical wish," said Mickie Knutson.

"God has promised victory in all things and through Chad being able to bring life to other people, we have seen victory. He's helped five other people with his heart, his eyes and his kidneys."

"Chad would sometimes astound us by the things he'd say," said Roy Knutson. "But when we thought about it, his wish to donate his organs wasn't that surprising."

"He was in the second grade where I teach (in Wrenshall). At a milk break, his teacher was passing around Oreo cookies and thought there'd be enough so each child would get two. When it became apparent that there weren't enough to go around, she (the teacher) said Chad's hand went immediately in the air and he said, 'I don't need a second one.'"

The Knutsons said they know the shock of the tragedy, which cost them their only two children and a neighbor they "cherished like a daughter," will linger. But they harbor no bitterness or anger, they said.

"We, as Christians, feel God has a plan for everyone," said Mickie Knutson. "We're thankful for the beautiful years he gave us with our boys and that Chad was allowed to help others."

"For us, that has been a joy."

It was one year ago this month that Jamie Fiske arrived at University

Hospitals to await the donor liver she needed to survive. After Jamie's father, Charles, made a dramatic national appeal, the donor liver came November 5 from a Utah boy who died in a car-train accident.

In Bridgewater, Massachusetts, yesterday, Jamie's mother, Marilyn, said in a telephone interview that her daughter, now 22 months old, is "doing terrific" with no problems from the transplanted liver. And she said that Jamie's role in Chad's donation of his organs after death "means an awfully lot to us," adding:

"We can truly learn from little kids. This boy learned something at age 6 that took me much longer to learn. He is a very special boy. We can learn from him like we have learned from Jamie. And his parents are very special people."

Funeral services for Chad and Trent Knutson were scheduled today at 10 a.m. at the Sandy Lake Baptist Church near Carlton. Services for Carol Jo Zack were set for 1 p.m. at the Barr Brothers Funeral Home in Cloquet.

Those wishing to contribute to the Chad and Trent Knutson Memorial Fund to Help Life Continue On may send donations to: Transplant Assistance Fund, Box 19, Mayo Building, University of Minnesota, Minneapolis, Minnesota 55455. The fund was established by the hospitals to help patients and their families meet housing, transportation and other nonmedical expenses associated with transplants.

Paul Levy & Lewis Cope, 1983. *Minneapolis Star and Tribune,* September 22, p. 1A. Reprinted with permission of the Star Tribune.

LIFE INSURANCE

The middle-class American value of planning ahead for the future is exemplified by the fact that the majority of Americans have life insurance. Life insurance is to protect one's dependents and to give the insured a feeling of security in knowing that his or her dependents will have some coverage in the event of death.

The amount of life insurance needed is related to the number of dependents one has. For example, if one is the primary provider in a family consisting of three small children, he or she would have a greater need for life insurance than a single person with no dependents. If the primary provider were to die, these dependents would have some financial coverage at least for the time being. At the time of death, the added burden of the loss of income is not needed.

If one's only purpose for life insurance is to provide for one's dependents, **term life insurance** is probably the best choice. Term life insurance tends to have the lowest premiums for the greatest amount of coverage. Group policies, such as those provided by one's place of employment, tend to have lower premiums than policies obtained outside of a group. Term life insurance is for a specific number of years, such as five or ten, with premiums going up as one ages. "My suggestion is to start with term, but if there is a permanent insurance need, convert to a good universal life policy," says Andrew Gross, a financial planner in Washington, DC (Smith, 1988:154).

Today, however, life insurance for many individuals is more than security for one's dependents. Some policies, universal life policies, for example, are a form of tax-deferred investment from which one can also borrow. Thus, one can have coverage in the event of death and can have the opportunity to build cash assets at the same time. These insurance policies are called *whole life* from which, for a set premium, one receives life insurance and a savings fund. **Universal life insurance** is more flexible, has investment opportunities, and allows one to raise or reduce premiums and the amount of coverage on one's life. *Variable life* insurance does not allow for the premium or minimum coverage on one's life to change, but one can switch the savings from among money-markets or various forms of stock.

It is advisable to shop around and compare the benefits of the different life insurance programs. Premiums vary considerably for the same coverage. Be cautious of high-powered salespersons trying to sell coverage not needed. Become informed about life insurance by talking with knowledgeable consumers or by reading consumer magazines before purchasing any life insurance. Comparison shopping should pay off.

LIFE EXTENSION

The American public has changed its lifestyle in recent years, according to the National Center for Health Statistics (1985). Between 1968 and 1983, the average American consumed 17 percent fewer eggs, 10 percent less butter, 35 percent less coffee, 40 percent less whole milk, and over 200 percent more low-fat milk. Red meat consumption has given way to more fish, poultry, and vegetables. Tobacco use has decreased, while aerobic exercise has increased. Many more Americans are aware of hypertension and are attempting to control it. According to experts, priorities for health promotion are smoking cessation, physical exercise, nutrition and weight control, stress management, and appropriate use of alcohol and other drugs (Hyner & Melby, 1987).

Exercise is one method of extending one's life through natural means.

Though it may not be the goal of everyone, most individuals enjoy life and prefer to live on and on. When the option is life or death, most persons would likely choose the former. As was noted in Chapter 10, the Abkhasians on the Black Sea seem to have a successful lifestyle that promotes long life. They practice what we *know*, but what we often fail to *execute*. While one's inheritance is something that cannot be controlled (hereditary tendencies to diseases or ailments, for example), one *can* control exercise, nutrition, and patterns of living.

Exercise

According to epidemiologist Ralph Paffenbarger (Ubell, 1988:8), "If you want to live longer, exercise. It's that simple." He studied 17,000 Harvard graduates and found that those who exercised more really did live longer.

The following points suggest how one can begin an exercise program (Ubell, 1988:8–9):

1. Write down the pros and cons of exercising.

2. The workout should be enjoyable and healthful so choose exercises that are both effective and fun.

3. Check with your physician before beginning, and begin exercising slowly.

4. Pick an exercise time and place that are convenient.

5. Get a friend to exercise with you.

6. Set your own goals.

7. Reward yourself for achieving short-term targets.

Before beginning any exercise program, *get a medical exam,* especially if you are overweight, a smoker, have heart trouble or any chronic ills, if you have seldom exercised, or are over age 40.

Some of the benefits of exercise are outlined by Vern Seefeldt and Paul Vogel (1986:1–2):

1. Promotes changes in brain structure and function in infants and young children.

2. Assists in the development and refinement of perceptual abilities involving vision, balance, and tactile sensations.

3. Enhances the function of the central nervous system through the promotion of a healthier neuronal network.

4. Fortifies the mineralization of the skeleton and promotes the maintenance of lean body tissue, while simultaneously reducing the deposition of fat.

5. Is an important regulator of obesity because it increases energy expenditure, suppresses appetite, increases metabolic rate, and increases lean body mass.

6. Is an effective deterrent to coronary heart disease due to its effects on blood lipids, blood pressure, obesity, and capacity for physical work.

7. Improves cardiac function as indicated by an increased stroke volume, cardiac output, blood volume, and total hemoglobin.

8. Is associated with a reduction in atherosclerotic diseases.

9. Promotes a more positive attitude toward physical activity and leads to a more active lifestyle during unscheduled leisure time.

10. Enhances self-concept and self-esteem as indicated by increased confidence, assertiveness, emotional stability, independence, and self-control.

11. Prevents the onset of some diseases and postpones the debilitating effects of old age.

Nutrition

Dietary recommendations for healthy Americans, as noted by the American Heart Association (Hyner & Melby, 1987:47), include the following:

1. Eat a variety of foods that will meet your daily needs.

2. Achieve and maintain your desirable weight.

3. Avoid eating too many foods containing saturated fat and cholesterol.

4. Substitute polyunsaturated fat for saturated fat wherever possible and yet do not eat too much of any kind of fat.

5. Limit your salt intake.

6. Make these changes gradually over a period of several months so they become a natural part of your permanent eating pattern.

Frequently eaten foods for a healthy diet, according to Hyner & Melby (1987:61), include the following: hot oatmeal cereal, 100% whole-grain bread, unsalted peanut butter, skinless chicken breast, potatoes, pasta, boiled or baked beans, skim milk, oranges, raisins, grapes, broccoli, apples, bananas, carrots, tomatoes, broiled fish (especially flounder, salmon, and mackerel), and mozzarella and cottage cheese.

BOX 14.5 **ORGANIC PRODUCE PREFERRED**

A large majority of Americans say they would buy organically grown food if it cost the same as fruits and vegetables grown with synthetic fertilizers or pesticides, and nearly half say they would pay more, according to a survey released Sunday.

The survey was conducted before the recent reports of poisoned grapes and apples treated with Alar, a chemical linked to cancer.

Louis Harris and Associates conducted the poll for Organic Gardening magazine and found that 84 percent of those surveyed said they would choose organically grown food if given the choice, 12 percent would not and 4 percent were not sure.

Perhaps more surprisingly, 49 percent said they would pay more for organic food, the poll showed.

The nationwide survey, which had a margin of sampling error of plus or minus 3 percentage points, was based on 1,250 telephone interviews with randomly selected adults throughout the continental United States between November 9 and 23.

(continued on next page)

The poll was taken well before Chilean fruit was temporarily banned last week when two grapes were found that had been injected with cyanide.

It also came before the most recent concerns raised over use on apples of Alar, a chemical that aids in ripening and helps preserve crispness. Some schools banned apples from their menus as a result of a report on Alar.

Associated Press. *The New York Times,* New York, March 21, 1989, p. 10.

Patterns of Living

Contrary to widespread impressions, not everything causes cancer. Most substances, in fact, do not. Factors in the general environment that cause or promote cancer are occupational exposures, food additives, and environmental pollutants—estimated to cause at most 7 percent of the 870,000 cases of cancer each year (Brody, 1984). Viruses and medical procedures are said to be responsible for another 6 percent. This leaves the overwhelming majority of cancers caused by factors within the control of individuals—tobacco (30 percent), overall diet (35 percent), heavy alcohol consumption (3 percent), and excessive exposure to sunshine (3 percent). Nonenvironmental factors are believed to account for the other 16 percent.

Cancer-prevention advice given by the National Cancer Institute includes the following:

1. Do not use tobacco in any form. Smoking greatly increases the risk of cancers of the lung, larynx, esophagus, pancreas, bladder, kidney, and mouth. Once an individual quits smoking, the risk of developing cancer begins to decrease immediately.

2. If you drink alcoholic beverages, do so only in moderation (one or two drinks per day). Heavy drinking, especially in conjunction with cigarette smoking, increases the risk of cancers of the mouth, throat, esophagus, and liver.

3. Eat low-fat foods since high-fat diets are associated with an increased risk of cancers of the breast and colon.

4. Include fresh fruits, vegetables, and whole-grain cereals in your daily diet. The fiber in these foods and in dried beans and peas is protective.

5. Avoid unnecessary X-rays.

6. Avoid too much sunlight, especially between 11 A.M. and 2 P.M. If out in the sun for prolonged periods, wear protective clothing or use a sunscreen with a high degree of protection.

INDIVIDUAL LIFE EXPECTANCY

The following method for calculating longevity not only points to the inevitability of dying but identifies specific ways of increasing one's chances for living longer.

The base number of years for computing life span in the United States: 75

If you are male, subtract 4; if you are female, add 4: _____

If you plan to live in an urban area for most of your life, subtract 2; if a town or a rural area is planned, add 2: _____

If you anticipate having a desk job for most of your life, subtract 3; if the work requires regular physical labor, add 3; if you anticipate working after 65, add 3: _____

If you anticipate earning over $50,000 or under $10,000 a year, subtract 2: _____

If you exercise vigorously several times weekly, add 3: _____

If you anticipate living with a spouse or friend for most of your life, add 4; if not, subtract 1 for each decade alone after reaching age 30: _____

If you are an extrovert, enjoying the society of others, add 2; if you are an introvert, preferring to be by yourself, subtract 2: _____

If you are intense, aggressive, and easily angered subtract 3; if you are relaxed, easygoing, and worry little, add 3: _____

If you have been given a ticket for speeding in recent years, subtract 2; if you regularly wear a seat belt while traveling, add 2: _____

If you anticipate finishing, or have finished, college, add 1; for a graduate degree, add 2: _____

If any grandparent lived to 85, add 2; if all four grandparents lived to 73, or are now living, add 3: _____

If either parent died of heart failure before 50, subtract 5; if any parent, brother, or sister under 50 has (or had) a heart condition, or has diabetes, subtract 3: _____

If you get intoxicated at least once a month, subtract 2; if a chronic alcoholic, subtract 8: _____

If you are overweight by more than 50 lbs., subtract 8; by 30–50 lbs, subtract 4; by 10–30, subtract 2: _____

(continued on next page)

If you smoke more than 2 packs a day, subtract 8; 1 or 2 packs, subtract 6; ½ to 1, subtract 3: _____

If you are over 30 make this adjustment: 31–40, add 2; 41–50, add
3; 51–70, add 4; over 70, add 5. _____

DEATH EDUCATION

With the majority of individuals in the United States today dying "offstage"
in the institutional setting of a hospital or nursing home away from the center
of the arena (in the home), death has largely been removed from kin and
friends and made into a taboo event, not to be seen or talked about. Since
death is inevitable—at present, we have a 100-percent chance of dying, with
the probability of change unlikely—coping skills and attitudes related to
death should definitely prove to be useful. With individuals being faced with
the occurrence of death throughout the life cycle, should not death education
be an important subject throughout our school curriculum?

Why Death Education?

Death education provides an opportunity to familiarize students and professionals with the needs and issues surrounding dying and death. This is
important because of the pervasiveness of formal death institutions, media
exposure to death, and haphazard experiences with death professionals,
notes Vanderlyn Pine (1986:212). One of the goals of death and dying
courses for all age groups is to increase knowledge about death and about
the professions involved with death—funeral directors, medical personnel,
and governmental organizations, for example (Gordon & Klass, 1979).
Another goal is to help students learn to cope with the death of significant
others, deal with one's own mortality, and be more sensitive to the needs of
others. A more abstract goal is to understand the social and ethical issues
concerning death with the value judgments involved with these issues.

A generation ago death was a subject even less likely than sex to be
found in the curricula of American public schools (Bordewich, 1988:30). If
death were acknowledged at all, it was likely to be discussed within the context of literary classics. Within the past decade, courses treating dying and
death far more explicitly have appeared in schools across the United States.

The exact number of offerings is not known, but thousands of schools are involved in death education ranging from a few hours duration to full-semester courses. While some schools offer specific courses on dying and death, others blend some of the philosophies and techniques of death education into health, social studies, literature, and home-economics courses.

Death Education for Health-Care Professionals and Clergy

The emotional conflicts related to dying and death are particularly acute for primary health-care professionals. While limited emphasis has historically been placed on death education in schools for the health-care professions in the United States, the current status of death education offerings in nursing, pharmacy, and medical programs is encouraging (Dickinson, Sumner, & Durand, 1987:60–61). Though few offer a full course in death education, the majority have some emphasis in their curricula on this topic. Most began their offerings since 1975, a time frame corresponding with society's increased interest in dying and death in the 1970s. Likewise, few dental schools currently offer anything in thanatology, yet plans for future offerings are encouraging (Dickinson & Sumner, 1989:564).

As more emphasis is placed on relating to terminally ill patients and their families in medical, nursing, dental, and pharmacy colleges, we would hope that more positive attitudes toward treatment of the dying patient will emerge when these students become practitioners. Helping students deal with their own anxieties about death at the time of actually facing terminally ill patients would seem to be an appropriate time for intervention. Such anxieties are expressed by Dawn McGuire (1988:341), a fourth-year medical student at Columbia Presbyterian Medical Center in New York City:

> I think the proper role for a physician with a dying patient is to enter into a partnership where there is a sense that that partnership is not going to end with the end of medical therapy. But we're not trained for that. Most of us feel totally inadequate and have found our own defenses, including abandoning the patient. It's been confusing to me and a constant source of frustration.

In the end, the young professional, the patient, and the patient's family should all benefit from this emphasis on death education.

The majority of theology schools in the United States do not offer courses on dying, death, and bereavement (Kalish & Dunn, 1976). When these courses are offered, the seminaries are responding to student demands for such a course. As with medical schools, theology schools not offering such courses noted that some death-related materials are covered in other courses such as pastoral counseling.

Death education should not only prove useful in coping with dying and death situations, but can actually improve the quality of our living. As Elisabeth Kübler-Ross notes, relating to the dying does not depress her but makes her both appreciate each day of life and be thankful each morning she awakes for the potential of another day. Learning more about dying and death should make one strive to make each day count in a positive way. It tends to make one "look for the good in others and dwell on it," as Alex Haley suggests, rather than constantly criticizing others.

Rather than wait until after the individual dies to make positive statements *after life,* why not tell those significant others in our lives *while they are alive* what they mean to us? If you cannot verbalize this face-to-face, drop that special person a note and simply state what you think of him or her. As Robert Kavanaugh (1972) notes, "It doesn't have to be a poem since most of us are not poets." Make it plain and simple, but do it. We hope that an awareness of the importance of gestures like this will result from death education.

CONCLUSION

It is our hope that this book has helped you in understanding and coping with dying, death, and bereavement and that you will therefore be able to assist others in doing the same. Our ultimate objective has been that this understanding will facilitate a more meaningful experience of life. Just as one cannot fully appreciate a beautiful day without experiencing its opposite, so too the richness of life is enhanced by the knowledge of its finitude.

SUMMARY

1. If one does not want the state to determine the distribution of one's property after death, a will is essential.

2. Certain criteria apply for making out a will, and the criteria vary with the states.

3. A living will is a document which states that one does not want medical intervention if the technology or treatment that keeps one alive cannot offer a reasonable quality of life or hope for recovery.

4. Life insurance protects one's dependents, gives the insured a feeling of security in knowing that dependents will have some coverage in the event of death, and can be a form of tax-deferred investment from which one can borrow.

5. Because of the sensitive nature of the topic, human organ transplants have not been widely discussed in society.

6. In recent years the American public has changed its lifestyle toward a more healthy existence.

7. Though one cannot control one's genetic inheritance, one can have something to say about exercise, nutrition, and patterns of living.

8. Death education provides an opportunity to familiarize students and professionals with the needs and issues surrounding dying and death.

9. Though death education is offered on a limited basis in many professional schools of medicine, nursing, pharmacy, dentistry, and theology, few offer a full course on relating to terminally ill patients and their families.

DISCUSSION QUESTIONS

1. Who should have a will?

2. What are some positive reasons for having a will?

3. What are the criteria generally required for making a will?

4. How can a will be broken?

5. What is a living will?

6. What are the reasons for having life insurance?

7. Distinguish between term life insurance and whole life insurance.

8. Discuss some of the problems affecting human transplantations.

9. Discuss the benefits of exercise, nutrition, and patterns of living toward the prolongation of life.

10. Discuss the pros and cons of requiring death education in health-related professional schools and theology schools.

GLOSSARY

Codicil An addition or supplement to a will made at a later date in accordance with the same formalities required for the validity of the original will.

Escheat The term describing the fact that property of a decedent goes to the state if not disposed of by a will and if the decedent has no heirs.

Holographic will   A will written wholly in one's own handwriting and generally requiring no witnesses; not recognized in all states.

Intestate   Describing a person who dies without a will.

Living will   A document in which the individual states while still healthy the conditions under which medical efforts to save his or her life should be stopped.

Term life insurance   A type of insurance policy covering the insured for a fixed period of time (five, ten, twenty or so years). Premiums are usually lower for a greater amount of coverage than for other types of life insurance policies.

Testator   A person who makes a will.

Universal life insurance   A policy that is flexible and allows one to raise or reduce premiums and the amount of coverage on one's life.

Variable life insurance   A type of insurance that does not allow for the premium or minimum coverage on one's life to change but allows one to switch the savings from among money-markets or various forms of stock.

Whole life insurance   A type of insurance in which, for a set annual premium, one receives life insurance coverage and, at the same time, invests one's money.

Will   A legal document in which a person states how he or she wants property and possessions distributed after death.

REFERENCES

Bordewich, Fergus M. 1988. "Mortal Fears: Courses in 'Death Education' Get Mixed Reviews." *Atlantic Monthly.* February, 261:30–34.

Brody, Jane E. 1984. "More Than 70 Percent of Cancers Are Caused by How People Live." *Lexington Herald.* Lexington, KY. April 15.

Cooper, D. K., & R. T. Lanza. 1984. *Heart Transplants: The Present Status of Orthotopic and Heterotopic Health Transplantation.* Boston: MTP Press.

Dickinson, George E., Edward D. Sumner, & Ronald P. Durand. 1987. "Death Education in U.S. Professional Colleges: Medical, Nursing, and Pharmacy." *Death Studies,* 11:57–61.

Dickinson, George E. and Edward D. Sumner. 1989. "Update on Death Education in U.S. Dental Schools." *Journal of Dental Education, 53* (October):564.

Ezell, Gene, David J. Anspaugh, & Judy Oaks. 1987. *Dying and Death: From a Health and Sociological Perspective.* Scottsdale, AZ: Gorsuch Scarisbrick Publishers.

Gordon, A. K., & D. Klass. 1979. *The Need to Know: How to Teach Children about Death.* Englewood Cliffs, N.J.: Prentice-Hall.

Hyner, Gerald C., & Christopher L. Melby. 1987. *Priorities for Health Promotion and Disease Prevention.* Dubuque, IA: Eddie Bowers.

Kalish, Richard A., & L. Dunn. 1976. "Death and Dying: A Survey of Credit Offerings in Theological Schools and Some Possible Implications." *Review of Religious Research,* 17:122–130.

Kavanaugh, Robert E. 1972. *Facing Death.* Baltimore: Penguin Books.

"Making A 'Living Will.'" 1985. *The New York Times.* November 23, p. 20.

Malcolm, Andrew H. 1986. "Taboo to Commonplace: Transplants Now Routine." *The New York Times.* February 15, p. 8.

McGuire, Dawn. 1988. "Medical Student, Fourth Year," 339–344. In Ina Yalof (Ed.) *Life and Death: The Story of a Hospital.* New York: Random House.

National Center for Health Statistics. 1985. *Health in the United States.* DHHS (PHS) Publication No. 86-1232. U.S. Government Printing Office.

Pine, Vanderlyn R. 1986. "The Age of Maturity for Death Education: A Socio-Historical Portrait of the Era 1976–1985." *Death Studies,* 10:209–231.

Schurenberg, Eric. 1987. "A Short Course in Estate Planning." *Money,* October, pp. 74–92.

Seefeldt, Vern, & Paul Vogel. 1986. *The Value of Physical Activity.* Reston, VA: American Alliance for Health, Physical Education, Recreation, and Dance.

Smith, Marguerite T. 1988. "Why You Might Go for a Cash-Value Policy." *Money.* December, pp. 153–161.

"Specific Instructions Needed in Living Wills." 1989. *The Times Picayune.* New Orleans. August 27, p. 9F.

Ubell, Earl. 1988. "Start Exercising—And Stick with It." *Parade.* December 4, pp. 8–9.

SUGGESTED READINGS

Sula Benet. 1974. *Abkhasians: The Long-Living People of the Caucasus.* New York: Holt, Rinehart and Winston.

An ethnography about a group of people who live long lives and who seem to practice good nutrition, exercise, and living patterns.

Gerald C. Hyner & Christopher L. Melby. 1987. *Priorities for Health Promotion and Disease Prevention.* Dubuque, IA: Eddie Bowers.

Provides information needed to make intelligent decisions regarding lifestyles and describes the potential impact that behavior changes may have on the health and well-being of an individual.

Jack B. Kamerman. 1988. *Death in the Midst of Life: Social and Cultural Influences on Death, Grief and Mourning.* Englewood Cliffs, N.J.: Prentice-Hall.

Has a good chapter on the health-care professions and the management of death and dying.

Gari Lesnoff-Caravaglia. 1987. *Realistic Expectations for Long Life.* New York: Human Sciences Press.

An anthology, written by international experts on gerontology, which concludes that expectations for long life are indeed realistic.

Photo Credits *continued*

Bettmann Newsphotos; **p. 114** UPI/Bettmann Newsphotos; **p. 140** Skeeter Hagler; **p. 148** ©
Frank Siteman MCMLXXXIII; **p. 180** © Joel Gordon 1989; **p. 186** © Joel Gordon 1988; **p. 201** ©
Joel Gordon 1988; **p. 210** Ergun Cagatay LIFE Magazine © 1982; **p. 227** Mike Vogl; **p. 234** ©
Joel Gordon 1984; **p. 242** Stanley J. Forman, Boston World-American 1978; **p. 245** © Jock
Pottle 1980; **p. 260** © Joel Gordon 1983; **p. 264** © Joel Gordon 1978; **p. 275** Robert Harbison; **p.
294** Reproduced from the Collections of the Library of Congress; **p. 297** Peter Buckley, Photo
Researchers, Inc.; **p. 300** Bernard Pierre Wolff © 1981; **p. 303** © Victor Englebert; **p. 311**
Bernard Pierre Wolff; **p. 324** Reproduced from the Collections of the Library of Congress; **p.
327** Reproduced from the Collections of the Library of Congress; **p. 331** Reproduced from the
Collections of the Library of Congress; **p. 371** Reproduced by courtesy of the British Museum;
p. 408 Joel Gordon 1978; **p. 417** Copyright Frank Siteman; **p. 420** Robert Harbison; **p. 432** ©
Corrections Magazine Photo by Bill Powers; **p. 438** © Joel Gordon 1986; **p. 451** © Joel Gordon
1981.

Acknowledgments

pp. 43, 240 From *The Social Reality of Death* by Kathy Charmaz. Copyright © 1980 by
McGraw-Hill, reproduced by permission.

p. 67 Copyright 1970, 1976 by Earl A. Grollman/Reprinted by permission of Beacon Press.

p. 74 From *Adolescence and Death,* Charles A. Corr and Joan N. McNeil, Eds. Copyright ©
Springer Publishing Company, Inc., New York 10012. Used by permission.

p. 82 From "Death and the Elderly" by Hannelore Wass in *Dying: Facing the Facts.* Hemisphere
Publishing Corp.

p. 110 From *Funeral Customs the World Over* by Robert W. Habenstein and William M. Lamers.
Reprinted with permission of the National Funeral Directors Association.

pp. 147, 150 Reprinted with permission of Macmillan Publishing Company, from *On Death
and Dying* by Elisabeth Kübler-Ross. Copyright © 1969 by Elisabeth Kübler-Ross.

p. 161 From NEWSWEEK 11/17/86, © 1986, Newsweek, Inc. All rights reserved. Reprinted
by permission.

p. 239 From Jack Douglas, *Social Meaning of Suicide.* Copyright © 1967 by Princeton University
Press. Excerpt, pgs. 39–40, reprinted by permission of Princeton University Press.

pp. 243, 244, 250 From *Death and Dying:* From a Sociological Perspective, by Gene Ezell,
David J. Anspaugh, and Judy Oaks. Gorsuch Scarisbrick Publishers, 1987.

pp. 296, 298, 300, 302 From *Celebrations of Death* by Richard Huntington and Peter Metcalf.
Cambridge University Press.

pp. 325–364 Chapter 11 originally written by James J. Farrell for the first edition of
Understanding Dying, Death, and Bereavement.

p. 416 "End of the World" lyrics by Sylvia Dee and Arthur Kent. Summit Music Corporation.

INDEX

Opper, Sylvia, 68, 263
Ordinary measures to preserve life, 217
Organ donations, 120, 443–449
Oswalt, W. H., 304n.
Otto, Melinda E., 175, 183
Oxley, J. MacDonald, 352

Paffenbarger, Ralph, 451
Pagli, Phyllis, 299
"Pain, Life, and Death," 339
Pain management in hospices, 175–176,
        190–191
Paradigms, theoretical, 35–36
Pardue, Peter, 115, 116
Parents of dying children, 280–282
    grieving for the loss of an infant, 424–
        428
    sudden infant death syndrome, 286–287
Parkes, Colin M., 201, 422, 423, 424
Parsons, Talcott, 147, 240, 410
Pascal, Blaise, 94
Passive euthanasia, 214–219
Pastoral care in hospices, 177, 204
Patient-family as unit of care for hospices,
        192–193
Patterson, R., 161
Pattison, E. Marshall, 77, 151
Paxton, Tom, 343–344
Pearlman, J., 160
Pearson, Algene, 158
Peers, adolescent suicide and relationship
        with, 249
Peplau, L. A., 45
Perinatal death, 425–428
Perion, Steve, 308–310
Pets, death of, 428–433
Phillips, David, 249
Phipps, William E., 443n., 456n.
Physical therapists, 187
Physicians:
    death education in medical school, 153–
        155, 457
    dying patient and, 149–150, 153–155,
        158–161
    grieving parents and, 425–426
    as part of hospice team, 176
Piaget, Jean, 68, 70, 263–264
Pike, Martha V., 351, 352
Pilling, Arnold R., 310
Pine, Vanderlynn, 158, 379, 381, 456
Pius XII, Pope, 216
Place of death, 85–86

"Pornography of Death, The," 359
Pospisil, Leopold, 301
Pratt, Clara, 282
Prearranging funerals, 400–402
Prefunding funerals, 400–402
Preneed funerals, 400–402
Professional Animal Disposal Advisory
        Council, 431–433
Propositions, 35
Pryor, Richard, 142
Psychiatrists as part of hospice team, 177
Psychoanalysis, 68
Psychologists as part of hospice team, 187
Public attitudes toward care of terminally
        ill, 200
Punishment of deviance, 156–157
Puritans, 327–330, 332, 374

Qemant people, 310
Quality of life:
    euthanasia from perspective of, 213–214
    hospice emphasis on, 190–192

Radcliffe-Brown, A. R., 48, 50, 51, 302
    on death anxiety and religion, 97–99,
        101, 313
Raether, Howard C., 388
Rahe, R. H., 128
Rahman, Fazlur, 109, 110, 216n.
Rambachan, Anant, 112–113n.
Ramsey, Michael Kirby, 177–179, 191
Ramsey, Paul, 9
Ramsminsky, Judy Sklar, 195–199
Raphael, Beverly, 424
Rappaport, Roy A., 299
Rational suicide, 250–253
Rawlings, Maurice, 125
Reece, R. M., 286
Re-establishment stage of bereavement
        process, 418
Reformed Tradition, 327–332
Reid, Lucie, 81–82
Reincarnation, 111
Relief stage of bereavement process, 417–
        418
Religion, 94–135
    death and the origin of, 94–96
    death anxiety and fear, 128–133
    as means of providing an understanding
        of death, 96–101
    near-death experiences and, 126–127